D1761154

TUDOR INTERLUDES VI

General Editors
Marie Axton   Richard Axton

THE PLAYS OF JOHN HEYWOOD

This complete collection the Heywood's plays is the first fully annotated edition in the original language. It makes possible revaluation of John Heywood's remarkable achievement as actor-playwright and an appreciation of his lively contribution to the English language. In all their experimental variety the comedies are seen to have the stamp of a distinctive, theatrical intelligence and of a surprising seriousness. As heir to Chaucer, French farce, and Erasmian humanism, 'witty' John Heywood emerges as a resourceful apologist for traditional Catholic doctrine in a time of Reformation. The plays are shown to shadow and foreshadow the polemical writings of his wife's uncle, Thomas More, but with a more genial tolerance. In arguing for a new chronology, the editors suggest that Henry VIII's servant and entertainer was capable of refreshing irreverence and political daring.

Frontispiece to The Spider and the Flie, 1556

THE PLAYS
OF JOHN HEYWOOD

Edited by
Richard Axton & Peter Happé

D.S. BREWER

First published 1991
D. S. Brewer, Cambridge

Transferred to digital printing

ISBN 978-0-85991-319-5

D. S. Brewer is an imprint of Boydell & Brewer Ltd
PO Box 9, Woodbridge, Suffolk IP12 3DF, UK
and of Boydell & Brewer Inc.
668 Mt Hope Avenue, Rochester, NY 14620, USA
website: www.boydellandbrewer.com

A CiP catalogue record for this book is available
from the British Library

This publication is printed on acid-free paper

CONTENTS

ACKNOWLEDGMENTS

It is a pleasure to record our thanks for help given over a number of years on a number of aspects of the edition. We were encouraged to begin by Richard Proudfoot, who generously turned over the proof sheets and notes for the Malone Society texts of *Pardoner and Frere* and *Foure PP*, together with his own interest in editing a complete Heywood. Martin Ashe-Jones, who edited *Foure PP* and *The Play of the Wether*, as an Oxford B.Litt. thesis in 1975, generously allowed us to cite some of his notes. The editing of *Witty and Witless* has benefitted from simultaneous preparation by Peter Happé of a diplomatic text for the Malone Society. We are grateful to John Pitcher and, again, to Richard Proudfoot, for their criticism and advice on interpreting a particularly difficult early Tudor hand. Elisabeth Leedham-Green also brought her palæographic expertise to bear on some of these problems of orthography. Our translation of *La farce du pasté* was improved greatly by Nigel Wilkins' unrivalled knowledge of the idiom and verse forms in late medieval French farce. To help with problems of dating Derek Bunker made a perpetual calendar for us as a computer programme.

Among others who have helped with expert knowledge or critical encouragement, we thank particularly Lucy Axton, Richard Beadle, Tony Hasler, Malcolm Jones, John N. King, Gordon Kipling, Richard Luckett as Pepys Librarian, Alan Nelson, Meg Twycross, and Greg Walker.

A substantial contribution to understanding the plays and helping the editorial process has been made by practical experiment and experience. Here, too, we have been fortunate in having friendly and expert advice and if the edition has not benefitted more, we have only ourselves to blame. David Parry brought an incomparable experience of playing Tudor interludes to the problems of performing *Pardoner and Frere* during a series of Cambridge seminars run jointly with Richard Axton. John Marshall and Peter Meredith, with other colleagues at the Medieval English Theatre meeting at York in 1987, contributed enthusiastically to the experiment. Carl Heap and the Medieval Players, having shown us so much about the performance qualities of *Johan Johan*, realised a brilliant production of our draft text of *Pardoner and Frere* in their 1987 tour. Difficulties of metre, sentence length, and punctuation in *Play of the Wether* were explored practically with help of the expert voices of Sandra Billington, Hilary Walston, and Alan Beck.

All the work in preparing the edition has been done in constant collaboration. Initially, Richard Axton took on the texts and notes to *Pardoner and Frere*, *Foure PP*, and *Play of the Wether*, while Peter Happé undertook the texts and notes to *Witty and Witless*, *Johan Johan*, and *Play of Love*. Labours of the Introduction and all other parts of the work have been fairly evenly divided. In the course of innumerable exchanges it soon became impossible to attribute particular insights or points of elucidation. At all stages the project has been improved by the eagle eye and careful, independent scholarship of Marie Axton.

In thanking these and other unnamed colleagues, we must stress that none of them is responsible for the errors and inconsistencies that undoubtedly remain. We shall gratefully bless the amending hand.

Cambridge
December 1990

ABBREVIATIONS

Altman	Joel B. Altman, *The Tudor Play of Mind: A Rhetorical Inquiry into the Development of Elizabethan Drama* (Berkeley and Los Angeles, 1978)
Anglo	Sydney Anglo, *Spectacle Pageantry and Tudor Policy* (Oxford, 1969)
Ashe-Jones	M.J. Ashe-Jones, 'An Edition of Two Plays by John Heywood: *Four PP* and *Play of the Wether*', Unpublished B.Litt thesis, Oxford University, 1975
Aston	Margaret Aston, *England's Iconoclasts* (Oxford, 1988)
Bale, *Plays*	*The Complete Plays of John Bale*, ed. Peter Happé, 2 vols. (Woodbridge, 1985–6)
Bang	*Materialien zur Kunde des älteren Englischen Dramas* ed. W. Bang (Louvain, 1902–)
Bevington	*Medieval Drama*, ed. David Bevington (Boston, 1975)
BL	British Library
Brigden	Susan Brigden, *London and the Reformation* (Oxford, 1989)
CSP Sp	*Calendar of State Papers, Spanish*, ed. G.A. Bergenroth, et al., 13 vols. (London, 1862–1964)
Calisto	*Calisto and Melebea* in *Rastell Plays*
Cambridge, REED	*Cambridge*, ed. Alan H. Nelson, REED, 2 vols. (Toronto, 1989)
Cameron, *Wether*	K.W. Cameron, *John Heywood's 'Play of the Wether'* (Raleigh, North Carolina, 1941)
Cameron, *Witty*	K.W. Cameron, *The Background of John Heywood's 'Witty and Witless'* (Raleigh, North Carolina, 1941)
Canzler, *Concordance*	David George Canzler, 'A Concordance to the Dramatic Works of John Heywood' Ph.D Dissertation, Oregon, 1961
Chaucer	*The Riverside Chaucer*, ed. Larry D. Benson (Boston, 1987)
Chester	*The Chester Mystery Cycle*, ed. R.M. Lumiansky and D. Mills, EETS s.s.3 (Oxford, 1974)
Cohen	*Recueil de farces françaises inedites du XVe siècle*, ed. G. Cohen (Cambridge, Mass., 1949)
Dent	R.W. Dent, *Proverbial Language in English Drama Exclusive of Shakespeare 1485–1616* (Berkeley and Los Angeles, 1984)
EETS	Early English Text Society
Erasmus, *Colloquies*	Desiderius Erasmus, *The Colloquies*, trans. C.R. Thompson (Chicago, 1965)
Erasmus, *Folly*	*The Praise of Folie*, trans. Sir Thomas Chaloner, ed. Clarence H. Miller, EETS (Oxford, 1965)
Farmer	*The Dramatic Writings of John Heywood*, ed. John S. Farmer (London, 1905)
Feuillerat	*Documents Relating to the Revels at Court in the Time of King Edward VI and Queen Mary*, ed. A. Feuillerat, in Bang vol. 44 (Louvain, 1914)
Fox	Alistair Fox, *Politics and Literature in the Reign of Henry VII and Henry VIII* (Oxford, 1989)

Foxe, AM	J. Foxe, *Acts and Monuments*, ed. S.R. Cattley and G. Townsend, 8 vols. (London, 1837–41)
Fulgens	*Fulgens and Lucres* in Medwall, *Plays*
Greene	Richard L. Greene, *Early English Carols*, 2nd edition (Oxford, 1977)
Greg	W.W. Greg, *A Bibliography of the English Printed Drama to the Restoration*, Bibliographical Society, vol.1 (London, 1939)
Heywood, *Dial. Provs.*	John Heywood's *A Dialogue of Proverbs*, ed. R.E. Habenicht (Berkeley and Los Angeles, 1963) STC 13291
Heywood, *300 Epigrams*	in Milligan
Johnson	R.C. Johnson, *John Heywood* (New York, 1970)
L&P	*Letters and Papers, Foreign and Domestic, of the Reign of Henry VIII*, ed. J.S. Brewer, et al., 21 vols. (London, 1862–1932)
La Rosa	*A Critical Edition of John Heywood's 'A Play of Love'*, ed. F.E. La Rosa (New York, 1979)
Lancashire	Ian Lancashire, *Dramatic Texts and Records of Britain: A Chronological Topography* (Cambridge, 1984)
Lydgate, *Minor Poems*	*Lydgate's Minor Poems*, ed. H.N. MacCracken, Part II, EETS o.s.192 (Oxford, 1932)
Mankind	in *The Macro Plays*, ed. Mark Eccles, EETS 262 (Oxford, 1969)
Maxwell	Ian Maxwell, *French Farce and John Heywood* (Melbourne and London, 1946)
MED	*Middle English Dictionary*, ed. Hans Kurath et al. (Ann Arbor, 1954–)
Medwall, *Plays*	*The Plays of Henry Medwall*, ed. Alan H. Nelson (Woodbridge, 1980)
Milligan	Burton A. Milligan, *John Heywood's 'Works' and Miscellaneous Short Poems* (Urbana, 1956)
More, *Confutation*	*The Confutation of Tyndale's Answer*, ed. L.A. Schuster, R.C. Marius, J.P. Lusardi, and R.J. Schoeck (1973) in More, *Works* VIII
More, *Works*	*The Yale Edition of the Complete Works of St Thomas More* (New Haven and London, 1963–)
More, *English Works*	*The English Works of Sir Thomas More*, ed. W.E. Campbell and A.W. Reed (London, 1931)
More, *Heresies*	*A Dialogue concerning Heresies* ed. T.M.C. Lawler, G. Marc'ladour, and R.C. Marius, 2 vols. (1981) in More, *Works* VI
MSR	Malone Society Reprints
OED	*The Oxford English Dictionary* (Oxford, 1933)
Piers Plowman	William Langland, *The Vision of Piers Plowman*, ed. A.V.C. Schmidt (London, 1978)
PL	*Patrologiae Cursus Completus [Patrologia Latina]*, ed. J.P. Migne (Paris, 1842–80)
PRO	Public Record Office
Rastell Plays	*Three Rastell Plays*, ed. R. Axton (Cambridge, 1979)
Reed	A.W. Reed, *Early Tudor Drama: Medwall, the Rastells, and the More Circle* (London, 1926)

Reed, *Canon*	A.W. Reed, 'The Canon of John Heywood's Plays', *The Library*, 3rd series, ix (1918)
REED	Records of Early English Drama
Respublica	*Respublica*, ed. W.W. Greg, EETS o.s.226 (Oxford, 1952)
Robinson	Vicki Knudsen Robinson, *A Critical Edition of 'The Play of the Wether' by John Heywood* (New York and London, 1987)
Roister Doister	N. Udall, *Roister Doister*, ed. W.W. Greg, MSR (Oxford, 1934)
Schoeck	R.J. Schoeck, 'Satire of Wolsey in Heywood's *Play of Love*', *Notes and Queries* 196 (1951), 113–14
Skelton, *Poems*	*John Skelton: The Complete English Poems*, ed. John Scattergood (Harmondsworth, 1983)
STC	*A Short-Title Catalogue of Books Printed in England, Scotland and Ireland, and of English Books Printed Abroad*, 2nd ed., ed. W.A. Jackson, F. J. Ferguson, and K.F. Panzer, 2 vols. (London, 1976, and 1986)
Stow, *Survey*	John Stow, *A Survey of London*, ed. C.L. Kingsford, 2 vols. (Oxford, 1908)
Tilley	M.P. Tilley, *A Dictionary of the Proverbs in England in the Sixteenth and Seventeenth Centuries* (Ann Arbor, 1950)
VCH	*The Victoria History of the Counties of England*
Welsford	Enid Welsford, *The Fool: His Social and Literary History* (London, 1935)
Whiting	B.J. and H.W. Whiting, *Proverbs, Sentences, and Proverbial Phrases* (Cambridge, Mass., 1968)
Whythorne	*The Autobiography of Thomas Whythorne*, ed. James M. Osborn, 2 vols. (Oxford, 1961)
Wit and Science	John Redford, *Wit and Science* in Bevington.

PREFACE

The six plays attributed to John Heywood are recognisably the offspring of a distinctive and witty theatrical imagination. This must be the principal justification for an edition (the first for half a century and the first ever with full critical apparatus) which gathers them together. For all the family resemblances, the interludes offer a stimulating diversity of entertainment. In Heywood's time they were highly experimental; they treated – albeit with a light hand – moral and intellectual issues of vital interest; and they were performed at or close to the centre of England's power.

The playwright's connection with the court of Henry VIII as a singing man, a player of virginals and a 'servant', has long been known, although the facts have not really advanced the understanding of his plays very much. In reviewing the biographical evidence and in discussing likely auspices for the plays we have tried not to stretch the records too far. Readers impatient for an introduction to the themes and conventions of the plays themselves may wish to turn first to the section on The Plays. Questions of dating and auspice required more detailed consideration of topical aspects of the plays and of Heywood's originality in relation to possible sources and other influences; these are therefore discussed in the third section of the Introduction: Sources and contexts of the plays.

Viewed as a whole, the plays do not strike one as predominantly 'courtly'. The text of *Witty and Witless*, probably the earliest, has some lines to be spoken in the presence of the King; yet the subject matter is an exploration of whether man's wit is truly a help to happiness and salvation. Its dedicatee was the monarch in his recently acquired role as defender of the faith. *The Play of the Wether*, possibly the latest in composition, presents a stage analogue to the King in the figure of Jupiter, to whom representatives of the estates of English society address suits for reforming the weather in their own particular interests. Yet whether Henry VIII himself would have watched the play, performed in all likelihood by Heywood and choirboy actors, is still a moot point.

Assumptions about likely auspices of the plays will inevitably affect any judgment of their topicality and tone, and any assessment of the risks that Heywood may have run. Like the proverbial mouse, he certainly had more than one hole. If, as we suspect, he performed in his own plays, this would have given them a distinct presence and there may be cross references for those in the know. He would have found his most sympathetic audience among those Catholic humanists firmly opposed to Lutheran doctrine, and hostile to Henry's divorce: Thomas More, William Rastell and the extended 'family circle' whose interests combined playing and printing, and the law. Specific historical records of performance of the six plays have not come to light. It has been suggested that *A Play of Love* was intended for lawyers at their Christmas revels in Lincoln's (More's own) Inn, offering them the spectacle of a parodic moot in which the pleasure and pain of love are ironically weighed.

In a court that was heavily Frenchified, Heywood undoubtedly learned a great deal from the contemporary French dramatists and players. It may be significant that the first of his plays to be printed was *Johan Johan*, a zestful translation of *La farce du pasté*. Heywood's closeness to the French farce can be seen from our modern English translation of it, included as Appendix II. At a stroke Heywood imported into English drama the strongly marked sexual stereotypes of late medieval anticlerical farce – the lustful shrew, the henpecked husband, the rapacious priest – compelling them with unflinching satire towards a noisy climax of violence and ridiculous pathos.

The two remaining plays, *The Foure PP* and *The Pardoner and the Frere*, are linked through satirical treatment of the figure of the Pardoner, and through Heywood's oblique engagement with the issues of contemporary belief. Granting the abuses of religion, of false pardons and preaching friars, of pilgrim shrines with their image-pedlers and patent relic-mongers, Heywood takes two distinct points of view and traces two different plot structures. The *Pardoner and the Frere* is violent, combative, and farcical, as the two religious charlatans attempt to drown each other's patter, and finally resort to bloodshed. *Foure PP* offers a more harmonious contest of quacks, using a fantastical competition of lies as an oblique approach to a serious theme: the need for tolerance and harmony within the Church of Mankind. Many of the theatrical elements and much of the intellectual 'doctrine' of Heywood's plays are traditional – as our account of the sources and backgrounds attempts to show; but the tension between the zany wit and the unforced seriousness, the balanced sense of the human comedy, is something uniquely John Heywood's that is present in all the plays.

With the exception of *Witty and Witless*, which remained in manuscript, all the plays were printed during Heywood's lifetime, four of them by his brother-in-law William Rastell during 1533 and 1534. *Foure PP* survives from a quarto ten years later than this. The dates of composition of the plays are not known and the present editors argue that they belong later than has usually been held, putting forward a chronology not dogmatically but deliberately.

Hitherto the plays as a whole have been available only in the modernized and bowdlerized edition of Farmer (1906) and in the plain transcriptions by de la Bère (1937). *Gentleness and Nobility*, whose authorship is disputed between John Heywood and his father-in-law John Rastell, has appeared in Richard Axton's edition of *Three Rastell Plays* in this series. Our purpose in bringing together the remaining six plays for the first time in a fully annotated, old-spelling edition, and in confirmation of the traditional canon, is to stimulate the appreciation of Heywood's output as a whole. We hope to have facilitated study of the connections between the plays, so that the individuality of his stagecraft and his dramatic idiom, as well as the coherence of his 'criticism of life' emerge more clearly than hitherto.

The original texts differ much in their state of readiness for performance (for instance, their provision of stage directions) and in their spelling. No attempt has been made to standardize the vagaries of spelling. The manuscript of *Witty and Witless* is not Heywood's holograph, but it may stand as evidence of the dynamic variation within early Tudor English. Four of the plays present fairly uniform aspect as a result of the spelling practice in the Rastell printing house. Further light on Heywood's own, irrecoverable, spelling may be shed by the short fragment from a lost play of Reason, preserved in his pupil Thomas Whythorne's phonetic orthography. The Glossary indicates earliest usages, some unnoted by the *Oxford English Dictionary*, and points to fuller discussion in the Explanatory Notes. One index of the special interest of Heywood's linguistic usage is the frequency with which he is cited by proverb dictionaries. It is in the nature of a proverb that its first use is impossible to establish for certain; however, in this area, too, Heywood seems to have been a great innovator.

It is a great pity that no music survives for the plays. This lack may, of course, be made good in modern performance; but the lost sense of a household dramatist acting in his own plays cannot so readily be recovered without much patient and imaginative experiment. For virtuoso actors who are historically informed the challenges and the rewards of Heywood's oeuvre are great.

A CHRONOLOGY OF THE LIFE OF JOHN HEYWOOD

Entries in square brackets [] are conjectural. Dates 1 Jan – 24 Mar are given modern style.

c. 1497	John Heywood born [London or Coventry].
1499	John & Thomas More in business association with John Rastell.
1508	William Rastell born [Coventry].
1509 Apr 22	Accession of Henry VIII.
	[Heywood a chorister?]
1512–	John Rastell printing at Paul's Chains.
[1513–14	Heywood at Broadgates Hall, Oxford.]
c. 1514	Medwall, *Fulgens and Lucres*, printed by J. Rastell.
1516	Thomas More, *Utopia* printed in Antwerp.
c. 1519	J. Rastell, *Four Elements* printed.
1519 Michaelmas – 1520 Christmas	
	King's household 6 quarterly payments of 100s to Heywood 'singer'.
1520	J. Rastell works on hall at Guisnes for Field of Cloth of Gold.
1521 Feb 12	Royal annuity of 10 marks granted to Heywood.
	Henry VIII's *Assertio* against Luther printed.
	Pope Leo X grants Henry title 'fidei defensor.'
1522	J. Rastell's Cheapside pageant for Emperor Charles V.
1523 Mar 3	Heywood admitted Freeman of City.
	Married by now to Joan Rastell.
1523	Parliaments (1) 15 Apr–21 May; (2) 10 Jun–29 Jul; (3) 31 Jul–13 Aug.
1524	J. Rastell builds a house and stage at Finsbury Fields.
1525	Michaelmas Royal payment of £6.13.4d to Heywood 'player of the virginals.'
	Eltham Reforms of Royal Household.
c. 1525	Will Somer is Henry VIII's fool at court.
	[Heywood writes *Witty and Witless*.]
c. 1526–30	*Gentleness and Nobility*, [? collaboration of Rastell & Heywood] and *Calisto and Melebea* printed by J. Rastell.
	[Heywood translates *Johan Johan* from *La farce du pasté*.]
1527	More gives Henry VIII in private his opinion against divorce.
	Ambassadors from France arrange marriage with Princess Mary.
1527 May 6	Greenwich. J. Rastell's pageant 'Father of Heaven' with Holbein.
	W. Rastell employed.
	[W. Rastell now printing with J. Rastell.]
1528 Christmas	Royal quarterly payments of 'annual pension' £10 p.a. to Heywood begin (recorded in existing books for 1528–31, 1538–41, 1545, 1547–51).

1529		Bishop Tunstall employs More to read heretical books. [? Heywood writes *Pardoner and Frere*.]
1529 Mar		Royal quarterly payments of 50s to Heywood 'player at virginals' and to a 'John de John, priest, organ maker.'
1529 Jun 21		John Skelton buried at St Margaret's Westminster. More's *Dialogue concerning Heresies* printed by J. Rastell. Cardinal Campeggio and Legatine Court at Blackfriars try legality of Henry's marriage.
1529 Sept		W. Rastell prints More's *Supplication of Souls*, using a new fount of secretary type and some black letter from J. Rastell.
	Oct 26	More becomes Chancellor on resignation of Wolsey.
	Nov 4–Dec 17	First Reformation Parliament. J. Rastell is MP. (7 sessions more – ending 14 Apr 1536.)
	Christmas	[? *A Play of Love* performed at Lincoln's Inn.]
1530 Jan 20		'J. Heywood citizen and Stationer of London and one of the king's servants' presented as Common Measurer in the Mercers' Company.
1530		Ellis Heywood born. Medwall's *Nature* and Cicero's *De Amicitia* printed by W. Rastell. Skelton's *Magnyfycence* printed by P. Treveris using some type from W. Rastell.
1530 Oct 10		J. Rastell's *New boke of purgatory* printed.
1530 Dec		Clergy charged under *praemunire*.
1531 Jan 16		Parliament (2) to 31 Mar. John Frith, *A disputacion of purgatorye* printed in Antwerp. About this time J. Rastell espouses Reformed faith. [? Heywood writes *Foure PP*.]
1532 Jan 15		Parliament (3) to 28 Mar. (4) 10 Apr to 14 May.
	May 16	More resigns as Chancellor.
	May	Part I More's *Confutation of Tyndale* printed by W. Rastell. W. Rastell admitted to Lincoln's Inn.
	Oct 10	Cranmer recalled to England, later to become Archbishop.
	Dec	Anne Boleyn pregnant. More silent about divorce.
1533	New Year's Day.	Henry VIII's gift to Heywood of a gilt cup.
	Jan 25	Cranmer marries Henry and Anne in secret.
	Feb 4	Parliament (5) – Apr 7.
	Feb 12	*Johan Johan* (Anon.) issued by W. Rastell. (F)
	[? Shrovetide	*Play of the Wether* performed.]
	March	*Act in Restraint of Appeals* [to Rome].
1533 Apr 5		*Pardoner and Frere* (Anon.) printed by W. Rastell. (F)
	Apr 15	Easter Sunday. Anne Boleyn's first appearance as Queen.
	May 23	Cranmer declares marriage with Katherine null.
	Jun 1	Anne crowned. Pageants in London.
	Sept 7	Elizabeth born. Mary no longer 'Princess'.
1533		W. Rastell prints More's *Apology, Letter against J. Frith, Debellation of Salem and Bizance*. Heywood named on t.p. of *Play of the Wether* printed by W. Rastell (repr. c.1544, c.1560, c.1573). (F) [? a first folio of *Foure PP* printed by W. Rastell.]

1534 New Year		More, *Answer to Tyndale*, printed by W. Rastell.
		W. Rastell called before Cromwell.
	Jan 15	Parliament (6) – Mar 30.
		Heywood named on t.p. of **Play of Love**, printed by W. Rastell (repr. c.1550). (F)
	Mar 23	*Act of Succession.*
		More restrained at home.
	Apr 17	More taken to Tower.
		Cromwell appointed Secretary.
		W. Rastell stops printing, pursues law at Lincoln's Inn.
	Jul 25	Richard Heywood (brother of JH) enters Lincoln's Inn.
	Nov 3	Parliament (7) – Dec 18.
		Act of Supremacy.
		Act upholding the Act of Succession.
		Act of Treasons.
		Bill of Attainder against More.
[1534		J. Heywood dedicates his ballad, 'Give place ye Ladies', to Princess Mary.]
1535		Jasper Heywood born in London.
		John Rastell imprisoned as zealot, examined by Cranmer.
	Jun 3	More and Fisher interrrogated.
	Jun 14	More interrogated.
	Jun 17	Trial of Fisher.
	Jun 22	Fisher beheaded.
	Jul 1	Trial of More.
	Jul 6	More beheaded.
1536 Jan 7		Katharine of Aragon dies.
	Apr	John Rastell dies.
	May 19	Anne Boleyn executed.
	May 30	Henry marries Jane Seymour.
1537 Jan		Payments suggest Heywood is making music for Princess Mary.
	Oct 12	Prince Edward born.
1538 Mar		Heywood paid for playing an enterlude with Children before Princess Mary.
1539 Shrovetide		Heywood's *Masque of King Arthur's Knights* for Cromwell.
	Feb 22	The same at Court.
	Trinity	W. Rastell called to the Bar.
1540 Jul 10		Cromwell executed.
1542–43		Heywood implicated with John More in a plot against Cranmer.
1544 Feb 15		Heywood indicted at Westminster.
1544 Apr 12		Bill of Attainder. John More recants and is pardoned.
	Jul 6	After also being pardoned Heywood reads a recantation at St Paul's Cross.
[1544]		Heywood named on t.p. of **Foure PP** printed by Middleton. (Q1)
		Heywood named on t.p. of **Wether** printed by Middleton. (Q1)
c. 1545–8		Thomas Whythorne as Heywood's 'servant and skoller'.
		Heywood writes play on 'Parts of Man' for Cranmer.

1546	Heywood's *Dialogue of Proverbes* pr. Berthelet, King's Printer (repr. 1549, 1556, 1561).
1547 Jan 28	Death of Henry VIII, accession of Edward VI.
1549 Dec 21	W. Rastell flees to Louvain.
1550	Heywood's *An hundred Epigrammes* printed by T. Berthelet (repr. 1556).
[1550]	*Love* printed by J. Waley. (Q)
1552 Feb 13	Heywood and Westcott (with children of St Paul's) play for Princess Elizabeth.
1552 Mar 4	Heywood's pension now £40; he is groom of the chamber.
1553 Candlemas/Shrovetide	
	Heywood's 'play of children' postponed to
Easter	(Office of Revels, with Baldwin, Ferrers, Chapel Royal).
1553 Jul 19	Accession of Mary I. Heywood's oration 'in a pageant'.
1555 Apr 5	Philip and Mary confirm Heywood's annuities of 1528 and 1551–2.
1555	Payment of £50 to Heywood 'player on the virginals.' Heywood's *Two hundred Epigrams* printed by T. Berthelet.
1556	Heywood's *Spider & flie* printed by T. Powell.
[1557	Heywood's *Breefe balet of Scarborow Castell* printed by T. Powell.]
1557 Apr 30	More's *Works* in English prefaced by W. Rastell, dedicated to Q. Mary, printed by Tottel.
Christmas	Jasper Heywood is Lord of Misrule at Lincoln's Inn.
1558 Nov 17	Accession of Elizabeth.
1559 Aug 7	Heywood's play of children of Paul's for Elizabeth at Nonsuch.
1560	Heywood's *A fourth hundred of Epygrams* printed by T. Berthelet.
[1560	*Wether* printed by A. Kytson.] (Q2)
	Foure PP, printed by W. Copland. (Q2)
1561 Jan	'Wytles' entered in Stationers Register.
1562	*John Heywoodes Woorkes* [excluding plays] printed by T. Powell (repr. 1566, 1577, 1598).
	Heywood's *A ballad against sklander & dectraccion* pr. J. Allde.
1562 Jan 3	W. Rastell, justice of common pleas, flees with Clements family to Louvain.
1563	*39 Articles of Religion.*
1564	*Act of Uniformity.*
Jul 20	Heywood and wife flee to Flanders.
1569	*Foure PP* printed by J. Allde. (Q3)
1573–4	Heywood at Malines in Brabant refuses to act on Elizabeth I's permission to return to England.
1575 Apr 18	Heywood writes to Burghley from Malines pleading poverty.
1576	Heywood sheltered at the Jesuit College Antwerp with son Ellis.
1577 Jan 16	Heywood's will.
1578	Heywood flees Antwerp to Cologne and Louvain.
c. 1578	After death of Ellis on Oct 2, John Heywood dies.

FAMILY CONNECTIONS OF JOHN HEYWOOD

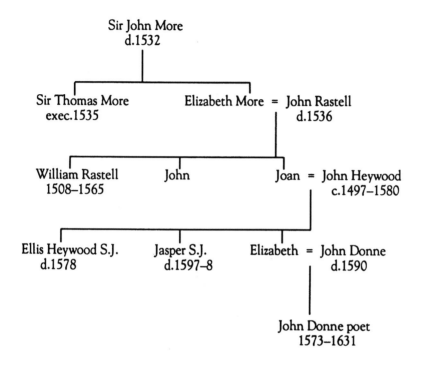

Sir John More
d.1532

Sir Thomas More
exec.1535

Elizabeth More = John Rastell
d.1536

William Rastell
1508–1565

John

Joan = John Heywood
c.1497–1580

Ellis Heywood S.J.
d.1578

Jasper S.J.
d.1597–8

Elizabeth = John Donne
d.1590

John Donne poet
1573–1631

LIFE AND WORKS

> Art thou Heywood that hath made many plaies?
> Ye many plaies, fewe good woorkes in all my daies.
> (Epigram 100, *Fifth Hundred of Epigrams*)

Heywood's long life (c.1497–1578) spans five reigns of doctrinal and social upheaval. As a loyal Catholic, related by marriage to the Rastells and the Mores, and by his daughter's marriage, to the Donnes, he narrowly escaped hanging in middle age. The last fourteen years of his old age were spent in exile, parted from a comfortable fortune. Yet his brilliance as an entertainer (singer, dancer, keyboard player, composer, playwright, poet, proverb-maker), made him welcome and rewarded at the courts of Henry VIII, Edward VI, Mary, and Elizabeth. A tall man of striking presence,[1] he seems, literally, to have lived by his wit; his playful intelligence, his sociability and his quickness in coining epigrams made him the Tudor epitome of a 'witty man'.

Among his contemporaries his reputation as a man-of-letters was very high. Bale praises his linguistic and musical skill, his power to evoke laughter;[2] Thomas Whythorne, who was Heywood's pupil between 1545 and 1548, emphasises his originality (his work came 'from his brain') and his copiousness, unrivalled in England since Chaucer:

> . . . I waz plased [wit]h mr John Haywood, to be both hiz servant and skoller, for hee waz not only very skylled in Muzik, and pleyeng on þe virʒinals but also such an english *poet*, az þe lyk, for hiz witt and invension, with þe quantite þat hee wrot, waz not az þen in England, nor befor hiz tym sinse Chawsers tym.[3]

Whythorne goes on to praise Heywood's skill as instrumentalist and composer of songs: 'In Muzik sweet [he] kan fram sweet nots to agree.' Gabriel Harvey, writing in the margin of his copy of Quintilian, ranks Heywood with Sidney and Spenser, contrasting these three 'natural geniuses' rather surprisingly with the lesser, 'lively talents' of Chaucer, More and Bishop Jewel.[4] Puttenham is more discriminating:

> for the myrth and quicknesse of his conceite more than for any good learning was in him [he] came to be well benefitted by the king.[5]

---

[1] To judge from the portrait on the frontispiece to *Spider and Flie* (T. Powell, 1556) STC 13308.

[2] John Bale, *Illustrium Majoris Britanniae Scriptorum Summarium*, Wesel, 1548, fol. 235; *Scriptorium Illustrium Maioris Brytannie Catalogus*, Basel, 1557–59, II 110. The pro-Catholic Pitts, praises his piety and the easy charm of his conversation (Iohannes Pitseus, *Relationem Historicarum de Rebus Anglicis*, Paris, 1619 p. 234; cited by Robinson p. 31).

[3] *The Autobiography of Thomas Whythorne* ed. James M. Osborn, Oxford, 1961, p. 13. The word 'quantite' here refers to poetic output rather than to Heywood's Chaucerian couplet versification. In the corresponding verses Whythorne says that no English poet 'somuch þis day can show.'

[4] Virginia Stern, *Gabriel Harvey: His Life, Marginalia and Library*, Oxford, 1979, pp. 149–50 & note).

[5] *The Arte of Poesie*, ed. G.D. Willcock and A. Walker, Cambridge, 1936, p. 60. Puttenham's comment may derive from Bale's 'sine doctrina ingeniosus' (*Catalogus* II p. 110).

John Florio regarded him as the great maker of English proverbs, Ben Jonson as 'Heywood the Epigrammatist'.[6]

Puttenham's implication of frivolity is misleading. Like many highly intelligent writers Heywood often understates the serious; much of his wit is oblique. His engagement in religious and political issues by virtue of publication, his involvement in the conspiracy against Cranmer, and the writing of *Spider and Flie* all show him as a committed Catholic, though never solemn or pompous about his beliefs. Our Explanatory Notes show how much 'good learning' there was in the plays, in particular how intimate Heywood was with the English writings of his wife's uncle Thomas More, and how intelligently he tracked the religious and social issues of his times. There is, literally, much more to the plays than meets the casual glance.

The 'merry conceited fellow' and the 'vir pius' are aspects of an authentic humanism, which has qualities appealing strongly to modern sensibilities: a good-natured balance of mind, religious tolerance and lack of factionalism, a quizzical eye and ear for pretensiousness or special pleading, a Chaucerian self-deprecation, a strong and kindly sense of the family of mankind. His plays, for all their fashionable intelligence, embody much traditional wisdom and down-to-earth humour – qualities found above all in the English proverbs, of which he was so fond.

A good deal of detail about Heywood's life has been gathered, particularly by A.W. Reed, to whom all later scholars are much indebted.[7] Many of the facts in the account that follows have been rehearsed before, although not with the interpretation and emphasis given here. In the shaping of John Heywood's professional career and fortunes three factors stand out: his native skill and charm as an entertainer; his family alliance with the Rastells, playmakers, lawyers and printers; and through them his affirmation of the Catholic ideas and attitudes of Thomas More.

From his own testimony, Heywood was born in about 1497, probably in Coventry, home of the Rastell family into which he married. It is likely that the William Heywood who temporarily succeeded Thomas Rastell, father of John, as Coroner of Coventry 1505–06, was father of John Heywood and three other sons.[8] John Rastell, father of Joan whom Heywood married in about 1522, had Coventry business associations with the Mores as early as 1499; by 1504 he was married to Elizabeth, Thomas More's sister. In London Rastell pursued a versatile and exhausting career at law, in royal service, printing, writing plays and polemics, producing pageants and scenic devices. He was to prove a powerful guide to his son-in-law.

Nothing certain is known about the first twenty-one years of John Heywood's life. He would have been twelve when Henry VIII came to the throne in 1509 and it is likely in view of later testimonies to his skill as a musician, that he was a chorister in the Chapel Royal, although this is unproven. Some time around 1513 he apparently studied, briefly and without taking a degree, at Broadgates

---

6 *Second Frutes*, 1591, 'To the Reader' sig. A6v; *Conversations With Drummond* in *Works* (ed. C. H. Herford and Percy Simpson, Oxford, 1925–) I 148.

7 A.W. Reed, *Early Tudor Drama*, 1926. See also Robert W. Bolwell, *The Life and Works of John Heywood*, New York, 1966.

8 Reed p. 9.

Hall (now Pembroke College), Oxford.[9] It is as a 'synger' that Heywood's name first appears in the King's Household Books, at a time when, according to the chronicler Edward Hall's contemptuous exaggeration, the courtiers of the King's privy chamber 'wer al Frenche'.[10] Identification of the 'Iohn Haywoode' who received payment made on Twelfth Night 1515 is impossible, but it is clearly the 'synger' who in 1519–20 was in receipt of quarterly payments of 100 shillings.[11] At Michaelmas 1525 a payment of £6.13.4d refers to him as 'player of the virginals'.[12] From February 1521 there is evidence of reward in the form of annual rents from lands in Essex, which had reverted to the Crown and which soon made Heywood prosperous and propertied. In 1523, with some assistance from the King he was granted Freedom of the City of London.[13] At about this time he married Joan Rastell. By 1525 her father, among his heavyweight legal titles, had printed three English interludes.

At Christmas 1528 Heywood received the first of numerous sums of 50 shillings, the quarterly payment of 'his annuell pencion after the rate of £10 by the yere . . . during his lyf.'[14] This record has usually been taken to signify his discharge from Court service, though R.C. Johnson suggests, without evidence, that it marks the beginning of his appointment as *dapifer camerae* or 'sewer' of the royal chamber. However, an 'annuell pencion' was a retainer, not a golden hand-shake, and Heywood received further payment as 'player of virginals' in March 1529.[15] Though he does not seem to have been in receipt of regular wages as a court servant, his involvement in court life is intermittently documented during the next two decades.

A year later (20 January 1530), Heywood transferred from the 'crafte' of Stationers to the wealthy Mercers Company, as 'Comen Mesurer or meter of Lynnen Clothes' and adjudicator of disputes.[16] This does not necessarily mean that he was fully employed at the cloth business; the wording of the presentation allowed him to substitute a 'sufficient depute' if he wished. Moreover, he is referred to as 'oon of the kynges ser[v]auntes'. During the next few years, which were fraught with political difficulty, Heywood seems to have kept in the King's good books. A record of royal New Year's gifts 1532/33 includes one 'To Heywood. Item a gilte cuppe with a cover weing xxiii oz'.[17] Whether or not there is any substance to the suggestion that Henry's handsome gift was in return for a manuscript of Heywood's dramatic works, one may be sure that the surviving plays associated with his name were virtually complete by this time. In the

---

[9] Anthony à Wood gives an account of Heywood in his *Athenae Oxoniensis*, 1691–92 (ed. Philip Bliss, 1813), I col. 348.

[10] Alistair Fox, *Politics and Literature in the Reigns of Henry VII and Henry VIII*, Oxford, 1989, p. 237.

[11] Reed p. 40. The earliest record we have confirmed is for Easter 1521, in 'The Kyngis boke of paymentis', PRO E36/216 p. 254.

[12] BL Egerton MS 2604 fol. 3. Reed p. 41. On Heywood's musical activities, see Stevens, *Music and Poetry*, pp. 282, 319–28.

[13] '. . . at the contemplacion of the Kynges letter, John Heywoode be admitted into the liberties of this citie, payinge the olde hanse [fee]'. Town Clerk's Records, Guildhall 22 May 1523, quoted by G.C. Moore Smith, 'John Heywood the Dramatist a Freeman of London', *N&Q* X (1914) 128.

[14] PRO E101/420 fol. 11. *L&P* V 306; Reed p. 43.

[15] Johnson p. 22. *L&P* V 309.

[16] Reed p. 46 cites Guildhall, Town Clerk's Records, Letter Book O.

[17] *L&P* VI 14. Reed p. 44.

course of the next year, four of the six plays were printed by Heywood's brother-in-law William Rastell.

Publication began anonymously six weeks into the New Year with *Johan Johan*, issued by William Rastell on 12 February 1533 (assuming, as seems probable, that Rastell began the New Year in legal and Roman style at January 1). *The Pardoner and the Frere*, also anonymous, followed on 5 April 1533. *The Play of the Wether* (1533) and *A Play of Love* (1534), both in folio, carried John Heywood's name. *Foure PP* was probably published around this time, though no Rastell edition survives; it was printed by Myddylton c.1544, at about the time he reprinted *Wether*. *Witty and Witless* (an eighteenth-century title) was apparently never printed but was copied and included in Harleian MS 367.[18] The manuscript bears Heywood's name, though the hand is not his, and the spelling is very different from that of the plays which went through Rastell's printing house. Watermarks suggest a date for the MS roughly contemporary with Myddleton's reprints.[19] One other play has frequently been attributed to Heywood; this is *Gentleness and Nobility*, printed by John Rastell c.1526.[20]

It is difficult to be certain how much earlier the plays had been composed, and it has generally been assumed that this was during the period 1520–28. Up to the point of his supposed 'departure' from Court none of the records associates Heywood's name with dramatic spectacles. During the next decade there is considerable evidence of his playmaking, but this comes too late to illuminate the context in which the extant plays must have been composed.

However, some sense of the context in which Heywood wrote his plays can be inferred from the activities of the Rastells up to William's printing of his brother-in-law's plays in 1533. The Rastell printing business was set up around 1509, after John Rastell moved from Coventry to London. His first book was a translation by his brother-in-law Thomas More, *The lyfe of Johan Picus erle of Mirandula* (? 1510). Rastell's printing trade flourished: in the course of twenty years he published over 60 titles, 15 of them law books, 14 were the work of family or friends, 33 were written, edited or translated by himself. Not only was Rastell the first English printer to bring out play texts, but plays continued to make up a significant proportion of his output: Medwall's twenty-year-old *Fulgens and Lucres* (c.1514) was followed by Rastell's own scientific morality *Four Elements* (c.1519) (which included the first music printed in England with moveable type) by *Gentleness and Nobility*, *Calisto and Melebea* (c.1525), and Medwall's *Nature* (c.1530). Skelton's *Magnyfycence* was printed by P. Treveris using Rastell's type.

Pageant making at court appears to have been for Rastell a natural extension of his engineering activity under the Clerk of the King's Works (another Coventry connection).[21] His special expertise in mechanical invention was soon employed in the design and construction of pageant devices for royal occasions: in 1520 at the Field of Cloth of Gold; in 1522 for the visit of Charles V and in 1527 for the entertainment of the French ambassadors at Greenwich, where he made a pageant 'Father in heaven' with 'zodiacke' machinery.[22]

By marrying Joan Rastell, John Heywood gained access to a 'family theatre'

18 *A Catalogue of the Harleian Manuscripts in the British Museum*, 3 vols., 1808–1812, I 213.
19 Personal communication from Dr John Pitcher. See *Two Moral Interludes*.
20 On authorship of *Gentleness and Nobility* see *Rastell Plays* pp. 20–6.
21 *Rastell Plays* pp. 4–8.
22 Reed pp. 165–6; Anglo pp. 197, 218–19.

and it would be surprising if this exposure played no part in fostering his interest in writing for the stage. When John Rastell built his own house at Finsbury Fields in 1524 he made a stage for plays; his wife, Elizabeth More, made costumes which were later hired out.[23] This, perhaps the least aristocratic of London's private playing places, provided a platform for Rastell's own serious ethical and philosophical ideas and, no doubt, also for his family and playwright friends. His brother-in-law Thomas More's enthusiasm for acting is legendary.[24] Ben Jonson's *Tale of a Tub*, set in Tottenham, associates 'old Iohn Haywood' with the mechanical craft of scene-making for masques.[25]

The links between publishing and playmaking are neatly illustrated in the case of Rastell's second or third play title: *Of gentylnes and nobylyte a dyaloge betwen the marchaunt, the knyght and the plowman* is a vigorous extension of the argument of Medwall's humanistic *Fulgens and Lucres*, which he had published about ten years earlier (c.1512–16). Most of *Gentleness* is written in a metre and dramatic language indistinguishable from Heywood's colloquial style, while the systematic philosophical argument in favour of a 'work ethic' and for reform are wholly congruent with Rastell's *Four Elements* and *Calisto and Melebea*. On both internal stylistic features and circumstantial evidence it must be highly probable that Heywood had a large hand in *Gentleness*. Heywood's debt to *Fulgens* is evident later in *The Play of the Wether* (see *Sources* 6). It thus seems likely that it was John Rastell who first steered Heywood's musical talents towards play making.

Whatever dependence Heywood had on his father-in-law must have been drastically reduced by Rastell's change of faith. During the 1520s John Rastell worked as a Chancery lawyer under Wolsey, but towards the end of the decade, he was drawn increasingly to engage in religious polemic, as writer as well as printer. In the course of his exchange with John Frith over purgatory (1529–31) he adopted the Protestant faith, enthusiastically espousing Cromwell's Reforming activities. The first version of More's *Dialogue concerning Heresies* (June 1529) issued from Rastell's printing house, but it probably was his staunchly Catholic son William who actually oversaw the printing, as he certainly did the new edition of 1530.[26]

Heywood's printer, William Rastell, born in 1508, had gone to Oxford in 1525. He had worked with his father and with Holbein on the 1527 Greenwich entertainment of the French ambassadors, preparatory to Princess Mary's betrothal.[27] Before entering Lincoln's Inn in 1532 he had learned the law printing from his father. Clearly he was a man of exceptional ability, rising to become judge in 1558. William remained Catholic and his intense loyalty to his uncle More, reinforced by his marriage in 1542 to his cousin Winifred (More's adopted daughter), is most evident in his monumental life task: editing and, finally, in Queen Mary's reign, publishing Thomas More's *Works* in English (1557).

23 *Rastell Plays* p. 8. 'Pleadings in a Theatrical Lawsuit, John Rastell v. Henry Walton' in *Fifteenth-Century Prose and Verse*, ed. A.W. Pollard, 1903, pp. 307–21.

24 See Lancashire, Nos. 258, 262, 267. E.K. Chambers, *Medieval Stage* II 193 n. 1.

25   'Ha' you nere a Cooper
    At London call'd *Vitruvius*? send for him;
    Or old Iohn Haywood, call him to you, to helpe.' (V ii 72–4)

26 STC 18084, 18085.

27 'The Reknyng of Johan Rastall' in *Treasurer's Accounts of Sir Henry Guldeford*, 19 Henry VIII, PRO E36/227 (unpaginated).

It was crucial for Heywood and for More that William Rastell remained firmly Catholic. As the King leaned towards 'heresy' in his determination to be free of Katherine and of Rome, questions of religious orthodoxy and authority in England became vexed, and printing became more dangerous. William Rastell, having 'elected himself the chief purveyor of Catholic works,'[28] published all the polemical writing by his uncle More that appeared after 1529. When More, who considered himself spokesman of the Queen's party and opposed to the drift of Henry's proposals, was allowed to resign as chancellor on 16 May 1532, Rastell's publication of Part I of the *Confutation of Tyndale* followed almost immediately. In the following year Rastell printed More's *Apology*, his *Letter against J. Frith* and *The Debellation of Salem and Bizance*. At the same time, he began printing Heywood's plays – in two pairs, the first pair anonymous. *Johan Johan* was dated 12 February 1533 (Rastell seems to have started the new year in January, legal fashion). *Pardoner and Frere* was dated 5 April 1533. Neither title page named John Heywood.

When Henry's break with Rome became public, events accelerated: Anne's appearance as Queen (15 April) was swiftly followed by Cranmer's declaration of the marriage with Katherine nul; Anne was crowned (1 June) and three months later gave birth to Princess Elizabeth. Soon after the King's order that Mary was no longer to be styled 'Princess of England', Heywood dedicated to her his ballad, 'Give place ye ladies.' Far from shunning danger, William Rastell, who was sharing a house with Heywood, increased his output. It may be that *Foure PP* was first printed at this time, though the first surviving edition is Middleton's of about 1544. At any rate, when Rastell printed the second pair of plays, *The Play of the Wether* 1533 (probably late in the year) and *A Play of Love* 1534 (probably soon after), both title pages named John Heywood.

The risk in printing these unpretentious and superficially non-controversial plays was slight, especially as there is evidence that the author enjoyed royal favour at the beginning of 1533. Printing the second part of More's *Confutation of Tyndale* was another matter. This seems to have been ready for sale around Christmas 1533, and Rastell dated it 1534 in anticipation of its release. Early in the New Year he was summoned before Cromwell to account for his part in an alleged reply by More to St German's pro-supremacy *Articles*.[29] More himself was first under investigation and then arrested. (In this connection it is worth noting that *A Play of Love* bears the colophon 'cum privilegio Regali', as if to claim some protection.) The upshot of Cromwell's pressure on More was that William Rastell stopped printing at this time, and devoted himself to the law at Lincoln's Inn, where he was joined in July 1534 by Heywood's brother Richard. Within a year John Heywood's son Jasper was born and Thomas More was executed. Things also went badly for old John Rastell, imprisoned as a zealot, examined by Cranmer, he died in April 1536, a year before his wife Elizabeth More.

The circumstances of printing Heywood's plays in 1533–34 may therefore be

---

[28] G.R. Elton, *Reform and Reformation 1509–1558*, London, 1977, p. 156. William Rastell's importance as a leading Catholic at Lincoln's Inn is indicated by a record that on 3 May 1554, as 'one of the benchers' he paid for a 'great image or pycture in a Table of the takyng downe of Chryste fro the Crosse for chapel Altar' at the Inn (*The Black Books of Lincoln's Inn: I 1422–1586* (London, 1897) pp. 308–9). His wife 'Wenefred' was dead by then.

[29] J. Guy, 'Thomas More and Christopher St German: The Battle of the Books' in *Reassessing the Henrician Age: Humanism, Politics and Reform*, ed. A. Fox and J. Guy, Oxford, 1986, pp. 95–120.

seen as part of an energetic campaign by William Rastell to support Thomas More after his resignation as Chancellor in his private stand for the old beliefs and loyalties, just as Cromwell's reformation seemed to have triumphed for the King.

John Heywood himself apparently weathered these difficult times with success, though men on such opposite tacks as John Rastell and Thomas More sank. The records suggest that he continued to prosper as musician and play-maker. He was associated with Princess Mary's household, possibly as music tutor, and in January 1537 her Book of Expenses shows a payment 'to Heywood's servant for bringing my lady graces Regalles to Greenwich xxd.'[30] In March 1538 he received 40s 'for pleyeng an enterlude with his Children bifore my ladies grace.' This may have been at Richmond.[31] There is no indication whether he devised and acted in the interlude as well as directing it. The 'children' are likely to have been choristers from the Chapel Royal or St Paul's, with whose Master, Sebastian Westcott, Heywood certainly collaborated some years later.[32]

Surprisingly, at about the same time as Cromwell paid the fiercely Protestant John Bale for a play performance, Heywood was also involved in dramatic production for Cromwell. This is indicated by Heywood's receipt of payment and his 'costes' for his part in producing a 'Masque of King Arthur's Knights' with hobby horses at Cromwell's house on 11 February 1539 (Shrove Tuesday).[33] On 22 February Cromwell paid 'the bargemen that carried Heywoods maske to the court and home again.'[34] Meanwhile, Heywood was active acquiring property in Essex, where it seems he benefitted from Cromwell's execution in 1540.[35] Jointly with his wife he conveyed property in Tottenham to William Rastell at the time of the latter's marriage to Winifred Clements, Thomas More's adopted daughter, in 1542.

Amidst what might look like trimming, Heywood's boldest intervention in religious affairs came in 1542–43, when he was involved with John More and other conservative Catholics in a plot to arraign Cranmer for heresy. With others he was found guilty at Westminster on 15 February 1544 of conspiring against the royal supremacy; John More was pardoned; on 7 March Heywood walked to the scaffold with other of the leading conspirators, but was not hanged. Following a pardon on 26 June, in which he is referred to as 'late of London, alias of North Mymmes' (Middlesex), on 6 July he dressed in a penitential gown and read a public recantation at St Paul's Cross. According to Sir John Harington, the King's favourite 'escaped hanging with his mirth'.[36]

---

30 Princess Mary's Privy Purse Accompt, BL Royal MS 17.B.xxviii fol. 7v. Reed p. 58. The accounts for February 1524 show payment of expenses to a 'Johannes haiwarde de henley super Tamisia et sociis suis' but this seems to have been a provisioner (PRO E36/222 p. 11).

31 Privy Purse expenses of Princess Mary, cited by Reed p. 58. Lancashire No. 1334.

32 A payment of 30s from Household Expenses of Princess Elizabeth, 13 February 1552, shows Heywood in collaboration with 'Sebastian', who was reimbursed for 'the charge of the children with the carriage of the plaiers garments' (Reed p. 59, Lancashire No. 754). An inscription in Thomas Mulliner's Book (Add MS 30513), containing some of Redford's music and his play *Wit and Science*, claims that Mulliner was a pupil of Heywood's, some of whose poems are written into the MS (fols. 56–62v).

33 *L&P* V.xiv.ii.340. Reed p. 44. Bale, *Plays* I, 4–5.

34 *L&P* V.xiv. 782. Reed pp. 61–2. Lancashire No. 1029.

35 Reed pp. 35–51.

36 Reed p. 63 cites Harington's *Metamorphosis of Ajax*. See also Foxe, *A&M* V 528; *L&P* XIX.i 444; Brigden pp. 353–54.

Soon after this recantation, according to Thomas Whythorne, his 'servant and skoller' in music from about 1545 to 1548, Heywood composed a metaphysical interlude for Cranmer. It sounds like a peace-offering:

At þe request of doktor (Thos.) Cranmer, lat archbyshop of Cantorbury hee mad A sertayn enterlude or play which waz devyzed vpon þe parts of Man at þe end wherof he lykneth and applieth þe sirkunstans þerof to þe vniuersall estat of Chrystes church.[37]

Whythorne transcribed (as prose) a speech in two rhyme royal stanzas from this lost moral play, which shows Heywood's style at its knottiest (see Appendix I). To this same period belong reprints of *Foure PP*, *Love* and *Wether*, and the manuscript copy of *Witty and Witless*. The reissue of the plays, whether it originated with Heywood or not, may reflect a confidence that these openly attributed plays would not be thought the work of a religious zealot. A *Dialogue of Proverbes*, also referred to by Thomas Whythorne, was published by Thomas Berthelet, the King's Printer, in 1546, and reprinted in 1549, 1556, 1561. Meanwhile, Heywood's personal wealth was boosted by fees from a disestablished priory.[38] In 1550 Berthelet printed his *An hundred Epigrammes* (reprinted 1556).

Though he can have felt little sympathy with the Protestant Reformation, Heywood's position at court seems to have continued secure. On 4 March 1552, on the death of Sir William Penyson, his pension was substantially increased to £40 a year and he was appointed (or reappointed) *dapifer camerae*, sewer of the King's chamber.[39] 'Apparell and furnyture' for 'another playe of the Chilldren made by Mr Hawood' were paid for by the Office of the Revels between January and April 1553 and included 'xij cotes for the boyes'. 'Heywoodes playe' was part of Shrovetide Court Revels, under the direction of George Ferrers. Along with a topical 'playe of the State of Ireland' made by the lawyer William Baldwin, it was postponed, probably till Easter.[40] At the young King's death (19 July 1553) Heywood was granted livery for himself and two servants, as 'sewer of the chamber', in charge of seating the King's guests at table.

While it cannot be claimed that Heywood suffered under Edward VI, the accession of Mary, his Catholic princess and pupil, must have brought great joy to him at the age of almost sixty. At her coronation on 30 September, Mary

rode forth and in Pauls Churchyard against the school [Colet's] one Master Haywood sate in a pageant under a vine and made to her an oration in Latin & in English.[41]

As the children of Paul's and other choirmen at Dean's gate 'sung dyverse staves in gratifying the quene', Heywood's pageant at Colet's school probably made use of older boys; at the 'commynge of the prynce of Spayne' in 1554, Heywood was similarly engaged.[42] The earlier annuities were confirmed.[43] To judge from Ben

---

37 Whythorne, *Autobiography* pp. 13–14; a few lines from the play are quoted on p. 74. Lancashire No. 136 dates this 1545–9.

38 *L&P* V.xxi.243.

39 Reed p. 51. Puttenham's story that 'merry John Heywood was allowed to sit at the tables end' at the Reformist Duke of Northumberland's board may also relate to this period (*Arte of Poesie*, pp. 275–6).

40 Anglo p. 315; Feuillerat pp. 134, 141–5; Lancashire No. 1081.

41 Stowe's *Annals* (1631 ed.) p. 617; Reed p. 59.

42 Lancashire No. 1083; Reed p. 60; Anglo p. 326.

43 Reed p. 51 cites Patent Rolls 1&2 Philip & Mary, P.8.m.40, P.4.m.16.

Jonson's *Conversations with Drummond*, Heywood's confidence in Queen Mary's favour showed itself in characteristic clowning.[44] In spite of the evident theatrical activity, no new plays of Heywood's were published. A further *Two hundred Epigrammes* were printed and Heywood completed *The Spider and the Flie* (printed by T. Powell 1556), taking up an allegory of legal intrigue in Westminster more than twenty years earlier and redirecting it to compliment the Queen.[45]

Meanwhile, William Rastell finished his great life work, of collecting and editing his uncle's writings, and Thomas More's *Workes . . . in the Englysh tonge* was printed by Tottel, dated 30 April 1557. In October 1558 he became a judge, three weeks before Queen Elizabeth's accession. That Christmas, Jasper Heywood, who had been a fellow of All Souls in Oxford, became Lord of Misrule at Lincoln's Inn.

At first nothing seems to have changed for Heywood. When Queen Elizabeth was at Nonsuch on 7 August 1559, according to Henry Machyn's *Diary*, she saw, 'a play of the chyldren of powlls and ther master S[ebastian Westcott], Mr Phelypes & Mr Haywode.'[46] A *fourth hundred of Epygrams* was printed in 1560. In January or February 1561 Thomas Hackett paid fourpence to enter 'a play of Wytless' in the Stationers' Register.[47] Thomas Powell printed *John Heywoodes Woorkes* (excluding the plays) in 1562.

The balance of Elizabeth's religious settlement shifted the fortunes of the Catholic families decisively. Faced with the impending 1563 Articles of Religion, William Rastell fled with his wife's Clements family to Louvain. After the establishment of the Commission to enforce the Act of Uniformity, Heywood and his wife left England on 20 July 1564 to settle in Brabant.[48] William Rastell died, leaving a ring to John Heywood and most of his estate to Heywood's son Ellis. The Heywood property amassed during a life-time of successful royal service was confiscated. John and his wife continued to live at Malines (Mechelen), though Queen Elizabeth granted him permission to return to England.[49] On 18 April 1575 he wrote from the poverty of exile in Malines to Lord Burghley, asking – with pathos and gallant wit, and also with success – for release of revenues from his estates in England.[50]

As he approached eighty John Heywood joined his son Ellis, a priest at the Jesuit College in Antwerp, making his will on 16 January 1577.[51] Fleeing the

---

[44] 'Heywood the Epigrammatist being apparelled in Velvet by Queen Mary with his cap on in the presence, in spight of all the Gentlemen, till the Queen herself asked him what he meaned, and then he asked her if he was Heywood, for she had made him so brave that he had almost misknowen himself.' (*Works* I 148).

[45] *Spider* STC 13308. Possibly this began as the story of how John Rastell was caught in Cromwell's web and altered to how Heywood himself was caught in Cranmer's web. But the Spider has been interpreted as Northumberland. See further John N. King, *English Reformation Literature*, Los Angeles, 1986, p. 252; de la Bère pp. 101–11.

[46] Reed p. 60.

[47] *A Transcript of the Registers of the Company of Stationers of London; 1554–1640*, ed. Edward Arber, 4 vols., London, 1875–77, I, 154. *Revels History of Drama* II 60.

[48] Reed p. 68.

[49] *CSP Dom.Eliz. 1566–79*, p. 581.

[50] Printed by Reed pp. 237–8.

[51] W. Bang, 'Acta Anglo-Lovaniensia: John Heywood und sein Kreis', *Englische Studien* 38 (1907), 234–49, at 236. On Heywood's last years see also ed. H. De Vocht (ed.), *Jasper Heywood and his Translations of Seneca*, Louvain, 1913, p. vii.

violence of the Orange party in 1578 he and Ellis took refuge in Louvain, where John died, shortly after his son's death on 2 October 1578.

The last fifteen years make a sad and strained conclusion to a life that was unusually long, fortunate, and creative. By the time of his death most of the extant plays were half-a-century old. Since publication in 1533 some had been printed at least three or four times. On 15 January 1582 J. Awdeley assigned to J. Charlewood the printing rights to *Foure PP* (last printed by J. Allde 1569), *A Play of Love* (last extant edition c.1550) and *The Play of the Wether* (last extant edition c.1573). Some spellings were modernized, some expressions were made metrically smoother, and some references to Catholic practice were changed (see note on 4P1163). It is unlikely and probably impossible that Heywood overlooked these later editions, which means that they cannot be afforded much authority. The plays belong to the 1520s and early 1530s and there is little in their subtle topical and doctrinal manoeuverings to alarm an Elizabethan reader looking to merry John Heywood for wit and proverbial wisdom.

From the biographical details sketched here it should be apparent that external evidence for composition and performance of the extant plays is meagre. However, discussion of the plays' source materials, as well as of their topicality and interrelations, will attempt to put into historical focus the canon attributed to Heywood and will suggest a tentative order of composition. First, however, the themes and conventions of the plays themselves merit description and analysis.

THE PLAYS

1. Common Features

In size and scope all the plays are suited as entertainment in private houses or at Court or Inns of Court, and are playable within about an hour-and-a-half, depending on the extent of additional song and music. The plays, however, come in two sizes – short (*Witty and Witless* 703 lines, *Johan Johan* 678, *Pardoner and Frere* 641) and long (*Foure PP* 1234 lines, *Love* 1577, *Wether* 1254). Size of cast varies considerably: the first two have three actors, the next three have four, while *Wether* requires ten – probably an indication of increased resources available to Heywood at different points in his career. *Wether* looks to be the odd one out; it may be the only survivor of his plays written for acting by boys of the Chapel Royal or St Paul's.

All the plays are comic, working satirically through exaggeration and ridicule. In all except the French-derived *Johan Johan*, which has a 'proper plot', the essence of dramatic action is a dispute for preeminence: debate of views (*Witty and Witless*), argument based on personal experience (*Play of Love*), trial of professional expertise (*Pardoner and Frere*, *Foure PP*), competing claims for social and economic priority (*Play of the Wether*). Conflict develops dynamically through the process of dialogue and mutual judgment, so that the audience's own judgment is awakened; argument and view point are critically manipulated towards resolution in which the rivalries are finally viewed as parts of a whole, diverse but unified. In *Pardoner and Frere* this resolution takes a parodic form in the last-minute alliance of the rogues against authority and the established Church. The characters themselves are little altered, but for the audience a pattern is revealed, so that they must confront their own selfish bias. In the two plays with violent farcical action (*Johan Johan*, *Pardoner and Frere*) decisive change in estate is likewise avoided and a strong sense conveyed of a repeatable cycle.

Analysis shows all the plays to be carefully constructed according to fairly simple principles of stagecraft: the entry or exit of a character marks a new stage in the process of the action. Except for *Witty* (which seems to begin in a conversational Erasmian fashion, as if the audience has just entered a room where discussion is already in progress), all the plays open with a long speech; in three cases (*Johan Johan*, *Pardoner and Frere*, *Play of the Wether*) this is also the longest speech in the play. The scenic units are often balanced with a fine sense of the symmetry and are interwoven to produce a pleasing diversity of mood and interest, while at the same time the main dramatic idea is constantly thrust forward.

There is much formality in the conduct of argument itself. Heywood's keen interest in displaying and exercising the mechanics of argument and showing the difficulty of resolving it gives support to Altman's emphasis on the widespread Tudor interest in dialectic.[1] Likewise, his structuring of argument by adept manipulation of rhetorical tropes to accentuate contrasts between speakers and between attitudes, has been noted.[2] In visual terms, Heywood's liking for symmetries and oppositions, paradoxes, contradictions, is highlighted by recur-

[1] Altman, pp.107–24.
[2] Robinson, pp.163–80.

11

rent dance-like antics which regroup the figures on stage, making new alliances and thematic patterns. This is specially true of the plays which make use of four actors.

Language and versification are significantly varied, so as to shift tone and pace, and to switch levels of social decorum. The 'highest' verse form, rhyme royal is used at the end of *Witty and Witless* and *Foure PP*, where the king or the court audience is addressed. In *A Play of Love* rhyme royal is used at beginning and end. Jupiter in *The Play of the Wether* speaks little else, while the verse forms and speech of the human figures is hierarchically graded. In the scurrilous *Johan Johan* Heywood was interested in the prosodic variety of his source, the *Pasté*, and in translating he uses a lively array of verses, including repetitive phrases reminiscent of the *rondeau*, and the subdivision of individual lines between different speakers. His most frequent verse form, the couplet, is used with great variety, especially in argument where rhymes are made to pick up keywords, or where the pace is varied as the speakers exploit opportunities for making points in debate.

These characteristics are enhanced by Heywood's skilful use of 'leashes' where a word may be turned inside out by frequent repetition, so that its meaning is destabilized. Many examples of this 'French' technique occur in *Witty and Witless* and in *A Play of Love*.[3]

The recurrence of proverbial language is usually integral to the argument where proverbs are often used as the voice of authority to strike an attitude or generalise a point. Nowhere do the plays attain the density of proverbial texture in the later virtuoso *Dialogue of Proverbs* where proverbs are swapped and matched, crowding upon one another sequentially in exhilarating display of ingenuity. Characteristically, the proverbs in the plays are used for their colloquial pithiness and ironic worldly wisdom; but the colourful 'scenic' quality of their figurative language also helps to create a literal and vivid visual world.

Because action centres on the conflict of ideas and social attitudes, the 'characters' required are usually types. Only Johan Johan, Tyb, Syr Johan, Jupiter, and Mery Report have 'proper' names, the rest being labelled, fixed in their estates: 'a Gentylwoman', 'the Pedler'. 'Lover unloved' and so on. Fixity of social position and outlook, economic, intellectual, or moral, is necessary to perpetuation of conflict. The greatest range is in *The Play of the Wether*, where the eight suitors use different verbal registers and speak from conflicting economic interests. Here and elswehere Heywood shows a Chaucerian pleasure in the detail of technical language for its own sake, as well as to create character and social function.

The paucity of local habitations and names for his characters is in some respects off-set by Heywood's liking for lists, especially of places and things, giving solidity to the outside world beyond the plays. This geographical world stretches as far as Jerusalem but is mostly located in the vicinity of Greater London, especially in Middlesex and Essex, where the playwright himself had property. Performance of the long monologues stretches the audience's sense of the world as well as testing its credulity and taxes the actor's ability to the full. Heywood's most fascinating experiments in this area of dramaturgy may be his use of the long monologue (following Chaucer in the *Canterbury Tales*) to make the audience judge story against teller. The Pardoner's descent to hell (*Foure PP*)

---

[3] E.g. Wy76–9, 128–32, 661–5, where the words 'witty' and 'witless' are consistently juxtaposed; and L941–4, 1102–45, 1362–71, which play upon 'will', 'contentacyon' and 'lie/love'.

and No lover nor loved's account of his own invulnerability to the folly of love (*A Play of Love*) are masterful in this respect.

In contrast to the strongly typical nature of most of Heywood's characters, some parts require extraordinary versatility and an almost bewildering range of mood and theatrical behaviour: the Pedler, the Potycary, Mery Report, No lover nor loved in particular. These last two are the first named 'Vices' (although the others share many Vice characteristics). In *Foure PP*, where a Vice is not designated, or perhaps even conceived, his functions are shared between the Pedler, who organises the proceedings, and the acrobatic Potycary.[4] Our sense of the Vice's role has been intensified by the suspicion that Heywood – by contemporary accounts a charming, witty, and versatile performer and an expert singer may have taken this part himself in *Wether*. If the possibility that John Bale played the Vice in his *Three Laws* and *King Johan* is also kept in mind, the case for playwright-actor is strengthened.

These Vice characters have an organising function – not to say a manipulative one – and a propensity to deflate others by irreverence. They are playmakers and go-betweens, not fixed in any social 'estate', but able to mimic any. They relate as easily to the audience as to the other players, taking liberties with both. Their capers and apparent improvisations add movement, dance perhaps, and song-like antics often reminiscent of children's games. But the Vice figures are the least innocent of Heywood's roles: knowing, verbally clever, and irrepressibly bawdy.

Recurrent and reductive joking, both scatological and sexual, is a notable common feature. This was part of the traditions of popular and courtly entertainment Heywood inherited, but he developed this line of entertainment from his acquaintance with the theatrical routines of French farce and *sottie*. Henrician court taste clearly countenanced a liking for double entendre and a good deal of grossness. In a theatrical context these features ensure that the audience's attention is refreshed in following serious argument; they also act as a foil to more dangerous objects of satire. In the terrifying, sometimes ridiculous, struggle of the Tudor Court enmeshed in the inseparable problems of Divorce and Reformation, wit was indispensible, and the making of jokes essential for survival. There can be no doubt about the seriousness of Heywood's orthodox beliefs, nor of his courage and consistency in restating them. Beyond the cogent sanity of their argument, the theatrical qualities of the plays, which were produced at – or close to – the centre of power, suggest a much more daring course, danced nimbly between diplomacy and subversion.

2. Witty and Witless

The play's dramatic mode is disputation – itself a form of humanist entertainment and intellectual exercise – on the great Erasmian theme of Folly. Direct argument between the first two protagonists, who are then joined by a third, is used to explore contradiction and paradox. Provisional acceptance of the folly of men's lives is then subjected to more searching scrutiny leading to an affirmation of deeper spiritual wisdom.

The dramatic construction is simple: two large dialogue scenes flank a central

---

4 Compare the Potycary's joke with that of Not lover nor loved, 4P499–503 and L1022–7.

short scene of three characters. The symmetry and progression reinforce the movement of the argument. Dialogue is entirely in 'heavy', long-line couplets (10–13 syllables, usually five-stress) with some repeated rhymes forming quatrains a dozen times at random intervals.[1] A brief epilogue to be used in the royal presence, is in rhyme royal.

Witty and Witless is unique among the plays in that Heywood plunges *in medias res*. It is possible that the beginning of the text has been lost from the manuscript, yet the Erasmian stylistic trick is neatly turned: 'I seay as I began' (Wy4) and the 'first' topic of review is introduced at Wy8, so that nothing appears lost from the argument. The question in debate is, Has the witty or the witless man more pleasure and less pain in life? The first section ends when John concedes to James, 'better to be a foole then a wyse man, sewre' (Wy408). Jerome's entry brings all three speakers on stage (Wy408–42), though dramatic convention allows the newcomer to have heard the preceding arguments. He distinguishes wit and wisdom, showing the necessity of wit to human beings. At this, the impertinent and scornful 'elfe' (Wy120) James exits in anger, thinking he has lost. In the third 'scene' (Wy443–703), at John's request, Jerome points out his errors in having conceded the arguments of James, and persuades him of the uses of reason. By introducing considerations of the soul he guides argument towards reinforcing a traditional Catholic position: man should use his wits to good purpose, 'Plant ymps of good woorcks' (Wy556) in hope of reward in heaven, because 'There are in heven dyvers degrees of glory' (Wy563). Lines 676–703 form an epilogue, four of the stanzas being addressed to the King.

Thus the apparently superficial issue of the first part becomes a consideration of the relation of good works to grace, and of salvation to degrees of glory (Wy559–73, 603–34). Jerome is forcefully persuasive, and contrasts with James's impertinent defence of folly; like Mery Report in *Wether*, James is an 'elfe' (Wy120), although the play's strict pursuit of argument allows him little scope for irrelevant antics.

Of all the plays this offers least information about action and plot – there is only one stage direction. Forceful conduct of the argument would no doubt be accomplished by gesture and positional play in the performance area. Noteworthy are the set pieces within the speeches, such as the description of the lot of the mill horse (Wy466–76), which may be one of the earliest examples of an Erasmian 'emblem' enacted. Miming the mockery of the 'sott' is reinforced by lengthy repetition of '*Some* beate hym . . .' (Wy31–41). In general the play is richest of all Heywood's in 'leashes' which strain a repeated word almost beyond sense. Significantly, these often initiate or end phases in the argument.[2] Rhyme is neatly used to clinch points in argument, as at Wy195–6. Taken together, these virtuoso passages of speech, reveal one of Heywood's interests in performance: the speaker's skill is in negotiating passages which are difficult to say because they depend upon tongue-twisting or feats of memory. In one case the word play follows the proverb 'Better one byrde in hand then ten in the wood,' and runs through nine succeeding lines (Wy594–602). Such dazzling dexterity can assist the argument, and it contrasts amusingly with occasional monosyllabic

---

1 Wy19, 105, 175, 181, 207, 245, 365, 395, 399, 437, 489, 615, 649.
2 E.g. at Wy307–12. Other leashes are noted at Wy76–9, 131–2, 207–10, 307–11, 329–35, 355–64, 595–602, 637–42, 661–5.

14

and sometimes extra-metrical lines. At one point the monosyllabic 'yes' draws a contemptuous comment (Wy365).

The central concept of folly in the play is epitomized by the references to Will Somer, the King's Fool and, perhaps, in some senses Heywood's theatrical rival (Wy43, 701, and notes). These jibes and the one direction about the possibility of the King's presence (Wy675) attest a royal or Court performance.

3. Johan Johan

The dramatic qualities of *Johan Johan* partly derive from its French source, so that discussion of it as a translation is postponed to the section on sources. Partly as a consequence of its origins, the play is closer to ordinary domestic circumstance than any of the other plays; it depends far more on physical objects and actions and is unique in its sustained representation of narrative. Its plot springs from the conspiracy of Tyb and the priest Syr Johan against her husband. The characters are traditional types (dithering cuckold, lustful shrew, sanctimonious adulterer) and functional, subservient to dramatic conflict.

Dramatic construction follows the French in its rapid linear clarity. Like most of Heywood's plays it has strong symmetry, having a 'prologue' scene of monologue, three 'scenes', and an 'epilogue'. In his long opening speech, addressed to the audience (J1–110) Johan Johan confides his suspicions and threatens to beat his straying wife. Though strictly speaking this is a monologue, Johan Johan's quotation of his neighbour's advice on how to treat his wife, together with his own cowardly vacillations, make it seem like dialogue.

Tyb's aggressive entry starts the first movement of the plot (J111–313), withering Johan Johan's resolve. He is made the unwilling agent of her plot to entertain the priest. Here, the simple conflict of marital strife gives an impression of being orchestrated for four voices, because both speakers use asides, often overheard and responded to by the other partner. The secret to Tyb's theatrical power is that she brazens out her asides; in contrast, Johan Johan's meek denial of his shows him impotent. Similarly, she ignores his commands, while he unwillingly carries out hers, setting the trestle table, washing the cups and so on. This comic inversion of 'normal' authority is very much funnier (and less offensive to modern audiences) if, as was probably the case historically, Tyb is played by a man.) Throughout the preparations, the husband's anxious and hungry solicitide establishes the pie as the goal of the characters' appetites in the play. Dramatic tension has been heightened by six false exits before Johan Johan is finally allowed to leave the house.

For the second 'scene' (J314–415) there is a second locus, the priest's house, to which Johan Johan is sent. Here a richness of vocal response is generated by mingling the oily double entendre of Syr Johan's professed virtue with the husband's gullible asides, through which his angry suspicions evaporate. Johan Johan's resumption of the threatening mode concludes the scene, as the two move back to his house for supper.

All the characters are now gathered at the original locus of hearth and pie for the longest scene (J416–664). At first the lovers are careful of Johan Johan's hovering presence, but as their confidence grows, their impositions on Johan Johan grow more flagrant as the dramatic tension mounts towards the climax. While the priest gorges himself on Tyb's pie, the husband is ritually humiliated.

It is not sufficient that he stand by the fire chafing the wax in a vain attempt to stop the 'cleft' of his wife's pail; he must be made to narrate his humiliation in a refrain which is repeated, with variations, sixteen times before his patience bursts into physical violence.

After the flight of the adulterous pair, in a brief monologue (J665–78) Johan Johan's glow of self-satisfaction at having beaten his wife soon cools to habitual nagging jealousy. He exits, fearing a never-ending tale of sexual deception.

An impression of speed is intensified by the use of couplets for the entire dialogue, save for one triplet (J328) and nine quatrains of alternating rhyme.[1] Individual lines are divided between speakers at the height of dramatic tension (J629–36) just before the breaking point. Further division of a line between the three of them – 'And thou lyest!' 'And thou lyest!' 'And thou lyest agayn!' (J659) – indicates a care for symmetry of the triangle even in the midst of the brawl. Pauses are equally important. Johan Johan's opening speech breaks into short 'paragraphs' (indicated in the folio by the use of a pilcrow) as he starts off in ludicrously self-contradictory directions.

The quality of colloquial speech is caught throughout: in the thorough Anglicization of the scene through reference to local saints and churches; in the false note of Tyb's simpering, 'By my soule, I love the too too' (J183); and in the characters' apt use of proverbs to relate their particular experience to the way of the world. Proverbs are sometimes realised literally, as in Johan Johan's complaint:

> The parysshe preest forgetteth that ever he was clarke. (J595)

They always carry a thematic burden, and there is rueful irony in Johan Johan's line:

> He must nedes go that the dyvell dryveth. [Exit] (J313)

Heywood's liking for punning allusions is evident in his choice of popular saints (see note on J146) and in his tracing of patterns of imagery. The outrageous sexuality of the plot is conveyed by elaboration of the idea of Tyb as a cat on heat who goes 'catter wawlyng' (J110 and note) and by pursuing such double entendre as 'tacle' (J554). Above all, the domestic stage properties are used to represent the elemental action; chafed wax candle, split bucket, and hot pie greedily devoured convey frustrated impotence and the satisfying of appetite in a directly physical – but also ridiculously oblique and mechanical – way.

This explicitness of sexual ideas in word and action derives from the *Farce* source. It was a technique Heywood was able to extend in other, more decorous play actions, particularly in *The Play of the Wether*, and *A Play of Love*, where Heywood mocks the follies of love. The dramatic effectiveness of building conflict into physical combat he used again in *The Pardoner and the Frere*, where the opponents also 'fyght by the erys'.

4. The Pardoner and the Frere

Though it is written for four actors, this is a virtuoso piece for two. The Pardoner, is taken directly from Chaucer's vehement and unscrupulous salesman, while the mendicant Frere, with his hackneyed diction of the friar song-books

---

1 Quatrains (abab) are at J341, 391, 487, 497, 525, 543, 581, 593, 641, so that metrically the play is very similar to *Witty and Witless*.

(his 'Lorde, clyped swete Jesus' PF35), develops the lisping preacher from the *Canterbury Tales* too. They have been simplified to the needs of crude confrontation with polemical undertones: separately and together they threaten the Church. The two vicious and avaricious rogues compete for the audience's attention and money until they come to blows; when finally challenged by authority in the form of the Curate and Prat, the constable, they join forces and escape to try their tricks another day. Condemnation is implicit.

The action is simply linear. The Frere enters first (PF1–78), is joined, unawares, by the Pardoner (PF79–188). Rivalry begins with their simultaneous address of the audience, indicated by the stage direction,

> Now shall the Frere begyn his sermon, and evyn at the same tyme the Pardoner begynneth also to shew and speke of his bullys, and auctorytes com from Rome:

and increases without slackening through a continuous 'dialogue' (PF189–544). There are five bursts of simultaneous speech, divided by brief exchanges which become increasingly threatening. In the first (PF189–209) the two charlatans pretend to be unaware of each other, pausing only long enough for each to make a two-line comment on the other's interruption, before resuming (PF214–51), so that the Frere completes his exemplum of Dives and Lazarus while the Pardoner simultaneously alleges Papal authority for pardons in the cause of collecting for St Leonard's chapel. In turn (PF252–315), the Frere curses his opponent for hindering the Word and the Pardoner threatens the Frere with excommunication, accusing him of heresy. The third 'bout' (PF316–43) is an open competition for the audience's attention, with the Frere's begging formula 'We freres' ringing against the Pardoner's 'This is the pardon'. In the brief pause (PF344–63), the Frere attempts formally to curse using words alleged to be from scripture. They fall to simultaneous sales patter (PF246–407) in praise, respectively, of poverty and pardons. In a further respite from the cacophany of simultaneous speech (PF408–35) the Pardoner openly accuses the Frere of the very 'covetyse' that he preaches against (an accusation Heywood has neatly turned round from Chaucer). The two resolve to a further and louder trial of voices (PF436–507) in which each decries the other's deeds; the Frere praises his services as intercessor with God, while the Pardoner, playing on the audience's fear of death, describes ceremonial wakes and chantry prayers. The contest now grows furious (PF508–44) and physical, as each incites the audience to help 'pull down' the other, so that after many a threat and dare, they fight – literally – 'by the ears'.

The entry of the Curate provokes speeches of self-justification and further vilification of each rival (PF545–77). Neybour Prat is called in to help arrest the knaves for punishment. With the full cast now on stage (PF578–641) Heywood springs one last surprise. The two rascals unite against authority and, having made 'reade blood' run, exit together. It is a final savage irony that, having spoken 252 lines simultaneously, their last utterance is spoken in unison:

> Than adew, to the devyll, tyll we come agayn! (PF640)

The traditional theatrical 'Vice' exit line here carries an ominous suggestion that the place they go to can only be hell.

There is little doubt from the stage direction at PF188 that the Pardoner and Frere are meant to speak simultaneously. Experiment has shown that the audience can follow both speeches at the same time quite successfully, though one must leave open the possibility that some variation would need to be introduced over the five bursts in performance. Clues in the dialogue show how the attention of the audience may be sustained and also switched from one speaker to the other. The formulaic quality of the speeches, repetition in the syntax, and metrical exactness all help the listener to engage with the sense of the individual speeches and yet be simultaneously aware. If the performers, building upon these clues as structural aids, then add variation, say in pitch of voice and in pace, not to mention physical posturing, we have an extraordinary *coup de théâtre* which encourages virtuoso performance. It seems the Pardoner may keep up a continuous noise while the Friar is speaking (PF347–9 and note). That the conflict grows more physical is hinted in the dialogue (PF515, 521) and detailed during the fight itself (PF539, 540, 543).

Heywood's skill in relating words and actions is very original here. The perception of the follies of avarice and heresy – neither character arouses sympathy from the audience – is sharpened by the carefully controlled tempo and by the inventiveness of the conflict. The audience, subjected to a double onslaught of trickery, is manipulated into making a judgment. It is a startling moment when the Parson reveals near the end of the play that all this chicanery has been perpetrated inside his church – a cleverly delayed and clinching condemnation. As in *Johan Johan*, simultaneous stage presence is exploited to convey interaction and reaction. The Pardoner's accusation that the Friar is avaricious is proved true, and its converse implied. Neither admits his heresy. There is an implicit warning in the escape which the tricksters make from the just condemnation of the Parson and the Constable.

The play may be seen as a variation of Heywood's continuous interest in presenting conflicting views. There are orthodox defences implied in the words of each speaker. What they say may be expected of them given their initial positions, but it is an additional irony that they condemn themselves out of their own mouths. The insistence with which the play turns its audience from game to earnest, towards the squalid violence and sacrilege of contemporary factionalism, reveals the underlying seriousness of Heywood's dramatic imagination.

5. The Foure PP

The play resembles *The Pardoner and the Frere* in the idea of a comic 'contest between shady wayfarers', but is different in tone and method and offers a positive and harmonious resolution instead of sinister violence. Heywood's preference for four actors (as in Pardoner and Frere but with the parts more evenly distributed) makes for variety of conflict and contrast, requiring a more complex resolution than do the plays scripted for three.

Although *Foure PP* is virtually plotless, its action is skilfully constructed by means of symmetries and contrasts. The interweaving of formal boasts or narratives with antic 'improvisations' creates four larger movements of roughly equal length. Lines 1–321 introduce the characters, establishing their animosities, and ending with their song. From 4P322–643 further argument, including formal boasts by the Pardoner and Potycary, about the merits of their professional skills in helping men to salvation, unearths a bone of contention: Which of the four should take social precedence? The third movement (4P644–1010) contains the formal lying contest, with the long narratives of the Potycary and the Pardoner, respectively scatological and escatological, ending with the clever, brief intervention of the Palmer. Finally (4P1011–1234) judgment is given by the Pedler, first on the trivial competition, then more seriously on the morality of the three contestants' chosen ways of life.

The characters (as in most of the plays) are clearly types, but they are strongly distinguished by temperament and moral outlook: one pair (Palmer, Pedler) is sunny, optimistic, orthodox; the other (Pardoner, Potycary) is cynical, aggressive, blasphemous, heretical. It accords with natural justice that the good-natured Palmer, whom the audience meets first, when he recommends pilgrimage to them, should carry the day (which he does by his apparently naive defence of women). As a good Christian, he accepts fortune, cheerfully turning the other cheek to insults from the defeated pair. He immediately gives up his 'maistry' over them. The Palmer's authority is underlined by the fact that he alone speaks in higher verse forms; he begins the play with quatrains and closes it with two stanzas of rhyme royal.

The Pardoner, who challenges him, is a shady figure, pursuing a licensed trade from despicable motives. His actual relics are ludicrous beyond the point of blasphemy – for instance the big toe of the Trinity; his jaw-bone of All Hallows associates him with the Protestant heresy preached at All Hallows, Honey Lane (see below p. 42). It is notable that in boasting of his own powers he claims 'more then heven [man] can nat get' (4P354), thus denying the degrees of beatitude of the saints. (In *Witty and Witless* Heywood puts the orthodox view that there are degrees in heaven in the mouth of the aptly named Jerome.) The Pardoner is sly and snobbish, showing some deference towards the Palmer only when he wins (4P1053–5) but taking the judgment in bad part (4P1102–5). He commands the audience's attention by his zany, egotistical imagination; his masterly story-telling bounds with energy –

And I from thens to hell that nyght (4P819)

– and abounds with delightful details: the incidental dispatch to heaven of the soul in purgatory who blesses the sneezer, the coincidence of his acquaintance with the devil-porter from the Corpus Christi play in Coventry, his observation of the devils' birthday-best livery and grooming, Margery's employment in the diabolical kitchen. The Pardoner's smug account of the deferential welcome he receives in Purgatory provides splendid scope for vocal mimicry and gesture; it contrasts nicely with his fawning admission to hell, where he needs the devil's authority in the form of a safe conduct. Clearly the Pardoner overreaches the limits of his own authority.

The Potycary, coarse, lively, and unpredictable, is equally interesting dramatically. He is originally conceived, though he may owe something to the medieval tradition of the *mercator* or quack doctor. Entering third, he immediately tries to prove the Palmer and Pardoner fools, and proceeds to trivialize the argument by claiming that his poisonous drugs send men to heaven. Later, he admits that he thus damns himself to hell (4P407). His most devout prayer is for perpetual wine from the Pardoner's antedeluvian glass. Totally unscrupulous, he tries to bribe the judge and then claims victory by a cheat. He has two strongly marked 'Vice' qualities: a vein of obscene double entendre, both sexual and scatological, and boundless physical energy: he hops manically in anticipation of victory and constantly invents acrobatic routines to disrupt the proceedings (4P1034, 1106). The Pedler's judgment concedes that the Potycary is 'well beloved' by the audience for his railing at pardons and relics, and his admission of 'no vertue at all' is the beginning of self-knowledge. As a sinner he is, perhaps, redeemable.

The fourth P sees himself not as contestant so much as umpire. He is without pretentiousness and offers his Pedler's trifles as 'tokens' of love, cheerfully accepting the lack of customers. It is he who proposes the 'pastyme' of singing. Side-stepping more weighty and contentious issues in a way that is perhaps characteristic of Heywood's own tact, he agrees to be judge in the contest for 'maistry', and suggests the suitably trivial contest of lies. His sense of fun is manifest in his proposal, with appropriate acrobatic arrangement, that the three others should form a sort of Trinity, as the best formula for salvation. He handles the lying contest firmly and with courtesy, judging in favour of the Palmer's lie with reasoned analysis. Finally, he proceeds to make judgments on the serious issues he at first eschewed, commending the Palmer and Pardoner to their practices, which he sees as symbolic of all human effort done with good will: alms giving, good works, the maintenance of chantry priests, loving one another. He even claims to see a gleam of hope for the incorrigible Potycary, but warns him against 'raylynge' on relics unless he knows for sure that they are 'counterfete'; otherwise, all personal judgments should be submitted to those of the Church. Here the voice is unmistakably that of the author.

Thus Heywood's defence of orthodox Catholic positions is worked through the interplay of the four well-matched wayfarers. The Palmer's final apology to the audience for any 'neglygence' may be taken to refer to the statement of doctrinal matters as much as to performance of the play itself.

In spite of its deliberately inconsequential plot, the play is inventive in its language and action. The business of setting up the group as a kind of watch is accompanied by alliteration and expressed in couplets with an occasional triplet (4P211–3). Leashes are frequent: the one ending in -ynge is split between two speakers (4P301–7); and the Pedler forcefully expresses his conviction that two women in three are shrews by means of a 'leash' on 'Thre' (4P1070–80). Stage business is enhanced by Heywood's enthusiasm for the recital of lists, which are cleverly handled and much developed. The Palmer lists the contents of his pack (4P232–42), and later elaborates in a leash of trinkets for women ending -ettes (4P257–62). In the description of the Pardoner's relics there are plenty of interruptions in which comic disbelief magnifies the outrageousness of what is on offer. The Pardoner drops his sanctimonious tone to describe one specially efficacious one as a 'whipper' (4P524). In reply to the Pardoner, the Poticary recites the qualities of his medicines (4P592–643). So the lists are more than just occasions for stage business: they become central to the play in provoking the audience to consider the bounds of credibility, and they lead naturally to the competition in lies.

Further linguistic set pieces take the form of extended bawdy jokes – on pyncase (4P243–53), tail pin (4P267–78), and spit (4P954–60). Proverbs are used frequently (see notes on 4P66, 109–10, 293, 351, 467s.d., 569, 1185–6, 1190–2, 1206–10), often with a cynical tone. They add verbal dexterity and a sense that what is shown here has been merely a sample of the world's trickery.

The inter-relationship between speech and action is much developed in the manipulation of pronouns. These indicate stage movement by pointing the attention of one character to another, or by shifting the attention of the audience (e.g. at 4P378–9). An extended play on I, you, us and he is tied together by a repetitive 'leash' on lied/lie/lier/laide (4P680–93). Such devices enclose the play-world tightly, yet skilfully manipulate the audience's viewpoint. Similar devices and gestural business is provided for the Potycary – further evidence, perhaps, for his being partly a Vice. There is his hopping game (4P467 s.d.), turning words into action, and the curtsy joke which surrounds the triumphant Palmer with mock respect, culminating a leash with double rhymes (see notes to 4P1106–10, 1115–8). In another number game he arranges and rearranges the others in formation as 'knaves' (4P1034–7).

These features, which draw the audience into a 'play' of active judgment (4P5–6, 158, 992, 1198), constitute a very accomplished stage technique. Heywood is confident enough to insert the very long narrative of the Pardoner's visit to Hell (4P771–976), which itself contains linguistic devices and games. It is a tale full of wit and invention, and includes many passages of direct speech inviting mimicry. If, as we suppose, there are satirical hits at the court of Henry VIII, in the tennis playing and the celebration of the Devil-king's birthday, the attention of the original audience would have been stimulated by the danger of the allusions.

Such a daring sequence gives an important clue to Heywood's conception of theatre, and it needs to be related to the underlying theological issues noted above. The disguising of serious doctrine in comic entertainment is a remarkable development of techniques found in *Fulgens and Lucres* and *Magnyfycence*. He probably owed something to these plays in their comic subplots, and in the way in which folly – in different disguises – is made to comment on the action. Heywood was not a superficial joker, and his ability to exploit comic routines seems to have improved with practice.

6. The Play of Love

Like *Foure PP*, Heywood's intellectual comedy of the pleasures and pains in love is scored for four actors. The complementary natures of the characters, variously loved and loving, forms the base for an intricate debate structure; in the end each pair judging the other can only find a draw. On the page the characters may be difficult to distinguish, yet the dramatic mode separates them clearly, and once they are identified visually, their contributions to the argument and their manner of speaking seem more distinct. The clues are that Loved not lovyng is the only woman, Lover not loved is melancholic, Lover loved is foolishly cheerful, and No lover nor loved is specifically a 'vyce' figure, who combines a quick, cynical wit and 'impromptu' capering about. The first (oddly valent) two are paired to judge the dispute between the last (evenly valent) two, and vice-versa. Patterns of opposition, contrast, symmetry are explored with logical – sometimes geometric – delight.

The process of the action falls conveniently into ten movements, of which the sixth occupies the centre and almost half the play's length. These sections are marked off by entrances or exits and may be further distinguished by shifts in verse form.

1.(L1–63) The Lover not loved is met first, and his complex, meandering sentences beautifully controlled in rhyme royal stanzas, establish a world of Petrarchan love and courtly lyric complaint.

2.(L64–245) The lady, Loved not lovyng joins him, belittling his sufferings with her irritiation. After some argument as to who suffers most, they agree to find arbitration; eyeing the audience, they can find 'here no judge mete,' and go out to find one.

3.(L246–301) A song introduces the demonstrative Lover beloved, solo, who explains enthusiastically that love is the highest pleasure. He too keeps to rhyme royal stanzas.

4.(L302–98) The mocking voice of No lover nor loved brings him down to earth in couplets interspersed with rondeau-like quatrains (abba). Until the end of the play couplets now remain the principal medium – an indication of the control excercised over the tone and conduct of affairs by this Vice character. In dubbing love a folly and the Lover a 'woodcock', the cynic includes the audience, 'this flock' (L322). His cynicism requires him to demonstrate his imperviousness to women and this he does in a double-edged leash of superlatives (L351–62). This pair agree, like the first, to find an 'indifferent herer' to judge their case.

5.(L399–690) The Lover loved's exit leaves the Vice holding the stage and he proposes to 'pass the time' with a 'mummyng' (408). After a reverie describing the ideal woman from top to toe, rapidly delivered in Skeltonic dimeter couplets, he proceeds to tell a story. In this virtuoso narrative he tells how his younger self engaged in an affair with a practised woman. 'Mock or be mockt' is the rule of the game they play, but the tale, guided by the proverb 'mockum mockabitur' backfires on him. His cynical superiority is finally seen to be self-deceiving as he confesses his hurt to the audience. The audience is thus prepared for the return of the others to form a complete set in the acting place for the big sixth scene.

6.(L691–1268) As Lover loved brings in the first pair, the decorousness of his rhyme royal and his courtly manner in leading the woman by the hand are abruptly deflated by the Vice's comment that one of the men at least might mount this 'nag'. For the first time, all the characters are together. This, the longest movement, conducted almost entirely in couplets, turns out to have a double structure, with the two cases proceeding seriatim. First, the Lover un-loved and the woman, Loved not lovyng, dispute; meanwhile No lover nor loved enlivens the proceedings from above, apparently perched on a throne, where he takes off Chancellor Wolsey's style of judgment: having no legal training he relies on the purity of his conscience (see L800 and note). After a deadlock of the judges (a 'demurrer in lawe'), further skilful pleading by the woman clarifies the moot point on which they agree to request judgment. In the second half of the scene roles are reversed and the first pair become judges. The contented Lover loved begins by distinguishing pleasure (positive and selfish) from 'con-tentacyon' which has regard to circumstance and to other people: he thus lays the foundation for a deeper, religious note at the play's ending. Lover loved's claim that love is good is countered by the Vice's 'proof' that it is evil. But the Vice is cornered by the charge that he is no better than an insensible 'post', and he improvises an excuse to exit, bringing the scene to a close.

7.(L1269–97) Heywood now skilfully precipitates a climax and instant reversal. In the presence of the unhappy pair, the Lover loved rashly rejoices in the height of his happiness, proposing to hasten to judgment.

8.(L1298–1335) The Vyce's spectacular entry, shooting fireworks from his hat, calling, 'Fire, fire', collapses the Lover, who exits in desperate hope of finding his mistress saved from her burning house.

9.(L1336–53) The ninth scene matches the seventh; the Vyve, rejoicing that his 'woodcock' is basted by fire, proposes summary judgment.

10.(L1354–1577) The Lover loved returns chastened in his own perfect happiness. He now attacks the Vice's ability to feel, using a traditional comparison (as in *Witty*) of tree and horse, and reducing him to perplexity. The second case is now brought to a single moot question (L1451–2). Judgment proceeds. The first pair's claims are found to be equal in 'just counterpaise'. Switching roles, the first pair become judges and reach a similar balanced judgment. From L1495 to the end, with only two brief exceptions, a more serious tone is underscored by the use of rhyme royal. After the second judgment, all the characters commend impartiality as in accordance with Christ's second commandment (L1547). The 'love' in dispute here is said not to be conducive to 'contentacyon'; men are urged to accept bad fortune uncomplainingly and to rejoice in each other's good fortune. It is the Lover not loved who recommends the audience,

> . . . seke the love of that lovyng Lorde
> Who to suffer passion for love was content. (L1566–7)

Of all the plays, the idiom of *Love* is the most formal, often tortuous in its syntax and strangely removed from common speech, capable of ambiguous interpretation. These features suggest deliberate imitation and parody of lawyers' language (see *Sources* 6). The polite, conversational idiom is polished into verbal neatness, and occasionally sprinkled with a commoner idiom –

> But I thus deckt at all poyntes poynt devyce
> At dore were this trull was I was at a tryce. (L513–4)

or, with sexual innuendo –

> Ye take to much upon ye' (L641)

to great effect. In the almost incessant wordplay is that on *hope* and *hop*, (L573), used also at 4P468 as a key to antic hopping. Among the set pieces of the play, the fourteen lines which analyse love as a conflict of Good and Bad Angels (L543–56) remarkably anticipate Shakespeare's Sonnet 144.

Of all the plays *Love* has most proverbs (the Notes identify 37 of them), used for critical and summative comment, to distil a moot point of argument. They may derive from the legal provenance of the play. Dazzling twists of argument, recalling *Witty and Witless*, are embellished by many leashes; for example, the play on content/contentacyon at a very late stage in the argument (L1104–46) emphasizes the key note of the ending; similarly, the punning which interweaves 'love' with 'lie' (L1362–71) reinforces perceptions the audience must make about the characters and their arguments. Within the Vice's narrative 'pastime' the verbal fireworks continue in the play on 'I love you', and conjugation of the verb 'to love' (L581–5). In general, the witty, surface play of words encourages swiftly changing and critical viewpoints on the speakers.

Within the formality a wide range of emotions is subtly discriminated. Altman (pp. 112–14) suggests that Heywood was interested in giving fictional depth to his argument, and these psychologically accurate details support his view. In performance there is a further psychological complexity in that each of the 'oddly valent' couple (Lover not loved and Loved not loving), complaining of the cruelty of another person not represented on stage, makes the other stand for that person; this raises a flickering suspicion in the minds of the audience that the two are indeed each other's bane. The Vice's prodigious narrative (L399–690), like those in *Foure PP*, has many mimetic elements. Here, again, a present and a reported fictional persona can be compared; the mocker of love is mocked and his proverbial motto *mockum moccabitur* is made to reflect on his own folly.

In spite of the apparent abstraction of the argument, and the fact that only two out of eight stage directions do more than indicate entrances and exits, the play is rich in visual incident. The Vyce's 'copintank' of squibs is an obvious *coup de théâtre*. His cries of alarm at first sight look improvised and hypermetric; they are in fact highly patterned and antithetical. An indefatigable entertainer, he does most to shape the visual appearance of the group and to keep up the audience's spirits and critical attentiveness. He has ready recourse to sexual innuendo and it seems likely that wordplay such as that on joyne/part (L775–92) would be accompanied by appropriate gestural play. The other characters are mocked in a routine of curtsying (L705–12), which has them whirling about, and a variation of the routine reoccurs at L1076–7. There is visual comedy in the heat and cold of Lover not loved's prolonged Petrarchan sufferings, which are reduced to absurdity by the Vice's clowning between head and arse (L1018–31). Further bawdy merriment is involved in the revival of Lover loved (L1316–35). In all these routines No lover nor loved controls the action. As judge he dominates the action (L1468–81), just as earlier he mimics Chancellor Wolsey (L801–12), no doubt much to the satisfaction of a lawyerly audience.

The Vice is less dominant in the argument, however. His withdrawal into a cynical rejection of love is quite contrary to the conclusion of the play, in which the two lovers appeal for toleration (L1543–77). The doctrinal precept which requires 'One man to joy the pleasure of another' (L1549) is linked to the passion of Christ in a passage woven round the word 'love' (L1565–8). Thus love fulfils the law (Rom 13:10). Such a message in such a form is appropriate for Christmas, a season of 'honest myrth', and specially valuable in a time of political uncertainty and religious faction.

7. The Play of the Wether

The cast of ten in *Wether* gives Heywood the opportunity to work with his greatest variety of character types, and to satirize the self-interest of the estates of England as they clamour for the ear of their ruler. Nor does Henry VIII himself escape Heywood's irony (though this has not previously been sufficiently noted); scepticism is expressed principally through the impudent way in which Jupiter's messenger Mery Report dances round important matters of state – the proposed divorce and the assumption of ever greater autocratic powers. Discussion of the play's likely date and auspices depending on a detailed account of its topicality will be found in the following chapter (*Sources* 7), so that the present account may concentrate on a straightforward account of its structure and themes.

The action presents conflicting claims for more stable weather, a subject for argument which is English enough, and one correspondingly settled by a compromise when the king of gods decrees no change amid general rejoicing. This basic plot is so simple and its outcome so anticlimactic that in less skilful hands the dramatic treatment might have become a mere hierarchical pageant of suitors. As it is, Heywood varies not only the themes, pace, and tone, but also the length and complexity of his scenes. This pleasing variety and interplay is articulated by a variety of voice patterns and with careful attention to a hierarchical use of metre. As a result, a simply episodic string of complaints is given a formal structure which is the most intricate and satisfying of all, and the theatrical interest is made to climax where the most dangerous topics are glanced at.

The 'process' of the play falls conveniently into twelve scenic units (appropriate, perhaps, to the theme of the weather), marked by changing the number of speakers on stage. First, Jupiter introduces himself, speaking in dignified and aureate rhyme royal, and proposes to hear suits concerning the weather, for which he will need a servant (We1–97). The preposterous entry of Mery Report at once lightens the tone and creates other expectations of 'pastime' (We98–185). His idiom of couplets (mostly four-stressed) now dominates the play as he attracts each new character into it. After Mery Report's exit to change his livery, Jupiter reasserts his ruffled dignity in rhyme royal, speaking in whole stanzas. The first and second suppliants, the hunting Gentylman (We186–328) and venturing Merchaunt (We329–95), are allowed to make their complaints in the royal presence. Both speak in long-line quatrains (rhyming abab); both are answered in rhyme royal by the god; both converse with Mery Report in couplets. The Gentylman's ideas of social precedence and 'heads' are turned arsey-versy by Mery Report's clowning. In the fifth scene (We396–441), the formula is varied; Mery Report prevents the Ranger, a plain-spoken woodsman from reaching the throne, receiving his homely request and despatching him briefly, so that the audience is made impatient for the double scene which follows (We442–761). The Water Miller addresses his request for steady rains directly to god's servant, using the higher quatrain form; but instead of seeing him off, Mery Report allows in the Wind Miller and leaves the two professional rivals together to argue the social and economic benefits of their alternative technologies. On Mery Report's reentry this technical mill talk is animated by double entendre, by which mills turn into insatiable wives and all men are inadequate millers, their pecking tools worn into disuse and impotence. Though this exchange happens 'under the stairs', as it were, and not in Jupiter's presence, it must have the effect of provoking the audience's sexual awareness in preparation for the entry of the Gentylwoman.

At the play's centre, the seventh scene (We762–981) turns out to have a similar double structure to the sixth, forming a symmetry with it. Before she has had a chance to state her case, the Gentylwoman is accosted in sexual banter by Mery Report, who offers her to Jupiter as a possible 'wife' and raises the audience's prurient curiosity about what the god-king is doing out of sight 'making new moons'. When she is finally allowed to, the Gentylwoman speaks her piece in quatrains, but she is at once returned to couplets by Mery Report's pressing her to sing and then to a kiss. The abrupt entry of the Launder – one confessedly past her prime – on this cue turns the kiss into *osculandum fundamentum*. With coarse vigour and self-righteous moralism of one who bleaches the world's underwear in the sun, she attacks the veiled Gentylwoman for her vanity. While the spirited exchange which ensues has some aspects of medieval debates of Occupation and Idleness, and of Age and Youth, Mery Report's banter from the sidelines keeps up the bawdy possibilities of one man contemplating a choice of sexual partners. With the Gentylwoman's exit, the tone becomes even more obscene.

A very short eighth scene, symmetrical with the third, follows (Wy982–1001): Mery Report *solus* complains of his own thankless estate of servant to Jupiter. His notion that he would do better serving the devil is suggestive in relation to the courtly devil-king in *Foure PP*. The charming next scene with 'Little Dick' (significantly named to keep up the sub-theme of impotence) shows Mery Report in his most kindly vein, his mockery in abeyance, except for the comic matter of their relative stature. The Boy's innocent pleasure in snowballs is conveyed in his fresh speech in eight-syllable couplets (We1002–49). Left alone for a very short space (We1050–68), Mery Report addresses all estates in the audience, enlivening his idiom with trimeter rime coueé. He now gives Jupiter a summary report of all the suits and is commended gravely in rhyme royal (We1069–1131).

The finale is in itself a miracle of dramatic composition which gathers up the themes into a formally patterned harmony. Jupiter *solus* speaks one stanza before Mery Report drives into his presence all eight suitors chanting an eight-line snatch. (This has yet another new form with five- and four-syllable lines, and double rhymes, and may be a song.) The god's judgment is delivered in measured rhyme royal, eight stanzas corresponding (though not addressed individually) to the eight suitors. It is preceded and followed by short speeches of praise by the Gentylman as head of the estates. The others, in order of their hierarchical appearance in the acting place, follow suit. The play concludes, as it began, with Jupiter speaking rhyme royal stanzas of self-praise before ascending to his heavenly throne, no doubt to the accompaniment of music.

Much would depend in performance on the emphasis of the playing, and the extent to which individual performances were caricatures. The vanity of this Jupiter, his concern with his own supreme power, his self-glorification, his references to Parliament, the national disagreement, and the solution of all by divine intervention invite identification with the King. A mask worn by Jupiter might add to this.

The Vice's part is notably large. Instead of occasional manipulations like those of the Potycary and Pedler, and of No Lover nor loved, Mery Report is deputed royal power and he conducts the entire business of the court. He controls access to the royal presence, and thus the theatrical space takes on the highly charged and politically sensitive atmosphere of the 'haut-pace at the King's chamber-doore' (We487 and note). He decides which suitors shall be privileged, and he behaves in an overbearing manner in his new (but unspecified) clothes, insisting on respect (We432–3, 483). From the moment he picks on a torch bearer on his first entrance (We98, see also 167, 249, 733, 1239), he keeps in close contact with the audience. Thus Heywood has conflated the role of playwright with that of stage manipulator. It is hard not to imagine that, as servant of the King and, possibly, groom of the chamber, he wrote the part for himself to act, knowing that he would draw on the resources of the Chapel Royal or St Paul's choir school and that the task of directing the large cast of boy actors would be made easier by his own presence on stage.

The Vice has a particularly strong line in bawdy. Heywood's predilection for sexual jokes has been remarked. Here they occur in what appear to be deliberate sequences. For example, in the argument between the two Millers, the Vice's mention of his wife at We722 leads into a scatalogical passage of such intensity that the audience must be providing sexual meanings for nearly every line. We cannot be quite certain, in such a lively context, what the underlying implications are: the importance lies in the increase of awareness, because the climax of this sexual comedy is the appearance of the Gentylwoman. Whoever she is – she may well have been veiled – Mery Report thinks the god (being Jupiter, or perhaps Henry) ought to be interested in her. The explicit imagery in the following lines may well allude to the King's great matter (see We782–5, and note), but the important theatrical aspect is the way the susceptibilities of the presumably well-informed audience are aroused. Mery sustains his own sexual overture to the Gentylwoman through a song, the mutual 'pleasure' of which is stressed (We849, 855–7), so that the repeated 'yt' of We860–1 – in another leash – has sexual implications. There is thus a sequential element in the Vice's antics and sexual jokes, by which an actual plot is promoted.

Apart from the arrival and departure of the suitors, there is plenty of stage action. Some of this may well be gestural, associated with the sexual jokes (We235, 737, 973–4). The pronounced switches at We735–6, and 754 invite gesture. There is by-play between the Gentleman and Mery Report, possibly involving a joke about physical size, and a threatened blow (We298–300). The heads-and-tails routine seems to give Mery Report pain in his neck (We310–5, 325). Looked at another way, this may be a gallows joke for an audience aware of the sensitive nature of the satire in a hierarchically conscious court.

In *Wether*, as in all the plays, Heywood's handling of his themes is determined by a constant awareness that the audience has to be entertained, its inhibitions removed, its attention stimulated and directed, and the pace of events managed so that interest does not flag. This delicate manipulation of theatrical interest demands nimbleness and resourcefulness from the actors, because it constitutes the very technique by which the playwright defends his satire.

8. Staging

The actors in Heywood's plays would most likely be drawn from the Court and its immediate environs. The plays do not seem to have been conceived with doubling (and hence professional players) in mind. Some of the actors would be boys available, through Heywood's connections as a musician, from St Paul's and the Chapel Royal. Adult actors may have been associated musicians and schoolmasters. This possibility is increased by the evidence from 1553 onwards of his working with 'children' and with Master Wescott later at Court. *Wether* clearly requires at least one boy. More's participation in plays at home, and Rastell's building a theatre in his house suggest that Heywood may have been able to draw upon the family for help.

The settings demand little in the way of scenery that would not be readily available in a Tudor banqueting hall. There are sometimes several locations. *Johan Johan* requires a table for the meal, and a fireplace at Johan Johan's house, and, some distance away, the house of Syr Johan, though nothing is required there except perhaps a door which could be provided simply, or mimed. In a hall, as Southern suggests (p. 249) the fireplace commonly located on one wall would be suitable. *Wether* has most clues about an extravagant or impressive setting, though it must be admitted that these do not amount to much in comparison with other known Court entertainments before and after Heywood. Mery

27

Report's comment to someone holding a torch on the side lines (We98) suggests a household auspice and evening performance, the occasion of a supper (We1027). Jupiter's throne could be placed at the screens end of the hall. A curtain seems necessary so that Jupiter may retire as if into a little chamber in order to make his new moon; and Mery Report, some way off, makes other characters aware of his master's presence without actually saying that he can be seen (We534). Most of the action takes place at some distance from the throne. The throne and its curtain has a back entrance (We770), possibly used for the re-entry of the suitors near the end of the play (We1138). The throne itself was probably raised on a few steps, so that Jupiter could ascend in state (We1254). An area screened from the audience is suggested in *Love* by the Vice's need to go offstage to prepare his spectacular costume and fireworks for an effect which would be spoiled if it was anticipated. He could withdraw from the hall altogether, of course.

Cues for **music** are found in *Wether* (four), *Love* (one), and *Foure PP* (one). In performance this could imply instrumentalists (keyboard, string or wind) in the musician's gallery of a banqueting hall. In *Wether* the stage direction 'the god hath a song played in his trone' (We178 s.d.) suggests that the musicians were behind the throne curtain. The play ends with Jupiter again calling for music and inviting 'ye that on yerth sojoune . . . to synge moste joyfully' (We1250–53), apparently an ensemble of the actors. On the three occasions when the actors are specifically required to sing, one is a quartet (4P321 s.d.), one a duet between Mery Report and the Gentylwoman, with a request for an accompaniment from the musicians (We854 and stage direction), and one a solo by Lover loved (L245 s.d.). Mery Report's jingle to round up the procession of suitors to await Jupiter's judgment (We1139–46) is possibly the only song lyric in the texts, though there is no instruction for him to sing here. Performance of the quartet is delayed by discussion of whether the Pedler is 'a ryght syngynge man' – a distinction which may support the suggestion that Heywood himself took this part of 'playmaker' and judge. The Potycary leads, inviting the others to follow, perhaps in harmony, though this may have been a round or a 'catch'. The occasion of this song is the Pedler's satisfaction with the company (4P290) and his conventional requirement for 'pastyme' (4P295). It follows jokes about drinking which may indicate subject matter.[1]

The duet in *Wether* comes in a sexual context (We845, 849) where the Gentylwoman seems both to want to evade Mery Report's proposition and to accept it (We856). Her part would be sung by a boy, possibly a chorister, one of Little Dick's hundred fellows (We1023).[2] On this occasion, 'Come kiss me Joan,' mentioned in *Nature* (Pt. 2, l.150) might have the right mood.[3] Similarly, Lover Loved sings of his satisfaction in love. A suitable mood is found in 'In youth is pleasure' (*Lusty Juventus*, lines 37–49).

Heywood usually writes with a strong sense of the **audience**. Even *Witty and*

---

[1] Drinking songs (without settings) are found in *Gammer Gurton's Needle* (ll. 237–9, a group offstage), *Tom Tiler* (ll. 254–77, three voices), and *Like Will to Like* (C1, solo; C2, solo; D1v, three voices).

[2] Love songs are common in interludes, as in *Magnyfycence* (ll. 2064–77, solo), *Wyt and Scyence* (ll. 989–1020, two groups of four singers), *Nice Wanton* (A4v, duet), and *Patient Grissell* (ll. 968–78, solo).

[3] The tune is in C.B. Simpson, *The British Broadside Ballad and Its Music*, New Brunswick, 1966, fig. 256, pp. 396–8.

Witless shows concern to tailor the play to the presence of the King by introducing three special stanzas of rhyme royal (Wy675 s.d.). In *Johan Johan* the husband's indecisive confidences are addressed directly to the audience, and the comedy of his deception and humiliation depends heavily on asides by all three characters. There is some speech directed to the audience in *La farce du Pasté*, and Heywood follows his source in the by-play about leaving the coat with a spectator, but he enlarges the joke by having Johan Johan suggest to the man, 'Whyle ye do nothyng – skrape of the dyrt' (J257). In *Pardoner and Frere* the audience is put to some strain in listening to the protagonists speak simultaneously, yet the characters address the audience as though they form a congregation in a church requiring instruction and salvation. This Babel of heretics must be meticulously synchronized if the actors are not to lose their way. The Palmer addresses a single spectator (4P61), and the Pedler picks out women separately seated in the audience for sexist ridicule (4P1082). The Vice in *Love* proposes to entertain the audience as a 'pastime', telling a tale about himself (L399–690). In *Wether* the Vice emerges from the audience, volunteering to be Jupiter's servant. His later bawdy jokes are addressed to them (We176–8); on his reentry he pushes through the crowd, impertinently demanding respect (We249). Further encounters of actor and audience at We249, 607, and 1239, sustain the view that in his play Heywood was particularly keen to arouse close attention and sympathy. Given the nature of *Wether*'s satirical objectives, this would be very necessary, and Heywood cultivates audience contact with more persistence than he does in any other play. The separate seating of the women is made the occasion of provocation here as in *Foure PP*: Mery Report introduces the Gentylman as a hunter who 'wolde hunte a sow or twayne out of this sorte. *Here he poynteth to the women*' (We249). The Pedler addresses 'the women in thys border,' numbering them off in threes and characterizing them all as shrews (4P1068–80).

The texts offer little direct information about **costume**. Except for Mery Report in his finery as God's servant, and No lover nor loved's alarming 'copyn tank' of squibs, there are no examples of the changes for dramatic purposes common in morality plays and interludes. However, since most of Heywood's characters are generalized types it seems likely that the visual impact of each would have helped to identify social function and rank. The cast of *Witty and Witless* however are not differentiated socially, though the impertinent 'elfe' James should look different from the more sober Jerome, who requires an ecclesiastical robe or doctor's gown. Appropriate clothing for the casts of *Johan Johan* and *Pardoner and Frere* should distinguish their professional roles; in the latter play the fact that the Pardoner and Frere are charlatans and heretics may be pointed by exaggeration.

Love and *Wether* give more distinct possibilities. Lover loved might be dressed in cheerful colours to distinguish him from Lover not loved whose aimlessness hints at an unkempt appearance. The Vice's bizarre behaviour and acrobatics suggest that appropriate clothing should be flashy but not physically constricting. Colour coding the four characters would reflect the balletic mode of the argument.

In *Wether* there are stronger reasons for costume by 'estate'. Mery Report responds very quickly when each new suitor appears, and at a time of sumptuary laws regulating the richness of cloth appropriate to various social degrees, it seems certain that they should be typically dressed. The Gentylman wears hunting clothes, with a horn prominent. The Ranger too is an outdoor man; he may wear livery, since he is a crown officer, and he needs a cap (We433). The Millers should be linked, though the Wind Miller's dress might reflect his alleged poverty (We522–3); and they may bear tools of their craft (e.g. a 'pecker' We744). Mery Report's wilful mistaking of the Marchaunt for a Parson suggests that he should wear a long gown.

The Gentylwoman is the sexual centrepiece of the play. Whether her costume would reflect the personality of someone at Court is speculative. Her concern to protect her complexion suggests a veil, perhaps a 'bongrace' (see 4P146 and note). Jupiter as a god would require a gilded mask. Both these 'disguises' might have been used to suggest a specific person at Court. The emphasis upon Jupiter's glory requires extravagance (even 'magnificence'). Mery Report is rebuked for his light array (We110), and appears in much more impressive, even pompous, clothing as 'goddes servaunt' (We483); a Mercury costume, with winged helmet and heels, might be suitably incongruous.

Properties are in general sparingly used, but hand properties are important in *Foure PP*, where each of the four has tokens of his trade: pilgrim badges, relics, patent medicines, knick-knacks. Practical experience shows that the production of visual items enlivens Heywood's lists and enthralls the audience. The Pardoner in *Pardoner and Frere* needs relics and bulls. Both these protagonists stand on stools to preach. The properties in *Johan Johan* are dictated by the source (trestle table, cups, stool, pot of ale, bread and, especially the pie), as is the method of exploiting them. The lovers' eating of the pie and the husband's handling of the wax candles and the pail require full exploitation of the bawdy possibilities. In *Love* the Vice has an unspecified book, perhaps a Fool's bible, while his trick played on Lover Loved requires a spectacular hat stuffed with fireworks. His take-off of Wolsey again suggests use of a stool to gain stage dominance (L801–12). In *Wether* the suitors may carry props consonant with social type – the Launder a basket, the Boy a pitfall trap and so on – but the only property specified is the horn blown by the Gentylman and carried by his companions, if any.

Stage directions in the text are sparse – only one in the manuscript copy of *Witty and Witless*. The earliest printed texts *Johan Johan* and *Pardoner and Frere* have respectively two and five; Middleton's *Foure PP* has only two. The longest texts have most: *Love*, eight and *Wether*, twenty. The status of these directions is suspect, since we can not be sure they are authorial. However some concern essential actions, as when Johan Johan brings the empty pail (J442), or when he is left on stage after the fight at the end (J664 – a modification of the source). In *Pardoner and Frere* the Frere 'kneleth downe' at his prayers while the newly entered Pardoner declares the vertue of his relics; the protagonists are directed to speak 'evyn at the same tyme' (PF188), and to fight (PF538, 627). Stage directions calling for songs occur at 4P321, L245, and We178 and 853.

The more plentiful use in *Love* and *Wether* is to mark the many exits and entrances (in the case of *Wether* occasioned by the large cast). Six of the stage directions are added in the margin in italic type (We185, 249, 328, 396, 551, 954). The remaining ones are fully integrated into the black letter text. Elsewhere, a few special incidents or movements are noted, as with the Potycary's hopping (4P467), the Vice's entry at L1297, one of Mery Report's sexist jokes (We249), and his leading in the suitors (We1138).

Taken together, however, the stage directions give only the slightest hint of the bustle and intricacy of stage movement in most of the plays. Previous discussion has shown that there are many actions implied in the dialogue. These may involve dance-like play with groupings, and a variety of gestures, some of them scatological, some perhaps indicating mannerisms of those in the audience or known to it, some purely entertaining, like the hopping. The curtsying routines and the use of nods and becks, and the extended description of the court of hell in in *Foure PP*, may all be making fun of Court ceremonial. Even in *Witty and Witless*, where it is difficult to pick up hints of performance from the manuscript text, Tudor acting conventions would have provided a good deal of rhetorical gesture. The leashes and insistent verbal patterns seem the most likely places for improvised action, not least because such passages are often markers at critical stages in the argument. The labours of the mill horse, for example, invite mimetic representation (Wy470–6). All of the actors' vocal resources and physical skills are needed to sustain the monologue narratives. In *Foure PP* the boasts of the Potycary and Pardoner offer opportunities for 'stage journeys' and visual antics, as well as for vocal mimicry of speakers within the stories. The same is true of *Love*, in the Vice's subtle and self-revealing tale of mocker mocked. The probable lampooning in that play of Wolsey's manner may serve as a reminder of the dangerous possibilities open to Heywood and his co-players as they sought to show the very age and body of the Henrician time by direct or oblique impersonation.

SOURCES AND CONTEXTS OF THE PLAYS

1. Introduction

By the formidable standards of his age Heywood was not a learned man. He was surrounded by examples of poet-dramatists who used plays in different ways to convey or display learning, whether this be classical (Udall), scholastic (Skelton), biblical-historical (Bale) or 'scientific' and philosophical (John Rastell). Yet his own plays make no overt pretence to learned authority, skipping instead lightly over the ground of his reading and leaving few traces. He was, nevertheless, well read, particularly in the English poets and in contemporary religious polemic. Like Shakespeare, Heywood was a habitual borrower, showing some of his inventiveness in transforming his reading into original designs for particular purposes.

Beyond grammar school classics, Aesop, 'Cato', he probably read Lucian's dialogues in the Latin translations of More and Erasmus. He was fond of Chaucer, quoting him without acknowledgment, and of Skelton, of whose verse there are frequent echoes in the plays. He shows a knowledge of contemporary French drama, particularly the farces and sotties, beyond the specific debt in *Johan Johan*. Among humanistic writers, he made use of Henry Medwall, Pico della Mirandola, Erasmus (the *Colloquies* and, particularly, *Praise of Folly*), and Thomas More. It is hardly surprising, though the fact has not sufficiently been noted,[1] that Heywood's plays often run parallel to More's polemical writings in their doctrinal arguments and in points of anecdotal and linguistic detail, as the references to *OED* in the Notes show. Unlike More in his later polemical writing, Heywood never sounds harsh or intolerant. Indeed, among English writers of the Reformation period he may be unique in displaying what Hemingway called 'grace under pressure'.

For his plot structures and many of his theatrical techniques Heywood is more indebted to the French than the English tradition. In the surviving plays, at least, he avoids the allegorical method and the temptation-fall-salvation paradigm of most of the surviving plays. He also avoids the straightforward didactic stance of the English playwrights, preferring 'lighter' conversational debate, cast within patterned forms of contest. Like the French *farceurs* and his older London contemporary John Skelton, Heywood favoured couplets to convey variety of pace and immediacy of dramatic speech. There are some set-pieces ('Some . . . Some' Wy31–42; 'So nice it is . . .' We860–1), but the real strength of the verse is in dialogue and rhetoric, giving the actor the opportunity for virtuoso theatrical peformance. He also made a place for song and dance in his interludes. As a consequence of these aspects, when the plays are seen in relation to the small corpus of earlier English printed drama, they have a marked 'Gallic air'.[2]

Heywood's originality and independence from his sources appear in paradoxical ways. Whilst *Pardoner and Frere* is arguably the most original piece in its theatrical conception, it is built on quotation from Chaucer's *Pardoner's Prologue*, using hints from French farce as well as from Chaucer's presentation of the begging Friar. Since the fairly recent discovery that *Johan Johan* is not merely

---

1   A recent exception is Alistair Fox (*Politics and Literature in the Reigns of Henry VII and Henry VIII*, Oxford, 1989, pp. 248–52), who discusses well the oblique 'Morian strategy' of *Foure PP*.
2   Ian Maxwell, *French Farce and John Heywood*, Melbourne and London, 1946, p. 115.

'based on' French farce, but is a close translation of *La farce du pasté*, some long-held assumptions about the 'development' of English drama and about the nature of Heywood's originality have had to be rethought. Close comparison of *Johan Johan* with its source reveals Heywood's masterly skill as adapter and his unrivalled subtlety in naturalizing the French idiom and stagecraft. For *The Play of the Wether* many sources have been claimed, including Lucianic *Dialogues* and the Portuguese plays of Gil Vicente, while the Chaucerian presence is again strong, as are the influences of John Rastell and Henry Medwall. From the latter's *Fulgens and Lucres* Heywood copied the structural interweaving of high and low characters and contrasting social discourses, marked by the use of stately rhyme royal and fast-flowing couplets. The predominance of native elements in the language of the plays is specially marked in Heywood's liking for proverbial expressions.

It is unlikely that the six plays span more than nine years in composition (c.1525–33, see below), a period that is known to have contained much dramatic activity. It would be rash to claim on this basis that Heywood 'developed' independence from particular sources in the course of writing these plays. And yet it is worth noting that *The Play of the Wether*, which we consider latest in the sequence, is structurally the most ambitious, and is composed for the largest cast. From the jesting reference to Sot Somer in *Witty and Witless* to the clowning with 'heads' and new wives in *The Play of the Wether*, all the interludes allude to real life people or places, and it may be suggested – without insistence – that there is an increasing boldness in Heywood's theatrical engagement with topical issues of religious and political importance.

2. Witty and Witless

The play is attributed to John Heywood in a single manuscript, idiosyncratically spelled;[1] this has been tentatively dated c.1544 and it therefore belongs to the period of the quarto reissues of *Foure PP* and *The Play of the Wether*. But composition and performance must have been much much earlier, and it is likely on grounds of style and subject matter to be the earliest play of those surviving.

The dramatic idea for *Witty* may have been a French *Dyalogue du Fol et du Sage*, printed c.1516–27.[2] A copy in the British Library, bears the name of John Donne – John Heywood's grandson.[3] There are no close resemblances between *Witty* and the *Dyalogue*, which has only two speakers and fits comfortably within the tradition of Solomonic dialogues. Heywood's aphorism, 'Better be sott Somer then sage Salamon' (repeated at Wy440, 658 and reversed at Wy660), shows his awareness of this medieval genre of wisdom contests which pitted king Solomon against the cunning 'fool' Marcolphus. A 'Dialogue of Wit and Wisdom' survives from the fifteenth century; an English translation from Latin of 'the dyalogus of communyng betwixt the wyse king Salomon and Marcolphus' was printed in Antwerp in 1492; and 'the sayinges or prouerbes of king Salomon, with the answers of Marcolphus' were translated from the French and printed by Pynson

---

1 See Editorial Notes, pp. 217–19.
2 Maxwell pp. 87–96.
3 Cameron, *Witty* p. 7.

in 1529.[4] Heywood's repeated preference for the word 'sot' rather than 'fool' suggests his awareness of the French tradition of theatrical *sottie*, or 'fools' plays'.[5] 'Sott Somer', the King's professional fool, against whom Heywood expresses some real or feigned animosity, is thought to have come to court in about 1525 (Wy43 and note). A date for the play around this time would fit with the themes and attitudes expressed.

In the discussion of the pain and pleasure of being human and possessing 'wit' many of the arguments used are Renaissance commonplaces. For instance, the passages on imagination (Wy277–95, 494–508) derive ultimately from Aristotle's *De Anima*. Similarly, the Aristotelian categories of pleasure and pain, deriving from *Nicomachean Ethics*, were very widely known and are also used in *Love*, with which *Witty* has some similarities. However, Pico della Mirandola, in his *On the Imagination*, had commented on one of Aristotle's exempla (*De Anima* 428b) and had given to Aristotle's anonymous men the names James and John, which Heywood uses for his interlocutors.[6] The third speaker, Jerome, bears the name of the great father of the Roman Catholic Church.

The main themes are unmistakably Erasmian, showing delight in revealing the world's folly and in exploring the advantages of 'witty' and 'witless' in relation to Christian salvation. Erasmus had asked, 'If you had to die tomorrow, would you rather die more foolish or more wise?'[7] Many points of argument found in *Witty* may be paralleled in the *Colloquies* (comparing fools to beasts, contrasting pleasure and pain, considering pain briefly suffered as a means to gaining eternity, comparing man and horse).[8] In *Praise of Folly* Heywood would have found the comparison of man and horse greatly elaborated and the argument that an unreasoning fool is incapable of sin (see note to Wy517).[9] A neat epitome of these Erasmian themes is found in a marginal note printed in the 1533 English translation of *Enchiridion Militis Christiani*:[10]

> Folyshnes is myserye. wysdome is felicite. Fooles also be wretches/ and vnhappy. wyse men also be happy and fortunate. Fylthynesse is folysshenes. Vertu is wysdom.

Heywood's pointing of the way to salvation is thoroughly conservative and, as if to signal the fact, his doctrinal dispute is arbitrated by Jerome, compiler of the Vulgate Bible. The provisional victory of Witless reached in the first step of the play's argument could not be allowed to stand, since it would have denied the efficacy of human effort ('good works') in the process of salvation; from an English point of view in the 1520s, this was the chief heresy of Luther and his followers.

It has been suggested that *Witty* was 'written for a court still admiring Henry

---

4 (1492) STC 22905, (1529) STC 22899. The Middle English fragment seems quite unrelated (see Bruce Dickins, *The Conflict of Wit and Will*, Leeds School of English Language. Texts and Monographs 4. Leeds, 1937). On the background see also Barbara Swain, *Fools and Folly during the Middle Ages and the Renaissance*, New York, 1932.
5 Maxwell, p. 95. For the French tradition see Heather Arden, *Fools' Plays*, Cambridge, 1980.
6 *Pico on the Imagination*, ed. Harry Caplan, Westport Conn. 1930, repr. 1957, p. 55.
7 'The Abbot and the Learned Lady' (1524) in *Colloquies*, trans. C.R. Thompson, Chicago, 1965, p. 222.
8 Cameron, *Witty* pp. 8–10.
9 *The Praise of Folie*, translated by Sir Thomas Chaloner, ed. Clarence H. Miller, EETS, Oxford, 1965; pp.44/1–4. 46/16–30.
10 [Wynken de Worde] 1533, STC 10479.

VIII's *Assertio Septem Sacramentorum Adversus M. Lutherum* published in 1526'.[11]
The vocabulary of *Witty* is certainly theologically textured and the concluding
rhyme royal stanzas in praise of the king's God-given gifts and 'grace' (Wy685–6
and note) point convincingly to composition in the 1520s. An additional point
in favour of early composition may be the echoes of Thomas More's *Four Last
Things* (1522). In discussing things 'which men for madness laugh at', More
imagines Bedlam with 'one knocking of his own head against a post' and a 'sage
fool' who 'laugheth at the casting of his own soul into the fire of hell'.[12] If the
play of *Witty* does indeed belong to the early 1520s, then it anticipated many of
More's conservative arguments in *Confutation of Tyndale* (see notes to Wy556,
620). Heywood emphasizes the importance of infant baptism, which 'sealythe us
all aquyttans generall' from original sin (Wy337–8 and note). Above all, in tacit
opposition to the writings of Luther and Tyndale or the Dutch version of *Every-
man*, he stresses the efficacy of good works as a means to grace and the reward of
salvation for 'Crystyane that wurkythe most in faythe' (Wy625). He speaks of
'the wytty wyse wurkes' which are 'commandyd' (Wy587) by God, of man's 'wyll
to wurk well' (Wy628) and of God's reward for the 'most faythfull wurker'
(Wy637). Like More, he reaffirms the importance of 'dew ordryd penytens'
(Wy629). The closeness of Heywood's religious position to More's is apparent in
the other plays.

Heavier-weight theological references in *Witty* seem to have been picked up
from polemical writings in which they were cited. Thus, the 'comfortable saying'
from Ezechiel 33:11 (Wy621–22) was probably taken from Gerson's *Alphabetum
Divini Amoris*.[13] The quotation (Wy519–26) from Gregorius Reisch's *Margarita
Philosophica Nova* was from a work previously used by John Rastell in his interlude of *Four Elements*.[14] St Augustine's interpretation of St John 14.2 ('In my
father's house are many mansions')[15] was much argued about in the Rastell/Frith
dispute about Purgatory at the end of the decade, and is affirmed at the play's end
(Wy566).

In view of the folly themes, the comments on the King's 'sot Somers', and the
straightforward praise of Henry as God's favourite in alleging matters of scripture, *Witty* seems to belong to the mid- rather than late 1520s. By 1533–4, when
the other plays were printed, its earnest reiteration of Henry's 'orthodox' views
in response to Luther would have seemed a bit passé and this may be why it
remained in manuscript. On the surface it appears quite unlike the first of the
printed plays, the Rastell-Heywood *Gentleness and Nobility* and Heywood's star-
tlingly novel farce *Johan Johan*.

3. Johan Johan

Publication of *Johan Johan the husband, Tyb and Syr Johan*, printed by William
Rastell on 12 February 1533, reveals little about the time of its composition.
Features which once were taken as signs of Heywood's maturity as a dramatist are

---

11 Cameron, *Witty* p. 30; Johnson p. 72.
12 *De quatuor novissimus* in *English Works* I 461–2.
13 Cameron, *Witty* p. 23.
14 (Argentine, 1512) Lib.XI.cap.xvii; *Rastell Plays* p. 11.
15 *PL* XXXV col. 1811.

now known to be part of the play's nature as a translation. The play is unlike anything else before or since in English drama.

Heywood's general debt to French farce was established by Maxwell. The husband's name may have been suggested by a French farce *Jehan Jenin*,[1] but the name John John is unusual in English. It seems not to have been noticed that one of Heywood's fellow servants, a musician in the King's household was 'John de John, priest, organ maker'.[2] In making his priest into a Syr Johan, Heywood has produced an amusing plethora of Johns. Since all the other plays make comic allusion to contemporary people, it is quite likely that there would have been possibilities for further satirical double entendre in this association. In the farce of *Pernet* we find wife and lover, a banquet served by the compliant cuckold husband, whose foolish impatience is greeted with a *refrain*, 'Chauffez le cire'. The same refrain is made literal in the action of *La farce nouvelle du pasté*.

Craik's discovery that *Johan Johan* is a very close rendering of a French *Farce du Pasté* printed in about 1500 confirms the broad thrust of Maxwell's argument with irrefutable evidence, and must also alter modern assessments of Heywood's dramatic achievement and development.[3] Comparison of the French and English has been made by Craik and by Norland.[4] In this edition a translation of the *Pasté* is included (Appendix II) so that readers can make their own judgments. In general Heywood kept very close to the structure of the French. He slightly shortened it (767 lines to 678), made Tyb delay the welcome of the priest-lover by drawing out the dialogue at J426–38, and by increasing the husband's frustration in his general cursing (*Pasté* 475 is moved to J517–20). Heywood altered the ending by extending the husband's epilogue so as to deny him any peace of mind and return him to the uncertainty of the opening speech.

Although Heywood copied the patterns of dialogue and most of the word-play in the French original, he made no attempt to imitate one of its most striking (and unnoticed) features: passages in *rondeau* form, which may have required some special style of song-and-dance performance, like the English 'jig'. There are three of these eight-line forms (rhyming ABaAabAB) in the *Pasté*: the first opens the farce (1–8) in the manner of a *demande d'amour* and answer. The second (463–70) pin-points the 'hole in my bucket' theme. The final one 694–701) juxtaposes the two central visual acts of the play: chafing wax and serving the pie. As the pace and violence of action increases, the French uses also apparently random repetition of the *refrain*, 'Je chauffe la cire'. This occurs a score of times at intervals of three to fifteen lines, and it is the feature which Heywood picks up.

In anglicizing the French setting of the action Heywood is strikingly successful. Whereas the contemporary translations of *Calisto and Melebea*[5] and of Terence's *Andria*[6] often feel foreign and do not locate the scene in England, *Johan Johan* evokes Tudor London by its alteration of dozens of small details in

---

1 Maxwell pp. 68–9.
2 The Treasurer of the Chamber's Accounts, 1 October 1529 records payments of 50 shillings to Heywood and to him; *L&P* V 306.
3 T.W. Craik, 'The True Source of John Heywood's *Johan Johan*', MLR XLV (1950), 289–95.
4 Howard B. Norland, 'Formalizing French Farce: *Johan Johan* and its French Connection', *Comparative Drama* 17 (1983), 1–18.
5 *Rastell Plays*.
6 *Terence in English*, ed. Meg Twycross (Medieval English Theatre Modern-Spelling Texts No. 6), Lancaster, 1987.

the original. Heywood introduces Temmes Strete (J114), with its Lenten Stockfish double entendre; he discards a dozen oaths by French saints (Jean, Nicolas, Maurice, Julien, Paul, Remy, Pierre, Martin, Arnoul, Jacob) and substitutes some of his own: 'our lady of Crome' (J10), 'saynt Mary' (J52), the punningly named 'swete saynt Dyryk' (J146). He keeps the original call to combat 'by saynt George' (J664), presumably because it relates instantly to the popular and widespread village plays of the Henrician period. But he turns St Paul into a reference to 'the churche of Poules' (J153). He expands St Anthony's association with pigs by reference to offerings made to Saint Modwin (J561) and by giving Johan Johan the proverbial 'pyg in the wors panyer' at the close of the play.

Heywood names the anonymous woman friend of the Wife in the French as Margery; she is described as 'the most bawde hens to Coventre' (J164) The choice of the name Margery, perhaps suggested by Skelton's *Colin Clout*, links her with Margery Corson (rhyming with 'horyson'), the friend whom the Pardoner claims to have sought in hell and found there in the kitchen merrily turning a spit. The choice of Coventry can hardly be fortuitous; it may have been the place of Heywood's birth, it certainly was the place of his father-in-law's; like Margery, Coventry is also mentioned in *Foure PP* (830–2).

The Wife in the *Pasté* is renamed Tyb. A brief and (in contrast to the priest's tale of 'miracles') innocent remark of the Wife about the fecundity of her cat is elaborated by Heywood and linked in a network of proverbial sayings about cats. From Chaucer's Wife of Bath Heywood took the idea of the stray wife as going 'catter wawlyng' (J110) and from this develops a coherent pattern of imagery suggesting Tyb as a cat-on-heat (see notes to J73, 100, 129, 588–9). Thomas More writes scornfully of priests, friars and monks who 'runne out a caterwawynge', linking this sexual licence to heretical Protestant teaching ('evangelycall lyberty').[7]

Heywood's choice of the *Pasté* needs little explanation. Its taut construction around a central proverb would appeal to a generation taught by Erasmus. Heywood's interest in English proverbs was lifelong. The French 'chauffer le cire' (which Cotgrave translates, 'To attend long for a promised good turne') does not seem to have become current in English, so that Heywood's translation loses the prudential meaning. However, the proverb gave him a literal image, a visual *double entendre* in which to encapsulate the whole action of the play.

The candle-as-penis occurs in a scurrilous tale about the 'miraculous' practices at the shrine of St Valerius in Picardy told by More in his *Dialogue concerning Heresies*, published in 1529 and 1531, two years before *Johan Johan*.[8] Another of

---

[7] (*Confutacyon of Tyndales Answere*, (1532) *Works* VIII i 8/16). More plays on the same idea in condemning Luther: 'for a shewe of holy matrymony, frere Luther and Cate calate hys nonne lye luskynge togyther in lechery' (*ibid.* 181/2–4).

[8] The story, told by More's interlocutor, concerns a newly-married English couple on holiday at Saynt Waleryes (Valerius) in Picardy:
> 'lyke as in other pylgrymages ye se hanged vp legges of waxe or armes or such other partes
> / so was in that chapell al theyr offrynges yt honge about the walles / none other thynge
> but mennes gere & womens gere made in waxe' (*Works* VI i 228/10–3).

The gentleman and his wife observe the males among the pilgrims testing the size of their members in the silver rings provided, while an officiating monk sells magical thread to cure 'the stone'. The husband is approached by a 'sadde woman' who offers him a certain remedy against the stone:
> 'She wolde haue ye length of his gere / & that sholde she make in a waxe candell / which
> sholde bren vp in the chapell / & certayne prayers sholde there be sayd ye whyle' (*ibid.*
> 229/3–6).

37

More's tales concerns a poor man who 'had founde þe preste over famylyer with his wyfe' and complained publicly until he was forced by the priest to stand up in high mass and recant with the words, 'Mouth thou lyest'.[9] The resemblance may be coincidental, but Heywood and More must in any case have been intimate with each other's writing. It is worth noting that Heywood's adaptation of the 'miracles' narrated in the French original is relatively free and very much in the spirit of many of thé scurrilous 'tales' that enliven the *Dialogue concerning Heresies*. In Heywood's satire of the priest there is no hint of factional considerations, and on these grounds alone the play's initial composition may belong to the mid-1520s, rather than later.

Though *Johan Johan* is a translation, and anonymous, there can be no doubt it is really Heywood's work: language and idiom, proverbial expressions, metrical practice, rhyme all cohere. As already noted, the metrical practice in the incidence of quatrains among the couplets, matches very closely that of *Witty and Witless*. The Glossary shows numerous words and phrases in common with the other plays, particularly *The Pardoner and the Frere* and *The Foure PP*: the stage direction 'They fyght by the erys' is literally what happens in PF515; the derogatory 'dryvyll' J655, PF420; the farcical cry in both plays that 'thou lettyst the worde of God' (J556, PF419; 'our lady of Crome' (J10, 4P48); 'your masshyp' (J401, 4P641). If Reed and Greg are correct in their interpretation of the colophons of the plays then *Johan Johan* and *Pardoner and Frere* were printed, in the same format, within a few weeks of one another. With the latter play Heywood ventured into an area of fierce controversy. But favourable reception of this first, anonymous pair of plays would have encouraged William Rastell to publish Heywood's name in future.

4. The Pardoner and Frere

William Rastell published the anonymous play in folio on 5 April 1533, at a time when his press was busy sounding a conservative alarm at the confusing and rapidly deteriorating religious situation in England. How much earlier *Pardoner and Frere* was composed is a matter for dispute in interpreting its relation to sources, as well as possible allusions in the text. Close links, theatrical, thematic, verbal, with the other plays (particularly *Johan Johan* and *Foure PP*) strongly suggest Heywood's authorship.

The idea of having religious professionals speak simultaneously for almost half the play (252/641 lines) is strikingly original (though it may have been suggested by a lost source play). From *La farce d'un Pardonneur, d'un Triacleur, et d'une Tavernière*, are copied some burlesque saints and relics.[1] But the major debt is to Chaucer's *Pardoner's Prologue* (lines 335–88), quoted verbatim in the Pardoner's opening speech (PF97–132, 170–82). A shift in tone is noticeable when Heywood stops quoting Chaucer and produces 'marvels of quite another colour':[2]

He consults his wife, who replies vehemently:
   'Burne vp quod A? Mary god forbede. It wold wast vp your gere vpon payne of my lyfe'
   (*ibid*. 229/12–3).
[9] *Ibid*. p. 69.

[1] *La farce nouvelle d'un Pardonneur, d'un Triacleur et d'une Tavernière* is printed by M. Viollet-Leduc, *Ancien théâtre françois*, 10 vols. Paris, 1854–57, II 50–63.
[2] Maxwell p. 76.

'Swete saynt Sondaye', (PF134) 'great too of the Holy Trynyte' (140), 'of Saynt Myghell, eke, the brayn pan' (162). From the *Canterbury Tales*, too, particularly the speech of the mendicant friar in the *Summoner's Tale*, Heywood reinvented the Pardoner's heretical economic rival. The Frere's reference to his 'place' where 'be fryers thre score and thre' (PF380 and note) identifies him as a member of the 'demoniacal friary' immortalised in Lydgate's *Order of Fools*. But this is clearly dangerous folly.

The use of Chaucer has led most commentators to assign the play an early date, and to see the satire as merely traditional, similar to Erasmus's and removed from the factionalism of the Reformation. Reference to Pope Leo X, who licensed selling pardons to raise money for building the Vatican, granted Henry VIII the title *Fidei Defensor* and died in 1521, has been taken to indicate a *terminus ad quem* for the play's composition.[3] However, Leo is not mentioned as living (PF193 and note), and the play plays tricks by mixing real and imaginary Popes. The quotation from Chaucer (just conceivably worked from memory) is textual, and the use of a virgule (/) to mark the mid-line caesura, helpful to the actors in marking time during the difficult feat of speaking simultaneously, may indicate that the playwright used a particular printed text of Chaucer from 1527 or even 1532. But he could have known his Chaucer in manuscript, so this line of approach cannot help with dating.

Two topical allusions point towards the later 1520s. The Pardoner's collection is ostensibly for repairs to the 'holy chapell of swete saynt Leonarde, / Whiche late by fyre was destroyed and marde' (PF207–9 and note). Suitable English candidates are lacking, and bearing in mind the Pardoner's specifically Roman allegiance, it is possible that the chapel of this disreputable saint may be one sacked by the Protestant forces at the invasion of Rome in 1527.[4] Secondly, the mockery 'Of all Helowes the blessyd jaw bone' (PF154), (as well as 4P497–506) may specifically refer to All Hallows Church in Honey Lane. This was a notorious pulpit for Lutheran views by 1528 and Heywood makes clear his scorn for such heretical 'jawing'. The violence of his play may be taken as a wry comment on a spectacle frequent in his London. In summer 1532, blood was shed in All Hallows, when two priests fought, and no services could be performed until they did penance before a general procession.[5] The entrance in the play of the Curate to complain that the brawling rogues 'polute my chyrche' is more than a theatrical shock and a revelation of sacrilege (comparable to that in Skelton's *Ware the hawk*); it is an urgent warning for the times. But what times?

The case for dating *Pardoner and Frere* closer to 1530 than 1520 depends also on perceiving the doctrinal distinctions that are made between the rivals; these differences are highlighted by a number of close parallels in wording between the play and Thomas More's *Dialogue concerning Heresies* (1529) and his *Confutation of Tyndale* (1532, 1533). While it is not improbable that More was recalling Heywood (a possibility that says much for Heywood's unrecognised originality), their close family association needs to be kept in mind. If the tone and specificity of satire is to count as evidence of the climate of a particular time, then the play and the polemic writing belong close together.

Heywood's Frere is associated specifically with Lutheran heresy. He enters

3 Farmer p. 245.
4 PF207 and note. Carlo Milanesi, *Il Sacco di Roma del 1527*, Firenze, 1867; *L&P* IV ii 1418–20.
5 Brigden p. 213.

first, to 'preche the gospel' (PF15–6) and bring the 'Lord's peace'. He wants to be sure that he has a welcome, 'yf that house be worthy and electe' (PF42). By introducing one of Luther's and Tyndale's key-words, 'electe' into this gloss of Matthew 10.12, Heywood suggests that the Frere looks to the audience as likely heretics, 'Which were dysposyd the worde of God to here' (PF62). He offers them 'grace' (PF68,76). He threatens excommunication and curses those 'that lettyth the worde'. His authority and theme-song are the Word: 'Our lorde in the gospell' is juxtaposed with the Pardoner's citing the 'Popys auctoryte' (PF529–30). At the end it is the Frere who fights with the Parson, who laments that 'The cursed frere dothe the upper hande wyn!' (PF637).

The Pardoner's prayer that the audience resemble 'the ymage' of their creator sounds the keynote of his traditional licensed trade – images and relics. The satire here differs from that of Chaucer and of Langland before him largely to the extent that the importation of fantastic relics from the French tradition make it seem less savage. In addition to Papal authority for his 'bullys', he also claims royal protection:

> And, eke, yf thou disturbe me any thynge
> Thou arte a traytour to the kynge!   (PF270–1)

and this probably reflects Henry's Defence of the Faith against Luther in his *Assertio* of 1521[6] and his *Letters* of 1526.[7]

Relatively speaking, the Pardoner seems less dangerous than his opponent. In one of the few speeches where his voice is heard alone without the confusing overlay of the Frere's speech, he accuses the Frere of heresy in offering his congregation 'no salve for theyr sore' (PF284–93). But the Pardoner's own doctrine is also implicitly heretical, since he promises 'clene remyssyon' and forgiveness 'without confessyon or contrycyon' (PF321). The picture of his 'fraternitie' is traditional, with its 'masse and dirige', its torches and tapers, bells, its 'prestes and clerkes' singing, ceremonials for the souls of the dead (PF463–75) is, surprisingly, unsatirical (though one suspects that the 'twelve pore people' received there (PF479) are not harboured and fed very well.) He accuses the Frere of apostacy (PF566), homycyde (PF567) and sexual perversion (PF569) – far worse crimes than the Frere can level at him. Unlike the Frere, he asks pardon for his offence within the parson's 'lybertye' (PF597). At the end he fights with the constable (who describes him as an 'elfe': a word in Heywood's plays denoting mischief rather than great wickedness) and makes his head bleed. Nevertheless it is clear that they both 'polute my chyrche' (PF547).

Among parallels between the play and More's *Dialogue concerning Heresies*, printed by Heywood's father-in-law John Rastell in June 1529,[8] More's recollection of Chaucer is particularly striking:

> For what reverent honoure is there dayly done . . . to some old rotten bone yt was happely some tyme as Chaucer sayth a bone of some holy Iewes shepe.[9]

More's view of Luther is repeatedly that of a 'furious' friar who made his first

---

6 STC 13078; (1522) STC 13079
7 STC 13084; English translation, *A Copy of the letters* (1527) STC 13086.
8 STC 18084; printed again in 1531 by William Rastell, STC 18085.
9 *Works* VI i 98/12–15.

heretical attack on the Catholic church by manipulating the abuse of pardons as a stalking horse.

> Fyrst he began quod I wyth pardons & wyth ye popys power . . . And sone after . . . he denyed all ye vii. sacraments.[10]

In explaining how Luther fell into heresy More writes,

> there was a pardon obtayned in Saxony / for whyche pardon as the maner ys there /Luther was the precheour. . . For anger wherof he fell in to suche a fury. . . from reasonyng than fell he to raylyng.[11]

Eventually, according to More, Luther taught the neglect of all ceremonies and freedom from 'all maner lawys spyrytuall or temporall / excepte the gospel onely'.[12] More goes on to paint a horrifying picture of the forces of Reformation marching on Rome and committing atrocities (May 1527), linking these with Luther's vehemence against pardons. The word More constantly applies to Luther and his English disciple Tyndale is 'frantyke'.

The *Confutacyon of Tyndales Answere* (1532, 1533) offers further examples of scornful reference to Luther as 'frere Frappe,'[13] 'frere Luther'.[14] In England, vilification of Luther appears to have become more popular and widespread as the 1520s went on. A Latin *farsa*, played by St Paul's boys on 10 November 1527, represented Luther as a 'party friar'.[15] There was much of this in the air, but it is plain that the idiom of invective in *The Pardoner and the Frere* is at times almost indistinguishable from that of More's polemical writing. Heywood's 'ragman roll with lyes' (PF553) matches More's 'Ragman roll of a rable of heretykes'[16] and 'all the heresyes that they haue in all theyr whole Ragmans roll'.[17] The Frere's insult 'thou slouche!' (PF519) is particularly suggestive. *OED* gives the first usage as 1511 and defines it as 'a term of disparagement without precise significance'. In the *Confutation* More's repeated use of the word 'slouche' forges a strong association with heresy. He imagines a heretic of Tyndale's faith as 'a great slouen slouche, that of hys boyes age is twenty wynter stepte into hys knavys age' and speaks of 'a nother slouche of hys acuayntaunce hys owne mayster Master Luther'.[18] Also suggestive in relation to the Pardoner's offer of pardon 'though ye had slayne bothe father and mother' (PF385) is More's 'ensample of Iak slouche' who commits 'auoutry with hys mother, poysenynge hys father, and murderynge hys brother.'[19]

More's sense of humour and his love of theatrical metaphor create a scene quite suggestive of Heywood's play:

> monkys & freres, and now apostatas & lyuynge wyth harlotes . . . Tyndale here . . . wolde [a man] not wene that yt were a sorte of freres folowynge an abbote of mysrule in a Christemas game that were prykked in blankettes,

---

10 *ibid.* 349/12–15.
11 *ibid.* 361/3–25.
12 *ibid.* 368/18–31.
13 *Works* VIII ii 925/27.
14 *Works* VIII i 181/3–4.
15 Lancashire No. 723.
16 *Works* VIII i 181/29.
17 *Works* VIII ii 657/13.
18 *ibid.* 492/30, 494/6–7.
19 *ibid.* 495/6–7.

and then sholde stande vp and preche vppon a stole and make a mowynge sermon.[20]

Heywood's Frere reveals his membership of a fraternity of fools (PF380); a stool (or stools) are used in the farcical preaching in the play (PF509–12).

More's polemics thus confirm a reading of Heywood's friar as specifically a Lutheran figure; under the guise of condemning pardons he teaches worse heresies based on 'the gospel'; when not allowed to preach 'by pardon' he falls 'into a fury'. Such a theme might, perhaps, have been struck early in the 1520s, but would be more urgent towards the end of the decade, as the popular perception of Luther and his followers grew more perturbed. The numerous verbal parallels with More's polemical interchange with Tyndale give a topical edge and energy to the language of the dispute. They must also, in view of the parallels found between More's writings and other plays of Heywood's, constitute circumstantial evidence of Heywood's authorship of the anonymous *Pardoner and Frere*. But the daring experiment for two virtuoso actors by no means exhausted Heywood's interest in religious roguery, nor in creating his own 'dialogues of heresies'.

5. The Foure PP

Although the earliest surviving text is Middleton's quarto of about 1544, it is likely that *Foure PP* was first printed c.1533 by William Rastell in the same period as the other plays. Its date of composition can be conjectured from the topicality of its themes and allusions. In some ways the play can be seen as an expansion of the idea of *Pardoner and Frere* – a comic contest between professionals offering ways to salvation. By recasting the Pardoner, Heywood re-used and expanded the joke of making All Hallows into a saint (PF154, 4P497–503 and notes). The protracted demonstration that 'All Halows breth stynketh' (4P503ff.) may well express disgust at the church of All Hallows in Honey Lane, whose notoriety as a pulpit for 'the secret sowing and setting forth of Luther's heresies' reached a peak in 1528; its rector was condemned by More in *Dialogue concerning Heresies*.[1] On these grounds alone *Foure PP* would seem to be later – though not necessarily much later – than *Pardoner and Frere*.

Heywood re-used the same French source, *La farce d'un Pardonneur, d'un Triacleur et d'une Tavernière*, plundering more of its absurd relics and remedies, its fantastic journeys. Only two of the P's, the professional charlatans, Pardoner and Potycary, have models in the French, but Heywood's Palmer and Pedler too are professional rather than fantastic.[2] In contrast to the desultory fantasy of the French Heywood sharpened the element of purely professional rivalry, using both satire and comic fantasy (in the lying contest) to approach his serious theme: the way to salvation.

The title draws attention to the (for Heywood normal) cast and wittily alludes to a matched set of religious professionals sharing the initial P (Tudor evidence indicates that the printer's plural 'PP' was pronounced 'Pees').

---

[20] *ibid.* 42/2–8.

[1] More, *Works* VI ii 714; Brigden p. 117.

[2] Maxwell pp. 74–84.

Heywood may have borrowed his conceit from Stephen Hawes' 'ppp thre' in *Conforte of Lovers*. More remote is the figure of Dante.[3] Before he entered Purgatory Dante had seven P's inscribed on his forehead with the tip of an angel's sword; the P's indicated sins (*peccati*) to be washed and purged. Though it may be a little fanciful to see Heywood's drama in parodic relationship with *Purgatorio*, there is certainly a confessional aspect to the encounter and the sinful rogues come to express some awareness of sin.

Much in the play's style and subject matter can be loosely paralleled in the French *farces*. Professional boasts, long dramatic narratives, routines of word-play and repetitive 'leashes' of couplets, sometimes monorhymed, also occur in the *sermons joyeux* and *dits*. The quack 'epicier' is a stock figure in French farce, though no precise textual parallels have been adduced.[4] By contrast, the hopping game arranged by the Potycary (4P467) seems purely English, with Lydgate's *Order of Fools* as Heywood's parent text. Lists of herbs and medicines occur in the medieval Chester *Shepherds' Play* and in the 'quack doctor scene' of the Croxton *Play of the Sacrament*.[5] It may be significant that neither of these English treatments is purely comic, and they anticipate *Foure PP* in metaphorically linking 'salve' with 'salvation'.

The traveller's spiel has ancestors in French *Jeu du Pelèrin*,[6] and in English drama: the merchant's list in the Croxton *Play of the Sacrament* is alliterative and partly alphabetical;[7] so is that in *Mundus et Infans*.[8] Rastell's *Four Elements* (c.1518) contains an illustrated lesson in 'cosmography', beginning with Jerusalem.[9] The topographical list in *Hickscorner* (c.1513–14) is more fantastic and includes 'the land of rumbelow, Three mile out of hell.'[10]

However, almost all Heywood's pilgrimage places are real, though some of the popular shrines were disreputable at his time. A cluster of the same pilgrimage haunts appears also in More's *Dialogue concerning Heresies*, 1529: 'the Rodes', 'Amyas', 'saynt Uncumber', Willesden and 'saynt Roke', patron of syphilis (see notes to 4P29, 30, 31, 40). Their incidence underlines the thematic similarities between Heywood and More in defence of harmless traditional practices. It indicates too the fundamental seriousness of Heywood's satirical fantasy, which lacks More's scornful harping on 'heresy'.

Thomas More may also be responsible for the conception of the Pedler. In the seventh 'Properte of a lover', appended to his *Lyfe of Johan Picus*, More writes:[11]

> 'There is . . . none so small a tryfle or conceyte,
> Lace, gyrdell, poynt or propre glove strayte,
> But that yf to his love it have ben nere,

---

3 *Conforte of Lovers*, ll. 139–40; *Purgatorio* IX 112–4, XII 121ff. See Explanatory Note to 4P Title.
4 A list of herbs including 'colloquintide et cassia' occurs in *La Condemnacion de Bancquet*. P.L. Jacob, *Recueil de farces, soties et moralités du quinzième siècle*, Paris, 1859, pp. 443–4. Cited by Ashe-Jones p. 44.
5 *Chester Plays* VII 17–28, 73–80; *Play of the Sacrament* 525–653 (ed. Bevington).
6 Cohen, *Recueil* No. V.
7 *Play of the Sacrament* 97–114.
8 *Mundus et Infans* 245–8 (ed. Schell and Schuchter, *English Morality Plays and Moral Interludes*, New York, 1969).
9 'Syr, yf a man have suche corage / Or devocyon in pylgrymage / Jheruzalem unto .˙. .' *Four Elements* 678–80.
10 *Hickscorner* 317–8, (ed. Lancashire, *Two Tudor Interludes*, Manchester, 1980).
11 Printed by J. Rastell c.1510, STC 19897.7 and by Wynkyn de Worde c.1525, STC 19898. *The XII Properties of a Lover*, in *English Works* I 389.

> The lover hath it precyous, leyfe & dere.
> So euery relyque, image or pycture,
> That doth pertayne to Goddes magnyfycence,
> The lover of God sholde wyth all besy cure
> Haue it in love, honoure and reverence . . .

Heywood's modest Pedler hawks his wares with:

> Who lyveth in love or love wolde wynne
> Even at this packe he must begynne. (4P231–2)

Through metaphor the Pedler is seen as dealing in images and relics of the divine Beloved.

The motif of a journey to purgatory or hell was very widespread in late medieval literature. A 'frere ravysshed . . . to helle' is mentioned in Chaucer's *Summoner's Prologue* (1676–7), while the fate of the lewd Margery Coorson (4P932) may have been suggested by Skelton's *Colin Clout* 876–8, where friars

> say propreli they ar sacerdotes
> To shryve, assoyle and reles
> Dame Margeries soule out of hell.[12]

Thomas Whythorne's Ballad of Robert the 'lechrouz frier' describes his final amorous escapade, a descent into hell to try (unsuccessfully) 'þe Divls dam'.[13] This light-hearted ballad by Heywood's pupil introduces a miniature discourse on purgatory.

Foure PP is notorious for the Rabelaisian obscenity and anti-feminism of the Potycary's tale of Margery. Such elements were popular in writing of the period and are found repeatedly, for example, in Skelton's *Eleanor Rumming* and in the interlude of *Thersites*. The latter was thought appropriate to mark the birth of Prince Edward in 1537. Scatological feats and 'miracles' involving a 'clyster' are stock-in-trade of French farces and fabliaux. In view of Heywood's epic expansion of the motif of scatological artillery (4P732ff.) the humorous little verse tale, *Mery geste of the frere and the boye* is worth noting.[14]

The satirical possibilities of an infernal journey are suggested by record of a farce acted in London in January 1531 showing Cardinal Wolsey going down to hell. This performance, arranged by Thomas Boleyn at his own house to entertain the French ambassador, must have given particular satisfaction to the father of the King's mistress. Order was given (possibly by the Duke of Norfolk) for the play to be printed.[15] The episode is a reminder that there were coterie 'theatres' available to Heywood beyond the confines of the court.

The delightful picture of hell (4P886ff.) may recall John Frith's polemical mockery of purgatory at the expense of Thomas More:

---

12 J.W. McCain Jr, 'Heywood's *The Foure PP*: a Debt to Skelton' *N&Q* CLXXIV (1938), 205.
13 Whythorne, *Autobiography* pp. 125–29.
14 Printed by Wynkyn de Worde, 1510–13, STC 14521. As a result of the Boy's magical powers, his wicked step-dame is made to

> . . . let go a blaste
> That they in the hall were agaste . . .
> Quod the boye well I wote
> That gonne was well shote
> As it had ben a stone. (A3v)

15 Lancashire No. 1014; *CSP Sp* IV ii (1882) no. 615, pp. 40–1.

Now, as touching the manner how this devil came into purgatory, laughing, grinning, and gnashing his teeth, in sooth it maketh me to see the merry antics of Master More.[16]

Perhaps the remark is to be taken as alluding to theatrical performance. *Foure PP* seems to have been associated with More and his household and in the play *Sir Thomas More* (scene 9) the 'foure Pees' is one of the titles offered to the Chancellor by the visiting players.[17]

Court forms – livery, verbal formulae, and etiquette are finely observed among the devils and the satirical possibilities of the shirt-sleeved tennis-playing fiends, presided over by the 'Master devil' in his fashionable jacket (4P881 and note) celebrating the anniversary of his fall into power, would not have escaped Heywood's audience. The text of *Foure PP* makes no allusion to royal presence. Private performance, among like-minded family and friends, might make such a glancing allusion safer, and would bring light relief to worried conservatives during the darkening days around 1530.

Heywood's defence of pilgrimage (4P1141 and note) and the good humoured treatment afforded the Pardoner, in contrast with *Pardoner and Frere*, may be signs of reaction to the threat of reform. The judicious Pedler comments that the Potycary, despire his claim to 'no vertue at all' is 'well beloved of all thys sorte / By your raylynge here openly / At pardons and relyques so leudly' (4P1198–1200). Clearly Heywood believed that criticism of Catholic practice had gone far enough in the circle surrounding the king, and would not have wanted to give further ammunition to the reformers. He concludes with the Pedler urging the submission of individual judgment to that of the Church. However, it is the Palmer who leads the prayer for God's grace, dignified by rhyme royal, and stating firmly the Catholic doctrine of man's ability to 'purchase / Hys love' (4P1223–4) by his efforts during his lifetime. The defence of pilgrimage and the dramatic authority given to the Palmer's final utterances align Heywood's point of view with that of More in *Dialogue concerning Heresies* and indicate roughly contemporary date of composition c.1528–30.

6. A Play of Love

The title page of the play, printed 'cum privilegio regali' in 1534 by William Rastell, ascribes *A Play of Love* to John Heywood. It was the last to be printed, appearing in the same format as *The Play of the Wether*, to which Rastell may have given a few months' priority. In its rhetorically structured debating and word-play *Love* resembles *Witty and Witless*.[1] Like *Foure PP* it uses four actors to make symmetrical patterns, and takes inset story-telling to extremes of length; in the developed clowning of the cynical Vice the play resembles *Wether*.[2] The play's formality and heavy reliance on debate structure have often been interpreted as signs of early work. But this is not necessarily so, any more than the

---

16 Cited by Foxe, AM IV 665.
17 *The Book of Sir Thomas More*, ed. W.W. Greg, MSR, Oxford, 1911, line 921.

1 Similarities include extensive use of the Aristotelian categories of pain and pleasure, the clock metaphor (L255ff. Wy276ff.), vocabulary and tricks of style (L1104, Wy540), arguments by choice of objects (horse/tree L1428, man/beast Wy456).
2 Similarities include the neck joke (L1267, We352–6, 998–9).

mature, colloquial vigour of *Johan Johan* is a sign of its lateness. Heywood merely adopted a different style to suit an audience of 'stately porte' (L7).

One striking aspect of the play, as well as a clue to its auspices and interest, is its formal legal language. A *case* (the word occurs 43 times) is *proved* (9 times), so as to gain an *indifferent* (5 times) *judgment* (24 times).[3] Slightly more technical expressions include: *attorney* (L1026), *demurrer* (L931), *denyeng Your pryncyple* (L207–8), *mater of recorde* (L1343), *proces* (L314, 915), *sarjaunt* (L810), *stande unto . . . judgement* (L738), *substaunce* (L672), *veryfy* (L61, 65, 70), *wytnes* (L311). The list, by no means exhaustive, indicates the interest of the play's action as a moot of love, in which the three who are touched by Love are schooled by the fourth – a would-be 'indifferent judge'.

The suggestion that *Love* was a seasonal piece, intended for an audience of lawyers, puts into focus the lawyerly language and the peculiar nature of the play's forms of argument. In the educational context of Inns of Court Christmas revels the parodic nature of Heywood's 'moot of love' becomes apparent, as does the possibility of specific personal satire. The sequence in which the Vice sanctimoniously claims to have prepared himself to give judgment by confession and shrift, vaunting his pure conscience in place of any legal qualifications (L801–12) has plausibly been seen as a take-off of Wolsey's style in the Court of Chancery. Heywood here aligns himself with the common lawyers' hatred of Wolsey, who had no training in either civil or canon law. On the basis of this passage Schoeck suggests as possible auspice for *Love* the Christmas Revels at Lincoln's Inn 1528 or 1529.[4] A further accusation of greed and corruption appears to be the point of allusion to Westminster Hall full of gold (L1423–24).

Heywood would have been safe in mocking him – as a dozen other English writers did – by Christmas 1529, since Wolsey resigned as Chancellor in October. The promotion of Heywood's kinsman Thomas More as Chancellor may possibly have been an additional stimulus for the King's servant to compose a Christmas play for his Inn. St Paul had written, 'Love is the fulfilling of the law' (Rom.13.10); and More himself had written on the 'points of a perfect lover' in the sonnet-like verses attached to his translation of the Life of Pico.[5]

Hunting sources for *Love* has so far proved fairly unrewarding and has shed no specific light on its date or context. Maxwell has claimed that dissection of amorous conditions was French rather than English, and that in form and detail *Love* stands closer to the French than the English tradition. Non-dramatic dialogues of love had been common in France since the *jeux partis* and *demandes d'amour* of the thirteenth century. In *Le jardin de plaisance* (printed 1501) an Absent and a Rejected Lover compare their plights, each arguing his case is worse, and agreeing to submit to two judges. In its 'logical' aspect the cast list of Heywood's play recalls the well-known morality *Bien avisé, Mal avisé*: 'Regnato, Regno, Regnavi, Sum sine Regno'.[6] The long monologues of fabliau type, with *graphie* lists and set descriptions couched in tripping verse, the leashes of antithetical clauses, rhyming and chiming, are all common in French drama and verse of the period.[7]

However, the pleasure and pain of love, together with the traditional debate

---

3 Details based on Canzler *Concordance*.
4 R.J. Schoeck, 'Satire of Wolsey in Heywood's *Play of Love*', *N&Q* 196 (1951), 112–14.
5 *English Works* I 389.
6 Maxwell p. 102.
7 Maxwell p. 115.

about whether women are 'true' lovers, occurs in two little-known English works published in the 1520s. The *Spectacle of Lovers* by Wyllyam Walter is a 'lytell contravers dyalogue bytwene loue and councell', entirely in rhyme royal stanzas.[8] Thomas Feylde's *Contrauersye bytwene a louer and a Jaye*[9] aligns itself with the tradition of Chaucer, Lydgate, and Hawes. It is written (like *A Play of Love*) in a mixture of rhyme royal and short-line couplets. Feylde's Amator complains, 'What payne it is/ To loue vnloued' (A4r) and the cynical Jaye's song warns that, 'To sette thy mynde/On one unkynde/Thy wyttes were blynde' (B1r). J. Rickes's *Ymage of Love*[10] turns out to be a 'goostly pamphlete' proving Christ to be the true image of love. While they can hardly be claimed as 'sources', these three contemporary English works show the ambivalence inherent in Heywood's title as to what 'kynde of love as here hath ben ment', for at the end he recommends: 'Let us seke the love of that lovyng Lorde' (L1565–6).

The influence of More's translation of Pico della Mirandola's *Life* with its 'Twelve Points of a Perfect Lover' has been argued by La Rosa, who makes the interesting suggestion that No lover nor loved (whom we have treated above as a purely theatrical 'Vice' character) is an incarnation of Pico's and Vivés' notion of man's Protean freedom to fashion roles for himself.[11] There are some parallels with Rastell's *Calisto and Melebea*: both plays satirize the Petrarchan lover, directly and in showing the young lady's rational scorn of him; both include a narrative 'pastime' concerning a wanton with a second lover, and an old 'mother' to keep the door.[12] A faint but unmistakable echo of Chaucer's *Miller's Tale* is heard in the episode at the window (L659–61).[13] In a more courtly vein, the influence of Skelton's *Garland of Laurel* is most felt in the Vice's dancing dimeter couplets (L427–66) evoking the ideal woman. It is interesting to note, too, that the subterfuges of love described in *Love* are close in language, idiom and attitude to the amorous adventures and moral warnings of Thomas Whythorne's *Autobiography*. Indeed, much of Whythorne could be read as informal commentary on themes suggested by Heywood's plays, a sort of autobiographical tribute to his master, complete with quotation from a lost play (see Appendix I) and recurrent allusion to Heywood's *Proverbs*.

7. The Play of the Wether

The Play the Wether, printed 'cum privilegio' by William Rastell in 1533, carries John Heywood's name. It is the most ambitious in scale of the surviving interludes by Heywood and has attracted most attention from modern editors and other scholars. Consequently, its sources and context require somewhat fuller discussion than do the five plays already considered. No single source has been advanced in which the play's structural and thematic elements are combined.[1] The conception of Jupiter as ruler (rather than lover) seems to have been fashionable in court entertainment of the early sixteenth century, partly as a result of human-

---

8   Printed by Wynkyn de Worde n.d. STC 25008.
9   Printed by Wynkyn de Worde [c.1522]
10 Printed by Wynkyn de Worde Oct 1525.
11 La Rosa p. civ, citing ed. J.M. Rigg, London, 1890.
12 Cf. L616–20 and *Calisto* 353–73.
13 L659–61, *MilT* 3470.

1   See the discussion by Cameron, *Wether*, Ashe-Jones, and Robinson.

ist popularising of the Dialogues of Lucian. The most relevant of these is *Ikaromenippus*, printed in Florence 1496, and translated into Latin by Erasmus by 1511.[2] By 1522 it had appeared in four editions of the Erasmus-More translations of the *Dialogues*. Menippus tells of his flight to heaven and admission to Jupiter's court by Hermes (Mercury), the doorkeeper, and of the contradictory petitions from earth dwellers that reach the ears of the king of gods. Jupiter orders various kinds of weather for different parts of earth. However, two important features of *Ikaromennipus* do not figure in *Wether*, although Heywood could easily have made use of them: the satire of philosophers and the banquet.[3]

Control of the Weather as a metaphor for government of conflicting human activities is a medieval commonplace, occuring at the beginning of the *Secretum Secretorum*.[4] A parliament of planets and constellations called by Jupiter was represented theatrically in *Cortés de Jupiter* by the Portuguese playwright Gil Vicente, and performed at the royal palace Lisbon in 1519, in honour of the Duchess of Savoy. Parallels between *Wether* and other plays of Gil Vicente have been made by Cameron,[5] and by Ashe-Jones, who suggests that Heywood may have known the Portuguese dramatist through Erasmus.[6]

As part of the entertainments of the English court at Greenwich on 6 May 1527 Heywood's father-in-law John Rastell made a 'pageant of the Father of Hevin'. A play by the Chapel children with disputes between Love/Cupid and Riches/Plutus was introduced by Mercury and judged by the King on the authority of Jupiter.[7] Mercury's blue taffeta gown sewn all over with eyes may be pertinent to Heywood's conception of Mery Report's costume (We186 and note). So may an earlier entertainment, recorded by Hall, in which a messenger called Reaport was 'appareled in Crymosyn satyn full of tonges, sitting on a flyeng horse with wynges and fete of gold called Pegasus.'[8] In these fictions presented to the English court there is an inevitable equation between Jupiter and the King. The same fiction had been used by Skelton in his *Speke Parott* (c.1522).[9]

French plays of the late fifteenth and early sixteenth centuries contain examples of suits presented by representatives of the various estates. Maxwell has suggested a number of parallels between *Wether* and the *sotties*, in particular *Sottie Nouvelle de l'Astrologue* (1498). Ashe-Jones draws attention to the conception of the attendant Fool figure in a number of 'mère sotte' plays, his relation with the audience, and his verbal games.[10] Farces in French were among entertainment offered by Wolsey during the visit of Cardinal Campeggio at Christmas

2 Cameron, *Wether* p. 20, Ashe-Jones p. 49.
3 Cameron, *Wether* p. 26 finds similar motifs in *Bis Accusatus*: Jupiter speaks of disagreement among the gods, Mercury volunteers his services and makes proclamation, only some of the petitioners are allowed to see Jupiter in person, they come in pairs and two women quarrel over a lover.
4 Ed. M.A. Manzalaoui, EETS Oxford, 1977, I 40–1: 'It is rad that a kynge in his reame is as rayne in the erthe . . .'
5 Cameron, *Wether* pp. 15–16.
6 Ashe-Jones pp. 58–61.
7 Lancashire No. 721. Sydney Anglo, 'La salle de banquet et le théâtre construits à Greenwich pour les fêtes franco-anglaises de 1527' in *Le lieu théâtral à la Renaissance*, ed. Jean Jacquot, Elie Konigson & Marcel Oddon, Paris, 1964, pp. 273–88.
8 Hall, *Chronicle* p. 595, cited by Cameron p. 20.
9 Henry VIII is Jupiter in Skelton's *Speke Parott* (c.1522 but not printed until 1545). Saturn, Aeolus also appear. See *Poems* ed. Scattergood, pp. 461–3 and notes on lines 398–99.
10 'I am I per se I' (We104) is heard as an echo of *Tout, Rien et Chascun* cited by Ashe-Jones p. 58.

1528.[11] Given the prestige of French culture at Henry's court, it is quite likely that dramatic models in French have been lost or remain to be discovered.

Closer to home is the tradition of seasonal dramatic performance. A Twelfth Night mumming in 1429 devised by Lydgate for the Mercers of London, had 'a poursuyaunt in wyse of mommers desguysed' who related a letter 'in wyse of balade' announcing to the Mayor the imminent arrival of Jupiter in London.[12] At Christmas the year before, Lydgate had devised Christmas revels for the court of Henry VI at Hertford. These were made,

> in maner of a bille by wey of supplicacioun putte to þe kyng holding his noble feest of Cristmasse in þe Castel of Hertford as in a disguysing of þe Rude upplandisshe people compleyning on hir wyves with þe boystous aunswere of hir wyves.[13]

At the end the King gave judgment that the partners must make the best of the status quo. The analogue is not close, but it points to a traditional subject which flickers beneath the surface of *Wether*, and which has not been emphasized by previous commentators – marriage.

In the line of English humanism an important ancestor of *Wether's* is Henry Medwall's 'godely [goodly] interlude' *Fulgens and Lucres* (c.1497), printed by John Rastell in about 1515 and deriving, as the title-page made clear, from the household of 'Johan Morton, cardynall and archebysshop of Caunterbury', where Thomas More had been a page. Fulgens provided Heywood with a model of entirely secular drama, free from allegory and doctrinal matter, in the form of suits presented and judged impartially. Its debate between aristocratic 'nobility' or 'gentleness' and plebeian 'virtue' carries its own underplot in the servants A and B.[14]

Class conflict in *Wether* focuses sharply in the dispute of the Gentylwoman and the Launder. In theatrical conception and idiom Mery Report owes much to A and B: his entry into the play world as volunteer from the crowd (We94, *Fulgens* 354), his ridiculous pretensions and inadequacies, his easy relation with the audience and vulgar amorousness. The sequence in which he 'woos' both the Gentlewoman and the Launder can be seen as a parodic inversion of A and B wooing the maid Jone. Both scenes make use of social embarassment at the public demand for a kiss and of reductive scatalogical humour. In a formal sense Medwall's care in separating high and low characters by means of rhyme royal and rime couée may have suggested to Heywood his principle of decorum, using rhyme royal and couplets.

For his types of the estates of England Heywood had, as well as Chaucer, dramatic models of the Knight, Merchant, and Ploughman in *Gentleness and Nobility*. Viewed within the tradition, it is striking that both plays lack a figure for Clergy (though there is a vestigial presence in *Wether*, where Mery Report deliberately mistakes the Merchant as a parson). Both plays sustain serious economic analysis (Ploughman, the Millers); both allow a Merchant to put the case for mercantilism as England's preeminent activity; both include voluble spokesmen for 'honest labour' from the lower orders (Ploughman, Launder). The verbal

---

[11] Lancashire No.725.
[12] *Minor Poems* ed. H.M. McCracken, II 695; Lancashire No. 930.
[13] *Minor Poems* II 675.
[14] 'Vertue! What the devyll is that? – *Fulgens* 842, cf. 4P1188.

skills by which they are presented and the ironic humanistic viewpoint of their claims are similar in the two cases. There may be a common debt to Chaucer here too.[15]

Dating the play

Previous attempts to date the play have assumed as *terminus ad quem* Heywood's supposed departure from Royal service in 1528. Yet, as has been noted, records for the previous ten years fail to show evidence of his dramatic activity (in contrast to those for 1530s and 1540s). Moreover, the King's gift at New Year 1532/33 shows that Heywood was still in favour at Court. From evidence within the text it seems at least possible that Heywood himself played the part of Mery Report (We121), so that his complaint to the audience, 'No "welcome home" nor "where have ye be?" ' (We193) may indicate a return to familiar surroundings. The inclusion in the cast of a school Boy, 'the lest that can play', chosen as spokesman by his hundred fellows, together with the use of music, suggests that the play may have been done with the collaboration of a choir school such as St Paul's. As mentioned in the account of Heywood's life, evidence from later in the 1530s shows Heywood working with Westcott and his boys. In any case, it seems better at first to retain as *terminus* for the play William Rastell's publication of the folio *Wether* in 1533, probably late in the year.

Issues mentioned in the text and thought to refer to contemporary events are the weather, especially heavy rains and the consequent high price of corn (We634–5); the restriction of access to the King's person by unworthy persons, specially 'boys' (We487), which has been held to post-date the Eltham Reforms of the household in 1525; the Merchant's proposal to travel to Chios 'by mid Lente' (We385), which has been held to be impossible during the Anglo-Spanish hostilities of 1527–28. None of these is conclusive and the play contains a great deal more worth considering as topical allusion.

On the question of heavy rainfall only one relevant comment seems clearly addressed to the audience: [16]

> And well it is knowen to the moste foole here
> How rayne hath pryced corne within this seven yere. (We634–5)

Corn prices rose in the 1520's. Great rains were chronicled in autumn 1526 and in spring 1527; the harvest failed badly and prices rose. But imports of grain from the continent reduced prices. A draft bill for Parliament in 1533 shows the King still concerned to pursue those who had raised the price of corn.[17] The 'proverbial' phrase 'this seven yere' is unlikely to be arithmetically exact (cf. 4P776)

---

15 Robinson pp. 86–8 sees 'skeletal resemblances' between *Wether* and Chaucer's gentle satire of the estates in *Parlement of Foulis*; a thematic precedent in his treatment of 'Juppiter the kynge, / That is prince and cause of alle thyng' (KnT 3035–6); and hints for his dramatic characters in the Canterbury Knight, Merchant, Wife of Bath, Prioress, Miller. In the light of the specific borrowings in PF these are likely.

16 Otherwise the evidence is inconclusive: Saturn and Phebus complain of Phebe's rainfall, but all three complain of Aeolus's winds. The Water Miller complains of lack of rain and the Water Miller of lack of wind and too much rain. Mery Report predicts that the 'new moon' will produce moderate rains, 'Not gushynge out lyke gutters of Noyes flood' (We805). But then moderation is the play's message.

17 Brigden p. 138.

and, even interpreted strictly, may have appropriately been spoken at any time between the years between 1526 and 1533.

In *Wether* direct access to the king is clearly governed by rules of social decorum which Mery Report self-importantly and comically breaches. The Articles of Eltham devised by Wolsey and Sir Henry Guildeford, Comptroller of the Household, and brought into effect by Christmas 1525, winnowed the household employees and restricted admittance to the Privy Chamber. They also regulated behaviour – none was

> to advaunce himselfe further in service than by the K's Heighnesse he shalbe appointed unto, nor presse his Gr in makinge of suites, nor intermeddle with causes or matters.[18]

The Eltham Articles command the Knight Marshall to 'have speciall respect to the exclusion of boyes and vile persons,' and Yeomen ushers to 'avoyde and purge the haute-pace at the King's chamber-doore of all manner servauntes, raskalles, boyes, and other.'[19] In the play Mery Report treats the Boy's entry as presumption (We484) and asks, 'Syr, who let you in, spake ye wyth the porter?' This problem was, however, a perennial one, and forms part of Heywood's awareness in making his stage space represent the 'haut-pace at the King's chamber-doore'. Interpreting the play's tone in this respect is inseparable from interpreting the role of Mery Report, in whom it is hard not to see Heywood's self-mocking of an upstart and officious servant of the chamber.

The Merchant's intention to sail to Chios (We385–8) shows that *Wether* was composed for performance around Shrovetide, but offers no help as to year. The voyage is evidently hazardous and Heywood's point in choosing Chios in the Eastern Mediterranean was presumably because of the ever-present possibility of Turkish piracy. Had he wanted to allude to troubles in Spanish waters he could have done so.

References in the play to Parliament offer some clues.[20] Jupiter claims that the gods and goddesses 'hath late assembled' before 'our presens in our hye parlyment' (We22–4) with satisfactory agreement of differences. His statement, 'We have clerely fynyshed our foresayd parlement' (We80) cannot refer to dissolution of Parliament by the King (which happened only 13 August 1523 and 14 April 1536), but could refer to the completion of a session: after six years without summoning Parliament there were six sessions between 4 November 1529 and 7 April 1533. The likeliest seems to be the fourth session (10 April to 14 May 1532), when Henry intervened to put his case for divorce directly to Parliament. Moreover, Jupiter clearly refers to his own newly extended absolute powers (We70–4, 1246–7). Mery Report's banter with the Gentleman about the latter's claim to be 'head' seems to hint at a period after 1531, when acceptance of the title 'supreme head' was in process of being enforced on different estates of England (see notes on We296–316 and 1246).

It is likely that the planetary gods were to be associated with important people in the realm, as in *Speke Parott*: the fall of 'father' Saturn (We6) could refer to

---

18 Cameron, *Wether* p. 45.
19 'Articles devised by the King's Highness . . . Apud Eltham (January 1526) PRO E/36/231 p. 25.
20 Alistair Fox, who thinks the play much inferior to *Foure PP*, argues that the parliament in question is the Reformation Parliament of November–December 1529 (*Politics* pp. 252–3).

Cardinal Wolsey, deprived of chancellorship in October 1529 for opposing the King's projected divorce. On this reading, his 'frosty mansion' would be associated with Wolsey's palace York Place (later Whitehall). Interpretation of Phoebe (We51) with Anne Boleyn would link with the extended bawdy passage concerning the 'new moon' and her revitalising effect on the reign/rain (We782–815 and notes). Similarly oaths by St Anne and humorous banter about sexual prowess and impotence would be highly pertinent in the period before Anne was publicly known to be pregnant (Easter 1533), and in accord with the grosser side of Henrician court taste. The extended play with the Gentlewoman as a sexual object and the joking about taking new marital partners all harp on the same string.

Interpretation of the play's tone depends on a hypothesis about auspices. Clearly the play would be much less complimentary about Jupiter and his new powers if one imagined it performed to a coterie of like-minded Roman Catholics in the London household of a baron of the realm than if it were presented before Henry VIII himself.

A small but possibly significant detail seems to have escaped previous commentators. The Wynde Myller recalls 'an old proverbe' (Heywood's use is, notably, the earliest recorded – see We621 and note): 'One bushell of March dust is worth a kynges raunsome.' It was in March 1533 that the Act in Restraint of Appeals 'ransomed' the King, enabling the divorce to be settled by Cranmer in May.[21] The Act would have been in preparation during the early months of the year. The fifth session of Parliament lasted from 4 February to 7 April 1533. If *Wether* was performed late in February 1533 the London audience would have been aware of the impending legislation and of its importance to the King. In 1533 Shrove Tuesday was on 4 March (thus making the Merchant's arrival time in Chios by mid-Lent – about 20 March), and there was a new moon on 24 February. Shrovetide marked the the end of the 'Christmas' revels season for plays. Two traditional Shrovetide motifs – the flouting of authority and scatological humour – occur in *Wether* (We1042 and note).

In conclusion, one may confidently say that composition of *Wether* was between 1527 and 1533; interpretation of its topical commentary on the affairs of the king point to completion towards the end of this period – later than has previously been thought and only a few months before publication. If these arguments are granted, then Heywood's most ambitious play is also his most politically audacious. For, while the dialogue and argument are redolent with diplomatic adulation of the great god-king, the wit and wordplay sparkle with irreverence and scepticism. There would have been every reason for Heywood to wish it printed as soon as possible.

---

[21] Elton, *England under the Tudors*, pp. 132–3.

REFERENCE AND FURTHER READING

Bernard, J.E., *The Prosody of the Tudor Interlude*, New Haven, 1939

Bevington, D.M., 'Is John Heywood's *Play of the Weather* Really about the Weather', *Renaissance Drama* 7 (1964), 11–9

Blamires, A., 'John Heywood and *The Four PP*', *Trivium* 14 (1979), 47–69

Bolwell, R.W., *The Life and Works of John Heywood*, New York, 1921

Craik, T.W., 'The True Source of John Heywood's *Johan Johan*', *Modern Language Review* 45 (1950), 289–95

—— *The Tudor Interlude*, Leicester, 1958

—— 'Experiment and Variety in John Heywood's Plays', *Renaissance Drama* 7 (1964), 6–11

Fox, Alan B., 'Chaucer's prosody and the non-pentameter line in John Heywood's comic debates', *Language and Style* X (1977), 23–41

Fryde, E.B., D.E. Greenway, S. Porter, and I. Roy, *The Handbook of British Chronology*, 3rd ed., London, 1986

Guy, J., *Tudor England*, Oxford, 1990

Hogrefe, P., *The Sir Thomas More Circle*, Urbana, 1959

Ives, E.W., *Anne Boleyn*, Oxford, 1986

Johnson, R.C., *John Heywood*, New York, 1970

Kolin, Philip C., 'Recent Work on John Heywood', *English Literary Renaissance* 13 (1983), 113–23

Mason, H.A., *Humanism and Poetry in the Early Tudor Period*, London, 1959

Miller, E.S., 'Guilt and Penalty in Heywood's Pardoner's Lie', *Modern Language Quarterly* 10 (1949), 58–60

Norland, H.B., 'Formalizing French Farce: Johan Johan and its French Connection', *Comparative Drama* 17 (1983), 1–18

Phy, W., 'The Chronology of John Heywood's Plays', *Englische Studien* 74 (1940), 27–41

Sanders, Norman, et alii, *The Revels History of Drama in English: Volume II, 1500–1576*, London, 1980

Scarisbrick, J.J., *Henry VIII*, London, 1968

Schoeck, R.J., 'A Common Tudor Expletive and Legal Parody in Heywood's *Play of Love*', *Notes and Queries* 201 (1956), 375–6

Southern, R., *The Staging of Plays before Shakespeare*, London, 1973

Stevens, John, *Music and Poetry in the Early Tudor Court*, Cambridge, 1961

Walker, Greg, *Plays of Persuasion: Drama and Politics at the Court of Henry VIII*, Cambridge, 1991

Westfall, Suzanne R., *Patrons and Performance: Early Tudor Household Revels*, Oxford, 1990

Wickham, Glynne, *Early English Stages 1300–1660*, vol. III, London, 1981

Wilson, F.P., *The English Drama 1485–1585*, Oxford, 1969

EDITORIAL PROCEDURE

The editors' aim has been to reproduce the spelling of the original texts free from the typographical and manuscript conventions of early Tudor versions. Thus *u* and *v*, *i* and *j* are regularised; scribal þ is rendered *th* and 3 by the more usual *gh*. Capitals are used sparingly according to modern practice. Although spelling in printed books and manuscripts had distinct styles, some irregularity is typical of the period; no attempt has been made to standardize word forms, except for the speakers' names where the originals give abbreviated forms. In general abbreviations and contractions are expanded to the forms most commonly found in each text. In the case of the plural ending (ꝭ), expansion to the forms *-ys* or *-es* is adopted. Roman numerals are given in words.

The word divisions of early Tudor printing were not standard. The editors have followed the copy-texts in most cases, but have joined or separated words where the original might impede a modern reader. A hyphen is used only very rarely.

Wherever there is possible justification, original readings are retained. Editorial conjectures and additional stage directions are placed in square brackets; other emendations are recorded in the Notes, which record variants from the copy text and substantive variants from later editions in Heywood's lifetime. Variant spellings which may affect rhyme or syllable count are also included. Minor printing errors such as turned type are not normally noted.

The punctuation is substantially editorial; it has been kept as light as possible without encouraging misunderstanding of the syntax. The force and frequency of marks in the originals has been taken into account, as have printers' paragraph signs in breaking up long speeches or indicating changes of metre or rhyme pattern. The unique edition of *The Pardoner and the Frere* uses a slash (/) with great regularity to mark a mid-line break; this may have helped the actors synchronize simultaneous delivery. We have registered the break by a space in the line, to avoid doing violence to the syntax while preserving the possibility that something about pace and phrasing in performance may thereby be learned.

Where speech headings have been expanded from contracted forms or have been supplied by the editors, the commonest spelling used in the copy text has been adopted. Each text has also been provided with a standardized title page, giving the players' names in these forms. The words of the original title pages are included at the head of each text.

Problems specific to individual plays are discussed at the beginning of each set of Notes.

WYTTY AND WITLESS

The Names of the Players

John
James
Jerome

John	A mervelus mater, marcyfull lorde,	f.110
	Yf reason whyth this conclewtyon acorde:	
	Better to be a foole then a wyse man.	
James	Better or wurs, I seay as I began:	
	Better ys for man that man be wyttles	5
	Then wytty.	
John	Ye schow some wytty wyttines.	
James	Experyens schall wyttnes my tale trewe,	
	And for temperall welthe let us fyrst vuewe:	
	And that experyens may schowe the trewer,	
	Accepte we reson to be owr vuewer.	10
	In whyche reson by experyens we knowe	
	That folke most wytty to whom ther dothe growe	
	By frenddes dedde before, nowght left them behynde,	
	Nor by lyvyng frendds no lyvynge asynyde,	
	Excepte they wyll storve, ther fyndyng must they fynde,	15
	By muche payne of body or more payne of myndde.	
	And as for the wyttles, as who saythe the sott,	
	The naturall foole calde or thydeote –	
	From all kyndes of labore that dothe payne constrayne,	
	As farre as suffycyency nedythe obtayne,	20
	In sewrty of lyvyng the sot dothe remayne.	
John	In sewrty of lyvyng, but not wythe owt payne,	
	For admyte all sotts in case, as be mayny,	
	That leve wythe owt labor, yet where ys any	
	But for that one plesewr he hathe more payne	25
	Then the wyty wurker in all dothe sustayne?	
	What wretche so ferythe payne havyng eny wytt	
	Lyke the wyttles wretche? None, yf ye marke hyt.	
	Who cumth by the sott, who cumth he by,	
	That vexyth hym not somewey usewally?	30
	Some beate hym, some bob hym,	
	Some joll hym, some job hym,	
	Some tugg hym by the heres,	
	Some lugg hym by the eares,	
	Some spet at hym, some spurne hym,	35
	Some tosse hym, some turne hym,	
	Some snape hym, some snatche hym,	
	Some crampe hym, some cratche hym,	
	Some cuff, some clowt hym,	
	Some lashe hym, some lowte hym,	f.110ᵛ
	Some whysk hym, some whype hym,	41

56

Wythe scharpe naylys some nype hym.
Not evyn mayster Somer the Kyngs gracys foole
But tastythe some tyme some nyps of new schoole.
And by syd thys kynde of frettyng and fewmyng   45
Another kynd of turment in consewmyng
The wytty to the wyttles oft invent.
After inventyon of yerfull entent
The foole by flatery to turment ys browght,
So farre over joyd and his brayne so wyde wrowght,   50
That by joy of a jewell skant wurthe a myght
The sott ofte slepythe no wynke in a whole nyght.
And for ensampyll wythe a Walsyngam rynge
Thys dystemperans to the sot ye may bryng,
And make hym joy theryn as hyt ware a thyng   55
Of pryce to peyse the rawnsome of a kynge.
In joying wherof, yf ony man got way
To get yt from hym as evry chylde may
Then man and chylde sethe the sot in suche case
That nowght but paynfull sorow takythe ony place.   60
By thys small prosses a small wytt may ges
That wyde were the wytty to wyshe them wyttles.

James   Theffecte of this yowr matter as ye spake yt
           Standyth muche yn two poynts as I take yt:
           Of whyche tweyne the tone ys that the sot hathe   65
           By jollynge and jobbynge and other lyke skathe
           Extreme payne wythe extremyte of yere;
           Thother ys after frettyng fewryus fyer
           That the foole wythe eche frewtles tryflyng toy
           Ys so dystempryd wythe dystemperat joy   70
           That as muche payne brynght his plesaunt pashyon
           As dothe the pynchynge of hys most paynfull fashyon.
           Thes two poynts consyderyd, the sot as ye saye
           Hathe some payne somtyme, but most tymes I say nay. f.111

John   Then from no payne to some payne the wyttles are browght.
James   Ye, but wytty and wyttles wytyly wrowght   76
           By some payne to suche payne that wytty fele most,
           Then wytty and wyttles eche parte his parte bost.
           Take of wytty the degrees and nombyr all
           And of that nombyr I thyngke the nombyr small   80
           But that eche one of them ys of nede asynde
           To labor sore yn body or ells yn mynde.
           And few to all that fortewne so dothe favor
           But yn body and mynde bothe they do labor,

And of [bothe] thes labors the most paynefullest
Ys the labor of mynde, I have harde gest.   86
And lest bothe paynes or most of twayne be to towgh
For yow to matche wythe, and the lest payne inowgh,
To the fyrst most payne of the wyttles nody
Joyne we the wyttyse least payne, payne of body.   90
Who sethe what payne labor bodyly bryngth
Schall easely se therby how the body wryngth.
Husbond mens plowyng, or earyng and sowyng,
Hedgyng and dychyng, wythe repyng and mowyng,
In cartyng such lyftyng, such burdenns bareyng   95
That payne of the body bryngthe [thy eyse] to stareyng.
And muche of thys done yn tyme of suche hete
That yn colde cave covryd the carcas must swete.
Some other use crafts in whyche wurcke ys so small
That yn somer plesaunttly they lyve all   100
Who in wynter when husbondmen warme wythe warke
In that they may not sturr, for colde ar evyn starke.
Some yn wynter fryse, some yn somer fry,
And the wyttles dothe nother, for comenly
Other whyche wurshypfull or honorabull   105
He temprately standth in howse at the tabyll;
And of all his labors, reckyn the hole rabyll,
Bygger burden barthe he none then his babyll.
So that from thes paynes or the lyke recytyd
The wyttles hathe warrant to be aquyghtyd;   110
And sewr the sotts pleasewre in this last aquyghtall   f.111ᵛ
Cownterwaylth his payne in yowr fyrst recyghtall.
Feor unto the sotts nyppyng and beatyng
Joyne the wytty laborers nypps and freatyng;
And whether ye cownt by yere, monthe or weke   115
Ye schall fynde thease of the wytty to seeke
As far as of the wyttles; and of bothe sorts
This ys the dyfferens that to me ymports:
Sotts are coylde of other, the wytty coylthe hym self.
What choyse thus aleagyd?

John   Small, ah horson elfe!   120
Some what he towchythe me now yn very deed;
How beyt to thys am not I yet full agreed.
The wytty who beate them selves by bysynes
May ofte yn beatyngs favowr them selves I ges.
Such oportewnyte by wytte ys ofte espyde   125
That labor by wytt ys ofte qualyfyd,
In takying tyme or place as best may stand
Most easelye to dyspatche things cumyng in hand.

Wytt hathe provytyon alwey for releefe
To provyde some remedy agaynst myscheef.   130
Wytty take bysynes as wytty wyll make yt
And as wytty beate wyttles, wyttles must take yt.

James   Tak yt howe ye lyst, ye can make yt no les
         But wytty have suche payne as my wordes wyttnes.
         For thowgh wytt for tyme sometyme may payne prevent,   135
         Yet yn most tymes theyre foreseyde payne ys present;   .
         Whych payne in the wytty wyttyly weyde
         May match payne of the wyttles by ye fyrst leyde.
         And to the second poynte, for dystemporate joyes,
         By havynge or hopynge of fancyes or toyes   140
         In wyttl[e]s or wytty, bothe tak I as one:
         For thowgh the thyngs that wytty have, or hope on,
         Are yn some kynde of acownt thyngs muche gretter
         Then thyngs of the sotts joyings, yet nowhyt better,
         Nor les payne bryngth that passhyon, but endyferent   145
         To bothe – excepte wytty have the woors turment.
         Thyn[k] yow a right good wytty havynge clerely
         A thowsand pownd sodaynly gyvyn hym yerely,   f.112
         Who before that owre myght dyspend no peny,
         Nor tyll that owre never lokyd for eny,   150
         Myght not joy as muche that soden recevyng
         As joythe the sott reseyte of hys Walsyngam rynge,
         And therby be kepte from quyet sleepe a weke?
         As well as the rynge makethe the sotts sleepe to seeke
         And in a soden leesyng that gyfte agayne,   155
         Myght not the wytty be presyd wythe payne
         As depe as the wyttles his ringe stolne or lost?
         And thowgh thys ensampyll chanse seelde when at most,
         Yet sometyme yt happyth, and dayly we see,
         That folke farr from wyttles passhynyd be   160
         By joyfull hope of thyngs to them lyk to hape,
         Or havyng of things plesaunt late lyght in the lap,
         As muche to theyre unrest for dystemprancy
         As ye showde the wyttles restles formerly,
         And oft tyme for cawse consydryd and weyde   165
         As lyght as yowr Walsyngam rynge afore leyde.
         Wytt in wytty hathe seelyd suche perfecshyon
         To bryng dysposyshyn full in abjeckshyon;
         And the dyfferens of dysposyshyon ys such
         Some wytts hope to lyttyll, some wytts hope to muche.   170
         By whyche over muche I sey, and sey must ye,
         That wytty and wyttles one in thys case be.

                        59

And thus in bothe casys reasonyng cawse showthe
Cawse to conclewde that to the wytty growth
As muche payne as to the wyttles, wherby   175
As good be wyttles as wytty say I.

John   That conclewcyon ys conclewdyd wysely.
          Yowr pryme proposycyon dyd put presysely:
          Better to be wyttles then wytty, and now
          As good to be wyttles as wytty sey yow.   180
          But that wytt, whych putth case in degre comparatyve
          And conclewdythe case in degre posytyve,
          Sall not in that case clayme degre sewperlatyve.
James   Ye pas in this tawnt yowr prerogatyve.
          But that wytt whyche bostythe the full of his wynnyng   185
          As thowgh he knewe thende of thing at begynnyng,
          That wytt schall schow wyttles ympedyment
          To be taken wytty wythe wytts excelent.
          I conclewde here not for thende but for the myds
          Whyche, yf ye wyll here to end as reason byds,   f.112ᵛ
          Ye schall perceyve and also condysend   191
          To grawnt me thanks then yn that I entende
          Yowr fall by feare handelynge to be the more fayre,
          To set ye downe feately stayer after stayer,
          And so by a fayer fygewre of ynduckshyn   195
          To bryng yowr parte softe and fayer to dystrucksshyn.
          For where ye grawnt fully for owght yowr wordes make
          That as muche payne wytty as wyttles do take,
          So from thys myds to the ende I schall pro[v]e
          That most payne of twayne to the wyttles dothe move.   200
          For as I lode egally paynes of body
          To wytty and wyttles, lyke wyse wyll I
          Over lode the wytty wythe payne of mynde
          In mater as playne as can be asynde,
          Whyche payne of mynde in mete mesewre to wey   205
          Ys more paynfull then payne of body I seay.

John   Ye sey so, and seyd so, but so seyde not I,
          Nor sey yt not yet, but that seynge deny;
          And tyll saynge prove yowr saynge more playnely
          I wyll asey to sey the contrary.   210
          I thynke paynes of body cowntyd in eche kynde
          May compare wythe all kyndes of paynes of mynde.
James   Yf ye assewrydly thynke as ye sey now,
          I thynke ye thynke as few men thynke but yow,

60

	Howbeyt that beyng but an ynsydent	215
	To pryncypall purpose presently ment.	
	Yet that excepshyn took yow wyttyly,	
	For had ye grawntyd that as ye schall schortly	
	Then forthwythe scholde owr pryncypall proses	
	Have concludyd in the parte that I profes:	220
	For a meane wherunto as mesewre may	
	Meet unmesewrabull thynges, as who say	
	Joyne in lyke proporshyn as may be ment	
	The meane laborer to the meane studyent;	
	And ye schall anon fynde the stewdyents payne	225
	More paynfull then the laborers labor playne.	

John   The stewdyents payne ys ofte plesauntly myxt
            In felynge what frewte by his study ys fyxt.

James   The laborers labor quyghthe that at a whyppe
            In felynge the frewte hys wurkmanshyp: f.113

As muche delyght carters oft in carts neate trymd   231
As do studyents yn bokes wythe golde neate lymd;
And as muche envy who may dreve hys carte best
As amonge stewdyents who may seme lernd hyest,
Wherby inwarde delyght to tolle forthe eche parte   235
Semthe me yndyfrent to arte or to cart.
And furder, meane labor in most common wyse
Ys most parte hansome and holsome excersyse
That purgythe hewmors, to mans lyfe and quycknes,
Whyche study bredythe to mans dethe or sycknes.   240
Also most kyndes of labor most comenly
Strene most grose owtewarde partes of the body
Where study sparyng scholders, fyngers and tose
To the hedde and hart dyrectly study gose.
Pervert ys yowr jugment yf ye judge not playne   245
That les ys the parell and les ys the payne,
The knockynge of knockylls, whyche fyngers dothe strayne,
Then dyggynge yn the hart, or drying of the brayne.

John   For comun meane kyndes in bothe parts now leyde
            I se not but reason saythe as ye have seyde.   250

James   The labor of body and mynde thus compare
            In what degrese ye can devyse to declare
Betwene bothe, beynge not knyt yn suche degre
But that thone from thother seperate may be;
And that bothe labors yn joynynge ye arecte   255
As lyke yn degre as wytt may conjecte,

| | And bothe ons serchyd, serche schall make warantyse | |
| | Yn labor of mynde the wurst payne dothe aryse. | |

John	Methynkthe I cowlde make yt otherwyse apere	
	Save I lacke tyme to dylate matter here;	260
	For tyme of reasonyng wolde be longe therin	
	And tyme of reasonynge must be short here in:	
	Whyche weyde wythe that, this standthe but insydently	
	To owr present porpose pryncypally.	
	I graunt to agre as ye have defynde	265
	Of labor of body and labor of mynde	
	That labor or payne of mynde ys the greter –	
	And thys nowe grawntyd, what be ye the better?	

James	So muche the bettyr and yow so muche the wurs	
	That ye may now put yowr toong in yowr purs;	270
	For ony woorde in defens yowr toonge schall tell,	
	After thes my next woordes gyve eare and marke well.	f.113ᵛ
	This labor of myndd, whyche we now agre	
	Above labor of body, we must decre	
	To joyne sole to the wytty, for possybly	275
	Cannot the wyttles take parte of that payne.	
John	Why?	

James	How can he have payne by imagynacyon	
	That lackythe all kynds of consyderatyon,	
	And yn al sencys ys so ynsofycyent	
	That nowght can he thynke in owght that may be ment	280
	By ony meane to devyce ony selfe thinge,	
	Nor devyse in thyng past, present or cumynge?	
	No more hathe he in mynde, other payne or care,	
	Then hathe other Cocke my hors or Gyll my mare.	
	Thys cawse wythe wyttles payne of mynde dyspensys,	285
	But the wytty havynge all vytall sensys	
	Hathe therby an inwarde clocke whyche marke who wyll	
	May oftymes go false, but yt never standythe styll:	
	The plummets of that clocke come never to grownd.	
	Imagynacyon ys watche, and gothe so rownde,	290
	To whyche consyderacyon gyvythe so quycke eare	
	That in the wytty mynde the restles rest ys there.	
	A small wytte may ges – no wone wytte can deme –	
	How many or how muche are theyre paynes extreme,	
	Nor how many contrary kyndes in some one brest.	295
	Yf ye perceyve thys tale, ye se yt wytnest	
	Thre thyngs, of whyche the fyrst ys that the wyttles	

	Off labor or payne of mynde have reles,	
	The seconde ys that the wytty have in ure	
	All paynes of mynde, and that wytty dothe that proocure;	300
	Thyrdly I glanset a[t] payne of mynde, alewdyng	
	That payne to be most payne as in for conclewdyng –	
	Perceyve ye this?	
John	Ye, and grawnt yt trew, to.	
James	Then must ye grawnt wytty to have most payne.	
John	So I do.	
James	Yf wytty have most payne of tweyne, ye must say	305
	Better to be wyttles then wytty.	
John	Nay!	
James	I say yes!	
John	I say nay, and wyll so envey	f.114
	That I wyll holde ye to wagge another wey.	
	As I grawnt wytty of twayne most payne endewre	
	So wyll I prove wytty to have most plesewre,	310
	Whych plesewre schall bothe drowne the wyttys payne	
	And the plesewer yn whyche the wyttles remayne.	

James	Thys promyse wyll hardly bryng good payment,	
	For yt ys a strange kynde of argewment	
	To prove hym in most plesewre who hathe most payne,	315
	Or hym yn least payne who least plesewre dothe sustayne.	

John	Let us reason all plesewrs on bothe sydes	
	And then let that syde have best that best provydes.	

James	All plesewrs on bothe sydes? That were a thynge	
	To make us make ende to morow mornyng.	320
John	A, now the best parte of my parte cumth on	
	Ye make marvelus hast, ye wolde fayne be gone!	

James	Right now your self cowld wey in right wytty sort	
	That resonyng here now of reason must be schort.	

John	Yt schalbe schort inowgh if ye take awey	325
	All that parte that for my part effeckte dothe ley!	

James	I wyll nother take awey all nor take all,	
	But for a meane betwene bothe, my self streyght schall	
	Alege not plesewrs all I sey, but such one	
	As over weythe other plesewrs evry chone.	330
	Whyche plesewre where yt in fyne dothe not remayne,	
	All plesewrs in all partts ar plesewrs but vayne;	

	Of whyche one plesewre the wyttles ar sewre evyr,	
	And of that plesewre wytty are sewre nevyr.	
John	What plesewre ys that?	
James	Plesewre of salvashyon.	335

John   What plesewre ys that?

James   Plesewre of salvashyon.   335

I thynke yowr selfe wyll affyrme affyrmashyon
That from owrr forfathers syn orygynall
Babtym sealythe us all aquyttans generall,
And faythe of ynfants whyle they infants abyde
In faythe of parents for the churche ys supplyde.   340
Wherby tyll wytt take roote of dysernynge,
And betwene good and yll geve perfyght warnynge,
Where ever innosents innosensy dyspewte,
For thowghts, woorddes or dedes, God dothe none yll ympewte.
Wher God gyvythe no dys[c]ernyng God takethe none acownte; f.114ᵛ
In whyche case of acownt the sot dothe amownt,   346
For no more dysernythe the sott at yeres thre score
Then thynosent borne wythe in yeres thre before.
This schort sayng yf ye yn mynde revolve
Then schall thys longe debate forthwythe dysolve.   350

John   Syr, I grawnt sottes schall be savyd as ye tell,
And safe schall wytty be to yf they do well.

James   Yff they do well? That yf altryth muche, lo,
Theffeckte of my sentens to wyttles!

John   How so?

James   That yf leyde for the wytty, purporthe a dowte,   355
But all dowtes in the wyttles are scrapte clene owte:
Sans dowte the wyttles ys sewer of salvashyon.
Wherby, to conclewde thys comynycashyon,
Make wytty sewer of all plesewrs can be leyde,
Dowtyng lacke of none but thys one plesewre last seyde,   360
And of all plesewrs wyttles to have none
Savynge he standthe in sewrte of this one,
Ys not the sewrte of thys one muche bettyr
Then of the rest, thowgh the nomber be grettyr?

John   Yes.

James   Lyke as a goose can say nothynge but 'hys',   365
So hathe he now nothynge, nothynge to say but 'yes'.
And in affyrmyng my saynge he saythe thys
In whyche he grawntthe his partt not partly amys
But all amys, as who saythe in all placys
The sum wherof in bothe partes standthe in thre casys.   370
Off whyche thre thargewment of the fyrst was thus:
In laboryus payne of body to dyscus
Who soferythe more the wytty or the sott,

Yn whyche, by bothe assents, we knyt thys knott:
That as muche payne of body in effeckte hathe the one 375
As thother, conclewdyng thus farre there uppon
As good to be wyttles as wytty; and then
We argewde labor or payne of mynde in men,
Wherin I, dryvyng hym to grawnt payne of mynde
More then payne or labor bodyly defynde. 380
In the seconde case I payne of mynde provyng
To wytty and not to wyttles to be movynge
Drave hym to grawnt furder that by that payne
Better wythe owte wytt then wythe wytt to remayne.
Now in thys thyrde case where ye made a bragge 385
By plesewrs in the wytty to holde me wagge f.115
And plesewrs of the wyttles to overwhelme,
I stamynge in wythe hym stacke so to the helme
That hys parte fynally to shypwracke ys browght.
The sewrte of all plesewrs in this worlde wrowght 390
Matche not the sewrte of plesewre eternall,
And thestate of sotts have none acownt so carrnall
That God ympewtthe any yll to them I say.
And the wyttyse acownt awgmenthe evry day;
And thawdytors wytt who schall take thacownt so clere 395
He forgethe not wone worde in a thowsand yere.
What nede mo woordes? I thynke the least wytt here
Sethe thes thre casys on my syde so apere,
That in the two fyrst casys temporally,
And in this thyrd and last case spyrytewally 400
Ys sene fully, I may conclewde fynally,
Better to be wyttles then to be wytty.

John   So sey I now to, by owr blyssyd lady!
I gyve uppe my part and take yowr part playnly.
Off wytty and wyttles I wysche now rather 405
That my chylde may have a foole to hys father.
The pythe of yowr conclewsyons be all so pewre
That better be a foole then a wyse man, sewre.

[Jerome, having heard all, joins the debate.]

Jerome   Not so! All thowgh yowr fancy do so surmyse:
Not better for a man to be wytles then wyse, 410
Nor so good to be wyttles as wytty nother.
Thus ys yowr wytt dysseyvyd in other.

John   Why, what dyffrens betwene wyse and wytty?
Jerome   As muche sometyme as betwene wysdom and folly.

John	Man can in nowyse be wyse wythe owte wytt.	415
Jerome	No, and man may have gret wytt and wysdom nowhyt.	
	Wytt ys the wurker of all perseyvyng	
	And indyferent to good or yll wurkyng.	
	And as muche wytt may be in thynges of most yll	
	As in the best thyngys wytt can aspyre untyll –	420
	In vertu or vyse I meane; and wytt hathe receyght	
	Off none yll where wytt uppon wysdom dothe weyght.	
	Wysdome governth wytt alwey vertu to use.	f.115ᵛ
	And all kynds of vyce alway to refewse.	
	Thus ys wysdom in good parte takyn alweyse,	425
	And gydythe wytt in all thynges beynge, thyngs of preyse.	
	Thus thowgh ye must (as ye nede not) graunt his grownd,	
	Whyche ys better wyttles then wytty to be fownd,	
	Yet as muche as wysdom above wytt schowth,	
	So muche grawntyd ye hym more then of nede growthe.	430

| James | Thys ys some yownge schooleman, a freshe comonar! | |
| | Harde ye the pryncypyll that plantyd thys jar? | |

Jerome	I harde all.	
James	And dothe not all on my syde fall?	
Jerome	No, yf ye had resonyd as I schall.	
James	Yf ye as ye say have harde all here sayde,	435
	And that ye that saying have so wydely wayd	
	To way my parte wurst herein in conclewsyon,	
	Then ar ye wyttles that we towe talkt on.	
	But babyll yowr wyll. Thys wyll I byde uppon:	
	Better be sott Somer then sage Salamon.	440

| Jerome | Geve ye sentens or ye here what I cane say? | |
| | Loo, how wyll carythe hym and hys wytt away! | |

[Exit James.]

John	Syr, yf ye harde all, in my part how say ye?	
	What dyd I graunt hym to farre? Schow, I pray ye.	
Jerome	All that ys grauntyd, welnye.	
John	Nay, I trow.	445
Jerome	Ye schall when we have done not trow but know;	
	For entre wherto, I pray ye, answere me	
	A questyon or twayne, or mo yf nede be.	
	And fyrst unto thys, answere as ye can:	
	Whether wolde ye be a resonable man	450
	Or an unresonabyll beast?	
John	By and sell!	
	I wolde be the symplest man betwene hevyn and hell,	

	Rather then the best beast that ever was bred.	
Jerome	Then yf ye of one of the twayne must be sped,	
	Ye woolde be a maltman, – ye, a myller,	455
	Rather then a mylhorse?	
John	Be ye my well wyller?	f.116
Jerome	Ye!	
John	Speke no more of thys then. What, man, fye!	

	I wold not be a beast for all this worlde, I,	
	Were yt for nowght ells but for this lyfe present.	
Jerome	The tyme of this lyfe in dede I meane and ment.	460
	But tell me why, by yowr faythe, evyn playnely,	
	Ye wyl not change estate wythe the myll horse.	
John	Why,	
	There be whyse and wherforrse I thyngke a thowsand	
	In cownt of two kynds of things cumyng in hande:	
	Sensybyll plesewre, and sensybyll payne.	465
	And fyrst for payne sustaynyd in thes twayne,	
	Begyn wythe the myll hors whom ye put for prefe,	
	Or ony lyke beast sustaynynge the lyke grefe,	
	And or I wolde take the payne the poore beasts take,	
	I wolde eche day be twygde and tyde to a stake:	470
	Carying fro the myll, carying to the myll,	
	Drawyng in the myll, poore jade he jetthe styll.	
	Ambyll he, trot he, go he a foote pase,	
	Walope he, galop he, racke he in trase,	
	Yf hys pase please not, be yt softe or faster,	475
	The spures or whypp schalbe hys pay master.	
	Were not a man, trow ye, in plesaunt case	
	Wythe a beast in thys case to change case or plase?	
	No man, excepte some few so ynfortewnate	
	That they be owt of thacownt of mans estate,	480
	That wolde agre to leve to change paynes I trow,	
	Wythe beasts payne beynge such as all men know.	
	Now to speke of plesewre in thes twayne asynde,	
	The beaste to compare ys to far behynde,	
	Plesewr dyscussybyll in thes thus dothe fall:	485
	The beast in effecte hathe none, the man hathe all.	
	The resonabyll manns imagynashyon,	
	Joynde wythe resonabyll consyderatyon,	
	Bryngthe man muche plesewre in consyderyng	
	The plesant proporte of eche plesaunt thynge	490
	Possesyd to mans behofe at commaundynge.	
	Beasts have thyngs of nede but no furder pleasynge,	
	Syns man hathe releefe for all nesessyte	
	As well as beast, and above beaste commodyte	

	Of plesewrs plantyd for mans recreatyon,	495
	In the hyest kynd to mans contentatyon –	
	Whereby plesewre in effecte betwene thes twayne	f.116ᵛ
	Showthe thus – man hathe all, beast hathe none; and more payne	
	Hathe beast then resonabyll man by thes bothe.	
	Change fro man to beast who wyll, I wolde be lothe.	500

Jerome Ye have yn my myndde thys right well defynde,
And for cawse kepe yt well a while yn your mynde.
Set we asyde man and beasts symylytewde,
And full dysposytyon in bothe se we vewde.
What thyng dysposythe most the varyete   505
Betwene man and beast?
John   Reson in man, perde.

Jerome That man who of reason ys as destytute
As a beast ys, what dyffrens schall we dyspewte?
John   Small in this case, excepte yt be this one:
The sott hathe a resonabyll sowle, beasts have none.   510

Jerome What helpyth the wytt of the sowle in the sott,
Syns the body ys suche yt usythe yt not?
Where ympotensy planthe suche ympedyments
That use of sensys are voyde to all yntents
For use of reason – so that for use of wytt   515
They ar as beasts wyttles, usyng wytt nowhyt –
In man thus wytles and thunresonabyll beaste
I se small dyffrens – for thys lyfe at leaste.

John   I grawnt the wyttles and the beast thus as one.
Jerome Then schall thes beasts, wyttles man and mylhors, draw on   520
Bothe yn one yoke: for thynke yow the nomber
Standthe as Somer dothe all day yn slomber?
Nay, Somer ys a sot, foole for a kynge,
But sots in many other mens howsyng
Beare water, beare woodde, and do yn drugery   525
In kychyn, cole howse, and in the norsery.
And dayly for fawtes whyche they cannot refrayne,
Evyn lyke the myll hors, they be whyppyd amayne.
Other fooles that labor not have other conseyts:
Uppon thydyll foole the flocke ever more weytes.   530
They tos hym, they turne hym, he is jobd and jolde,
Whythe frettyng and fewmyng as ye a fore tolde:
Excepte mayster Somer, of sotts not the best,
But the myllhors may compare wythe hym for rest.
The[re]for plesewr conceyvyng or receyvyng,   535

The wyttles and mylhors are bothe as one thyng.
Yowr last tale and thys tale to gether conferd,   f.117
By matter of bothe let yowr answere be harde
Whether ye wolde be a man r[e]sonabyll
Or unresonabyll: and excepte ye fabyll,   540
Thys answere schall schow playne and undowtydly
Whether ye wolde be wyttles or wytty.

John   In good faythe I take thys conclewcyon so full
That I may geve over, and evyn so I wull,
For thys lyfe.

Jerome   Well then for the lyfe to come,   545
Few woords where reason ys may knyt uppe the sum.
Concernyng plesewre after thys lyfe present,
By whyche he and yow dyssolvyd argewment,
Bothe parts by bothe partyse were so endyd
That yowr part full fayntly ye defendyd.   550
Thowgh the mere meryte of owr redemtyon
Stande in Cristys passyon, yet in exemsyon
Therof schall we stand by Gods justyce, excepte,
Havynge tyme and wytt, hys commandments be kept.
And who in whyche dothe most dylygently   555
Plant ymps of good woorcks gyvyn by God chefely,
Most hyly of God schall he have rewarde.

John   How prove ye that?

Jerome   By scrypture. Have in regarde
Cryst in the gospell of John dothe thys declare:
In the howse of my father, sayth Crist, ther are   560
Dyvers and many mantyons. That ys to say,
As thexposytyon of Saynt Awstyne dothe way,
There are in hevyn dyvers degrees of glory
To be receyvyd of men acordyngly.
Eche man as he usythe Gods gyfts of grace   565
So schall he have in hevyn hys degre or place.
But marke thys chefe grownd, the sum of scrypture saythe
We must walke wythe thes gyfts in the pathe of faythe,
In whyche walke who wurkthe most in Gods commandment
He schall have most. And Seynt Powle schowthe lyke entent: 570
As one starre dyfferthe from an other in schynynge
So the resurrectyon of the ded, whyche lyke thynge
Aperthe in other placys of scrypture.

John   I grawnt; and what than?

Jerome   That what cumth streyght in ure: f.117ᵛ
Syns he that usythe Gods gyfts best schall have best,   575
And he next who dothe next, and so forthe the rest;

And that the wytty do dayly wurke or may,
And the wyttles nowght wurkythe by no way
So that hys rewarde may compare in degre.
Yf wytty have thys a vantage, thynkythe me   580
The wyse wyttyse place wysche I desyrusly
Rather then place of the wyttles.

John   So do I,
Yff wyshe wolde wyn yt; but where the sot ys sewre
The wytty standthe in hasardous adventewre
To lees all, and so in fyne, fayre and well   585
In sted of way to hevyn to take the waye to hell.
In wurks commandyd who in faythe walkthe not
By Gods justyce he hathe damnatyon in lott;
And what other folks fele I can not tell
But suche frayle falls fele I in my selfe to dwell   590
And by them to lees hevyn I am so adrad.
The sotts sewrte of least joy there wolde God I hadde!
An olde proverb makythe wythe thys whyche I take good:
Better one byrde in hand then ten in the wood.

Jerome   What yf of the ten byrds in the woode eche one   595
Were as good as that one in yowr hand alone,
And that ye myght cache them all ten yf ye wolde?
Wolde ye not leve one byrde for the ten now tolde?
John   Yes.
Jerome   Wolde ye not, havynge helpe, take resonabyll payne
For thencres of ten byrds for one in gayne?   600
John   Yes.
Jerome   Then in Gods name, feare not! Let fle thys one!
Ye schall, I trust, catche thes ten byrds evry chone.
Yowr fleshly frayle falls are suche that ye drede
As muche as hope in havynge hevynly mede;
By whyche dred sewrte of joyes there the most small,   605
Wysche ye rather, then byd venture to have joyes all
And the soner by this ye chose thys I deme,
The least joy there ys more then man can esteme.
But now to remove thys blocke, yowr grett drede,   f.118
We have a lever that removethe drede wythe spede.   610
God sofereth but not wylthe ony man to syne,
Nor God wylthe no synners dethe but he be yn
Suche endles males that hys fynall estate
In lacke of penytens make hym selfe reprobate.
In tyme of this lyfe at eche penytent call   615
Owrr marcyfull maker remytthe synns all
From the perpetewall peyne infernall,

70

What ever they be from least to most carnall.
By whyche goodnes of God we are set in hopes chayer,
Not to brede presumpsyon but to banyshe dyspayre.   620
The grace of God alwey to grace alewrthe man,
And when man wyll call for grace, of grace asewrthe man,
To assyst man Gods commandments to fulfyll
At all tymes, yf man cast owte yll wyllynge wyll.
Nowe syns the Crystyane that wurkythe most in faythe   625
Schall have most in rewarde, as the scrypture saythe,
And that Gods grace by grace cald for, wyll asyst
Mans wyll to wurke well alwey when men lyst,
And at instant of dew ordryd penytens
Man hathe Gods mercy of all former offens   630
Whyche schowthe for mercy man ys not more gredy
To ax then God to grawnt mercy ys redy –
Thys sene, what schow yow to mayntayne the feare
Whyche ye towarde desperatyon were in whyle eare?

John   What schow I? Nay the schow of that feare ys extyngkt   635
Evyn by thys praty tale thus pythyly lynkt.
Syns God to the most faythfull wurker gyvythe most,
And to make man wurke muche God hasthe as in post,
And where man hathe not wrowght, at contrytyon
God grawnthe man of damnatyon remytyon –   640
  Makynge man sewre of frewte of Crystys passyon,
Excepte mans wylfull wyll mar all good fascyon –
By this I drede God as standthe wythe love and hope;
But no desperate drede dothe my hart now grope.
Jerome   Ten byrds in the wood or one in hande alone,   645
      Whych chose ye now?
John   I wyll not change ten for one   f.118ᵛ
Syns the byrder wyl helpe me to tak them all,
As sewre to myne use as the one byrde cowld fall.

Jerome   Well for conclewsyon, syns ye sowndly se
That wytty have plesewre here in more degre   650
Then wytles, and also wytty wyse se ye
In hevyn by scrypture in hyer joyes be
Then the wyttles, yow seyng thys clerely,
Whether wold ye now be wyttles or wytty?

John   Wytty! And the more wytty am I for yow,   655
Of whych hartyly I thanke yow: and now
Where my mate, my lords, sayde, that ys gone,
Better be sot Somer then sage Salomon,

71

In for sakynge that I woolde now rather be
Sage Saloman then sot Somer, I assewre ye.   660

Jerome   As ye schow wyt in change of former mynd,
           Beyng now from wytles to wytty enclynde,
           So aply yowr wytt in what wytt schall devyse,
           As in good use of wytt by grace ye may ryse
           To be bothe wytty and wyttyly wyse   665
           In governans of Gods gyfts in suche syse
           As wysdom alwey gydyth, wherby thys schall fall:
           Gods gyfts to Gods glory bothe ye may use and schall.

           Thes woords of cowncell in whyche I now wadyd
           To hym whom I tolde them I onely asyne: 670
           I am by all cyrcumstance full perswadyd
           This sort beyng sortyd in sort thus fyne,
           Nede none exortatyon, or at least not myne.
           Thys sort have not onely by natewre hys wytt
           But also by grace lyk wysdom joynde to yt.   675

                                   Thes thre stave next folowyng in the
                                   Kyngs absens are voyde.

           And as in them therby Gods gyfts schyne most ma[y]   f.119
           So stand ther affayres wherby they so schyne schall.
           Yf the glos of Gods schyne not bryght eche way
           In them, who havyng a realme in governall
           Set forthe theyre governans to Gods glory all,   680
           Charytably aydynge subjects in eche kynde,
           The schynyng of Gods gyfts wheer schall we then fynde?

           And of this hye sort the hy hed most excelent
           Ys owr most loved and drade supreme soferayne,
           The schynynge of whose most excellent talent   685
           Ymployde to Gods glory above all the trayne
           Syns wytt wantyth here recytall to retayne,
           And that all hys faythfull fele the frewte of hys fame.
           Of corse I pray pardon in passyng the same.

           Prayng that pryns, whome owr pryns hys grett grace gave 690
           To grawnt hym longe lengthe of encres in estate,
           At full fyne wherof hys most hy gyfts to have,
           By his most faythfull use, rewarde in suche rate
           As ys promysyd in scrypture alegyd late:
           The joyes not allonely inestymabyll   695
           But more the degre of joyes incomparabyll.

                                   72

Contynewans wherof wythe frewtfull encrese
I hartyly wysche for encrese of rewarde;
As scrypture alegyd late doth wytnes
The wytty wyse wurker to be prefarde   700
Above thydyll sot, and ye to regarde
Eche man hym selfe so to aply in thys
As ye all may obtayne the hye degre of blys.

   Amen q[uo]d John Heywod.

JOHAN JOHAN

The Names of the Players

Johan Johan the husband
Tyb
Syr Johan the preest

A *mery play betwene John Johan the husbande, Tyb his wyfe,*
and Syr Johan the preest.

Johan Johan the husbande

    God spede you, maysters, everychone!
    Wote ye not whyther my wyfe is gone?
    I pray God the dyvell take her.
    For all that I do I can not make her
    But she wyll go a gaddynge very myche   5
    Lyke an Anthony pyg with an olde wyche
    Whiche ledeth her about hyther and thyther,
    But by our lady I wote not whyther.
    But by gogges blod, were she come home
    Unto this my house, by our lady of Crome,   10
    I wolde bete her or that I drynke.
    Bete her, quoth a? Yea, that she shall stynke,
    And at every stroke lay her on the grounde
    And trayne her by the here about the house rounde.
    I am evyn mad that I bete her not nowe,   15
    But I shall rewarde her hardly well ynowe –
    There is never a wyfe betwene heven and hell
    Whiche was ever beten halfe so well.

    Beten, quoth a? Yea, but what and she therof dye?
    Than I may chaunce to be hanged shortly.   20
    And whan I have beten her tyll she smoke,
    And gyven her many a[n] hundred stroke,
    Thynke ye that she wyll amende yet?
    Nay, by our lady, the devyll spede whyt!
    Therfore I wyll not bete her at all –   25

    And shall I not bete her? No, shall.
    Whan she offendeth and doth a mys,
    And kepeth not her house, as her duetie is,
    Shall I not bete her if she do so?
    Yes, by cokkes blood, that shall I do.   30
    I shall bete her and thwak her I trow,
    That she shall beshyte the house for very wo.

    But yet I thynk what my neybour wyll say than:
    He wyll say thus, 'Whom chydest thou, Johan Johan?'
    'Mary,' wyll I say, 'I chyde my curst wyfe,   35
    The veryest drab that ever bare lyfe,
    Whiche doth nothyng but go and come,
    And I can not make her kepe her at home.'
    Than I thynke he wyll say by and by,

'Walke her cote, Johan Johan, and bete her hardely.'   40
But than unto hym myn answere shalbe,
'The more I bete her, the worse is she:
And wors and wors make her I shall.'

He wyll say than, 'bete her not at all.'
'And why?' shall I say, 'this wolde by wyst: 45
Is she not myne to chastice as I lyst?'

But this is a nother poynt, worst of all:
The folkes wyll mocke me whan they here me brall.
But for all that shall I let therfore
To chastyce my wyfe ever the more,   50
And to make her at home for to tary?
Is not that well done? Yes, by Saynt Mary,
That is a poynt of an honest man
For to bete his wyfe well nowe and than.

Therfore I shall bete her, have ye no drede,   55
And I ought to bete her tyll she be starke dede.
And why? By God, bicause it is my pleasure.
And if I shulde suffre her, I make you sure,
Nought shulde prevayle me, nother staffe nor waster,
Within a whyle she wolde be my mayster.   60

Therfore I shall bete her, by cokkes mother,
Both on the tone syde and on the tother,
Before and behynde – nought shall be her bote –
From the top of the heed to the sole of the fote.

But masters, for Goddes sake do not entrete   65
For her, whan that she shalbe bete,
But for Goddes passion let me alone
And I shall thwak her that she shall grone.
Wherfore I beseche you, and hartely you pray,
And I beseche you say me not nay   70
But that I may beate her for this ones,   A2
And I shall beate her by cokkes bones
That she shall stynke lyke a pole kat.
But yet, by gogges body, that nede nat,
For she wyll stynke without any betyng.   75
For every nyght ones she gyveth me an hetyng –
From her issueth suche a stynkyng smoke
That the savour therof almost doth me choke.
But I shall bete her nowe without fayle:
I shall bete her toppe and tayle,   80

Heed, shulders, armes, legges, and all,
I shall bete her I trowe that I shall,
And by gogges boddy I tell you trewe
I shall bete her tyll she be blacke and blewe.

But where the dyvell, trowe ye, she is gon?   85
I holde a noble she is with Syr Johan.
I fere I am begyled alway
But yet in fayth I hope well nay.
Yet I almost enrage that I ne can
Se the behavour of our gentylwoman.   90
And yet I thynke thyther as she doth go
Many an honest wyfe goth thyther also
For to make some pastyme and sporte.
But than my wyfe so ofte doth thyther resorte
That I fere she wyll make me weare a fether.   95
But yet I nede not for to fere nether,
For he is her gossyp, that is he.

But abyde a whyle, yet let me se:
Where the dyvell hath our gyssypry begon?
My wyfe had never chylde, doughter nor son.   100

Nowe if I forbede her that she go no more
Yet wyll she go as she dyd before,
Or els wyll she chuse some other place,
And then the matter is in as yll case.

But in fayth all these wordes be in wast,   105
For I thynke the matter is done and past.
And whan she cometh home she wyll begyn to chyde,
But she shall have her payment styk by her syde
For I shall order her for all her brawlyng
That she shall repent to go a catter wawlyng.   110

                                                [Enter Tyb]

Tyb   Why, whom wylt thou beate, I say, thou knave?
Johan   Who, I, Tyb? None so God me save.
Tyb   Yes, I harde the say thou woldest one bete.
Johan   Mary, wyfe, it was stokfysshe in Temmes Strete
           Whiche wyll be good meate agaynst Lent.   A2v
           Why, Tyb, what haddest thou thought that I had ment? 116
Tyb   Mary, me thought I harde the bawlyng.
           Wylt thou never leve this wawlyng?
           Howe the dyvell dost thou thy selfe behave?
           Shall we ever have this worke, thou knave?   120

Johan	What, wyfe! Howe sayst thou? Was it well gest of me
	That thou woldest be come home in safete
	As sone as I had kendled a fyre?
	Come warme the, swete Tyb, I the requyre.
Tyb	O Johan Johan, I am afrayd by this lyght 125
	That I shalbe sore syk this nyght.
Johan	By cokkes soule, nowe I dare lay a swan
	That she comes nowe streyght fro Syr Johan:
	For ever whan she hath fatched of hym a lyk,
	Than she comes home, and sayth she is syk. 130
Tyb	What sayst thou?
Johan	Mary I say
	It is mete for a woman to go play
	Abrode in the towne for an houre or two.
Tyb	Well gentylman, go to, go to.
Johan	Well, let us have no more debate. 135
Tyb	If he do not fyght, chyde, and rate,
	Braule and fare, as one that were frantyke,
	There is nothyng that may hym lyke.
Johan	If that the parysshe preest, Syr Johan
	Dyd not se her nowe and than, 140
	And gyve her absolution upon a bed,
	For wo and payne, she wolde sone be deed.
Tyb	For Goddes sake, Johan Johan, do the not displease:
	Many a tyme I am yll at ease.
	What thynkest nowe? Am not I somwhat syk? 145
Johan	Nowe wolde to God and swete saynt Dyryk
	That thou warte in the water up to the throte,
	Or in a burnyng oven red hote,
	To se and I wolde pull the out.
Tyb	Nowe Johan Johan, to put the out of dout 150
	Imagyn thou where that I was
	Before I came home.
Johan	M[ar]y, percase
	Thou wast prayenge in the churche of Poules
	Upon thy knees for all chrysten soules.
Tyb	Nay.
Johan	Than if thou wast not so holy 155
	Shewe me where thou wast, and make no lye.
Tyb	Truely, Johan Johan, we made a pye,
	I and my gossyp Margery,
	And our gossyp the preest, Syr Johan, A3
	And my neybours yongest doughter An. 160
	The preest payde for the stuffe and the makyng,
	And Margery, she payde for the bakyng.

Johan	By kokkes lylly woundes, that same is she	
	That is the most bawde hens to Coventre.	
Tyb	What say you?	
Johan	Mary, answere me to this:	165
	Is not Syr Johan a good man?	
[Tyb]	Yes, that he is.	
Johan	Ha Tyb, if I shulde not greve the	
	I have somwhat wherof I wolde meve the.	
Tyb	Well husbande, nowe I do conject	
	That thou hast me somwhat in suspect;	170
	But, by my soule, I never go to Syr Johan	
	But I fynde hym lyke an holy man,	
	For eyther he is sayenge his devotion	
	Or els he is goynge in processyon.	

Johan	Yea, rounde about the bed doth he go,	175
	You two to gether and no mo;	
	And for to fynysshe the processyon	
	He lepeth up, and thou lyest downe.	
Tyb	What sayst thou?	
Johan	Mary I say he doth well,	
	For so ought a shepherde to do, as I harde tell,	180
	For the salvation of all his folde.	
Tyb	Johan Johan.	
[Johan]	What is it that thou wolde?	
Tyb	By my soule, I love the too too,	
	And I shall tell the or I further go	
	The pye that was made, I have it nowe here,	185
	And therwith I trust we shall make good chere.	
Johan	By kokkes body, that is very happy.	
Tyb	But wotest who gave it?	
Johan	What the dyvel rek I?	
Tyb	By my fayth and I shall say trewe than,	
	The dyvell take me and it were not Syr Johan.	190
Johan	O holde the peas wyfe, and swere no more,	
	But I beshrewe both your hartes therfore.	
Tyb	Yet peradventure thou hast suspection	
	Of that that was never thought nor done.	
[Johan]	Tusshe wyfe, let all suche matters be:	195
	I love the well, though thou love not me.	
	But this pye doth nowe catche harme;	
	Let us set it upon the harth to warme.	
Tyb	Than let us eate it as fast as we can.	
	But bycause Syr Johan is so honest a man	200
	I wolde that he shulde therof eate his part.	
[Johan]	That were reason, I the ensure.	

[Tyb]	Than syns that it is thy pleasure	
	I pray the than, go to hym ryght	A3v
	And pray hym come sup with us to nyght.	205
Johan	Shall he cum hyther? By kokkes soule, I was a curst	
	Whan that I graunted to that worde furst.	
	But syns I have sayd it, I dare not say nay,	
	For than my wyfe and I shulde make a fray;	
	But whan he is come, I swere by Goddes mother,	210
	I wold gyve the dyvell the tone to cary away the tother.	
Tyb	What sayst?	
Johan	Mary, he is my curate, I say,	
	My confessour and my frende alway;	
	Therfore go thou and seke hym by and by,	
	And tyll thou come agayne, I wyll kepe the pye.	215
Tyb	Shall I go for hym? Nay I shrewe me than!	
	Go thou and seke as fast as thou can,	
	And tell hym it.	
Johan	Shall I do so?	
	In fayth it is not mete for me to go.	
Tyb	But thou shalte go tell hym for all that.	220
Johan	Than shall I tell hym, wotest what?	
	That thou desyrest hym to come make some chere.	
Tyb	Nay, that thou desyrest hym to come sup here.	
Johan	Nay by the rode, wyfe, thou shalt have the worshyp	
	And the thankes of thy gest that is thy gossyp.	225
Tyb	Full ofte I se my husbande wyll me rate	
	For this hether commyng of our gentyll curate.	
Johan	What sayst, Tyb? Let me here that agayne.	
Tyb	Mary, I perceyve very playne	
	That thou hast Syr Johan somwhat in suspect:	230
	But, by my soule, as far as I conject,	
	He is vertuouse and full of charyte.	
Johan	In fayth, all the towne knoweth better that he	
	Is a hore monger, a haunter of the stewes,	
	An ypocrite, a knave, that all men refuse,	235
	A lyer, a wretche, a maker of stryfe,	
	Better than they knowe that thou art my good wyfe.	
Tyb	What is that, that thou hast sayde?	
Johan	Mary, I wolde have the table set and layde	
	In this place or that, I care not whether.	240
Tyb	Than go to brynge the trestels hyther.	
Johan	Abyde a whyle, let me put of my gown.	
	But yet I am afrayde to lay it down,	
	For I fere it shalbe sone stolen –	
	And yet it may lye safe ynough unstolen.	245

It may lye well here and I lyst –
But by cokkes soule here hath a dogge pyst.
And if I shulde lay it on the harth bare   A4
It myght hap to be burned or I were ware,
Therfore I pray you take ye the payne   250
To kepe my gowne tyll I come agayne.

But yet he shall not have it by my fay,
He is so nere the dore he myght ron away;
But bycause that ye be trusty and sure
Ye shall kepe it and it be your pleasure;   255
And bycause it is arayde at the skyrt,
Whyle ye do nothyng – skrape of the dyrt.
Lo nowe am I redy to go to Syr Johan
And byd hym come as fast as he can.

[Tyb]   Ye, do so without ony taryeng.   260
               But I say harke, thou hast forgot one thyng;
               Set up the table, and that by and by.

*[He sets up the table, but she
repeatedly prevents him leaving.]*

               Nowe go thy ways.
Johan   I go shortly,
               But se your candelstykkes be not out of the way.
Tyb   Come agayne and lay the table I say.   265
               What! Me thynkes ye have sone don.
Johan   Nowe I pray God that his malediction
               Lyght on my wyfe, and on the baulde preest.
Tyb   Nowe go thy ways and hye the! Seest?
Johan   I pray to Christ, if my wyshe be no synne,   270
               That the preest may breke his neck whan he comes in.
Tyb   How? Cum agayn.
Johan   What a myschefe wylt thou fole?
Tyb   Mary, I say brynge hether yender stole.
Johan   Nowe go to, a lyttell wolde make me
               For to say thus, a vengaunce take the.   275
Tyb   Nowe go to hym and tell hym playn
               That tyll thou brynge hym, thou wylt not come agayn.
Johan   This pye doth borne here as it doth stande.
Tyb   Go washe me these two cuppes in my hande.
Johan   I go with a myschyefe lyght on thy face.   280
Tyb   Go and byd hym hye hym a pace,
               And the whyle I shall all thynges amende.

Johan	This pye burneth here at this ende.	
	Understandest thou?	
Tyb	Go thy ways, I say.	
Johan	I wyll go nowe as fast as I may.	285
Tyb	How, come ones agayne, I had forgot –	
	Loke and there be ony ale in the pot.	
Johan	Nowe a vengaunce and a very myschyefe	
	Lyght on the pylde preest, and on my wyfe,	
	On the pot, the ale, and on the table,	290
	The candyll, the pye, and all the rable,	
	On the trystels and on the stole:	A4v
	It is moche ado to please a curst fole.	
Tyb	Go thy ways nowe, and tary no more,	
	For I am a hungred very sore.	295
Johan	Mary, I go.	
Tyb	But come ones agayne yet;	
	Brynge hyther that breade, lest I forget it.	
Johan	Iwys it were tyme for to torne	
	The pye, for ywys it doth borne.	
Tyb	Lorde, howe my husbande nowe doth patter,	300
	And of the pye styl doth clatter.	
	Go nowe and byd hym come away.	
	I have byd the an hundred tymes to day.	
Johan	I wyll not gyve a strawe I tell you playne	
	If that the pye waxe colde agayne.	305
Tyb	What art thou not gone yet out of this place?	
	I had went thou haddest ben come agayne in the space.	
	But by cokkes soule and I shulde do the ryght,	
	I shulde breke thy knaves heed to nyght.	
Johan	Nay than if my wyfe be set a chydyng	310
	It is tyme for me to go at her byddyng.	
	There is a proverbe, whiche trewe nowe preveth:	
	He must nedes go that the dyvell dryveth.	

[He goes to the priest's house.]

	How mayster curate, may I come in	
	At your chamber dore without ony syn?	315
Syr Johan	Who is there nowe that wolde have me?	
the Preest	What Johan Johan, what newes with the?	
Johan	Mary syr, to tell you shortly,	
	My wyfe and I pray you hartely	
	And eke desyre you with all our myght	320
	That ye wolde come and sup with us to nyght.	
Syr Johan	Ye must pardon me, in fayth I ne can.	

Johan	Yes I desyre you good Syr Johan	
	Take payne this ones, and yet at the lest	
	If ye wyll do nought at my request	325
	Yet do somwhat for the love of my wyfe.	
Syr Johan	I wyll not go for makyng of stryfe,	
	But I shall tell the what thou shalte do:	
	Thou shalt tary and sup with me or thou go.	
Johan	Wyll ye not go than? Why so?	330
	I pray you tell me, is there any dysdayne	
	Or ony enmyte betwene you twayne?	
Syr Johan	In fayth to tell the betwene the and me,	
	She is as wyse a woman as any may be.	
	I know it well, for I have had the charge	B1
	Of her soule, and serchyd her conscyens at large.	336
	I never knew her but honest and wyse,	
	Without any yvyll or any vyce,	
	Save one faut, I know in her no more,	
	And because I rebuke her now and then therfore	340
	She is angre with me, and hath me in hate;	
	And yet that that I do, I do it for your welth.	
Johan	Now God yeld it yow, good master curate,	
	And as ye do, so send you your helth,	
	Ywys I am bound to you a plesure.	345
Syr Johan	Yet thou thynkyst amys peradventure	
	That of her body she shuld not be a good woman,	
	But I shall tell the what I have done, Johan	
	For that matter: she and I be somtyme aloft,	
	And I do lye uppon her, many a tyme and oft	350
	To prove her, yet could I never espy	
	That ever any dyd wors with her than I.	
Johan	Syr that is the lest care I have of nyne,	
	Thankyd be God, and your good doctryne;	
	But yf it please you, tell me the matter	355
	And the debate betwene you and her.	
Syr Johan	I shall tell the, but thou must kepe secret.	
Johan	As for that syr, I shall not let.	
Syr Johan	I shall tell the now the matter playn:	
	She is angry with me, and hath me in dysdayn	360
	Because that I do her oft intyce	
	To do some penaunce, after myne advyse	
	Because she wyll never leve her wrawlyng	
	But alway with the she is chydyng and brawlyng,	
	And therfore I knowe she hatyth m[y] presens.	365
Johan	Nay in good feyth, savyng your reverens.	

Syr Johan	I know very well she hath me in hate.	
Johan	Nay, I dare swere for her, master curate.	
	But was I not a very knave?	[Aside]
	I thought surely, so God me save,	370
	That he had lovyd my wyfe, for to dyseyve me,	
	And now he quytyth hym self, and here I se	
	He doth as much, as he may for his lyfe,	
	To styn[t] the debate betwene me and my wyfe.	
Syr Johan	If ever she dyd or though[t] me any yll	375
	Now I forgyve her with m[y] fre wyll.	
	Therfore Johan Johan, now get the home,	
	And thank thy wyfe, and say I wyll not come.	
Johan	Yet let me know now good Syr Johan	Blv
	Where ye wyll go to supper than.	380
Syr Johan	I care nat greatly and I tell the.	
	On saterday last, I and two or thre	
	Of my frendes made an appoyntement	
	And agaynst this nyght we dyd assent	
	That in a place we wolde sup together;	385
	And one of them sayd he wold brynge thether	
	Ale and bread, and for my parte I	
	Sayd that I wolde gyve them a pye,	
	And there I gave them money for the makynge.	
	And an other sayd she wolde pay for the bakyng,	390
	And so we purpose to make good chere	
	For to dryve away care and thought.	
Johan	Than I pray you, syr, tell me here	
	Whyther shulde all this geare be brought?	
Syr Johan	By my fayth and I shulde not lye,	395
	It shulde be delyvered to thy wyfe, the pye.	
Johan	By God it is at my house standyng by the fyre.	
Syr Johan	Who bespake that pye, I the requyre?	
Johan	By my feyth and I shall not lye,	
	It was my wyfe and her gossyp Margerye,	400
	And your good masshyp, called Syr Johan,	
	And my neybours yongest doughter An.	
	Your masshyp payde for the stuffe and makyng,	
	And Margery she payde for the bakyng.	
Syr Johan	If thou wylte have me nowe, in faithe I wyll go.	405
Johan	Ye mary, I beseche your masshyp do so.	
	My wyfe taryeth for none but us twayne,	
	She thynketh longe or I come agayne.	
Syr Johan	Well nowe, if she chyde me in thy presens	

85

	I wylbe content and take in pacyens.	410
Johan	By cokkes soule and she ones chyde	
	Or frowne, or loure, or loke asyde	
	I shall brynge you a staffe as myche as I may heve,	
	Than bete her and spare not; I gyve you good leve	
	To chastyce her for her shreude varyeng.	415

[They return to Johan Johan's house.]

Tyb	The devyll take the for thy longe taryeng!	
	Here is not a whyt of water, by my gowne,	
	To washe our handes, that we myght syt downe.	
	Go and hye the as fast as a snayle,	
	And with fayre water fyll me this payle.	420
Johan	I thanke our Lorde of his good grace	
	That I can not rest longe in a place.	
Tyb	Go fetche water I say at a worde,	B2
	For it is tyme the pye were on the borde;	
	And go with a vengeance, and say thou art prayde.	425
Syr Johan	A! good gossyp, is that well sayde?	
Tyb	Welcome myn owne swete harte,	
	We shall make some chere or we departe.	
Johan	Cokkes soule, loke howe he approcheth nere	
	Unto my wyfe – this abateth my chere.	430
Syr Johan	By God I wolde ye had harde the tryfyls	
	The toys, the mokkes, the fables, and the nyfyls	
	That I made thy husbande to beleve and thynke!	
	Thou myghtest as well in to the erthe synke	
	As thou coudest forbeare laughyng any whyle.	435
Tyb	I pray the let me here parte of that wyle.	
Syr Johan	Mary I shall tell the as fast as I can.	
	But peas, no more – yonder cometh thy good man.	
Johan	Cokkes soule, what have we here?	
	As far as I sawe, he drewe very nere	440
	Unto my wyfe.	
Tyb	What art come so sone?	
	Gyve us water to wasshe nowe – have done.	

Than he bryngeth the payle empty.

Johan	By kockes soule, it was even nowe full to the brynk,	
	But it was out agayne or I coude thynke;	
	Wherof I marveled by God almyght	445
	And than I loked betwene me and the lyght	
	And I spyed a clyfte, bothe large and wyde.	
	Lo, wyfe, here it is on the tone syde.	

Tyb	Why dost not stop it?
Johan	Why, howe shall I do it?
Tyb	Take a lytle wax.
Johan	Howe shal I come to it? 450
Syr Johan	Mary, here be two wax candyls I say,
	Whiche my gossyp Margery gave me yesterday.
Tyb	Tusshe let hym alone, for by the rode
	It is pyte to helpe hym or do hym good.
Syr Johan	What, Johan Johan, canst thou make no shyfte? 455
	Take this waxe and stop therwith the clyfte.
Johan	This waxe is as harde as any wyre.
Tyb	Thou must chafe it a lytle at the fyre.

[Johan goes to the fireside.]

Johan	She that broughte the these waxe candelles twayne
	She is a good companyon certayn. 460
Tyb	What, was it not my gossyp Margery?
Syr Johan	Yes, she is a blessed woman surely.
Tyb	Nowe wolde God I were as good as she,
	For she is vertuous and full of charyte.

Johan	Nowe so God helpe me, and by my holydome	465
	She is the erranst baud betwene this and Rome.	B2v

Tyb	What sayst?
Johan	Mary, I chafe the wax,
	And I chafe it so hard that my fyngers krakkes.
	But take up this py that I here torne;
	And it stand long, ywys it wyll borne. 470
Tyb	Ye but thou must chafe the wax I say.
Johan	Byd hym syt down I the pray –
	Syt down, good Syr Johan, I you requyre.
Tyb	Go, I say, and chafe the wax by the fyre
	Whyle that we sup, Syr Johan and I. 475

[She forces him back to the fire repeatedly.]

Johan	And how now, what wyll ye do with the py?
	Shall I not ete therof a morsell?
Tyb	Go and chafe the wax whyle thou art well,
	And let us have no more pratyng thus.
Syr Johan	Benedicite.
Johan	Dominus. 480
Tyb	Now go chafe the wax with a myschyfe.
Johan	What, I come to blysse the bord, swete wyfe.

87

	It is my custome now and than.	
	Mych good do it you, master Syr Johan.	
Tyb	Go chafe the wax, and here no lenger tary.	485
Johan	And is not this a very purgatory	
	To se folkes ete, and may not ete a byt.	
	By kokkes soule, I am a very wodcok.	
	This payle here, now a vengaunce take it!	
	Now my wyfe gyveth me a proud mok.	490
Tyb	What dost?	
Johan	Mary I chafe the wax here,	
	And I ymagyn, to make you good chere,	
	That a vengaunce take you both as ye syt,	
	For I know well, I shall not ete a byt.	
	But yet in feyth, yf I myght ete one morsell	495
	I wold thynk the matter went very well.	
Syr Johan	Gossyp Johan Johan, now mych good do it you.	
	What chere make you – there by the fyre?	
Johan	Master person, I thank yow now,	
	I fare well inow after myne own desyre.	500
Syr Johan	What dost, Johan Johan, I the requyre?	
Johan	I chafe the wax here by the fyre.	
Tyb	Here is good drynk, and here is a good py.	
Syr Johan	We fare very well, thankyd be our lady.	
Tyb	Loke how the kokold chafyth the wax that is hard,	505
	And for his lyfe daryth not loke hetherward.	
Syr Johan	What doth my gossyp?	
Johan	I chafe the wax,	
	And I chafe it so hard that my fyngers krakkes,	
	And eke the smoke puttyth out my eyes two.	
	I burne my face, and ray my clothys also	B3
	And yet I dare nat say one word,	511
	And they syt laughyng, yender at the bord.	
Tyb	Now by my trouth, it is a prety jape	
	For a wyfe – to make her husband her ape.	
	Loke of Johan Johan, which maketh hard shyft	515
	To chafe the wax, to stop therwith the clyft.	
Johan	Ye, that a vengeaunce take ye both two	
	Both hym and the, and the and hym also,	
	And that ye may choke with the same mete	
	At the furst mursell that ye do ete.	520
Tyb	Of what thyng now dost thou clatter,	
	Johan Johan, or wherof doth thou patter?	
Johan	I [c]hafe the wax, and make hard shyft	
	To stop herwith of the payll the ryft.	
Syr Johan	So must he do, Johan Johan, by my father kyn,	525

	That is bound of wedlok in the yoke.	
Johan	Loke how the pyld preest crammyth in –	
	That wold to God he myght therwith choke.	
Tyb	Now, master person, pleasyth your goodnes	
	To tell us some tale of myrth or sadnes	530
	For our pastyme in way of communycacyon.	
Syr Johan	I am content to do it for our recreacyon,	
	And of thre myracles I shall to you say.	
Johan	What, must I chafe the wax all day,	
	And stond here rostyng by the fyre?	535
Syr Johan	Thou must do somwhat at thy wyves desyre.	

	I know a man which weddyd had a wyfe,	
	As fayre a woman as ever bare lyfe,	
	And within a senyght after, ryght sone,	
	He went beyond se, and left her alone,	540
	And taryed there about a seven yere.	
	And as he cam homeward, he had a hevy chere,	
	For it was told hym that she was in heven.	
	But when that he comen home agayn was	
	He found his wyfe, and with her chyldren seven,	545
	Whiche she had had in the mene space;	
	Yet had she not had so many by thre	
	Yf she had not had the help of me.	
	Is not this a myracle, yf ever were any,	
	That this good wyfe shuld have chyldren so many	550
	Here in this town, whyle her husband shuld be	
	Beyond the se, in a farre contre?	
Johan	Now in good soth, this is a wonderous myracle –	
	But for your labour, I wolde that your tacle	B3v
	Were in a skaldyng water well sod!	555
Tyb	Peace I say, thou lettest the worde of God.	

	An other myracle eke I shall you say	
Syr Johan	Of a woman whiche that many a day	
	Had ben wedded, and in all that season	
	She had no chylde, nother doughter nor son.	560
	Wherfore to Saynt Modwin she went on pilgrimage	
	And offered there a lyve pyg, as is the usage	
	Of the wyves that in London dwell,	
	And through the vertue therof, truly to tell,	
	Within a moneth after ryght shortly	565
	She was delyvered of a chylde as moche as I.	
	How say you? Is not this myracle wonderous?	
Johan	Yes in good soth syr, it is marvelous;	

89

	But surely after myn opynyon	
	That chylde was nother doughter nor son.	570
	For certaynly, and I be not begylde,	
	She was delyvered of a knave chylde.	
Tyb	Peas, I say, for Goddes passyon,	
	Thou lettest Syr Johans communication.	

Syr Johan	The thyrde myracle also is this:	575
	I knewe a nother woman eke ywys,	
	Whiche was wedded, and within fyve monthis after	
	She was delyvered of a fayre doughter	
	As well formed in every membre and joynt,	
	And as perfyte in every poynt	580
	As though she had gone fyve monthis full to thende.	
	Lo, here is fyve monthis of advantage.	
Johan	A wonderous myracle so God me mende!	
	I wolde eche wyfe that is bounde in maryage	
	And that is wedded here within this place	585
	Myght have as quicke spede in every suche case.	
Tyb	Forsoth, Syr Johan, yet for all that	
	I have sene the day that pus, my cat,	
	Hath had in a yere kytlyns eyghtene.	
Johan	Ye, Tyb my wyfe, and that have I sene.	590
	But howe say you, Syr Johan, was it good, your pye?	
	The dyvell the morsell that therof eate I.	
	By the good Lorde, this is a pyteous warke!	
	But nowe I se well the olde proverbe is treu:	
	The parysshe preest forgetteth that ever he was a clarke.	595
	But Syr Johan, doth not remembre you	
	How I was your clerke, and holpe you masse to syng,	
	And hylde the basyn alway at the offryng?	B4
	Ye never had halfe so good a clarke as I!	
	But not withstandyng all this, nowe our pye	600
	Is eaten up, there is not lefte a byt,	
	And you two together there do syt	
	Eatynge and drynkynge at your owne desyre,	
	And I am Johan Johan, which must stande by the fyre	
	Chafyng the wax, and dare none other wyse do.	605
Syr Johan	And shall we alway syt here styll, we two?	
	That were to mych.	
Tyb	Then ryse we out of this place.	
Syr Johan	And kys me than in the stede of grace,	
	And fare well, leman, and my love so dere.	

Johan	Cokkes body, this waxe it waxte colde agayn here.	610
	But what, shall I anone go to bed,	
	And eate nothyng, nother meate nor brede?	
	I have not be wont to have suche fare.	
Tyb	Why, were ye not served there as ye are,	
	Chafyng the waxe, standyng by the fyre?	615
Johan	Why what mete gave ye me, I you requyre?	
Syr Johan	Wast thou not served, I pray the hartely,	
	Both with the brede, the ale, and the pye?	
Johan	No, syr, I had none of that fare.	
Tyb	Why were ye not served there as ye are,	620
	Standyng by the fyre chafyng the waxe?	
Johan	Lo, here be many tryfyls and knakkes!	
	By kokkes soule, they wene I am other dronke or mad.	
Tyb	And had ye no meate, Johan Johan, no had?	
Johan	No, Tyb my wyfe, I had not a whyt.	625

[He edges back to the table.]

Tyb	What, not a morsell?	
Johan	No, not one byt.	
	For honger I trowe I shall fall in a sowne.	
Syr Johan	O, that were pyte, I swere by my crowne.	
Tyb	But is it trewe?	
Johan	Ye, for a surete.	
Tyb	Dost thou ly?	
Johan	No, so mote I the!	630
Tyb	Hast thou had nothyng?	
Johan	No, not a byt.	
Tyb	Hast thou not dronke?	
Johan	No, not a whyt.	
Tyb	Where wast thou?	
Johan	By the fyre I dyd stande.	
Tyb	What dydyst?	
Johan	I chafed this waxe in my hande,	
	Where as I knewe of wedded men the payne	635
	That they have, and yet dare not complayne.	
	For the smoke put out my eyes two,	
	I burned my face, and rayde my clothes also	
	Mendyng the payle, whiche is so rotten and olde	
	That it wyll not skant together holde;	640
	And syth it is so, and syns that ye twayn	
	Wold gyve me no meate for my suffysaunce	B4v
	By kokes soule I wyll take no lenger payn.	
	Ye shall do all your self, with a very vengaunce	
	For me, and take thou there thy payle now,	645

	And yf thou canst mend it, let me se how.	
Tyb	A, horson knave, hast thou brok my payll?	
	Thou shalt repent, by kokes lylly nayll!	
	Rech me my dystaf, or my clyppyng sherys:	
	I shall make the blood ronne about his erys.	650
Johan	Nay, stand styll, drab, I say, and come no nere,	
	For by kokkes blood, yf thou come here,	
	Or yf thou onys styr toward this place,	
	I shall throw this shovyll full of colys in thy face.	
Tyb	Ye, horson dryvyll, get the out of my dore!	655
Johan	Nay, get the out of my house, thou prestes hore!	
Syr Johan	Thou lyest, horson kokold, evyn to thy face.	
Johan	And thou lyest, pyld preest, with an evyll grace.	
Tyb	And thou lyest!	
Johan	And thou lyest!	
Syr Johan	And thou lyest agayn!	
Johan	By kokkes soule, horson preest, thou shalt be slayn.	660
	Thou hast eate our pye, and gyve me nought.	
	By kokkes blod, it shalbe full derely bought.	
Tyb	At hym, syr Johan, or els God gyve the sorow.	
Johan	And have at you, hore and thefe, Saynt George to borow!	

Here they fyght by the erys a whyle and than
the preest and the wyfe go out of the place.

Johan	A! syrs, I have payd some of them even as I lyst;	665
	They have borne many a blow with my fyst.	
	I thank God I have walkyd them well,	
	And dryven them hens. But yet can ye tell	
	Whether they be go? For, by God, I fere me	
	That they be gon together, he and she	670
	Unto his chamber, and perhappys she wyll	
	Spyte of my hart, tary there styll,	
	And peradventure there he and she	
	Wyll make me cokold, evyn to anger me:	
	And then had I a pyg in the wors panyer.	675
	Therfore, by God, I wyll hye me thyder	
	To se yf they do me any vylany:	
	And thus fare well this noble company!	

Finis.

IMPRYNTYD BY WYLLYAM RASTELL, THE TWELFTH DAY OF
FEBRUARY,
THE YERE OF OUR LORD 1533.

CUM PRIVILEGIO.

THE PARDONER AND THE FRERE

The Names of the Players

Pardoner
Frere
Curate
Neybour Pratte

[*The Frere enters.*]

The Frere	*Deus hic!* The holy trynyte
	Preserve all that nowe here be!
	Dere bretherne yf we wyll consyder
	The cause why I am come hyder,

Deus hic!   The holy trynyte
Preserve all   that nowe here be!
Dere bretherne   yf we wyll consyder
The cause why   I am come hyder,
Ye wolde be glad   to knowe my entent,   5
For I com not hyther   for monye nor for rent,
I com not hyther   for meate nor for meale,
But I com hyther   for your soules heale.
I com not hyther   to poll nor to shave,
I com not hyther   to begge nor to crave,   10
I com not hyther   to glose nor to flatter,
I com not hyther   to bable nor to clatter,
I com not hyther   to fable nor to lye,
But I com hyther   your soules to edyfye.
For we freres   are bounde the people to teche,   15
The gospell of Chryst   openly to preche,
As dyd the appostels   by Chryst theyr mayster sent
To turne the people   and make them to repent.
But syth the appostels   fro heven wolde not come,
We freres now   must occupy theyr rome.   20
We freres are bounde   to serche mennes conscyens;
We may not care for grotes   nor for pens;
We freres have professed   wylfull poverte:
No peny in our purse   have may we.
Knyfe nor staffe   may we none cary,   25
Excepte we shulde   from the gospell vary.
For worldly adversyte   may we be in no sorowe:
We may not care to day   for our meate to morowe.
Bare fote and bare legged   must we go also:
We may not care   for frost nor snowe.   30
We may have   no maner care, ne thynke
Nother for our meate   nor for our drynke,
But let our thoughtes   fro suche thynges be as free
As be the byrdes   that in the ayre flee.
For why, our Lorde,   clyped swete Jesus,   35
In the gospell   speketh to us thus:
'Through all the worlde   go ye', sayth he,   A1v
'And to every creature   speke ye of me,
And shew of my doctryne   and connynge.
And that they may   be glad of your comynge,   40
Yf that you enter   in any hous any where,

Loke that ye salute them, and byd my peas be there.
And yf that house be worthy and electe,
Thylke peace there than shall take effecte;
And yf that hous be cursyd or parvert, 45
Thylke peace than shall to your selfe revert.
And furthermore, yf any suche there be
Which do deny for to receyve ye,
And do dyspyse your doctryne and your lore,
At suche a house tary ye no more, 50
And from your shoes scrape away the dust
To theyr reprefe; and I, bothe trew and just,
Shall vengeaunce take of theyr synfull dede.'

Wherfore, my frendes, to this text take ye hede.
Beware how ye despyse the pore freres, 55
Which ar in this worlde Crystes mynysters;
But do them with an harty chere receyve,
Leste they happen your houses for to leve —
And than God wyll take vengeaunce in his yre.
Wherfore I now, that am a pore frere, 60
Dyd enquere were any people were
Which were dysposyd the worde of God to here.
And as I cam hether, one dyd me tell
That in this towne ryght good folke dyd dwell,
Which to here the worde of God wolde be glad. 65
And as sone as I therof knolege had,
I hyder hyed me as fast as I myght,
Entendyd by the grace of God almyght —
And by your pacyens and supportacyon —
Here to make a symple colacyon. 70
Wherfore I requyre all ye in this prese[nce]
For to abyde and gyve dew audyence.

But fyrst of all,
Now here I shall
To God my prayer make, 75
To gyve ye grace
All in thys place
His doctryne for to take. A2

> *And than kneleth downe the Frere*
> *sayenge his prayers, and in the meane*
> *whyle entreth the Pardoner with all his*
> *relyques, to declare what eche of them*
> *ben, and the hole power and vertu therof.*

The Pardoner   God and saynt Leonarde sende ye all his grace,
As many as ben assembled in this place!   80
Good, devoute people that here do assemble,
I pray God that ye may all well resemble
The ymage after whiche you are wrought,
And that ye save that Chryst in you bought.

Devoute, Chrysten people, ye shall all wytte   85
That I am comen hyther ye to vysytte.
Wherfore, let us pray thus, or I begynne:
Our savyoure preserve ye all from synne,
And enable ye to receyve this blessed pardon –
Whiche is the greatest under the son,   90
Graunted by the Pope in his bulles under lede,
Whiche pardon ye shall fynde when ye are dede
That offreth outher grotes or els pens
To these holy relyques, whiche, or I go hens,
I shall here shewe in open audyence,   95
Exortynge ye all to do to them reverence.

But fyrst ye shall knowe well that I com fro Rome –
Lo, here my bulles, all and some!
Our lyege lorde seale here on my patent
I bere with me my body to warant,   100
That no man be so bolde, be he preest or clarke,
Me to dysturbe of Chrystes holy warke,
Nor have no dysdayne nor yet scorne
Of these holy relyques whiche sayntes have worne.

Fyrst here I shewe ye of a holy Jewes shepe   105
A bone – I pray you take good kepe
To my wordes and marke them well:
Yf any of your bestes belyes do swell,
Dyppe this bone in the water that he dothe take
Into his body, and the swellynge shall slake.   110
And yf any worme have your beestes stonge,
Take of this water and wasshe his tonge,
And it wyll be hole anon; and furthermore,
Of pockes and scabbes, and every sore,
He shall be quyte hole that drynketh of the well   A2v
That this bone is dipped in: it is treuth that I tell!   116
And yf any man, that any beste oweth,
Once in the weke, or that the cocke croweth,
Fastynge, wyll drynke of this well a draughte,
As that holy Jew hath us taught,   120

His beestes and his store   shall multeply.
And, maysters all,   it helpeth well
Thoughe a man be foule   in jelous rage:
Let a man with this water   make his potage,
And nevermore shall he   his wyfe mystryst –   125
Thoughe he in sothe the faut by her wyst,
Or had she be take with freres two or thre.

Here is a mytten eke,   as ye may se.
He that his hande wyll put in this myttayn,
He shall have   encrease of his grayn   130
That he hathe sowne,   be it wete or otys –
So that he offer pens   or els grotes.
And another holy relyke   eke here se ye may:
The blessed arme   of swete saynt Sondaye!
And who so ever is blessyd   with this ryght hande   135
Can not spede amysse   by se nor by lande.
And yf he offereth   eke with good devocyon,
He shall not fayle   to come to hyghe promocyon.

And another holy relyke here may ye see:
The great too   of the Holy Trynyte.   140
And who so ever   ones dothe it in his mouthe take,
He shall never be dysseasyd   with the tothe ake;
Canker nor pockys shall there none [brede] –
This that I shewe ye   is matter in dede.

And here is of Our Lady   a relyke full good: 145
Her bongrace   which she ware with her french hode,
Whan she wente oute   alwayes for sonne bornynge.
Women with chylde,   which be in mournynge,
By vertue therof   shalbe sone easyd,
And of theyr travayll   full sone also releasyd   150
And yf this bongrace   they do devoutly kys,
And offer therto   as theyr devocyon is.

Here is another relyke,   eke a precyous one:
Of All Helowes   the blessyd jaw bone,
Which relyke   without any fayle   155
Agaynst poyson   chefely dothe prevayle;
For whom so ever it toucheth,   without dout,   A3
All maner venym   from hym shall issue out,
So that it shall hurt   no maner wyghte.
Lo, of this relyke   the great power and myghte,   160
Which preservyth from poyson every man!

97

Lo, of Saynt Myghell, eke, the brayn pan –
Which for the hed ake is a preservatyfe
To every man or beste that beryth lyfe.
And, further, it shall stande hym in better stede, 165
For his hede shall never ake whan that he is dede!
Nor he shall fele no maner grefe nor payn,
Though with a sworde one cleve it than a twayn!
But be as one that lay in a dede slepe.
Wherfore, to these relykes now com crouche and crepe: 170
But loke that ye offerynge to them make,
Or els can ye no maner profyte take.
But one thynge, ye women all, I warant you:
Yf any wyght be in this place now
That hathe done syn so horryble that she 175
Dare nat, for shame, therof shryven be;
Or any woman, be she yonge or olde,
That hathe made her husbande cockolde,
Suche folke shall have no power nor no grace
To offer to my relykes in this place; 180
And who so fyndyth her selfe out of suche blame,
Com hyther to me, on Crystes holy name!

And bycause ye
Shall unto me
Gyve credence at the full, 185
Myn auctoryte
Now shall ye se:
Lo here the Popes bull!

Now shall the Frere begyn his sermon,
and evyn at the same tyme the Pardoner
begynneth also to shew and speke of his
bullys, and auctorytes com from Rome.

Frere	*Date et dabitur vobis*	
	Good devout people, this place of scrypture	190
Pardoner	Worshypfull maysters, ye shall understand	
Frere	Is to you that have no litterature –	
Pardoner	That Pope Leo the tenth hath granted with his hand,	
Frere	Is to say in our englysshe tonge –	
Pardoner	And by his bulles confyrmed under lede,	A3v
Frere	As 'departe your goodes the poorefolke amonge'	196
Pardoner	To all maner people, bothe quycke and dede,	
Frere	And God shall than gyve unto you agayne:	
Pardoner	Ten thousande yeres and as many lentes of pardon	

Frere	This in the gospell so is wryten playne.	200
Pardoner	Whan they are dede, theyr soules for to guardon,	
Frere	Therfore gyve your almes in the largest wyse;	
Pardoner	That wyll with theyr peny or almes dede	
Frere	Kepe not your goodes – fye, fye on covetyse!	
Pardoner	Put to theyr handes to the good spede	205
Frere	That synne with God is most abhomynable,	
Pardoner	Of the holy chapell of swete Saynt Leonarde,	
Frere	And is eke the synne that is most dampnable.	
Pardoner	Whiche late by fyre was destroyed and marde.	

Frere	In scrypture eke – but I say, syrs, how?	210
Pardoner	Ay, by the mas, one can not here	
Frere	What a bablynge maketh yonder felow!	
Pardoner	For the bablynge of yonder folysshe frere.	

Frere	In scrypture, eke, is there many a place	
Pardoner	And also, maysters, as I was aboute to tell,	215
Frere	Whiche sheweth that many a man so farforth lacketh grace	
Pardoner	Pope July the sixth hath graunted fayre and well,	
Frere	That whan to them God hathe abundaunce sent,	
Pardoner	And doth twelve thousande yeres of pardon to them sende	
Frere	They wolde dystrybute none to the indygent;	220
Pardoner	That ought to this holy chapell lende.	
Frere	Wherat, God havynge great indygnacyon,	
Pardoner	Pope Bonyface the ninth also,	
Frere	Punysshed these men after a dyvers facyon,	
Pardoner	Pope July, Pope Innocent, with dyvers popes mo,	225
Frere	As the gospell full nobly dothe declare	
Pardoner	Hathe graunted to the susteynynge of the same	
Frere	How Dives Epulus, reygnynge in welfare,	
Pardoner	Fyve thousand yeres of pardon to every of you by name.	
Frere	And on his borde dysshes delycate,	230
Pardoner	And clene remyssyon also of theyr syn,	
Frere	Pore Lazarus cam beggynge at his gate,	
Pardoner	As often tymes as you put in	
Frere	Desyrynge som fode his honger to releve.	
Pardoner	Any monye into the pardoners cofer,	235
Frere	But the ryche man nothynge wolde hym gyve –	
Pardoner	Or any money up unto it offer.	A4
Frere	Not so moche as a fewe crommys of breade –	
Pardoner	Or he that offeryth peny or grote;	
Frere	Wherfore, pore Lazarus of famyn strayth was dede,	240
Pardoner	Or he that gyveth the pardoner a new cote;	
Frere	And angels hys soule to heven dyd cary.	

Pardoner	Or take of me outher ymage or letter
Frere	But now the ryche man, of the contrary,
Pardoner	Wherby thys pore chapell may fayre the better,
Frere	Whan he was dede went to mysery and payne
Pardoner	And God wote it ys a full gracyous dede,
Frere	Where for evermore he shall remayne
Pardoner	For whych God shall quyte you well your mede!
Frere	In brennyng fyre whych shall never cease!
Pardoner	Now helpe our pore chapell, yf it be your wyll!

245

250

Frere	But I say, thou pardoner, I byd the holde thy peace!
Pardoner	And I say, thou frere, holde thy tonge styll!
Frere	What standest thou there all the day smatterynge?
Pardoner	Mary, what standyst thou there all day clatterrynge?
Frere	Mary, felow, I com hyder to prech the word of God,

255

Whych of no man   may be forbode,
But harde wyth scylence and good entent
For why it techeth them evydent
The very way and path that shall them lede
Even to heven gatys, as strayght as any threde.
And he that lettyth the worde of God of audyence
Standeth accurst in the greate sentence –
And so arte thou, for enterruptynge me!

260

[*Pardoner*]	Nay, thou art acurst, knave – and that shalt thou se!

265

And all suche that to me   make interrupcyon,
The Pope sendes them   excommunycacyon
By hys bullys, here redy to be redde,
By bysshoppes and hys cardynalles confyrmed.
And, eke, yf thou dysturbe me any thynge
Thou arte also a traytour to the kynge;
For here hath he graunted me, under hys brode seale,
That no man, yf he love hys hele,
Sholde me dysturbe or let in any wyse.
And yf thou dost the kynges commaundement dispise,
I shall make the be set fast by the fete!
And where thou saydyst that thou arte more mete
Amonge the people here for to preche,
Bycause thou dost them the very way teche
How to com to heven above –
Therin thou lyest, and that shall I prove,
And by good reason I shall make the bow
And knowe that I am meter than arte thou.

270

275

[A4v]
280

For thou, whan thou hast taught them ones the way,
Thou carest not whether they com there, ye or nay.

285

100

But whan that thou　has done all togyder,
And taught them the way　for to com thyther,
Yet all that thou canst ymagyn
Is but to use vertue,　and to abstayne fro syn.
And yf they fall ones,　than thou canst no more:　　　　290
Thou canst not gyve them　a salve for theyr sore.
But these my letters　be clene purgacyon,
All thoughe never so many synnes　they have don.
But whan thou hast taught them the way and all,
Yet, or they com there,　they may have many a fall　　　295
In the way,　or that they com thyther.
For why the way　to heven is very slydder.
But I wyll teche them after another rate,
For I shall brynge them to heven gate,
And be theyr gydes,　and conducte all thynges,　　　　300
And lede them thyther　by the purse strynges,
So that they shall not fall,　though that they wolde.

Frere　　　　Holde thy peace, knave!　Thou arte very bolde.
　　　　　　Thou pratest, in fayth,　even lyke a pardoner!
Pardoner　Why despysest thou　the Popes mynyster?　　　　305
　　　　　　Maysters,　here I curse hym openly,
　　　　　　And therwith warne　all this hole company
　　　　　　By the Popes　great auctoryte,
　　　　　　That ye leve hym　and herken unto me!
　　　　　　For, tyll he be assoyled,　his wordes take none effecte –　　310
　　　　　　For out of holy chyrche　he is now clene rejecte.
Frere　　　　My maysters,　he dothe but gest and rave –
　　　　　　It forseth not　for the wordes of a knave!
　　　　　　But to the worde of God do reverence,
　　　　　　And here me forthe,　with dewe audyence:　　　　315

Frere　　　　Maysters, I shewed you　ere whyle of almes dede,
Pardoner　　Maysters, this pardon　whiche I shewed you before
Frere　　　　And how ye shulde gyve poore folke at theyr nede,
Pardoner　　Is the greatest that ever was　syth God was bore,
Frere　　　　And yf of your partes　that thynge ones were don,　　　320
[Pardoner]　For why without confessyon or contrycyon　　　　B1
[Frere]　　　Dout not but God sholde gyve you retrybucyon,
[Pardoner]　By this shall ye have　clene remyssyon,
[Frere]　　　But now further　it ought to be declared:
[Pardoner]　And forgyven of the synnes seven.　　　　325
[Frere]　　　Who be thes pore folke that shold have your reward?
Pardoner　　Come to this pardon,　yf ye wyll come to heven!
Frere　　　　Who be those pore folk　of whome I speke and name?

101

Pardoner	Come to this pardon, yf ye wyll be in blys!	
Frere	Certes, we pore freres are the same.	330
Pardoner	This is the pardon which ye can not mysse!	
Frere	We freres dayly take payn, I say,	
Pardoner	This is the pardon which shall mens soules wyn!	
Frere	We frears dayly do bothe fast and pray!	
Pardoner	This is the pardon the rydder of your synne!	335
Frere	We freres travayle and labour every houre!	
Pardoner	This is the pardon that purchaseth all grace!	
Frere	We freres take payne for the love of our Savyour!	
Pardoner	This is a pardon for all maner of trespas!	
Frere	We freres also go on lymytacyon,	340
Pardoner	This is the pardon of which all mercy dothe sprynge!	
Frere	For to preche to every crysten nacyon.	
Pardoner	This is the pardon that to heven shall ye brynge!	

Frere	But, I say, thou pardoner, thou wylt kepe sylens sone!	
Pardoner	Ye, it is lyke to be whan I have done.	345
Frere	Mary, therfore the more knave art thou, I say,	
	That parturbest the wordes of God, I say,	
	For neyther thy selfe wylt here Goddys doctryne	
	Ne suffre other theyr earys to enclyne.	
	Wherfore, our Savyour in his holy scrypture	350
	Gyveth the thy jugement, thou cursyd creature,	
	Spekynge to the after this maner:	
	Maledictus qui audit verbum dei negligenter –	
	'Wo be that man', sayth our Lord, 'that gyveth no audiens,	
	Or heryth the worde of God with negligens'.	355

Pardoner	Now thou haste spoken all, syr daw,	
	I care nat for the an olde straw!	
	I had lever thou were hanged up with a rope	
	Than I, that am comen from the Pope –	
	And therby Goddes minister – whyle thou standest and prate,	360
	Sholde be fayn to knocke without the gate.	
	Therfore preche hardely thy bely full –	
	But I nevertheles wyll declare the Popes bull!	B1v

Frere	Now, my frendes, I have afore shewed ye	
Pardoner	Now, my maysters, as I have afore declared	365
Frere	That good it is to gyve your charyte,	
Pardoner	That pardoners from you may not be spared,	
Frere	And, further, I have at lenghte to you tolde	
Pardoner	Now here after shall folow and ensew	
Frere	Who be these people that ye receyve sholde –	370

102

Pardoner	That foloweth of pardons the great vertew.	
Frere	That is to say us freres pore,	
Pardoner	We pardoners for your soules be as necessary	
Frere	That for our lyvynge must begge fro dore to dore.	
Pardoner	As is the meate for our bodys hungry.	375
Frere	For of our own propre we have no propre thynge	
Pardoner	For pardons is the thynge that bryngeth man to heven.	
Frere	But that we get of devout peoples gettynge;	
Pardoner	Pardons delyvereth them from the synnes seven!	
Frere	And in our place be fryers thre score and thre,	380
Pardoner	Pardons for every cryme may dyspens!	
Frere	Which onely lyve on mens charyte –	
Pardoner	Pardon purchasyth grace for all offence –	
Frere	For we fryars wylfull charyte professe –	
Pardoner	Ye, though ye had slayne bothe father and mother!	385
Frere	We may have no money, nother more nor lesse,	
Pardoner	And this pardon is chefe above all other,	
Frere	For wordly treasure we may nought care:	
Pardoner	For who to it offeryth grote or peny,	
Frere	Our soules must be ryche and our bodyes bare.	390
Pardoner	Though synnes he had done never so many,	
Frere	And one thynge I had almoste left behynde	
Pardoner	And though that he had all his kyndred slayn,	
Frere	Which before cam not to my mynde	
Pardoner	This pardon shall ryd them fro ever lastynge payne.	395
Frere	And doutles it is none other thynge	
Pardoner	There is no syn so abhomynable,	
Frere	But what ye wyll gyve your almes and offerynge	
Pardoner	Which to remyt this pardon is not able –	
Frere	Loke that ye dystrybute it wysely	400
Pardoner	As well declareth the sentence of this letter.	
Frere	Not to every man that for it wyll crye	
Pardoner	Ye can not therefore bestow your money better.	
Frere	For yf ye gyve your almes in that wyse	
Pardoner	Let us not here stande ydle all the daye –	B2
Frere	It shall not bothe to them and us suffyse.	406
Pardoner	Gyve us some money or that we go our way!	

Frere	But I say, thou lewde felowe, thou,	
	Haddest none other tyme to shewe thy bulles but now?	
	Canst not tary and abyde tyll sone,	410
	And rede them than, when prechynge is done?	
Pardoner	I wyll rede them now – what sayest thou therto?	
	Hast thou any thynge therwith to do?	

	Thynkest that I wyll stande and tary for thy leasure?	
	Am I bounde to do so moche for thy pleasure?	415
Frere	For my pleasure? Nay, I wolde thou knewyst it well!	
	It becometh the, knave, never a dell	
	To prate thus boldely in my presence,	
	And let the worde of God of audience!	
Pardoner	'Let the word of God,' quod a! Nay, let a horson drevyll	420
	Prate here all day, with a foule evyll!	
	And all thy sermon goth on covetyce,	
	And byddest men beware of avaryce,	
	And yet in thy sermon dost thou none other thynge	
	But for almes stande all the day beggynge.	425

Frere	Leve thy realynge, I wolde the advyse!	
Pardoner	Nay, leve thou thy bablynge, yf thou be wyse!	
Frere	I wolde thou knewest it, knave, I wyll not leve a whyt!	
Pardoner	No more wyll I, I do the well to wyt!	
Frere	It is not thou shall make me holde my peas!	430
Pardoner	Than speke on hardly, yf thou thynkyst it for thy eas –	
Frere	For I wyll speke, whyther thou wylt or no	
Pardoner	In faythe I care nat, for I wyll speke also –	
Frere	Wherfore hardely let us bothe go to –	
Pardoner	Se whiche shall be better harde of us two.	435

Frere	What? Sholde ye gyve ought to pratyng pardoners?	
Pardoner	What? Sholde ye spende on these flaterynge lyers	
Frere	What? Sholde ye gyve ought to these bolde beggars?	
Pardoner	As be these bablynge monkes and these freres	
Frere	Let them hardely labour for theyr lyvynge:	440
Pardoner	Which do nought dayly but bable and lye,	
Frere	It moche hurtyth them, good mennys gyvynge,	
Pardoner	And tell you fables dere inoughe a flye –	
Frere	For that maketh them ydle and slouthfull to warke,	
Pardoner	As dothe this bablynge frere here to day!	445
Frere	That for none other thynge they wyll carke.	
Pardoner	Dryve hym hence, therfore, in the twenty devyll waye!	B2v
Frere	Hardely, they wolde go bothe to plow and carte	
Pardoner	On us pardoners hardely do your cost –	
Frere	And if of necessitie ones they felte the smarte.	450
Pardoner	For why? Your money never can be lost,	
Frere	But we freres be nat in lyke estate,	
Pardoner	For why, there is in our fraternitie,	
Frere	For our handes with such thinges we may nat maculate;	
Pardoner	For all bretheren and sisteren that thereof be,	455
Frere	We freres be nat in lyke condicion:	

Pardoner	Devoutly songe every yere –	
Frere	We may have no prebendes ne exhibition;	
Pardoner	As he shall know well that cometh there –	
Frere	Of all temporall service are we forbode,	460
Pardoner	At every of the fyve solempne festes,	
Frere	And onely bounde to the service of God,	
Pardoner	A masse and dirige to pray for the good rest	
Frere	And therwith to pray for every christen nation	
Pardoner	Of the soules of the bretheren and sisteren all	465
Frere	That God witsafe to save them fro dampnation.	
Pardoner	Of our fraternitie in generall,	
Frere	But some of you so harde be of harte	
Pardoner	With a herse there standynge well arayed and dyght,	
Frere	Ye can nat wepe, though ye full sore smarte.	470
Pardoner	And torches and tapers aboute it brennynge bright,	
Frere	Wherfore some man must ye hyre nedes,	
Pardoner	And with the belles, eke, solempnely ryngynge,	
Frere	Whiche must intrete God for your misdedes.	
Pardoner	And prestes and clerkes devoutly syngynge!	475
Frere	Ye can hyre no better, in myne oppinion,	
Pardoner	And furthermore, every nyght in the yere	
Frere	Than us, Goddes servantes, men of religion.	
Pardoner	Twelve pore people are received there,	
Frere	And specially, God hereth us pore freres	480
Pardoner	And there have bothe harborow and food	
Frere	And is attentife unto our desyres –	
Pardoner	That for them is convenient and good.	
Frere	For, the more of religion, the more herde of our Lorde –	
Pardoner	And furthermore, if there be any other	485
Frere	And that i[t] so shulde, good reason doeth accorde.	
Pardoner	That of our fraternitie be sister or brother	
Frere	Therfore doute nat, maisters, I am even he	
Pardoner	Whiche hereafter happe to fall in decay,	B3
Frere	To whom ye shulde parte with your charitie:	490
Pardoner	And yf he than chaunce to come that way	
Frere	We freres be they that shulde your almes take,	
Pardoner	Nygh unto our forsayd holy place,	
Frere	Whiche for your soules helth do both watche and wake;	
Pardoner	Ye shall there tary for a monethes space,	495
Frere	We freres pray, God wote, whan ye do slepe;	
Pardoner	And be there founde of the places cost.	
Frere	We for your synnes do bothe sobbe and wepe	
Pardoner	Wherfore now, in the name of the Holy Goost,	
Frere	To pray to God for mercy and for grace –	500
Pardoner	I advise you all that now here be	

105

Frere	And thus do we dayly with all our hole place!	
Pardoner	For to be of our fraternitie.	
Frere	Wherfore, distribute of your temporall welthe,	
Pardoner	Fye on covetise! – sticke nat for a peny,	505
Frere	By whiche ye may preserve your soules helthe.	
Pardoner	For whiche ye may have benefites so many!	

Frere	I say, wylt thou nat yet stynt thy clappe?	
Pardoner	Pull me downe the pardoner with an evyll happe!	
Pardoner	Maister Frere, I holde it best	510
	To kepe your tonge while ye be in rest.	
Frere	I say, one pull the knave of his stole!	
Pardoner	Nay, one pull the frere downe lyke a fole!	
Frere	Leve thy railynge and babbelynge of freres,	
	Or, by Jys, Ish'lug the by the swete eares!	515
Pardoner	By God, I wolde thou durst presume to it!	
Frere	By God, a lytell thynge might make me to do it!	
	[ ]	517a
Pardoner	And I shrew thy herte and thou spare!	
Frere	By God, I wyll nat mysse the moche, thou slouche!	
	And yf thou playe me suche another touche,	520
	Ish' knocke the on the costarde, I wolde thou it knewe.	
Pardoner	'Mary, that wolde I se!' quod blynde Hew.	
Frere	Well, I wyll begyn – and than let me se	
	Whether thou darest agayne interrupte me,	
	And what thou wolde ones to it say.	525
Pardoner	Begyn, and prove whether I wyll, ye or nay!	

Frere	And to go forthe where as I lefte right now –	
Pardoner	Because som percase wyll thynke amysse of me –	
Frere	Our lorde in the gospell sheweth the way how –	
Pardoner	Ye shall now here the Popys auctoryte.	B3v
Frere	By gogges soule, knave, I suffre the no lenger!	531
Pardoner	I say some good body lende me his hengar,	
	And I shall hym teche, by God almyght,	
	How he shall another tyme lerne for to fyght:	
	I shall make that balde crown of his to loke rede!	535
	I shall leve hym but one ere on his hede!	
Frere	But I shall leve the never an ere, or I go!	
Pardoner	Ye, horeson Frere, wylt thou so?	

Than the[y] fyght.

Frere	Lose thy handes away from myn earys!	
Pardoner	Than take thou thy handes away from my heres!	540

	Nay, abyde thou horeson, I am not downe yet –	
	I trust fyrst to lye the at my fete!	
Frere	Ye, horeson, wylt thou scrat and byte?	
Pardoner	Ye, mary wyll I, as longe as thou doste smyte!	

The Curate [enters].

Parson	Holde your handes! A vengeaunce on ye bothe two,	545
	That ever ye came hyther to make this a do,	
	To polute my chyrche – a myschyefe on you lyght!	
	I swere to you, by God all myght,	
	Ye shall bothe repente every vayne of your harte	
	As sore as ye dyd ever thynge, or ye departe.	550
Frere	Mayster Parson, I marvayll ye wyll gyve lycence	
	To this false knave, in this audience	
	To publysh his ragman rolles with lyes.	
	I desyred hym, ywys, more than ones or twyse	
	To holde his peas tyll that I had done,	555
	But he wolde here no more than the man in the mone.	
Pardoner	Why sholde I suffre the more than thou me?	
	Mayster Parson gave me lycence before the,	
	And I wolde thou knewyst it. I have relykes here –	
	Other maner stuffe than thou dost bere:	560
	I wyll edefy more with the syght of it	
	Than wyll all the pratynge of holy wryt.	
	For that, except that the precher hym selfe lyve well,	
	His predycacyon wyll helpe never a dell.	
	And I know well that thy lyvynge is nought.	565
	Thou art an apostata, yf it were well sought:	
	An homycyde thou art, I know well inoughe,	
	For my selfe knew where thou sloughe	
	A wenche with thy dagger in a couche.	
	And yet, as thou saist in thy sermon, [thou] no man shall touch.	B4
Parson	No more of this wranglyng in my chyrch!	571
	I shrewe your hartys bothe for this lurche!	
	Is there any blood shed here betwen these knaves?	
	Thanked be God they had no stavys	
	Nor egetoles, for than it had ben wronge.	575
	Well, ye shall synge another songe:	
	Neybour Prat, com hether, I you pray!	

[Prat enters.]

Prat	Why, what is this nyse fraye?	
Parson	I can not tell you: one knave dysdaynes another.	
	Wherfore, take ye the tone and I shall take the other.	580

	We shall bestow them there as is most convenyent	
	For suche a couple. I trow they shall repente	
	That ever they met in this chyrche here.	
	Neyboure, ye be constable – stande ye nere;	
	Take ye that laye knave, and let me alone	585
	With this gentylman. By God and by Saynt Johan	
	I shall borowe upon prestholde somwhat	
	For I may say to the, neybour Prat,	
	It is a good dede to punysh such to the ensample	
	Of suche other, how that they shall mell	590
	In lyke facyon as these catyfes do.	
Prat	In good fayth, Mayster Parson, yf ye do so	
	Ye do but well to teche them to beware.	

Pardoner	Mayster Prat, I pray ye me to spare,	
	For I am sory for that that is done.	595
	Wherfore, I pray ye forgyve me sone	
	For that I have offendyd within your lybertye,	
	And by my trouthe, syr, ye may trust me,	
	I wyll never come hether more	
	Whyle I lyve, and God before!	600

Prat	Nay, I am ones charged with the:	
	Wherfore, by Saynt Johan, thou shalt not escape me	
	Tyll thou hast scouryd a pare of stokys.	

Parson	Tut, he weneth all is but mockes!	
	Lay hande on hym – and com ye on, Syr Frere:	605
	Ye shall of me hardely have your hyre!	
	Ye had none suche this seven yere,	
	I swere by God and by our Lady dere.	

[Frere]	Nay, Mayster Parson, for Goddys passyon,	
	Intreate not me after that facyon,	610
	For, yf ye do, it wyll not be for your honesty!	

Parson	Honesty or not, but thou shall se	B4v
	What I shall do by and by.	
	Make no stroglynge: com forthe soberly,	
	For it shall not avayle the, I say.	615

Frere	Mary, that shall we trye even strayt way!	
	I defy the, churle preeste – and there be no mo than thou,	
	I wyll not go with the, I make God a vow!	
	We shall se fyrst which is the stronger:	
	God hath sent me bonys – I do the not fere.	620

108

Parson	Ye, by thy fayth, wylt thou be there?
	Neybour Prat, brynge forthe that knave!
	And thou, Syr Frere, yf thou wylt algatys rave –

Frere	Nay, chorle, I the defy –
	I shall trouble the fyrst!	625
[Parson]	Thou shalt go to pryson by and by.
	Let me se now – do thy worste!

Prat with the Pardoner,
and the Parson with the Frere.

Parson	Helpe, helpe, neybour Prat, neybour Prat!
	In the worshyp of God, helpe me somwhat!

Prat	Nay, deale as thou canst with that elfe!	630
	For why? I have inoughe to do my selfe.
	Alas, for payn I am almoste dede!
	The reede blood so ronneth downe about my hede.
	Nay, and thou canst, I pray the helpe me!

Parson	Nay, by the mas, felowe, it wyll not be –	635
	I have more tow on my dystaffe than I can well spyn.
	The cursed frere dothe the upper hande wyn!
Frere	Wyll ye leve than, and let us in peace departe?

Parson & Prat	Ye, by Our Lady, even with all our harte.
Frere & Pardoner	Than adew, to the devyll, tyll we come agayn!	640
Parson & Prat	And a myschefe go with you bothe twayne!

IMPRYNTED BY WYLLYAM RASTELL THE 5 DAY
OF APRYLL, THE YERE OF OUR LORDE
1533

CUM PRIVILEGIO

THE FOURE PP

The Names of the Players

Palmer
Pardoner
Potycary
Pedler

[The Palmer enters.]

Palmer	Nowe God be here! Who kepeth this place?	A1v

        Nowe God be here! Who kepeth this place?
        Now by my fayth I crye you mercy!
        Of reason I must sew for grace,
        My rewdnes sheweth me [now] so homely.
          Wherof your pardon axt and wonne,   5
        I sew you as curtesy doth me bynde
        To tell thys, whiche shal be begonne
        In order as may come beste in mynde.
          I am a palmer as ye se,
        Whiche of my lyfe much part hath spent   10
        In many a fayre and farre countre,
        As pylgrymes do of good intent.
          At Hierusalem have I bene
        Before Chrystes blessed sepulture.
        The mount of Calvery have I sene –   15
        A holy place ye may be sure.
          To Josophat and Olyvete
        On fote, God wote, I wente ryght bare –
        Many a salt tere dyde I swete
        Before thys carkes coulde come there.   20
          Yet have I bene at Rome also
        And gone the stacions all arow;
        Saynt Peters shryne and many mo
        Then yf I tolde all ye do know –
          Except that there be any suche   25
        That hath ben there and diligently
        Hath taken hede and marked muche,
        Then can they speke as muche as I.

        Then at the Rodes also I was
        And rounde about to Amyas,   30
        At Saynt Toncomber and Saynt Tronion,
        At Saynt Bothulph and Saynt Anne of Buckston,
        On the hylles of Armony where I see Noes arke,
        With holy Job and Saynt George in Suthwarke,
        At Waltam and at Walsyngam,   35
        And at the good rood of Dagnam,   A2
        At Saynt Cornelys, at Saynt James in Gales,
        And at Saynt Wynefrydes well in Walles,
        At Our Lady of Boston, at Saynt Edmundes Byry
        And streyght to Saynt Patrykes purgatory.   40

	At Rydybone and at the blood of Hayles,	
	Where pylgrymes paynes ryght muche avayles,	
	At Saynt Davys and at Saynt Denis,	
	At Saynt Mathew and Saynt Marke in Venis,	
	At mayster Johan Shorne, at Canterbury,	45
	The great God of Katewade, at Kynge Henry,	
	At Saynt Savyours, at our lady of Southwell,	
	At Crome, at Wylsdome and at Muswell,	
	At Saynt Rycharde and at Saynt Roke,	
	And at Our Lady that standeth in the oke.	50
	To these with other many one	
	Devoutly have I prayed and gone,	
	Prayeng to them to pray for me	
	Unto the blessed Trynyte,	
	By whose prayers and my dayly payne	55
	I truste the soner to obtayne	
	For my salvacyon grace and mercy.	
	For be ye sure, I thynke surely,	
	Who seketh sayntes for Crystes sake –	
	And namely suche as payne do take	60
	On fote to punyshe thy frayle body –	
	Shall therby meryte more hyely	
	Then by any thynge done by man.	

[Pardoner enters.]

Pardoner	And when ye have gone as farre as ye can,	
	For all your labour and gostely entente,	65
	Yet welcome home as wyse as ye wente.	

| Palmer | Why syr, dyspyse ye pylgrymage? | |

Pardoner	Nay, for God, syr, then dyd I rage.	
	I thynke ye ryght well occupyed	A2v
	To seke these sayntes on every syde;	70
	Also your payne I nat disprayse it	
	But yet I discomende your wit	
	And, or we go, even so shall ye	
	If ye in this wyl answere me.	
	I pray you shew what the cause is	75
	Ye wente al these pylgrymages.	

Palmer	Forsoth this lyfe I dyd begyn	
	To rydde the bondage of my syn,	
	For whiche these sayntes rehersed or this	
	I have both sought and sene iwys,	80

113

	Besechynge them to be recorde	
	Of all my payne unto the Lorde	
	That gyveth all remyssyon	
	Upon eche mans contricyon	
	And by theyr good mediacyon,	85
	Upon myne humble submyssion	
	I trust to have in very dede	
	For my soule helth the better spede.	

Pardoner   Nowe is your owne confessyon lyckely
To make your selfe a fole quyckely   90
For I perceyve ye wolde obtayne
No nother thynge for all your payne
But onely grace your soule to save.
Nowe marke in this what wyt ye have
To seke so farre and helpe so nye –   95
Even here at home is remedy.
For at your dore my selfe doth dwell,
Who coulde have saved your soule as well
As all your wyde wandrynge shall do
Though ye wente thryes to Jericho.   100
Nowe syns ye myght have spedde at home,
What have ye wone by ronnyng at Rome?

Palmer   If this be true that ye have moved,   A3
Then is my wyt in dede reproved.
But let us here fyrste what ye are.   105
Pardoner   Truly I am a pardoner.

Palmer   Truely a pardoner that may be true
But a true pardoner doth nat ensew.
Ryght selde is it sene or never
That treuth and pardoners dwell together.   110
For be your pardons never so great,
Yet them to enlarge ye wyll nat let
With suche lyes that oftymes, Cryste wot,
Ye seme to have that ye have nat.
Wherfore I went my selfe to the selfe thynge,   115
In every place and without faynynge
Had as muche pardon there, assuredly,
As ye can promyse me here doutefully.
Howe be it I thynke ye do but scoffe,
But yf ye hadde all the pardon ye kepe of,   120
And no whyt of pardon graunted
In any place where I have haunted,

Yet of my labour I nothynge repent.
God hathe respect how eche tyme is spent
And, as in his knowlege all is regarded,   125
So by his goodnes all is rewarded.

Pardoner   By the fyrste parte of this laste tale
It semeth you come late from the ale
For reason on your syde so farre doth fayle
That ye leve reasonyng and begyn to rayle,   130
Wherin ye forget your owne parte clerely.
For ye be as untrue as I
And in one poynte ye are beyonde me,
For ye may lye by aucthoryte,
And all that hath wandred so farre   A3v
That no man can be theyr controller.   136
And where ye esteme your labour so muche,
I say yet agayne my pardons be suche
That yf there were a thousande soules on a hepe,
I wolde brynge them all to heven as good chepe   140
As ye have brought your selfe on pylgrymage
In the leste quarter of your vyage –
Whiche is farre a thys syde heven, by God,
There your labour and pardon is od.
With smale cost and without any payne   145
These pardons bryngeth them to heven playne.
Geve me but a peny or two pens
And, as sone as the soule departeth hens,
In halfe an houre or thre quarters at moste
The soule is in heven with the Holy Ghost.   150

[*Potycary enters*]

Potycary   Sende ye any soules to heven by water?
Pardoner   If we dyd, syr, what is the mater?

Potycary   By God, I have a drye soule shulde thyther
I praye you let our soules go to heven togyther!
So bysy you twayne be in soules helth,   155
May nat a potycary come in by stelth?
Yes, that I wyll, by Saynt Antony,
And by the leve of thys company
Prove ye false knaves bothe or we goo,
In parte of your sayenges as thys, lo: 160
Thou by thy travayle thynkest heven to gete,
And thou by pardons and relyques countest no lete
To sende thyne owne soule to heven sure

115

And all other whome thou lyste to procure.
If I toke an accyon then were they blanke, 165
For lyke theves the knaves rob away my thanke.
All soules in heven havynge relefe
Shall they thanke your craftes? Nay, thanke myn chefe. A4
No soule, ye knowe, entreth heven gate
Tyll from the bodye he be separate. 170
And whome have ye knowen dye honestlye
Without helpe of the potycary?
Nay, all that commeth to our handlynge,
Except ye happe to come to hangynge –
That way perchaunce ye shall nat myster 175
To go to heven without a glyster.
But be ye sure I wolde be wo
If ye shulde chaunce to begyle me so.
As good to lye with me a nyght
As hange abrode in the mone lyght. 180
There is no choyse to fle my hande
But, as I sayd, into the bande!
Syns, of our soules, the multitude
I sende to heven when all is vewed,
Who shulde but I then all togyther 185
Have thanke of all theyr commynge thyther?

Pardoner   If ye kylde a thousande in an houre space,
When come they to heven, dyenge from state of grace?

Potycary   If a thousande pardons about your neckes were teyd,
When come they to heven yf they never dyed? 190

Palmer   Longe lyfe after good workes in dede
Doth hynder mannes receyt of mede,
And deth before one dewty done
May make us thynke we dye to sone.
Yet better tary a thynge, then have it, 195
Then go to sone and vaynly crave it.

Pardoner   The longer ye dwell in communicacion,
The lesse shall you lyke thys ymagynacyon,
For ye may perceyve even at the fyrst chop
Your tale is trapt in such a stop A4v
That at the leste ye seme worste then we. 201

Potycary   By the masse, I holde us nought all thre.

116

Pedler	By Our Lady, then have I gone wronge!	
	And yet to be here I thought longe.	
Potycary	Brother ye have gone wronge no wyt.	205
	I prayse your fortune and your wyt,	
	That can dyrecte you so discretely	
	To plante you in this company –	
	Thou palmer and thou a pardoner,	
	I a potycary.	
Pedler	And I a pedler.	210
Potycary	Nowe on my fayth full well watched!	
	Were the devyll were we foure hatched?	
Pedler	That maketh no mater syns we be matched.	
	I coulde be mery yf that I catchyd	
	Some money for parte of the ware in my packe.	215
Potycary	What the devyll hast thou there at thy backe?	
Pedler	Why, dost thou nat knowe that every pedler	
	In every tryfull must be a medler?	
	Specyally in womens tryflynges –	
	Those use we chefe above all thynges.	220
	Whiche thynges to se, yf ye be disposed,	
	Beholde what ware here is disclosed.	
	Thys gere sheweth it selfe in suche bewte	
	That eche man thynketh it sayth, 'come bye me'.	
	Loke were your selfe can lyke to be chooser	225
	Your selfe shall make pryce though I be looser.	
	Is here nothynge for my father Palmer?	B1
	Have ye nat a wanton in a corner	
	For your walkyng to holy places?	
	By Cryste, I have herde of as straunge cases!	230
	Who lyveth in love or love wolde wynne	
	Even at this packe he must begynne,	
	Where is ryght many a proper token	
	Of whiche by name parte shall be spoken:	
	Gloves, pynnes, combes, glasses unspottyd,	235
	Pomanders, hookes, and lasses knotted,	
	Broches, rynges, and all maner bedes,	
	Lace rounde and flat for womens hedes,	
	Nedyls, threde, thymbell, shers, and all suche knackes	
	(Where lovers be, no suche thynges lackes)	240

Sypers, swathbondes, rybandes and sleve laces
Gyrdyls, knyves, purses, and pyncases.

| Potycary | Do women bye theyr pyncases of you? |
| Pedler | Ye, that they do, I make God a vow. |

Potycary	So mot I thryve, then for my parte	245
	I beshrewe thy knaves nakyd herte	
	For makynge my wyfeys pyncase so wyde	
	The pynnes fall out – they can nat abyde.	
	Great pynnes must she have one or other,	
	Yf she lese one she wyll fynde an other;	250
	Wherin I fynde cause to complayne,	
	New pynnes to her pleasure and my payne.	

Pardoner	Syr, ye seme well sene in womens causes	
	I praye you tell me what causeth this,	
	That women after theyr arysynge	255
	Be so longe in theyr apparelynge?	

Pedler	Forsoth women have many lettes	
	And they be masked in many nettes,	B1v
	As frontlettes, fyllettes, partlettes, and barcelettes,	
	And then theyr bonettes and theyr poynettes.	260
	By these lettes and nettes the lette is suche	
	That spede is small whan haste is muche.	

Potycary	An other cause why they come nat forwarde,	
	Whiche maketh them dayly to drawe backwarde,	
	And yet is a thynge they can nat forbere:	265
	The trymmynge and pynnynge up theyr gere,	
	Specyally theyr fydlyng with the tayle pyn,	
	And when they wolde have it prycke in,	
	If it chaunce to double in the clothe,	
	Then be they wode and swereth an othe,	270
	Tyll it stande ryght they wyll nat forsake it.	
	Thus though it may nat, yet wolde they make it,	
	But be ye sure they do but defarre it,	
	For when they wolde make it ofte tymes they marre it.	
	But prycke them and pynne them as myche as ye wyll,	275
	And yet wyll they loke for pynnynge styll.	
	So that I durste holde you a joynt,	
	Ye shall never have them at a fall poynt.	

| Pedler | Let womens maters passe and marke myne. | |
| | What ever theyr poyntes be, these poyntes be fyne, | 280 |

118

	Wherfore, yf ye be wyllynge to bye,
	Ley downe money, come of quyckely!
Palmer	Nay, by my trouth, we be lyke fryers:
	We are but beggers, we be no byers.

Pardoner Syr, ye maye showe your ware for your mynde   285
          But I thynke ye shall no profyte fynde.

Pedler   Well, though thys journey acquyte no coste,
          Yet thynke I nat my labour loste,
          For by the fayth of my body   B2
          I lyke full well thys company.   290
          Up shall this packe, for it is playne
          I came not hyther al for gayne.
          Who may nat play one day in a weke
          May thynke hys thryfte is farre to seke.
          Devyse what pastyme ye thynke beste   295
          And make ye sure to fynde me prest.

Potycary Why, be ye so unyversall
          That you can do what so ever ye shall?
Pedler   Syr, yf ye lyste to appose me
          What I can do then shall ye se.   300

Potycary Than tell me thys, be ye perfyt in drynkynge?
Pedler   Perfyt in drynkynge as may be wysht by thynkyng.
Potycary Then after your drynkyng how fall ye to wynkyng?
Pedler   Syr, after drynkynge, whyle the shot is tynkynge,
          Some hedes be swymmyng but myne wyl be synkynge,   305
          And upon drynkynge myne eyse wyll be pynkynge,
          For wynkynge to drynkynge is alway lynkynge.

Potycary Then drynke and slepe ye can well do
          But yf ye were desyred therto
          I pray you tell me, can you synge?   310
Pedler   Syr, I have some syght in syngynge.

Potycary But is your brest any thynge swete?
Pedler   What ever my breste be, my voyce is mete.

Potycary That answere sheweth you a ryght syngynge man   B2v
          Now what is your wyll, good father, than?   315

Palmer   What helpeth wyll where is no skyll?
Pardoner And what helpeth skyll where is no wyt?

Potycary	For wyll or skyll, what helpeth it Where frowarde knaves be lackynge wyll?

Leve of thys curyosytie   320
And who that lyste synge after me.

Here they synge.

Pedler	Thys lyketh me well, so mot I the.
Pardoner	So helpe me God, it lyketh nat me!

Where company is met and well agreed
Good pastyme doth ryght well in dede –   325
But who can syt in dalyaunce?
Men syt in suche a variaunce
As we were set or ye came in,
Whiche stryfe thys man dyd fyrst begynne,
Allegynge that suche men as use   330
For love of God and nat refuse
On fot to goo from place to place
A pylgrymage callynge for grace,
Shall in that payne with penitence
Obtayne discharge of conscyence;   335
Comparynge that lyfe for the beste
Enduccyon to our endles reste.
Upon these wordes our mater grewe
For, yf he coulde avow them true,
As good to be a gardener   340
As for to be a pardoner!
But when I harde hym so farre wyde,
I then aproched and replyed,
Sayenge this: that this indulgence,   B3
Havyng the forsayd penitence,   345
Dyschargeth man of all offence
With muche more profyt then this pretence.
I aske but two pens at the moste –
Iwys this is nat very great coste.
And from all payne without dyspayre,   350
My soule for his, kepe even his chayre!
And when he dyeth, he may be sure
To come to heven even at pleasure.
And more then heven he can nat get,
How farre so ever he lyste to jet.   355
Then is hys payne more then hys wit,
To wa[l]ke to heven syns he may syt.
Syr, as we were in this contencion,

120

	In came thys daw with hys invencyon,	
	Revelynge us – hym selfe avauntynge –	360
	That all the soules to heven assendynge	
	Are most bounde to the potycary	
	Bycause he helpeth most men to dye;	
	Before whiche deth, he sayeth in dede,	
	No soule in heven can have hys mede.	365

| Pedler | Why, do potycaries kyll men? |
| Potycary | By God, men say so, now and then. |

| Pedler | And I thought ye wolde nat have myst |
| | To make men lyve as longe as ye lyste. |

| Potycary | As longe as we lyste, nay, longe as they can! | 370 |
| Pedler | So myght we lyve without you than. |

Potycary	Ye, but yet it is necessary	
	For to have a potycary;	
	For when ye fele your conscyens redy,	B3v
	I can sende you to heven quyckly.	375
	Wherfore concernynge our mater here,	
	Above these twayne I am best clere,	
	And yf he lyste to take me so,	
	I am content you and no mo	
	Shall be our judge as in thys case:	380
	Whiche of us thre shall take the best place?	

Pedler	I neyther wyll judge the beste nor worste,	
	For be ye bleste or be ye curste	
	Ye know it is no whyt my sleyght	
	To be a judge in maters of weyght.	385
	It behoveth no pedlers nor proctours	
	To take on them judgemente as doctours.	
	But yf your myndes be onely set	
	To worke for soule helthe, ye be well met,	
	For eche of you somwhat doth showe	390
	That soules towarde heven by you do growe.	
	Then yf ye can so well agree	
	To contynue togyther all thre,	
	And all you thre obey on wyll,	
	Then all your myndes ye may fulfyll	395
	As yf ye came all to one man.	
	Who shulde goo pylgrymage more then he can?	

[to Palmer]	In that, ye, palmer, as debite	
	May clerely dyscharge hym, parde;	
[to Pardoner]	And for all other syns ones had contryssyon	400
	Your pardons geveth hym full remyssyon.	
[to Potycary]	And then ye, mayster potycary,	
	May sende hym to heven by and by.	

Potycary	Yf he taste this boxe nye aboute the pryme,	
	By the masse, he is in heven or evensonge tyme.	405
	My craft is suche that I can ryght well	
	Sende my fryndes to heven and my selfe to hell.	
	But syrs, marke this man, for he is wyse	B4
	Who coulde devyse suche a devyce.	
	For, yf we thre may be as one,	410
	Then be we lordes everychone.	
	Betwene us all coulde nat be myste	
	To save the soules of whome we lyste.	
	But for good order, at a worde,	
	Twayne of us must wayte on the thyrde.	415
	And unto that I do agree,	
	For bothe you twayne shall wayt on me.	

| [Pardoner] | What chaunce is this that suche an elfe | |
| | Commaunded two knaves be, besyde hym selfe? | |

| Pardoner | Nay, nay, my frende that wyll nat be | 420 |
| | I am to good to wayt on the. | |

| Palmer | By Our Lady, and I wolde be loth | |
| | To wayt on the better on you both! | |

Pedler	Yet be ye sewer for all thys dout,	
	Thys waytynge must be brought about.	425
	Men can nat prosper wylfully ledde;	
	All thynge decayed where is no hedde.	
	Wherfore, doutlesse, marke what I say:	
	To one of you thre twayne must obey,	
	And synnes ye can nat agree in voyce	430
	Who shall be hed, there is no choyse	
	But to devyse some maner thynge	
	Wherin ye all be lyke connynge	
	And in the same, who can do beste.	
	The other twayne to make them preste	435
	In every thynge of hys entente,	
	Holly to be at commaundement.	
	And now have I founde one mastry	

	That ye can do indyfferently;	
	And is nother sellynge nor byenge,	440
	But even only very lyenge.	B4v
	And all ye thre can lye as well	
	As can the falsest devyll in hell.	
	And though afore ye harde me grudge	
	In greater maters to be your judge,	445
	Yet in lyeng I can some skyll,	
	And yf I shall be judge, I wyll.	
	And be ye sure without flatery,	
	Where my consciens fyndeth the mastrye,	
	Ther shall my judgement strayt be founde,	450
	Though I myght wynne a thousande pounde.	

Palmer   Syr, for lyeng though I can do it,
          Yet am I loth for to goo to it.

Pedler   Ye have nat cause to feare to be bolde,
[to Palmer] For ye may be here uncontrolled.   455
[to Pardoner] And ye in this have good avauntage
          For lyeng is your comen usage.
[to Potycary] And you in lyenge be well spedde
          For all your craft doth stande in falshed.
          Ye nede nat care who shall begyn,   460
          For eche of you may hope to wyn.
          Now speke all thre evyn as ye fynde:
          Be ye agreed to folowe my mynde?

Palmer   Ye, by my trouth, I am contente.
Pardoner Now in good fayth, and I assente.   465

Potycary If I denyed I were a nody,
          For all is myne, by Goddes body!

                    Here the Potycary hoppeth.

Palmer   Here were a hopper to hop for the rynge!
          But syr, thys gere goth nat by hoppynge.
Potycary Syr, in this hopynge I wyll hop so well   C1
          That my tonge shal hop as well as my hele.   471
          Upon whiche hoppynge, I hope and nat doute it,
          To hop so that ye shall hope without it.

Palmer   Syr, I wyll neyther boste ne brawll,
          But take suche fortune as may fall,   475
          And yf ye wynne this maystry
          I wyll obaye you quietly.

                    123

	And sure I thynke that quietnesse,	
	In any man is great rychesse	
	In any maner company	480
	To rule or be ruled indifferently.	

Pardoner	By that bost thou semest a begger in dede.	
	What can thy quyetnesse helpe us at nede?	
	Yf we shulde starve, thou hast nat, I thynke,	
	One peny to bye us one potte of drynke.	485
	Nay, yf rychesse myght rule the roste,	
	Beholde what cause I have to boste:	
	Lo here be pardons halfe a dosyn –	
	For gostely ryches they have no cosyn,	
	And more over to me they brynge	490
	Sufficient succour for my lyvynge.	
	And here be relykes of suche a kynde	
	As in this worlde no man can fynde.	
	Knele down all thre, and when ye leve kyssynge,	
	Who lyste to offer shall have my blyssynge.	495
	Frendes, here shall ye se evyn anone	
	Of All Hallows the blessyd jaw bone –	
	Kys it hardely with good devocion!	

Potycary	Thys kysse shall brynge us muche promocyon –	
	Fogh! By Saynt Savyour, I never kyst a wars!	500
	Ye were as good kysse All Hallows ars,	
	For by All Halows, me thynketh	C1v
	That All Halows breth stynketh.	

Palmer	Ye judge All Halows breth unknowen –	
	Yf any breth stynke it is your owne.	505
Potycary	I knowe myne owne breth from All Halows,	
	Or els it were tyme to kysse the galows.	

Pardoner	Nay, syrs, beholde, here may ye se	
	The great toe of the Trinite.	
	Who to thys toe any money voweth,	510
	And ones may role it in his moueth,	
	All hys lyfe after, I undertake,	
	He shall be ryd of the toth ake.	

Potycary	I praye you torne that relyke aboute –	
	Other the Trinite had the goute	515
	Or elles bycause it is thre toes in one,	
	God made it muche as thre toes alone.	

[*Pardoner*]	Well lette that passe and loke upon thys.	
	Here is a relyke that doth nat mys	
	To helpe the leste as well as the moste:	520
	This is a buttocke bone of Pentecoste.	
Potycary	By Chryste, and yet for all your boste,	
	Thys relyke hath beshyten the roste.	

Pardoner	Marke well thys relyke, here is a whipper.	
	My frendes unfayned, here is a slypper	525
	Of one of the Seven Slepers, be sure.	
	Doutlesse thys kys shall do you great pleasure,	
	For all these two dayes it shall so ease you	
	That none other savours shall displease you.	

Potycary	All these two dayes? Nay, all thys two yere!	C2
	For all the savours that may come here	531
	Can be no worse; for, at a worde,	
	One of the seven slepers trode in a torde.	

| *Pedler* | Syr, me thynketh your devocion is but smal. | |

| *Pardoner* | Small! Mary, me thynketh he hath none at all. | 535 |

| *Potycary* | What the devyll care I what ye thynke? | |
| | Shall I prayse relykes when they stynke? | |

Pardoner	Here is an eye toth of the great Turke.	
	Whose eyes be ones sette on thys pece of worke	
	May happely lese parte of his eye syght,	540
	But nat all, tyll he be blynde out ryght.	

Potycary	What so ever any other man seeth,	
	I have no devocion to Turkes teeth;	
	For all though I never sawe a greter,	
	Yet me thynketh I have sene many better.	545

Pardoner	Here is a box full of humble bees	
	That stonge Eve as she sat on her knees	
	Tastynge the frute to her forbydden.	
	Who kysseth the bees within this hydden	
	Shall have as muche pardon of ryght	550
	As for any relyke he kyst thys nyght.	

| *Palmer* | Syr, I wyll kysse them with all my herte. | |

Potycary	Kysse them agayne and take my parte,
	For I am nat worthy. Nay, lette be,
	Those bees that stonge Eve shall nat stynge me. 555

Pardoner	Good frendes, I have [yest] here in thys glas
	Whiche on the drynke at the weddynge was C2v
	Of Adam and Eve undoutedly.
	If ye honor this relyke devoutly,
	All though ye thurste no whyt the lesse, 560
	Yet shall ye drynke the more, doutlesse.
	After whiche drynkynge ye shall be as mete
	To stande on your hede as on your fete.

Potycary	Ye, mary, now I can ye thanke –
	In presents of thys the reste be blanke. 565
	Wolde God this relyke had come rather!
	Kysse that relyke well, good father.
	Suche is the payne that ye palmers take
	To kysse the pardon bowle for the drynke sake.
	O holy yeste, that loketh full sowr and stale, 570
	For Goddes body helpe me to a cuppe of ale.
	The more I beholde the, the more I thurste,
	The oftener I kysse the, more lyke to burste.
	But syns I kysse the so devoutely
	Hyre me and helpe me with drynke tyll I die! 575
	What, so muche prayenge and so lytell spede!

Pardoner	Ye, for God knoweth whan it is nede
	To sende folkes drynke, but by Saynt Antony,
	I wene he hath sent you to muche all redy.

Potycary	If I have never the more for the, 580
	Then be the relykes no ryches to me
	Nor to thy selfe, excepte they be
	More benefycyall then I can se.
	Rycher is one boxe of this tryacle
	Then all thy relykes that do no myrakell. 585
	If thou haddest prayed but halfe so muche to me
	As I have prayed to thy relykes and the,
	Nothynge concernynge myne occupacion
	But streyght shulde have wrought in operacyon.
	And as in value I pas you an ace, C3
	Here lyeth muche rychesse in lytell space: 591
	I have a boxe of rebarb here,
	Whiche is as deynty as it is dere.

So helpe me God and hollydam,
Of this I wolde nat geve a dram   595
To the beste frende I have in Englandes grounde,
Though he wolde geve me twenty pounde.
For though the stomake do it abhor
It pourgeth you clene from the color
And maketh your stomake sore to walter,   600
That ye shall never come to the halter.

Pedler   Then is that medycyn a soverayn thynge
          To preserve a man from hangynge.

Potycary If ye wyll taste but thys crome that ye se,
          If ever ye be hanged, never truste me.   605
          Here have I diapompholicus,
          A speciall oyntement as doctours discuse
          For a fistela or a canker.
          Thys oyntement is even shot anker,
          For this medecyn helpeth one and other   610
          Or bryngeth them in case that they nede no other.
          Here is syrapus de Byzansis,
          A lytell thynge is inough of this,
          For even the weyght of one scryppull
          Shall make you stronge as a cryppull.   615
          Here be other, as diosfialios,
          Diagalanga and sticados,
          Blanka manna, diospoliticon,
          Mercury sublyme and metridaticon,
          Pelitory and arsefetita,   620
          Cassy and colloquintita;
          These be the thynges that breke all stryfe
          Betwene mannes sycknes and his lyfe.
          From all payne these shall you delever   C3v
          And set you even at reste for ever.   625
          Here is a medecyn no mo lyke the same,
          Whiche comenly is called thus by name:
          Alikakabus or Alkakengy –
          A goodly thynge for dogges that be mangy.
          Suche be these medycynes that I can   630
          Helpe a dogge as well as a man.
          Nat one thynge here partycularly
          But worketh universally,
          For it doth me as muche good when I sell it
          As all the byers that taste it or smell it.   635
          Now syns my medycyns be so specyall

127

	And in operacion so generall	
	And redy to worke when so ever they shall,	
	So that in ryches I am principall;	
	Yf any rewarde may entreat ye,	640
	I besech your mashyp be good to me	
	And ye shall have a boxe of marmelade,	
	So fyne that ye may dyg it with a spade.	

Pedler	Syr, I thanke you, but your rewarde	
	Is nat the thynge that I regarde.	645
	I muste and wyll be indifferent,	
	Wherfore procede in your intente.	

| *Potycary* | Nowe yf I wyst thys wysh no synne, | |
| | I wolde to God I myght begynne. | |

Pardoner	I am content that thou lye fyrste.	650
Palmer	Even so am I, and say thy worste.	
	Now let us here of all thy lyes	
	The greatest lye thou mayst devyse,	
	And in the fewyst wordes thou can.	
Potycary	Forsoth ye be an honest man.	C4

Palmer	There sayde ye muche but yet no lye.	656
Pardoner	Now lye ye bothe, by Our Lady,	
	Thou lyest in bost of hys honestie,	
	And he hath lyed in affyrmynge the.	

Potycary	Yf we both lye and ye say true,	660
	Then of these lyes your parte adew!	
	And yf ye wyn, make none avaunt	
	For ye are sure of one yll servaunte –	
	Ye may perceyve, by the wordes he gave,	
	He taketh your mashyp but for a knave.	665
	But who tolde true or lyed in dede,	
	That wyll I knowe or we procede.	
	Syr, after that I fyrste began	
	To prayse you for an honest man,	
	When ye affyrmed it for no lye,	670
	Now by our fayth, speke even truely:	
	Thought ye your affyrmacion true?	

Palmer	Ye mary, I, for I wolde ye knewe	
	I thynke my selfe an honest man.	
Potycary	What thought ye in the contrary than?	675

Pardoner	In that I sayde the contrary,
	I thynke from trouth I dyd nat vary.

Potycary	And what of my wordes?	
Pardoner	I thought ye lyed.	
Potycary	And so thought I, by God that dyed.	
	Nowe have you twayne, eche for hym selfe, layde	680
	That none hath lyed out but both truesayd;	C4v
	And of us twayne none hath denyed,	
	But both affyrmed that I have lyed.	
	Now syns both your trouth confes,	
	And that we both my lye so witnes	685
	That twayne of us thre in one agree;	
	And that the lyer the wynner must be,	
	Who coulde provyde suche evydens	
	As I have done in this pretens?	
	Me thynketh this mater sufficient	690
	To cause you to gyve judgement	
	And to gyve me the mastrye,	
	For ye perceyve these knaves can nat lye.	

Palmer	Though nother of us as yet had lyed,	
	Yet what we can do is untryed,	695
	For yet we have devysed nothynge,	
	But answered you and geven hyrynge.	

Pedler	Therfore I have devysed one waye	
	Wherby all thre your myndes may saye.	
	For eche of you one tale shall tell,	700
	And whiche of you telleth most mervell	
	And most unlyke to be true,	
	Shall most prevayle what ever ensew.	

Potycary	If ye be set in mervalynge,	
	Then shall ye here a mervaylouse thynge;	705
	And though in dede all be nat true,	
	Yet suer the most parte shall be new.	
	I dyd a cure no lenger ago	
	But *Anno domini millesimo*	
	On a woman yonge and so fayre	710
	That never have I sene a gayre –	
	God save all women from that lyknes!	
	This wanton had the fallen syknes,	
	Whiche by dissent came lynyally,	D1
	For her mother had it naturally,	715
	Wherfore this woman to recure	

129

It was more harde ye may be sure.
But though I boste my crafte is suche
That in suche thynges I can do muche,
How ofte she fell were muche to reporte.   720
But her hed so gydy and her helys so shorte,
That with the twynglynge of an eye
Downe wolde she falle evyn by and by.
But or she wolde aryse agayne,
I shewed muche practyse, muche to my payne.   725
For the tallest man within this towne
Shulde nat with ease have broken her sowne.
All though for lyfe I dyd nat doute her,
Yet dyd I take more payne about her
Then I wolde take with my owne syster.   730
Syr, at the last I gave her a glyster;
I thrust a thampyon in her tewell
And bad her kepe it for a jewell.
But I knewe it so hevy to cary
That I was sure it wolde nat tary,   735
For where gonpouder is ones fyerd
The tampyon wyll no lenger be hyerd.
Whiche was well sene in tyme of thys chaunce:
For when I had charged this ordynaunce,
Sodeynly, as it had thonderd,   740
Even at a clap losed her bumberd.
Now marke, for here begynneth the revell:
This tampion flew ten longe myle levell
To a fayre castell of lyme and stone –
For strength I knowe nat suche a one –   745
Whiche stode upon an hyll full hye,
At fote wherof a ryver ranne bye
So depe, tyll chaunce had it forbyden,
Well myght the Regent there have ryden.
But when this tampyon on thys castell lyght,   D1v
It put the castels so farre to flyght   751
That downe they came eche upon other,
No stone lefte standynge, by Goddes mother,
But rolled downe so faste the hyll
In suche a nomber and so dyd fyll   755
From botom to bryme, from shore to shore,
Thys forsayd ryver so depe before,
That who lyste nowe to walke therto,
May wade it over and wet no shoo.
So was thys castell layd wyde open   760
That every man myght se the token

130

	But in a good houre maye these wordes be spoken!	
	After the tampyon on the walles was wroken,	
	And pece by pece in peces broken,	
	And she delyvered, with suche violens	765
	Of all her inconveniens,	
	I left her in good helth and luste –	
	And so she doth contynew, I truste.	

Pedler   Syr, in your cure I can nothynge tell,

But to our purpose ye have sayd well.   770

Pardoner   Well syr, then marke what I can say.

I have ben a pardoner many a day,
And done greater cures gostely
Then ever he dyd bodely,
Namely thys one whiche ye shall here,   775
Of one departed within thys seven yere,
A frende of myne, and lykewyse I
To her agayne was as frendly,
Who fell so syke so sodeynly
That dede she was even by and by,   780
And never spake with preste nor clerke
Nor had no whyt of thys holy warke,
For I was thens – it coulde nat be.
Yet harde I say she asked for me.   D2
But when I bethought me howe thys chaunced,   785
And that I have to heven avaunced
So many soules to me but straungers,
And coude nat kepe my frende from daungers,
But she to dy so daungerously,
For her soule helth especyally –   790
That was the thynge that greved me soo,
That nothynge coulde release my woo,
Tyll I had tryed even out of hande
In what estate her soule dyd stande.
For whiche tryall, shorte tale to make,   795
I toke thys journey for her sake.
Geve eare, for here begynneth the story.

From hens I went to purgatory
And toke with me thys gere in my fyste,
Wherby I may do there what I lyste.   800
I knocked and was let in quyckly
But, lorde, how lowe the soules made curtesy!
And I to every soule agayne

Dyd gyve a beck, them to retayne,
And axed them thys question than: 805
Yf that the soule of suche a woman
Dyd late amonge them there appere?
Wherto they sayd she came nat here.
Then ferd I muche it was nat well.
Alas, thought I, she is in hell!   810
For with her lyfe I was so acqueynted,
That sure I thought she was nat saynted.
With thys it chaunced me to snese;
'Christe helpe!' quoth a soule, that ley for his fees.
'Those wordes,' quoth I, 'thou shalt nat lees.   815
Then, with these pardons of all degrees,
I payed hys tole and set hym so quyght
That strayt to heven he toke his flyght.
And I from thens to hell that nyght,
To help this woman yf I myght –   D2v
Nat as who sayth by outhorite,   821
But by the waye of entreate.
And fyrst the devyll that kept the gate
I came, and spake after this rate:
'All hayle, syr devyll,' and made lowe curtesy.   825
'Welcome,' quoth he, thys smillyngly –
He knew me well and I at laste
Remembred hym syns longe tyme paste.
For as good happe wolde have it chaunce,
Thys devyll and I were of olde acqueyntaunce,   830
For oft in the play of Corpus Cristi
He hath played the devyll at Coventry.
By his acqeyntaunce and my behavoure
He shewed to me ryght frendly favoure.
And to make my returne the shorter,   835
I sayd to this devyll, 'Good mayster porter,
For all olde love, yf it lye in your power,
Helpe me to speke with my lorde and your.'
'Be sure,' quoth he, 'no tongue can tell
What tyme thou coudest have come so well,   840
For thys daye Lucyfer fell,
Whiche is our festyvall in hell.
Nothynge unreasonable craved thys day
That shall in hell have any nay.
But yet be ware thou come nat in,   845
Tyll tyme thou may thy pasporte wyn.
Wherfore stande styll, and I wyll wyt
Yf I can get thy save condyt.'

132

He taryed nat but shortely gat it,
Under seale and the devyls hande at it   850
In ample wyse, as ye shall here.

Thus it began: 'Lucyfere,
By the power of God chyefe devyll of hell,
To all the devyls that there do dwell
And every of them, we sende gretynge,   855
Under streyght charge and commaundynge   D3
That they aydynge and assystent be
To suche a pardoner – and named me –
So that he may at lybertie
Passe save without hys jeopardy,   860
Tyll that he be from us extyncte
And clerely out of helles precincte;
And hys pardons to kepe savegarde,
We wyll they lye in the porters warde.
Gevyn in the fornes of our palys,   865
In our hye courte of maters of malys,
Suche a day and yere of our reyne.'

'God save the devyll!' quoth I for playne.
'I truste thys wrytynge to be sure?'
'Then put thy truste', quoth he, 'in eure,   870
Syns thou art sure to take no harme.'
Thys devyll and I walket arme in arme
So farre, tyll he had brought me thyther,
Where all the devyls of hell togyther
Stode in aray, in suche apparell   875
As for that day there metely fell:
Theyr hornes well gylt, theyr clowes full clene,
Theyr taylles well kempt and, as I wene,
With Sothery butter theyr bodyes anoynted –
I never sawe devyls so well appoynted.   880
The mayster devyll sat in his jacket,
And all the soules were playnge at racket;
None other rackettes they hadde in hande,
Save every soule a good fyre brande,
Wherwith they played so pretely   885
That Lucyfer laughed merely,
And all the resedew of the feendes
Dyd laugh full well togytther lyke frendes.
But of my frende I sawe no whyt,
Nor durst nat axe for her as yet.   890
Anone all this rout was brought in silens,

133

And I by an usher brought in presens.
Then to Lucyfer, low as I coude
I knelyd, whiche he so well alowde
That thus he beckte, and by Saynt Antony, 895
He smyled on me well favoredly,
Bendynge hys browes as brode as barne durres,
Shakynge hys eares as ruged as burres,
Rolynge hys yes as rounde as two bushels,
Flastynge the fyre out of his nose thryls, 900
Gnashynge hys teeth so vaynglorousely,
That me thought tyme to fall to flatery.
Wherwith I tolde as I shall tell:

'O plesant pycture, O Prince of Hell,
Feutred in fashyon abominable! 905
And syns that is inestimable
For me to prayse the worthyly,
I leve of prays, unworthy
To geve the prays, besechynge the
To heare my sewte, and then to be 910
So good to graunt the thynge I crave.
And to be shorte, thys wolde I have:
The soule of one whiche hyther is flytted,
Delivered hens and to me remitted.
And in thys doynge, though al be nat quyt, 915
Yet some parte I shall deserve it,
As thus: I am a pardoner
And over soules as a controller,
Thorough out the erth my power doth stande,
Where many a soule lyeth on my hande 920
That spede in maters as I use them,
As I receyve them or refuse them;
Wherby, what tyme thy pleasure is,
I shall requyte any part of thys:
The leste devyll here that can come thyther 925
'Nowe,' quoth the devyll, 'we are well pleased.
Shall chose a soule and brynge hym hyther'.
What is hys name thou woldest have eased?'
'Nay,' quoth I, 'be it good or evyll,
My comynge is for a she devyll!' 930
'What calste her' quoth he, 'thou horyson?'
'Forsoth,' quoth I, 'Margery Coorson.'
'Now by our honour,' sayd Lucyfer,
'No devyll in hell shall witholde her.
And yf thou woldest have twenty mo, 935
Were nat for justyce they shulde goo;

For all we devyls within thys den
Have more to do with two women
Then with all the charge we have besyde.
Wherfore, yf thou our frende wyll be tryed,   940
Aply thy pardons to women so
That unto us there come no mo.'

To do my beste I promysed by othe,
Whiche I have kepte, for as the fayth goth
At thys dayes to heven I do procure   945
Ten women to one man, be sure.
Then of Lucyfer my leve I toke,
And streyght unto the mayster coke
I was hadde into the kechyn –
For Margaryes offyce was ther in.   950
All thynge handled there discretely,
For every soule bereth offyce metely,
Whiche myght be sene to se her syt
So bysely turnynge of the spyt.
For many a spyt here hath she turned,   955
And many a good spyt hath she burned,
And many a spyt full hote hath tosted,
Before the meat coulde be halfe rosted.
And or the meate were halfe rosted in dede,
I toke her then fro the spyt for spede.   960
But when she sawe thys brought to pas,
To tell the joy wherin she was,
And of all the devyls for joy how they
Dyd rore at her delyvery,   D4v
And how the cheynes in hell dyd rynge,   965
And how all the soules therin dyd synge,
And how we were brought to the gate,
And how we toke our leve therat,
Be suer lacke of tyme sufferyth nat
To reherse the twentieth parte of that.   970
Wherfore, thys tale to conclude brevely,
Thys woman thanked me chyefly
That she was ryd of thys endles deth,
And so we departed on New Market heth.
And yf that any man do mynde her,   975
Who lyste to seke her, there shall he fynde her.

Pedler   Syr, ye have sought her wonders well,
And where ye founde her as ye tell,
To here the chaunce ye founde in hell,
I fynde ye were in great parell.   980

135

Palmer	His tale is all muche parellous,	
	But parte is muche more mervaylous,	
	As where he sayde the devyls complayne	
	That women put them to suche payne	
	By theyr condicions so croked and crabbed,	985
	Frowardly fashonde, so waywarde and wrabbed,	
	So farre in devision and sturrynge suche stryfe	
	That all the devyls be wery of theyr lyfe.	
	This in effect he tolde for trueth,	
	Wherby muche murvell to me ensueth,	990
	That women in hell suche shrewes can be	
	And here so gentyll as farre as I se.	
	Yet have I sene many a myle	
	And many a woman in the whyle,	
	Nat one good cytye, towne, nor borough	995
	In cristendom but I have ben through,	
	And this I wolde ye shulde understande,	
	I have sene women fyve hundred thousande	E1
	[ ]	[998a]
	And oft with them have longe tyme maryed,	
	Yet in all places where I have ben,	1000
	Of all the women that I have sene,	
	I never sawe nor knewe, to my consyens,	
	Any one woman out of paciens.	
Potycary	By the masse, there is a great lye!	
Pardoner	I never harde a greater, by Our Lady.	1005
Pedler	A greater! Nay, knowe ye any so great?	
Palmer	Syr, whether that I lose or get,	
	For my parte judgement shall be prayed.	
Pardoner	And I desyer as he hath sayd.	
Potycary	Procede and ye shall be obeyed.	1010
Pedler	Then shall nat judgement be delayd.	
	Of all these thre, yf eche mannes tale	
	In Poules Churche yarde were set on sale	
	In some mannes hande, that hath the sleyghte,	
	He shulde sure sell these tales by weyght,	1015
	For as they wey so be they worth.	
	But whiche weyth beste – to that now forth.	
	Syr, all the tale that ye dyd tell	
	I bere in mynde, and yours as well,	
	And as ye sawe the mater metely,	1020
	So lyed ye bothe well and discretely.	

Yet were your lyes with the lest, truste me,
For yf ye had sayd ye had made fle
Ten tampyons out of ten womens tayles
Ten tymes ten myle to ten castels or jayles, 1025
And fyll ten ryvers ten tymes so depe
As ten of that whiche your castell stones dyde kepe, E1v
Or yf ye ten tymes had bodely
Fet ten soules out of purgatory
And ten tymes so many out of hell, 1030
Yet, by these ten bonnes, I coulde ryght well
Ten tymes sonner all that have beleved,
Then the tenth parte of that he hath meved.

Potycary Two knaves before one lacketh two knaves of fyve,
Then one and then one, and bothe knaves alyve! 1035
Then two and then two and thre at a cast,
Thou knave and thou knave and thou knave at laste!

Nay knave, yf ye tryme by nomber,
I wyll as knavyshly you accomber.
Your mynde is all on your pryvy tythe, 1040
For all in ten me thynketh your wit lythe.
Now ten tymes I beseche hym that hye syttes,
Thy wyfes ten commaundementes may serch thy fyve wittes!
Then ten of my tordes in ten of thy teth,
And ten of thy nose, whiche every man seth, 1045
And twenty tymes ten, this wyshe I wolde
That thou haddest ben hanged at ten yere olde –
For thou goest about to make me a slave.
I wyll thou knowe yf I am a gentylman, knave –
And here is an other shall take my parte! 1050
Pardoner Nay, fyrste I beshrew your knaves herte
Or I take parte in your knavery,
I wyll speke fayre by Our Lady:
Syr, I beseche your mashyp to be
As good as ye can be to me. 1055

Pedler I wolde be glade to do you good
And hym also, be he never so wood.
But dout you nat, I wyll now do
The thynge my consciens ledeth me to.
Both your tales I take farre impossyble, E2
Yet take I his farther incredyble; 1061
Nat only the thynge it selfe alloweth it,
But also the boldenes therof avoweth it.

137

I knowe nat where your tale to trye,
Nor yours, but in hell or purgatorye.   1065
But hys boldnes has faced a lye
That may be tryed evyn in thys companye.
As yf ye lyste to take thys order
Amonge the women in thys border,
Take thre of the yongest and thre of the oldest,   1070
Thre of the hotest and thre of the coldest,
Thre of the wysest and thre of the shrewdest,
[Three of the cheefest and thre of the lewdest,   1072a]
Thre of the lowest and thre of the hyest,
Thre of the farthest and thre of the nyest,
Thre of the fayrest and thre of the maddest,   1075
Thre of the fowlest and thre of the saddest;
And when all these threes be had a sonder,
Of eche thre two justly by nomber
Shall be founde shrewes – excepte thys fall,
That ye hap to fynde them shrewes all.   1080
Hym selfe for trouth all this doth knowe
And oft hath tryed some of thys rowe,
And yet he swereth by his consciens,
He never saw woman breke paciens.
Wherfore consydered with true entente,   1085
Hys lye to be so evident
And to appere so evydently,
That both you affyrmed it a ly.
And that my consciens, so depely,
So depe hath sought thys thynge to try,   1090
And tryed it with mynde indyfferent,
Thus I awarde by way of judgement:
Of all the lyes ye all have spent,
Hys lye to be most excellent.

Palmer/ Syr, though ye were bounde of equyte   E2v
         To do as ye have done to me,   1096
         Yet do I thanke you of your payne,
         And wyll requyte some parte agayne.
Pardoner Mary, syr, ye can no les do
         But thanke hym as muche as it cometh to,   1100
         And so wyll I do for my parte.
         Now a vengeaunce on thy knaves harte!
         I never knewe pedler a judge before,
         Nor never wyll truste pedlynge knave more.
         What doest thou there, thou horson nody?   1105

138

Potycary	By the masse, lerne to make curtesy.
	Curtesy before, and curtesy behynde hym,
	And then on eche syde the devyll blynde hym!
	Nay, when I have it perfytly
	Ye shall have the devyll and all of curtesy. 1110
	But it is nat sone lerned, brother,
	One knave to make curtesy to another.
	Yet when I am angry that is the worste –
	I shall call my mayster 'knave' at the fyrste.
Palmer	Then wolde some mayster perhappes clowt ye. 1115
	But as for me, ye nede nat doute ye;
	For I had lever be without ye
	Then have suche besynesse aboute ye.
Pardoner	So helpe me God, so were ye better
	What, shulde a begger be a jetter? 1120
	It were no whyt your honestie
	To have us twayne jet after ye.
Potycary	Syr, be ye sure he telleth you true;
	Yf we shulde wayte, thys wolde ensew:
	It wolde be sayd, truste me at a worde, 1125
	Two knaves made curtesy to the thyrde. E3
Pedler	Now by my trouth, to speke my mynde,
	Syns they be so loth to be assyned,
	To let them lose I thynke it beste –
	And so shall ye lyve beste in rest. 1130
Palmer	Syr, I am nat on them so fonde
	To compell them to kepe theyr bonde
	And syns ye lyste nat to wayte on me
	I clerely of waytynge dyscharge ye.
Pardoner	Mary syr, I hertely thanke you. 1135
Potycary	And I lyke wyse, I make God avowe.
Pedler	Now be ye all evyn as ye begoon:
	No man hath loste nor no man hath woon.
	Yet in the debate wherwith ye began,
	By waye of advyse I wyll speke as I can. 1140
[to Palmer]	I do perceyve that pylgrymage
	Is chyefe the thynge ye have in usage,
	Wherto in effecte for love of Chryst
	Ye have, or shulde have bene, entyst,
	And who so doth with suche entent 1145
	Doth well declare hys tyme well spent.

139

[to Pardoner] And so do ye in your pretence,
             If ye procure thus indulgence
             Unto your neyghbours charytably,
             For love of them in God onely.   1150
             All thys may be ryght well applyed
             To shewe you both well occupyed.
             For though ye walke nat bothe one waye,
             Yet walkynge thus, thys dare I saye:
             That bothe your walkes come to one ende.   1155
             And so for all that do pretende,
             By ayde of Goddes grace, to ensewe   E3v
             Any maner kynde of vertue –
             As some great almyse for to gyve,
             Some in wyllfull povertie to lyve,   1160
             Some to make hye wayes and suche other warkes,
             And some to mayntayne prestes and clarkes
             To synge and praye for soule departed –
             These with all other vertues well marked,
             All though they be of sondry kyndes,   1165
             Yet be they nat used with sondry myndes,
             But as God only doth all those move;
             So every man, onely for his love,
             With love and dred obediently
             Worketh in these vertues unyformely.   1170
             Thus every vertue, yf we lyste to scan,
             Is pleasaunt to God and thankfull to man.
             And who that by grace of the holy goste
             To any one vertue is moved moste,
             That man by that grace that one apply   1175
             And therin serve God most plentyfully.
             Yet nat that one so farre wyde to wreste,
             So lykynge the same to myslyke the reste.
             For who so wresteth hys worke is in vayne.
             And even in that case I perceyve you twayne   1180
             Lykynge your vertue in suche wyse
             That eche others vertue you do dyspyse.
             Who walketh thys way for God wolde fynde hym,
             The farther they seke hym, the farther behynde hym.
             One kynde of vertue to dyspyse another   1185
             Is lyke as the syster myght hange the brother.

Potycary   For fere lest suche parels to me myght fall,
             I thanke God I use no vertue at all.

Pedler	That is of all the very worste waye!	
	For more harde it is, as I have harde saye,	1190
	To begynne vertue where none is pretendyd,	E4
	Then where it is begonne, the abuse to be mended.	
	How be it ye be nat all to begynne,	
	One syne of vertue ye are entred in,	
	As thys: I suppose ye dyd saye true,	1195
	In that ye sayd ye use no vertue.	
	In the whiche wordes, I dare well reporte,	
	Ye are well beloved of all thys sorte,	
	By your raylynge here openly	
	At pardons and relyques so leudly.	1200

Potycary	In that I thynke my faute nat great,	
	For all that he hath I knowe conterfete.	

Pedler	For his and all other that ye knowe fayned,	
	Ye be nother counceled nor constrayned	
	To any suche thynge in any suche case	1205
	To gyve any reverence in any suche place.	
	But where ye dout, the truthe nat knowynge,	
	Belevynge the beste, good may be growynge.	
	In judgynge the beste no harme at the leste;	
	In judgynge the worste, no good at the beste.	1210
	But beste in these thynges it semeth to me,	
	To make no judgement upon ye.	
	But as the churche doth judge or take them,	
	So do ye receyve or forsake them.	
	And so be sure ye can nat erre,	1215
	But may be a frutfull folower.	

Potycary	Go ye before and, as I am true man,	
	I wyll folow as faste as I can.	

Pardoner	And so wyll I, for he hath sayd so well,	
	Reason wolde we shulde folowe hys counsell.	1220

Palmer	Then to our reason God gyve us his grace	
	That we may folowe with fayth so fermely	E4v
	His commaundementes, that we maye purchace	
	Hys love, and so consequently	
	To byleve hys churche, faste and faythfully,	1225
	So that we may accordynge to his promyse	
	Be kepte out of errour in any wyse.	

And all that hath scapet us here by neglygence,
We clerely revoke and forsake it.
To passe the tyme in thys without offence   1230
Was the cause why the maker dyd make it.
And so we humbly beseche you take it,
Besechynge our lorde to prosper you all
In the fayth of hys churche universall.

FINIS

IMPRYNTED AT LONDON IN FLETESTRETE AT THE
SYGNE OF THE GEORGE BY WYLLYAM
MYDDYLTON.

A PLAY OF LOVE

The Names of the Players

Lover not loved
Loved not lovyng
Lover loved
No lover nor loved

A PLAY OF LOVE. *A newe and a mery enterlude concernyng pleasure and*
payne in love. Made by Johan Heywood. The players names: A man, a
lover not beloved. A woman beloved not lovyng. A man, a lover and
beloved. The vyse, nother lover nor beloved.

[Lover not loved enters.]   A2

Lover not loved	Lo syr, who so that loketh here for curtesy

Lo syr, who so that loketh here for curtesy
And seth me seme as one pretendyng none,
But as unthought uppon thus sodenly
Approcheth the myddys amonge you everychone
And of you all seyth nought to any one,   5
May thynke me rewde, perceyvyng of what sorte
Ye seme to be and of what stately porte.

But I beseche you in most humble wyse
To omytte dyspleasure and pardon me;
My maner is to muse and to devyse   10
So that some tyme my selfe may cary me
My selfe knowyth not where, and I asure ye
So hath my selfe done nowe, for our Lorde wot
Where I am or what ye be – I knowe not.

Or whence I cam, or whyther I shall: 15
All this in maner as unknowen to me.
But evyn as fortune guydeth my fote to fale
So wander I, yet where so ever I be
And whom or howe many so ever I se,
As one person to me is everychone,   20
So every place to me but as one.

And for that one persone every place seke I,
Which one ones founde, I fynde of all the rest
Not one myssyng, and in the contrary
That one absent, though that there were here prest   25
All the creatures lyvyng most and lest,
Yet lackyng her I shulde and ever shall
Be as alone syns she to me is all.

And alone is she without comparyson
Consernyng the gyftys gyvyn by nature;   30
In favour, fayrnes and porte as of person
No lyfe beryth the lyke of that creature,
Nor no tonge can attayne to put in ure
Her to dyscryve, for howe can wordes expres
That thyng, the full wherof no thought can ges?   35

And as it is thyng inestymable
To make reporte of her bewty fully,
So is my love towarde her unable
To be reportyd, as who seyth ryghtly,
For my soole servyce and love to that lady   A2v
Is gyven under such haboundant fashyon   41
That no tonge therof can make ryght relashyon.

Wherin I suppose this well supposed
Unto you all, that syns she perceyvyng
As much of my love as can be dysclosed,   45
Evyn of very ryght in recompensyng
She ought for my love agayne to be lovyng.
For what more ryght to graunt when love love requireth
Then love for love, when love nought els desyreth?

But evyn as farre wurs as otherwyse then so   50
Stande I in case, in maner desperate.
No tyme can tyme my sewt to ease my wo
Before none to erely and all tymes els to late.
Thus tyme out of tyme mystymeth my rate,
For tyme to bryng tyme to hope of any grace,   55
That tyme tymyth no tyme in any tyme or place.

Wherby tyll tyme have tyme so farre extyncte
That deth may determyne my lyfe thus dedly,
No tyme can I reste. Alas I am so lyncte
To greves both so greate and also many   60
That by the same I say and wyll veryfy
Of all paynes the moste incomparable payne
Is to be a lover not lovyd agayne.

The woman belovyd not lovyng entreth.

Loved not lovyng Syr, as touchyng those wordes of comparyson
Whiche ye have seyd and wolde seme to veryfye,   65
If it may please you to stande therupon
Hearyng and answeryng me pacyently,
I doubt not by the same incontynently
Your selfe to see, by wordes that shall ensue,
The contrary of your wordes veryfyed for true.   70

Lover not loved Fayre lady, pleasyth it you to repayre nere
And in this cause to shewe cause reasonable
Wherby cause of reformacyon may appere;
Of reason I muste and wylbe reformable.

145

Loved not lovyng	Well syns ye pretende to be confyrmable 75
	To reason, in avoydyng circumstaunce,
	Brefely by reason I shall the truthe avaunce.

Ye be a lover no whyt lovyd agayne,   A3
And I am lovyd of whom I love nothyng:
Then standyth our question betwene these twayne   80
Of lovyng not lovyd, or lovyd not lovyng,
Which is the case moste paynfull in sufferyng
Wherto I saye that the moste payne doth move
To those belovyd of whome they can not love.

Lover not loved	Those wordes approved, lo, myght make a chaunge 85
	Of myne opinion, but verely
	The case as ye put it I thynke more straunge
	Then true, for though the belovyd party
	Can not love agayne, yet possybly
	Can I not thynke, nor I thynke never shall, 90
	That to be lovyd can be any payne at all.

Loved not lovyng	That reason perceyvyd and receyvyd for trouth
	From proper comparyson sholde clere confounde me:
	Betwene payne and no payne, no such comparyson growth.
	Then, or I can on comparyson grounde me, 95
	To prove my case paynefull ye have fyrst bounde me:
	To which syns ye dryve me by your denyall,
	Marke what ensueth before ferther tryall.

I saye I am lovyd of a certayne man
Whom for no sewt I can favour agayne   100
And that have I tolde hym syns his sewt began,
A thousand tymes but every tyme in vayne.
For never seaseth his tonge to complayne,
And ever one tale whiche I never can flee,
For ever in maner where I am is he.   105

Nowe if you to here one thyng every where
Contrary to your appetyte sholde be led,
Were it but a mouse, lo, sholde pepe in your ere
Or alway to harpe on a crust of bred,
Howe coulde you lyke such harpyng at your hed?   110

Lover not loved	Somewhat dyspleasaunt it were, I not deny.
Loved not lovyng	Then somewhat payneful as well seyd, say I.

Dyspleasure and payne be thynges joyntly anext,
For as it is dyspleasaunt in payne to be,
So it is paynefull in dyspleasure to be vext.   115
Thus by dyspleasure in payne ye confes me,
Wherby syns ye part of my payne do see
In my ferther payne I shall nowe declare
That payne by whyche with your payne I compare.   A3v

Smale were the quantyte of my paynfull smerte   120
Yf hys jangelynge percyd no further then myne erys,
But thorough myne erys dyrectly to myne harte
Percyth his wordys evyn lyke as many sperys;
By whyche I have spent so many and suche terys
That were they all red as they be all whyte,   125
The blood of my harte had be gone or thys quyte.

And almoste in case as though it were gone
Am I, except hys sewt take end shortely
For it doth lyke me evyn lyke as one
Shold offer me servyce most humbly   130
Wyth an axe in hys hande, contynually
Besechynge me gentylly that thys myght be sped
To graunte hym my good wyll to stryke of my hed.

I alledge for generall thys one symylytude,
Avoydyng rehersale of paynes partyculer,   135
To abreveate the tyme and to exclude
Surplusage of wordes in thys our mater;
By whyche ensaumple yf ye consydere
Ryghtly my case, at lest wyse ye may see
My payne as paynfull as your payne can bee.   140

And yet for shorter end, put case that your payne
Were oft tymes more sharpe and sore in degre
Then myne ys at any tyme, yet wyll I prove playne
My payne at lenght suffycyent to match ye.
Whiche profe to be true your selfe shall agre   145
Yf your affeccyon in that I shall resyght
May suffer your reason to understande ryght.

You stand in plesure, havyng your love in syght,
And in her absens hope of syght agayne
Kepyth moste tymes possessyon of some delyght.   150
Thus have you oft tymes some way ease of payne,
And I never no way, for when I do remayne

147

In hys presens, in dedly payne I sojorne,
And absent, halfe ded in feare of hys retourne.

Syns presens nor absens absenteth my payne   155
But alway the same to me is present,
And that by presens and hope of presens agayne
Ther doth appere myche of your tyme spente
Out of payne, me thynke this consequent,   A4
That my payne may well by meane of the length   160
Compare with your shorter payne of more strength.

Lover not loved   Maystres, if your long payne be no stronger
Then is your longe reason agaynst my shorte payne,
Ye lacke no lycklyhod to lyve much longer
Then he that wolde stryke of your hed so fayne.   165
Yet lest ye wolde note me your wordes to dysdayne,
I am content to agree for a season
To graunt and enlarge your latter reason.

Amytte by her presens halfe my tyme pleasaunt
And all your tyme as paynefull as in case can be,   170
Yet your payne to be most, reason wyl not graunt;
And for ensample I put case that ye
Stood in colde water all a day to the kne,
And I halfe the same day to myd leg in the fyer:
Wolde ye chaunge places with me for the dryer?   175

Loved not lovyng   Nay that wolde I not, be ye assuered.
Lover not loved   Forsoth and my payne above yours is as yll
As fyre above water thus to be endewred.
Came my payne but at tymes and yours contynue styll,
Yet shold myne many weys, to whome can skyll,   180
Shewe yours in comparyson betwene the twayne
Skantly able for a shadowe to my payne.

Felt ye but one pang such as I fele many –
One pang of dyspayre, or one pang of desyre,
One pang of one dyspleasaunt loke of her eye,   185
One pang of one worde of her mouth as in yre,
Or in restraynt of her love which I requyre –
One pang of all these, felt ones in all your lyfe,
Sholde quayle your opinyon and quench all our stryfe.

Which panges I say, admytted short as ye lyst,   190
And all my tyme besyde pleasaunt as ye please,
Yet coulde not the shortnes the sharpnes so resyst

148

The percyng of my harte in the lest of all these;
But much it overmacheth all your dysease,
For no whyt in effecte is your case dyspleasaunt   195
But to deny a thyng which ye lyst not to graunt.

Or to here a sewter by dayly peticyon,
In humble maner as wyt can devyse,
Requyre a thyng so standyng in condyshyon   A4v
As no porcyon of all his enterpryse   200
Without your consent can spede in any wyse.
This sewt thus attempted never so long,
Doubt ye no deth tyll your payne be more strong.

Nowe syns in this mater betwene us dysputed,
Myne admyttance of your wordes notwithstandyng,   205
I have thus fully your part confuted,
What can ye say nowe I come to denyeng
Your pryncyple, graunted in my foresayeng
Which was this, by the presens of my lady
I graunted you halfe my tyme spent pleasauntly?   210

Although myne affeccyon ledyth me to consent
That her selde presens is my relefe onely,
Yet as in reason appereth, all my torment
Bred by her presens – and marke this cause why:
Before I sawe her I felt no malydy,   215
And syns I sawe her I never was fre
From twayne the greatest paynes that in love be.

Desyre is the fyrst upon my fyrst syght,
And despayre the nexte upon my fyrst sewt.
For upon her fyrst answere hope was put to flyght,   220
And never came syns in place to dyspewt.
Howe bryngeth then her presens to me any frewt?
For hopeles and helpeles, in flames of desyre
And droppes of despayre I smolder in fyre.

These twayne beyng endeles syns they began,   225
And both by the presens of her wholly
Begon and contynued, I wonder if ye can
Speke any worde more, but yelde ymmedyately:
For had I no mo paynes but these, yet clerely
A thousande tymes more is my grefe in these twayne   230
Then yours in all the case by which ye complayne.

149

Loved not lovyng	That is as ye say, but not as I suppose
	Nor as the treuth is, which your selfe myght se
	By reasons that I coulde and wolde dysclose,
	Savyng that I see such parcyalyte 235
	On your parte, that we shall never agre,
	Unlesse ye wyll admyt some man indyfferent
	Indyfferently to heare us, and so gyve judgement.

Lover not loved	Agred! For though the knowledge of all my payne B1
	Ease my payne no whyt, yet shall it declare 240
	Great cause of abashement in you to complayne
	In counterfet paynes with my payne to compare:
	But here is no judge mete, we must seke elles where.
Loved not lovyng	I holde me content the same to condyscende,
	Please it you to set forth and I shall attend. 245

Here they go both out and the lover belovyd
entreth with a songe.

Lover loved	By comen experyence who can deny
	Inpossibylyte for man to showe
	His inward entent, but by sygnes outwardly,
	As wrytyng, speche, or countenaunce, wherby doth growe
	Outwarde perceyvynge inwardly to knowe 250
	Of every secrecy in mans brest wrought,
	Fro man unto man the effecte of eche thought.

These thynges well weyd in many thynges shewe nede
In our outwarde sygnes to shewe us, so that playne
Accordyng to our thoughtes, wordes and sygnes procede;   255
For in outwarde sygnes where men are sene to fayne
What credence in man to man may remayne?
Mans inwarde mynde with outward sygnes to fable,
May sone be more comen than commendable.

Much are we lovers then to be commendyd,   260
For love his apparence dyssembleth in no wyse,
But as the harte felyth, lyke sygnes alway pretendyd,
Who fayne in apparence are loves mortall enmyes
As in dyspayr of spede who that can myrth devyse
Or havyng graunt of grace can shewe them as morners,   265
Such be no lovers but evyn very skorners.

The true lovers harte that can not obteyne
Is so tormentyd that all the body
Is evermore so compelde to complayne,

That soner may the sufferer hyde the fury   270
Of a fervent fever, then of that malady
By any power humayne he possyble may
Hyde the leste payne of a thousande I dare say.

And he who in lovyng hath lot to suche lucke
That love for love of his love be founde,   275
Shalbe of power evyn as easely to plucke
The mone in a momet with a fynger to grounde,
As of his joy to enclose the rebounde,   Blv
But that the refleccion therof from his harte
To his beholders shall shyne in eche parte.   280

Thus be a lover in joy or in care,
All though wyll and wyt his estate wolde hyde,
Yet shall his semblaunce as a dyale declare
Howe the clocke goeth, which may be well applyed
In abrygement of circumstaunce for a guyed,   285
To leade you in fewe wordes by my byhavour
To knowe me in grace of my ladyes favour.

For beyng a lover, as I am in dede,
And therto dysposyd thus pleasauntly
Is a playne apparence of my such spede   290
As I in love cowld wysh, and undoubtedly
My love is requyted so lovyngly,
That in every thyng that may delyght my mynde
My wyt can not wyshe it so well as I fynde.

Which thyng at full consydred, I suppose   295
That all the whole worlde must agree in one voyce,
I beyng beloved as I nowe dysclose,
Of one beyng chefe of all the hole choyce,
Must have incomparable cause to rejoyce;
For the hyest pleasure that man may obtayne   300
Is to be a lover beloved agayne.

Nother lover nor loved entreth.

No lover nor loved   Nowe God you good evyn, mayster woodcock.
Lover loved   Cometh of rudenesse or lewdenesse that mock?
No lover nor loved   Come wherof it shall, ye come of such stock
                     That God you good evyn, mayster woodcock.   305
Lover loved   This losell by lyke hath lost his wyt.
No lover nor loved   Nay, nay, mayster woodcock, not a whyt,
                     I have knowen you for a woodcock or this,

151

	Or els lyke a woodcock I take you a mys.	
	But though for a woodcock ye deny the same,	310
	Yet shall your wyt wytnes you mete for that name.	
Lover loved	Howe so?	
No lover nor loved	Thus lo:	
	I do perceyve by your formare proces	
	That ye be a lover, wherto ye confes	315
	Your selfe beloved in as lovyng wyse	
	As by wyt and wyll ye can wyshe to devyse;	
	Concludyng therin determinately	B2
	That of all pleasures plesaunt to the body,	
	The hyest pleasure that man may obtayne	320
	Is to be a lover beloved agayne:	
	In which conclusyon, before all this flock,	
	I shall prove you playne as wyse as a woodcock.	
Lover loved	And me thynke this woodcock is tornd on thy syde,	
	Contrary to curtsy and reason to use	325
	Thus rudely to rayle or any worde be tryed	
	In profe of thy parte, wherby I do refuse	
	To answere the same. Thou canst not excuse	
	Thy foly in this, but if thou wylt say ought,	
	Assay to say better for this seyng is nought.	330
No lover nor loved	Well, syns it is so that ye be dyscontent	
	To be called fole or further matter be spent,	
	Wyll ye gyve me leave to call ye fole anone,	
	When your selfe perceyveth that I have proved you one?	
Lover loved	Ye, by my soule, and wyll take it in good worth.	335
No lover nor loved	Nowe, by my fathers soule, then wyll we evyn forth.	
	That parte rehersed of your seyng or this	
	Of all our debate the onely cause is.	
	For where ye afore have fastly affirmed	
	That such as be lovers agayne beloved	340
	Stande in most pleasure that to man may move,	
	That tale to be false truthe shal truely prove.	
Lover loved	What folke above those lyve more plesauntly?	
No lover nor loved	What folke? Mary, evyn such folke as am I.	
Lover loved	Beyng no lover what man may ye be?	345
No lover nor loved	No lover? No, by God, I warraunt ye	
	I am no lover in such maner ment	
	As doth appere in this purpose present,	
	For as touchyng women, go where I shall,	
	I am at one poynt with women all:	350
	The smothest, the smyrkest, the smallest,	

The trewest, the trymest, the tallest,
The wysest, the wylyest, the wyldest,
The meryest, the manerlyest, the myldest,
The strangest, the strayghtest, the strongest,   355
The lustyest, the lest, or the longest,
The rashest, the ruddyest, the roundest,
The sagest, the salowest, the soundest,
The coyest, the curstest, the coldest,
The bysyest, the bryghtest, the boldest,   360
The thankfullest, the thynest, the thyckest,
The sayntlyest, the sewrest, the syckest;
Take these with all the reste and of everychone
So God be my helpe I love never one.   B2v

Lover loved	Then I beseche the this one thynge tell me:	365
	Howe many women thynkest thou doth love the?	
No lover nor loved	Syr, as I be saved, by ought I can prove	
	I am beloved evyn lyke as I love.	
Lover loved	Then as appereth by those wordes rehersed,	
	Thou art nother lover nor beloved.	370
No lover nor loved	Nother lover nor beloved that is even true.	
Lover loved	Syns that is true I merveyll what can ensue	
	For profe of thy parte in that thou madest avaunt	
	Of both our estates to prove thyne most plesaunt.	
No lover nor loved	My parte for most plesaunt may sone be gest	375
	By my contynuall quyetyd rest.	
Lover loved	Beyng no lover who may quyet be?	
No lover nor loved	Nay, beyng a lover what man is he	
	That is quyet?	
Lover loved	Mary I.	
No lover nor loved	Mary, ye lye!	
Lover loved	What! Pacyens my frende, ye are to hasty;	380
	If ye wyll paciently marke what I shall say	
	Your selfe shall perceyve me in quyet alway.	
No lover nor loved	Say what thou wyll, and I therin protest	
	To beleve no worde thou sayst, most nor lest.	
Lover loved	Than we twayne shall talke both in vayne I see,	385
	Except our mater awarded may be	
	By judgement of some indifferent herer.	
No lover nor loved	Mary, go thou and be an inquerer,	
	And if thou canst bryng one any thyng lyckly,	
	He shalbe admytted for my parte quyckly.	390
Lover loved	Nowe by the good God, I graunt to agree;	
	For be thou assewred, it scorneth me	
	That thou shuldest compare in pleasure to be	

	Lyke me, and surely I promyse the	
	One way or other I wyll fynde redres.	395
No lover nor loved	Fynde the best and next way thy wyt can ges	
	And except your nobs for malous do nede ye	
	Make brefe returne – a felyshyp, spede ye!	

The lover loved goth out.

No lover nor loved	My merveyll is no more then my care is small	
	What knave this foole shall bryng, beyng not perciall.	400
	And yet be he false and a folyshe knave to –	
	So that it be not to much a do	
	To bryng a daw to here and speke ryght –	
	I forse for no man the worth of a myte.	
	And syns my doubt is so small in good spede	405
	What shulde my studye be more then my nede?	B3
	Tyll tyme I perceyve this woodcock commyng	
	My parte hereof shulde pas evyn in mummyng –	
	Savyng for pastyme, syns I consyder	
	He beyng a lover and all his mater	410
	To depende on love, and contrary I	
	No lover, by which all such standyng by	
	As favour my parte, may feare me to weyke	
	Agaynst the lovyng of this lover to speyke,	
	I shall for your confort declare suche a story	415
	As shall perfetly plant in your memory	
	That I have knowledge in lovers laws	
	As depe as some dosyn of those dotyng daws.	
	Which tolde, all ye whose fansyes styck nere me	
	Shall knowe it causeles in this case to feare me,	420
	For though as I shewe I am no lover now	
	Nor never have ben, yet shall I shewe yow	
	How that I ones chaunced to take in hande	
	To fayne my selfe a lover, ye shall understande,	
	Towarde such a swetyng as by swete Sent Savour	425
	I knowe not the lyke in fashyon and favour.	
	And to begyn	
	At settyng in	
	Fyrst was her skyn	
	Whyt, smoth and thyn,	430
	And every vayne	
	So blewe sene playne,	
	Her golden heare –	
	To see her weare,	
	Her weryng gere –	435

Alas I fere
To tell all to you:
I shall undo you.
Her eye so rollyng,
Ech hart controllyng,   440
Her nose not long,
Nor stode not wrong
Her fynger typs
So clene she clyps,
Her rosy lyps,   445
Her chekes gossyps;
So fayre, so ruddy,
It axeth studdy
The hole to tell
It dyd excell,   450
It was so made
That evyn the shade   B3v
At every glade
Wolde hartes invade;
The paps so small   455
And rounde with all,
The wast not myckyll
But it was tyckyll;
The thygh, the kne
As they sholde be   460
But suche a leg
A lover wolde beg
To set eye on,
But it is gon.
Then syght of the fote   465
Ryft hartes to the rote.
And last of all, sent Katheryns whele
Was never so round as was her hele.
Asawt her harte and who coulde wynne it,
As for her hele, no holde in it.   470

Yet over that her beawty was so muche,
In pleasaunt qualytes her graces were such
For dalyaunt pastaunce, pas where she sholde,
No greater dyfference betwene lede and golde
Then betwene the rest and her, and suche a wyt   475
That no wyght I wene myght matche her in it.
If she had not wyt to set wyse men to scole
Then shall my tale prove me a starke fole.
But in this matter to make you mete to ges

155

Ye shall understand that I with this maystres 480
Fyll late acquaynted and for love no whyt,
But for my pleasure to approve my wyt
Howe I coulde love to this trycker dyssymble
Who in dyssymelyng was perfyt and nymble;
For where or whan she lyst to gyve a mock 485
She coulde and wolde do it beyonde the nock.
Wherin I thought that if I trysed her
I shulde therby lyke my wyt the better,
And if she chaunsed to tryp or tryse me
It sholde to learne wyt a good lesson be. 490

Thus for my past tyme I dyd determyn
To mock or be mockt of this mockyng vermyn,
For which her presens I dyd fyrst obtayne,
And that obtayned forthwith fell we twayne
In great acquayntaunce and made as good chere 495
As we has ben acquaynted twenty yere;
And I through fayre flatteryng behavour
Semed anone so depe in her favour, B4
That though the tyme then so farre passed was
That tyme requyred us asonder to pas 500
Yet could I no pasport get of my swettynge
Tyll I was full woed for the next dayes metynge.
For sewrauns wherof I muste as she bad
Gyve her in gage best juell I there had,
And after mych myrth as our wyttes coulde devyse 505
We parted and I the nexte morne dyd aryse
In tyme not to tymely, suche tyme as I coulde –
I alowe no love where slepe is not alowde.
I was or I entred this jorney vowd
Deckt very clenly but not very prowd, 510
But trym must I be, for slovenly lobers
Have ye wot well no place amonge lovers.
But I thus deckt at all poyntes poynt devyce
At dore were this trull was I was at a tryce;
Wherat I knocked her presens to wyn, 515
Wherwith it was opened and I was let yn.
And at my fyrste commyng my mynyon semed
Very mery, but anone she mysdemed
That I was not meryly dysposed;
And so myght she thynke, for I disclosed 520
No worde nor loke, but such as shewed as sadly
As I in dede inwardly thought madly
And so must I shewe for lovers be in rate
Somtymes mery but most tymes passyonate.

156

In gevyng thankes to her of over nyght   525
We set us downe, an hevy couple in syght,
And therwithall I fet a sygh such one
As made the forme shake which we both sat on.
Wherupon she without more wordes spoken
Fell in wepyng as her harte shulde have broken   530
And I in secret laughyng so hartely
That from myne eyes cam water plenteously.
Anone I turned with loke sadly that she
My wepyng as watery as hers myght se.
Which done these wordes anone to me she spake: 535
'Alas, dere harte, what wyght myght undertake
To shewe one so sad as you this mornyng,
Beyng so mery as you last evenyng?
I so farre then the meryer for you,
And without desert thus farre the sadder now.'   540
'The selfe thyng,' quoth I, 'which made me then gladde,
The selfe same is thynge that maketh me nowe sadde.
The love that I owe you is origynale
Grounde of my late joy and present payne all,   B4v
And by this meane, love is evermore lad   545
Betwene two angels, one good and one bad,
Hope and Drede, which two be alway at stryfe
Which one of them both with love shall rewle most ryfe.
And Hope that good angell fyrst parte of last nyght
Drawe Drede that bad angell out of place quyght.   550
Hope sware I sholde streyght have your love at ones
And Drede this bad angell sware bloud and bones
That if I wan your love all in one howre
I sholde lose it all agayne in thre or fowre;
Wherin this good angell hath lost the mastry   555
And I by this bad angell won this agony.
And be ye sewer I stande nowe in such case
That if I lacke your contynued grace
In hevyn, hell, or yerth, there is not that he
Save onely God, that knoweth what shall come on me   560
I love not in rate all the common flock
I am no fayner nor I can not mock
Wherfore I beseche you that your rewarde
May wytnesse that ye do my truthe regarde.'

'Syr, as touchyng mockyng', quoth she, 'I am sewer   565
Ye be to wyse to put that here in ure,
For nother gyve I cause why ye so shulde do,
Nor nought coulde ye wynne that way wurth an old sho;
For who so that mocketh shall surely stur

157

This olde proverbe *mockum moccabitur*. 570
But as for you, I thynke my selfe assewred
That very love hath you hyther alewred,
For which,' quoth she, 'let Hope hop up agayne
And vaynquysh Dred so that it be in vayne
To dred or to doubt; but I in every thyng 575
As cause gyveth cause wylbe your owne derlyng.'
'Swere harte,' quoth I 'after stormy colde smertes,
Warm wordes in warm lovers bryng lovers warm hartes,
And so have your wordes warmed my harte evyn nowe
That dredles and doubtles now must I love you.' 580
Anone there was 'I love you' and 'I love you' –
Lovely we lovers love eche other –
'I love you' and 'I for love love you'.
My lovely lovyng loved brother,
Love me, love the, love we, love he, love she, 585
Depper love apparent in no twayne can be
Quyte over the eares in love and felt no ground –
Had not swymmyng holpe, in love I had byn dround.
But I swam by the shore the vauntage to kepe,
To mock her in love semyng to swym more depe. C1
Thus contynued we day by day, 591
Tyll tyme that a moneth was passed away.
In all the which tyme suche awayt she toke
That by no meane I myght ones set one loke
Upon any woman in company, 595
But streyght way she set the fynger in the eye
And by that same aptnes in jelousy
I thought sewer she loved me perfetly,
And I to shewe my selfe in lyke lovyng
Dyssimyled lyke chere in all her lyke lokyng. 600
By this and other lyke thynges then in hande
I gave her mockes me thought above a thousand,
Wherby I thought her owne tale lyke a bur
Stack to her owne back – *mockum moccabitur*.

And upon this I fell in devysyng 605
To brynge to ende this ydell dysgysyng,
Wherupon sodaynly I stale away,
And when I had ben absent halfe a day
My harte mysgave me, by God that bought me,
That if she myst me where I thought she sought me 610
She sewer wolde be madde by love that she ought me;
Wherin not love, but pety so wrought me
That to returne anone I bethought me;

And so returned tyll chaunse had brought me
To her chamber dore and hard I knocked.   615
'Knock softe,' quoth one who the same unlocked,
An auncyent wyse woman who was never
From this sayd swetyng but about her ever.
'Mother,' quoth I, 'howe doth my dere darlyng?'
'Dede, wretch!' cryed she, 'evyn by thyne absentyng'.   620
And without mo wordes the dore to her she shyt,
I standyng without, halfe out of my wyt
In that this woman sholde dye in my faute.
But syns I coulde in there by none assawte,
To her chamber wyndowe I gat about,   625
To see at the lest way the cors layd out,
And there lokyng in, by Godes blessed mother,
I sawe her naked a bed with an other,
And with her bedfelowe laught me to scorne
As meryly as ever she laught beforne.   630

The which when I saw, and then remembryd
The terryble wordes that Mother B rendryd,
And also bethought me of every thyng
Shewed in this woman true love betokenyng,
My selfe to see served thus prately   635
To my selfe I laughed evyn hartely,   C1v
With my selfe consyderyng to have had lyke spede
If my selfe had ben a lover in dede.
But nowe, to make som matter wherby
I may take my leve of my love honestly,   640
'Swete hart', quoth I 'ye take to much upon ye'.
'No more then becomes me, knowe thou well,' quoth she.
'But thou hast takyn to much upon the
In takyng that thou toke in hande to mock me,
Wherin from begynnyng I have sene the jet   645
Lyke as a foole myght have jettyd in a net,
Belevyng hymselfe save of hym selfe onely
To be perceyved of no lyvyng body;
But well saw I thyne entent at begynnyng
Was to bestow a mock on me at endyng,   650
When thou laughedest dyssymulyng a wepyng hart
Then I with wepyng eyes played evyn the lyke part,
Wherwith I brought in *moccum moccabitur*.
And yet thou beyng a long snowted cur
Coulde no whyt smell that all my meanyng was   655
To gyve mock for mock as now is come to pas,
Which now thus passed if thy wyt be handsome

159

May defende the from mockes in tyme to come
By clappyng fast to thy snowt every day
Moccum moccabitur for a nosegay.'   660
Wherwith she start up and shyt her wyndowe to;
Which done I had no more to say nor do
But thynke my selfe or any man elles a foole
In mockes or wyles to set women to scoole.
But nowe to purpose wherfore I began.   665
All though I were made a fole by this woman
Concernyng mockyng, yet doth this tale approve
That I am well sene in the arte of love,
For I entendyng no love but to mock,
Yet coulde no lover of all the hole flock   670
Circumstaunce of love dysclose more nor better
Then dyd I, the substaunce beyng no greater.
And by this tale afore ye all may see
All though a lover as well loved be
As love can devyse hym for pleasaunt spede,   675
Yet two dyspleasures, jelousy and drede,
Is myxt with love wherby love is a drynk mete
To gyve babes for wormes for it drynkth bytter swete.
And as for this babe our lover, in whose hed
By a frantyk worme his opinion is bred,   680
After one draught of this medsyn mynystryd
In to his brayne by my brayne apoyntyd,   C2
Reason shall so temper his opinion
That he shall see it not worth an onyon;
And if he have any other thyng to ley   685
I have to convynse hym every way.
And syns my parte nowe doth thus well appere
Be ye my parteners now all of good chere –
But sylence, every man upon a payne,
For mayster woodcock is nowe come agayne.   690

The lover loved entreth.

Lover loved   The olde seyng seyth, he that seketh shall fynde,
Which after long sekyng true have I founde;
But for suche a fyndyng my selfe to bynde
To such a sekyng as I was now bounde
I wolde rather seke to lesse twenty p[o]unde   695
Howe be it I have sought so farre to my payne
That at the last I have founde and brought twayne.

No lover nor loved	Come they a horse back?
Lover loved	Nay, they come a fote,
	Which thou myght see here, but for this great myst.
No lover nor loved	By jys, and yet see I, thou blynde balde cote, 700
	That one of those twayne myght ryde if he lyst.
Lover loved	How?
No lover nor loved	Mary, for he ledyth a nag on his fyst.
	Maystres, ye are welcome, and welcome ye be.
Loved not lovyng	Nay, welcome be ye, for we were here before ye.

No lover nor loved	Ye have ben here before me before now, 705
	And nowe I am here before you,
	And nowe I am here behynde ye,
	And nowe ye be here behynde me,
	And nowe we be here evyn both to gether,
	And nowe be we welcome evyn both hyther; 710
	Syns nowe ye fynde me here with curtsy I may
	Byd you welcome hyther as I may say.
	But settyng this asyde, let us set a broche
	The mater wherfore ye hyther approche,
	Wherin I have hope that ye both wyll be 715
	Good unto me, and especyally ye;
	For I have a mynde that every good face
	Hath ever some pyte of a pore mans case,
	Beyng as myne is a mater so ryght
	That a fole may judge it ryght at fyrst syght. 720
Lover not loved	Syr, ye may well doubt howe my wyt wyll serve,
	But my wyll from ryght shall never swarve.
Loved not lovyng	Nor myne, and as ye sew for helpe to me C2v
	Lyke sewt have I to sewe for helpe to ye,
	For as much nede have I of helpe as yow. 725
No lover nor loved	I thynke well that, dere hart, but tell me how.
Loved not lovyng	The case is this: ye twayn seme in pleasure
	And we twayn in payne, which payne doth procure
	By comparyson betwene hym and me
	As great a conflyct which of us twayn be 730
	In greatest payne, as is betwene ye twayne
	Whiche of you twayne in most pleasure doth remayne;
	Wherin we somewhat have here debated
	And both to tell trueth so gredyly grated
	Upon affeccion eche to our owne syde, 735
	That in conclusion we must nedes provyde

	Some such as wolde and coulde be indyfferent,	
	And we both to stande unto that judgement.	
	Wherupon for lacke of a judge in this place	
	We sought many places and yet in this case	740
	No man coulde we mete that medyll wyll or can,	
	Tyll tyme that we met with this gentylman,	
	Whome in lyke errand for lyke lacke of ayd	
	Was dryven to desyre our judgement, he sayd.	

Lover loved   Forsoth it is so, I promysyng playne,   745
They twayn betwen us twayn gevyng judgement playne,
We twayn betwen them twayn shuld judge ryght agayne.

No lover nor loved   That promysse to performe I not dysdayne;
For touchyng ryght, as I am a ryghteous man,
I wyll gyve you as muche ryght as I can.   750

Loved not lovyng   Nothyng but ryght desyre I you among,
I wyllyngly wyll nother gyve nor take wronge.

No lover nor loved   Nay in my conscyens I thynke by this boke,
Your conscyens wyll take nothyng that cometh a croke
For as in conscyens what ever ye do   755
Ye nothyng do but as ye wolde be done to.
O hope of good ende, O Mary mother!
Maystres, one of us may nowe helpe a nother.
But syr, I pray you some mater declare
Wherby I may knowe in what grefe ye arre.   760

Lover not loved   I am a lover not loved, which playne
Is dayly not dolefull but my dedly payne.

No lover nor loved   A lover not loved! Have ye knyt that knot?

Lover not loved   Ye, forsoth.

No lover nor loved   Forsoth, ye be the more sot.
Nowe, maystres, I hartely besech ye   765
Tell me what maner case your case may be.

Loved not lovyng   I am beloved not lovyng, wherby
I am not in payne but in tormentry.

No lover nor loved   Is this your tormentour? God turne hym to good!   C3

Loved not lovyng   Nay there is another man [on] me as wood   770
As this man on a nother woman is.

No lover nor loved   Ye thynke them both mad, and so do I, by jys,
So mot I thryve, but who that lyst to marke
Shall perceyve here a praty peyce of warke.
Let us fall somewhat in these partes to skannyng: 775
Lovyng not loved, loved not lovyng,
Loved and lovyng, not lovyng nor loved
Wyll ye see these foure partes well joyned?
Lovyng not loved, and loved not lovyng:
Those partes can joyne in no maner rekenyng.   780

Lovyng and loved, loved nor lover:
These partes in joynyng in lykewyse dyffer.
But in that ye love ye twayne joyned be,
And beyng not loved ye joyne with me,
And beyng no lover with me joyneth she,   785
And beyng beloved with her joyne ye:
Had I a joyner with me joyned joyntly,
We joyners shulde joyne joynt to joynt quyckly;
For fyrst I wolde parte these partes in fleses
And ones departed these parted peses   790
Parte and parte with parte I wolde so partlyke parte
That eche parte shulde parte with quyet harte.

Lover not loved   Syr, syns it passeth your power that part to play
Let passe, and let us partly nowe assay
To brynge some parte of that purpose to ende   795
For which all partyes yet in vayne attende.

Loved not lovyng   I do desyre the same and that we twayne
May fyrst be harde that I may knowe my payne.

Lover loved   I graunt for my parte, by fayth of my body.
Why where the devyll is this horeson nody?   800

No lover nor loved I never syt in justyce but ever more   [*Aloft*]
I use to be shryven a lyttell before,
And nowe syns that my confessyon is done
I wyll depart and come take penaunce sone.
When conscyens prycketh, conscyens must be sercht by God
In dyschargyng of conscyens or els gods forbod;   806
Which maketh me mete when conscyens must come in place
To be a judge in every comen case.
But who may lyke me his avaunsement avaunt?
Nowe am I a judge and never was serjaunt,   810
Which ye regarde not much by ought that I see
By any reverence that ye do to me.
Nay yet I prayse women; when great men go by
They crowch to the grounde, loke here how they ly:
They shall have a beck by saynt Antony.   C3v
But alas, good maystres, I crye you mercy   816
That you are unanswered, but ye may see
Though two tales at ones by two eares hard may be,
Yet can not one mouth two tales at ones answer,
Which maketh you tary; but in your mater   820
Syns ye by hast in havyng ferdest home
Wolde fyrst be sped of that for which ye come,
I graunt as he graunted your wyll to fulfyll
You twayne to be harde fyrst: begyn when you wyl.

163

Lover not loved	As these twayne us tweyn nowe graunt fyrst to breke,	825

Lover not loved As these twayne us tweyn nowe graunt fyrst to breke, 825
Syns twayn to be harde, at ones can not speke
I now desyre your graunt, that I may open
Fyrst tale which nowe is at poynt to be spoken;
Which I crave no whyt my parte to avaunce
But with the pyth to avoyde circumstaunce. 830

Loved not lovyng Speke what and whan so ever it please you;
Tyll reason wyll me, I wyll not dysease you.

Lover not loved Syrs, other here is a very weyke brayne
Or she hath, if any, a very weyke payne;
For I put case that my love I her gave 835
And that for my love, her love I dyd crave
For which though I dayly sew day by day
What losse or payne to her if she say nay?

No lover nor loved Yes, by saynt Mary, so the case may stande
That some woman had lever take in hande 840
To ryde on your errand an hundreth myle,
Then to say nay one Pater noster whyle.

Lover not loved If ye on her parte any payne defyne,
Which is the more paynefull, her payne or myne?

No lover nor loved Your payne is most if she say nay and take it; 845
But if that she say nay and forsake it
Then is her payne a great way the greater.

Loved not lovyng Syr, ye alledge this nay in this mater
As though my denyal my sewter to love
[Were] all or the most payne that to me doth move; 850
Wherin the treuth is a contrary playne,
For though to ofte spekyng one thyng be a payne,
Yet is that one worde the full of my hopyng
To bryng his hopyng to dyspayre at endyng.
Thus is this nay which ye take my most grefe 855
Though it be paynefull yet my most relefe.
But my most payne is all an other thyng
Which though ye forget or hyde by dyssymylyng
I partely shewed you, but all I coulde nor can.
But maysters to you, with payne of this man 860
That payne that I compare is partely this: C4
I am loved of one whome the treuth is
I can not love, and so it is with me
That from hym in maner I never can flee,
And every one worde in sewt of his parte 865
Nyps through myne eares and rons through my harte.
His gastfull loke so pale that unneth I
Dare for myne eares cast towarde hym an eye,
And whan I do, that eye [his] thought presentyth

Streyght to my hart and thus my payne augmentyth.   870
One tale so ofte, alas, and so importune;
His exclamacions somtyme on fortune
Some tyme on hym selfe, some tyme upon me,
And for that thyng that if my deth sholde be
Brought streyght in place except I were content   875
To graunt the same, yet coulde I not assent;
And he seyng this yet seasyth not to crave –
What deth coulde be worse than this lyfe that I have?

Lover not loved   This tale to purpose purporteth no more
But syght and hearyng. Complaynt of his sore   880
Is onely the grefe that ye do susteyne.
Alas tender hart, syns ye dye in payne,
This payne to perceyve by syght and hearyng,
Howe coulde you lyve to knowe our payne by felyng?
Marke well this question and answere as ye can: 885
A man that is hanged or that mans hangman
Which man of those twayne suffereth most payne?

Loved not lovyng   He that is hanged.
No lover nor loved   By the masse it is so playne.
Lover not loved   Well sayd for me, for I am the sufferer,
And ye the hangman understande as it were.   890
These cases vary in no maner a thyng
Savyng this serves in this mannes hangyng
Comenly is done agaynst the hangmans wyll,
And ye of delyghtfull wyll, your lover kyll.

Loved not lovyng   Of delyghtfull wyll? Nay, that is not so   895
As ye shall perfetly perceyve or we go.
But of those at whose hangyng have hangmen by
Howe many have ye knowen hang wyllyngly?

No lover nor loved   Nay, never one in his lyfe, byr lady.
Loved not lovyng   In this, lo, your case from our case doth vary   900
For ye that love where love wyll take no place,
Your owne wyll is your owne leder a playne case.
And not onely uncompelled without alewre,
But sore agaynst her wyll your sewt ye endewre.
Nowe syns your wyll to love dyd you procure   905
And with that wyll, ye put that love in ure,   C4v
And nowe that wyll by wyt seth love such payne
As wytty wyll wolde wyll love to refrayne;
And ye by wyll that love in eche condicion
To extynct may be your owne phesicion,   910
Except ye be a foole or wolde make me one,
What seyng cowd set a good ground to syt on
To make any man thynke your payne thus strong

165

	Makyng your owne salve your owne sore thus long?	
Lover not loved	Maystres, muche parte of this proces purposed	915
	Is matter of truth truely dysclosed.	
	My wyll without her wyll brought me in love,	
	Which wyll without her wyll doth make me hove	
	Upon her grace to see what grace wyll prove.	
	But where ye say my wyll may me remove	920
	As wel from her love as wyll brought me to it	
	That is false; my wyll can not wyll to do it.	
	My wyl as farre therin out weyth my power	
	As a sow of led out weyth a saforne flowre.	
Loved not lovyng	Your wyl out weyth your power, then where is your wyt?	925
	I merveyll that ever ye wyll speke it.	
Lover loved	Nay, merveyll ye maystres therat no whyt,	
	For as farre as this poynt may stretch in verdyt	
	I am clerely of this mans opinion.	
No lover nor loved	And I contrary with this mynion.	930
Lover loved	Then be we come to a demurrer in lawe.	
No lover nor loved	Then be ye come from a woodcock to a daw,	
	And by God it is no small connyng, brother,	
	For me to turne one wylde foole to a nother.	
Lover not loved	Nay, maysters, I hartely pray you both,	935
	Banyshe contencyon tyll ye see howe this goth.	
	I wyll repet and answere her tale forthwith,	
	The pyth for your part wherof pretendyth	
	A profe for your payne to be more then myne,	
	In that my wyll not onely dyd me enclyne	940
	To the same, but in the same by the same wyll	
	I wyllyngly wyll to contynue styll.	
	And as wyll brought me and kepeth in this bey	
	When I wyll, ye say wyll wyll bryng me awey;	
	Concludyng therby that if my payne were	945
	As great as yours that I sholde suerly bere	
	As great and good wyll to flee my love thus ment,	
	As do ye your sewters presens to absent.	
Loved not lovyng	This tale sheweth my tale perseyved every dell.	
Lover not loved	Then for entre to answere it as well	950
	Answere this: put case ye as depely nowe	
	Dyd love your lover as he doth love yow	D1
	Shulde not that lovyng, suppose ye, redres	
	That payne whiche lack of lovyng doth posses?	
Loved not lovyng	Yes.	955
Lover not loved	Syns love gyvyn to hyme gyveth your selfe ease, than	
	Except ye love payne, why love ye not this man?	
Loved not lovyng	Love hym? Nay, as I sayd, must I streyght chose	

	To love hym or els my hed here to lose,	
	I knowe well I coulde not my lyfe to save	960
	With lovyng wyll graunt hym my love to have.	
Lover not loved	I thynke ye speke truely for wyll wyll not be	
	Forced in love, wherfore the same to ye:	
	Syns this is to you such dyffyculte	
	Why not a thyng as dyffycult to me	965
	To wyll the let of love where wyll my love hath set	
	As you to wyll to set love where wyll is your let?	
Loved not lovyng	Well sayd, and put case it as harde nowe be	
	For you to wyll to leve her, as for me	
	To love hym, yet have ye above me a meane	970
	To learne you at length to wyll to leve love cleane,	
	Which meane many thousandes of lovers hath brought	
	From ryght fervent lovyng to love ryght nought –	
	Which long and oft approved meane is absens;	
	Wherto when ye wyll ye may have lycens	975
	Whiche I crave and wyshe and can not obtayne,	
	For he wyll never my presens refrayne.	

Lover not loved	This is a medsyn lyke as ye wolde wyll me –	
	For thyng to kewre me the thyng that wolde kyll me;	
	For presens of her, though I selde whan may have	980
	Is soole the medsyn that my lyfe doth save.	
	Her absens can I with as yll wyll wyll	
	As I can wyll to leve to love her styll;	
	Thus is this wyll brought in insydently;	
	No ayde in your purpose worth tayle of a fly.	985
	And as concernyng our pryncypall mater,	
	All that ye lay may be layd evyn a water.	
	I wonder that shame suffereth you to compare	
	With my payne, syns ye are dryven to declare	
	That all your payne is but syght and hearyng	990
	Of hym, that as I do, dyeth in payne felyng.	
	O payne upon payne, what paynes I sustayne!	
	No crafte of the devyll can expresse all my payne:	
	In this body no lym, joynt, senow, nor veyne,	
	But martreth eche other, and this brayne	995
	Chefe enmy of all, by the inventyng	
	Myne unsavery sewte to her dyscontentyng.	
	My speakyng, my hearyng, my lokyng, my thynkyng,	D1v
	In syttyng, in standyng, in wakyng, or wynkyng,	
	What ever I do, or where ever I go,	1000
	My brayne and myshap in all these do me wo,	
	As for my senses, eche one of all fyve	

Wondreth as it can to fele it selfe a lyve;
And than hath love goten all in one bed
Hym selfe and his servauntes to lodge in this hed: 1005
Vayne hope, dyspayre, drede, and audacite,
Hast, wast, lust without lykyng or lyberte,
Dilygence, humilyte, trust, and jelousy,
Desyre, pacyent sufferaunce, and constansy –
These with other in this hed lyke swarmes of bees   1010
Styng in debatyng theyr contraryetees;
The venym wherof from this hed dystylleth
Downe to this brest and this hart it kylleth.
All tymes in all places of this body
By this dystemperaunce thus dystempored am I,   1015
Sheveryng in colde and yet in hete I dye
Drowned in moysture, parched perchment drye.

No lover nor loved Colde, hote, [moyste], drye, all in all places at ones!
Mary, syr, this is an agew for the nones.
But or we gyve judgement I must serch to vew   1020
Whether this evydens be false or trew.
Nay, stande styll, your part shall prove never the wars
Fo! by Saynt Savour here is a whot ars!
Let me fele your nose – nay fere not, man, be bolde!
Well, though this ars be warme and this nose colde   1025
Yet these twayne by attorney brought in one place
Are as he seyth colde and whot both in lyke case.
O what payne drought is! See how his dry lyps
Smake for more moyster of his warme moyst hyps.
Breath out! These eyes are dull but this nose is quycker   1030
Here is most moyster, your breath smelleth of lycker.

Loved not lovyng Well syns ye have opened in this tale tellyng
The full of your payne, for spede to endyng
I shall in fewe wordes such one question dysclose,
As if your answere gyve cause to suppose   1035
The hole of the same to be answered at full
We nede no judgement, for yelde my selfe I wull.
Put case this man loved a woman such one
Who were in his lykyng the thyng alone,
And that his love to her were not so myckyll   1040
But her fancy towarde hym were as lyttyll,
And that she hyd her selfe so day and nyght
That selde tyme whan he myght come in her syght;
And then put case that one to you love dyd bere –   D2
A woman that other so ugly were   1045

168

That eche kys of her mouth called you to Gybbes fest,
Or that your fancy abhorred her so at lest
That her presens were as swete to suppose
As one shulde present –

No lover nor loved   A torde to his nose.

Loved not lovyng   Ye, in good fayth, wherto the case is this   1050
That her spytfull presens absent never is.
Of these two cases if chaunce shulde dryve you
To chose one, which wolde ye chuse? Tell trouth now.
What, ye study?

No lover nor loved   Tary, ye be to gredy!

Men be not lyke women, alway redy.   1055

Lover not loved   In good soth, to tell treuth of these cases twayne
Which case is the wurst is to me uncertayne.

Loved not lovyng   Fyrst case of these twayne I put for your parte,
And by the last case apereth myne owne smarte.
If they proced with thys fyrst case of ours   1060
Then is our mater undoubtedly yours;
And if judgement passe with this last case in fyne
Then is the mater asewredly myne.
Syns by these cases our partes so do seme
That which is most paynefull your selfe can not deme,   1065
If ye nowe wyll all circumstaunce eschew,
Make this question in these cases our yssew,
And the payne of these men to abrevyate
Set all our other mater as frustrate.

Lover not loved   Agreed.

Loved not lovyng   Then further to abredge your payne,   1070
Syns this our yssew apereth thus playne,
As folke not doubtyng your consciens nor connyng,
We shall in the same let passe all resonyng,
Yeldyng to your judgement the hole of my parte.

Lover not loved   And I lykewyse myne, with wyll and good harte.   1075

No lover nor loved So, lo, make you low curtsy to me now,
And streyght I wyll make as lowe curtsy to you.
Nay, stande ye nere the upper ende I pray ye,
For the neyther ende is good ynough for me.
Your cases which enclude your grefe eche whyt   1080
Shall dwell in this hed.

Lover loved   And in myne, but yet
Or that we herein our judgement publysh,
I shall desyre you that we twayne may fynysh
As farre in our mater towarde judgement
As ye have done in yours, to the entent   1085
That we our partes brought to gether thyther

D2v

169

	May come to judgement fro thens to gyther.	
No lover nor loved	Byr lady, syr, and I desyre the same.	
Loved not lovyng	I wolde ye began.	
Lover not loved	Begyn then, in Goddes name.	
Lover loved	Shall I begyn?	
No lover nor loved	Syns I loke but for wynnyng,	1090
	Gyve me the ende and take you the begynnyng.	
Lover loved	Who shall wynne the ende, the ende at ende shall try.	
	For my parte wherof nowe thus begyn I	
	I am as I sayd a beloved lover,	
	And he no lover nor beloved nother,	1095
	In which two cases he maketh his avaunt	
	Of both our partes to prove his most pleasaunt,	
	But be ye assuered by ought I yet se	
	In his estate no maner pleasure can be.	
No lover nor loved	Yes, two maner pleasures ye must nedes confes:	1100
	Fyrst I have the pleasure of quyetnes,	
	And the secounde is I am contented.	
Lover loved	That seconde pleasure now secondly invented;	
	To compare with pleasure by contentashyon	
	Is a very seconde ymagynashyon.	1105
No lover nor loved	Then shewe your wyt for profe of this in hande	
	Howe may pleasure without contentacyon stande?	
Lover loved	Pleasure without contentacyon can not be,	
	But contentacyon without pleasure we se	
	In thynges innumerable every day,	1110
	Of all which marke these which I shall nowe ley:	
	Put case that I for pleasure of some frende	
	Or some thyng which I longed to se at ende	
	Wolde be content to ryde thre score myle this nyght	
	And never wolde bayte nor never alyght;	1115
	I myght be ryght well content to do this,	
	And yet in this doyng no pleasure there is.	
	Moreover, ye by pacyent sufferaunce	
	May be contented with any myschaunce,	
	The losse of your chylde, frende, or any thyng	1120
	That in this worlde to you can be longyng,	
	Wherin ye contented never so well,	
	Yet is your contentacyon pleasure no dell.	
No lover nor loved	These two exsamples, by ought that I se,	
	Be no thyng the thynges that any thynge touch me.	1125
	With deth of my chylde my beyng contented	
	Or payne with my frende wyllyngly assented	
	Is not contentacyon voluntary,	
	For that contentacyon cometh forceably.	

170

	But my contentacion standeth in such thyng	D3
	As I wolde fyrst wyshe if it went by wyshyng.	1131
Lover loved	Syr, be ye contented even as ye tell,	
	Yet your contentacyon can nother excell	
	Nor be compared egall to myne estate,	
	For touchyng contentacyon I am in rate	1135
	As hyely contented to love as ye se,	
	As ye to forbere love can wyshe to be.	
	Had I no more to say in this argument	
	But that I am as well as you content,	
	Yet hath my parte nowe good approbacyon	1140
	To match with your even by contentacyon.	
	But contentacion is not all the thyng	
	That I for my love have in recompencyng.	
	Above contentacyon pleasures felyng	
	Have I so many, that no wyght lyvyng	1145
	Can by any wyt or tonge the same reporte.	
	O the pleasaunt pleasures in our resorte!	
	After my beyng from her any whyther,	
	What pleasures have we in commyng to gyther!	
	Eche tap on the grounde towarde me with her fote	1150
	Doth bathe in delyght my very harte rote,	
	Every twynke of her aluryng eye	
	Revyveth my spirites even thorowoutly,	
	Eche worde of her mouth not a preparatyve	
	But the ryght medicyne of preservatyve.	1155
	We be so joconde and joyfully joyned,	
	Her love for my love so currantly coyned,	
	That all pleasures yerthly, the treuth to declare,	
	Are pleasures not able with ours to compare.	
	This mouth in maner receyveth no food,	1160
	Love is the fedyng that doth this body good,	
	And this hed dyspyseth all these eyes wynkyng	
	Longer then love doth kepe this harte thynkyng	
	To dreame on my swete harte. Love is my feader,	
	Love is my lorde, and love is my leader.	1165
	Of all myne affayres in thought, worde, and dede	
	Love is the Christs crosse that must be my spede.	
No lover nor loved	By this I perceyve wel ye make rekenyng	
	That love is a goodly and a good thyng.	
Lover loved	Love good? What yll in love canst thou make apere?	1170
No lover nor loved	Yes, I shal prove this love at this tyme ment here	
	In this mans case as yll as is the devyll,	
	And in your case I shall prove love more evyll.	

What tormentry coulde all the devylles in hell
Devyse to his payne that he doth not tell?   1175

What payne bryngeth that body those devyls in that hed   D3v
Which mynysters alway by love are led?
He frysyth in fyre, he drowneth in drought,
Eche parte of his body love hath brought abought,
Where eche to helpe other shulde be dylygent,   1180
They marter eche other the man to torment.
Without stynt of rage his paynes be so sore
That no fende may torment man in hell more.
And, as in your case, to prove that love is
Wurs than the devyll, my meanyng is this: 1185
Love dystempereth hym by torment in payne,
And love dystempereth you as farre in joy playne.
Your owne confession declareth that ye
Eate, drynke, or slepe evyn as lyttell as he,
And he that lacketh any one of those three,   1190
Be it by joy or by payne clere ye see,
Deth must be sequell howe ever it be.
And thus are ye both brought by loves induccyon,
By payne or by joy, to lyke poynt of dystruccyon.
Which poynt aproveth love in this case past   1195
Beyonde the devyll in turmentry to have a cast.
For I trowe ye fynde not that the devyll can fynde
To turment man in hell by any pleasaunt mynde,
Wherby as I sayd I say of love styll.
Of the devyll and love, love is the more yll   1200
And at begynnyng I may say to yow
If God had sene as much as I say now,
Love had ben Lucyfer, and doubt ye no whyt
But experyens nowe hath taught God such wyt
That if ought come at Lucyfer other then good,   1205
To whyp soules on the brech love shalbe the blood.
And sewer he is one that can not lyve long,
For aged folke ye wot well can not be strong.
And an other thyng his phisicyon doth ges
That he is infecte with the blak jawndes.   1210

Lover loved   No ferther then ye be enfecte with folye;
For in all these wordes no worde can I espye
Such as for your parte any profe avoucheth.
No lover nor loved For profe of my parte, no, but it toucheth
The dysprofe of yours, for where you alledged   1215
Your parte above myne to be compared

172

By pleasures in which your dyspleasures are such
That ye eate, drynke, nor slepe, or at most not much,
In lacke wherof my tale proveth playnly
Eche parte of your pleasure a turmentry,   1220
Wherby your good love I have proved so evyll
That love is apparauntly wors then the devyll.   D4
And as touchyng my parte there can aryse
No maner dyspleasures nor tormentryes
In that I love not, nor am not loved.   1225
I move no dyspleasures nor none to me moved
But all dyspleasures of love fro me absent
By absens wherof I quyetly content.

Lover loved   Syr, where ye sayd and thynke ye have sayd wel
That my joy by love shall bryng deth in sequell,   1230
In that by the same in maner I dysdayne
Fode and slepe, this proverbe answereth you playne:
Loke not on the meat, but loke on the man.
Nowe loke ye on me and say what ye can.

No lover nor loved   Nay for a tyme love may puffe up a thynge.   1235
But lackyng fode and slepe deth is the endyng.

Lover loved   Well, syr, tyll such tyme as deth approve it
This part of your tale may slepe every whyt,
And where ye by absent dyspleasure wolde
Match with my present pleasure ye seme more bolde   1240
Then wyse, for those twayne be farre dyfferent sewer.

No lover nor loved   Is not absens of dyspleasure a pleasure?

Lover loved   Yes, in lyke rate as a post is pleased,
Which as by no meane it can be dyseased
By dyspleasure present, so is it trew   1245
That no pleasure present in it can ensew.
Pleasures or dyspleasures felyng sensybly
A post ye knowe well can not fele possybly,
And as a post in this case I take you
Concernynge the effecte of pleasure in hande now: 1250
For any felyng ye in pleasure indure
More then ye say ye fele in dyspleasure.

No lover nor loved   Syr, though the effecte of your pleasure present
Be more pleasaunt then dyspleasure absent,
Yet howe compare ye with myne absent payne   1255
By present dyspleasures in which ye remayne?

Lover loved   My present dyspleasures? I knowe none such.

No lover nor loved   Knowe ye no payne by love lytell nor much?

Lover loved   No.   1259

No lover nor loved   Then shall I shewe such a thyng in this purs   1260
As shortly shall shewe herein your parte the wurs.

	Nowe I pray God, the devyll in hell blynde me –	
	By the masse I have lefte my boke behynde me!	
	I beseche our Lorde I never go hens	
	If I wolde not rather have spent forty pens,	1265
	But syns it is thus, I must go fetch it –	
	I wyll not tary – a, syr, the devyll stretch it!	
Lover loved	Farewell dawcock.	D4v
No lover nor loved	Farewell woodcock.	
	[*Exit*]	
Lover loved	He is gone.	
Loved not lovyng	Gone, ye, but he wyll come agayne anone.	
Lover loved	Nay this nyght he wyll no more dyssease you.	1270
	Gyve judgement hardely even whan it please you,	
	Which done syth he is gone my selfe streyght shall	
	Ryghtously betwene you gyve judgement fynall.	
	But lorde, what a face this fole hath set here	
	Tyll shame defaced his foly so clere!	1275
	That shame hath shamfully in syght of you all	
	With shame dryven hym hens to his shamefull fall,	
	Wherin all though I nought gayne by wynnyng	
	That ought may augment my pleasure in lovyng	
	Yet shall I wyn therby a pleasure to see	1280
	That ye all shall see the mater pas with me.	
	What though the profyte may lyghtly be lodyn,	
	It greveth a man to be over trodyn.	
	Nay whan I saw that his wynnyng must growe	
	By payne pretendyng in my parte to shewe,	1285
	Then wyst I well the nody must cum	
	To do as he dyd or stande and play mum.	
	No man, no woman, no chylde in this place	
	But I durst for judgement trust in this case:	
	All doubt of my payne by his profe by any meane	1290
	His ronnyng away hath nowe scrapt out cleane.	
	Werfore gyve judgement and I shall returne	
	In place hereby where my dere hart doth sojurne,	
	And after salutacion betwene us had	
	Such as is mete to make lovers hartes glade,	1295
	I shall to rejoyce her in mery tydynges	
	Declare the hole rable of this fooles lesynges.	

*Here the vyse cometh in ronnyng sodenly aboute the place
among the audyens with a hye copyn tank on his hed full of
squybs fyred, cryeng 'Water, water, fyre, fyre, fyre, water,
water, fyre,' tyll the fyre in the squybs be spent.*

Lover loved	Water and fyre?
No lover nor loved	Nay water for fyre I meane.
Lover loved	Well thanked be God it is out nowe cleane.
	Howe cam it there?
No lover nor loved	Syr, as I was goyng 1300
	To fet my boke for which was my departyng
	There chaunced in my way a house hereby
	To fyre which is burned pyteously E1
	But mervelously the people do mone
	For a woman, they say a goodly one – 1305
	A sojoner whome in this house burned is;
	And shoutyng of the people for helpe in this
	Made me runne thyther to have done some good,
	And at a wyndowe therof as I stood
	I thrust in my hed and evyn at a flush 1310
	Fyre flasht in my face and so toke my bush.
Lover loved	What house?
No lover nor loved	A house paynted with red oker,
	The owner wherof they say is a broker.
Lover loved	Then brek hart! Alas, why lyve I this day?
	My dere hart is dystroyd, lyfe and welth away! 1315
No lover nor loved	What man? Syt downe and be of good chere.
	Gods body, mayster woodcock is gone clere.
	O mayster woodcock, fayr mot be fall ye –
	Of ryght mayster woodcock I must nowe call ye.
	Maystres stande you here afore and rubbe hym 1320
	And I wyll stande here behynde and dubbe hym.
	Nay, the chylde is a slepe, ye nede not rock.
	Mayster woodcock! Mayster wood wood woodcock!
	Where folke be farre within a man must knock
	Is not this a pang, trow ye, beyonde the nock? 1325
	Speke, mayster woodcock, speke parot I pray ye.
	My leman your lady ey wyll ye see
	My lady your leman one un[d]ertakes
	To be safe from fyre by slyppyng through a jakes.
Lover loved	That worde I harde but yet I see her not. 1330
No lover nor loved	No more do I, mayster woodcock, our Lorde wot.
Lover loved	Unto that house where I dyd see her last
	I wyll seke to see her, and if she be past
	So that to apere there I can not make her
	Then wyll I burne after and overtake her. 1335

The lover loved goeth out.

No lover nor loved	Well ye may burne to gyther for all this
	And do well ynough for ought that is yet amys.

175

For Gods sake one ronne after and bast hym –
It were great pyte the fyre shulde wast hym,
For beyng fatte, your knowledge must recorde,   1340
A woodcock well rost is a dyshe for a lorde.
And for a woodcock ye all must nowe knowe hym
By mater of recorde that so doth shewe hym.
And brevely to bryng you all out of dowt
All this have I feyned to brynge abowt,   1345
Hym selfe to convynce hym selfe even by acte,   E1v
As he hath done here in doyng this facte.
He taketh more thought for this one woman nowe
Then coulde I for all in the worlde, I make avowe,
Which hath so shamefully defaced his parte   1350
That to returne nother hath he face nor harte.
Which sene, whyles he and she lese tyme in kyssyng,
Gyve ye with me judgement a Godes blessyng.

                         [Lover loved returns.]

Lover loved   The profe of my sayeng at my fyrst entre
                       That wretch bryngeth now in place in that I leyde,   1355
                       Dyssimblyng mans mynde by apparence to be
                       Thyng inconvenyent, which thyng as I seyd
                       Is proved nowe true: howe was I dysmeyd
                       By his false facyng the deth of my darlyng,
                       Whome I thanke God is in helth and eyleth nothyng.   1360
No lover nor loved   Syr, I beseche you of all your dysmaying
                       What other cause can ye ley then your lovyng?
Lover loved   My lovyng? Nay all the cause was your lyeng.
No lover nor loved   What had my lye done if ye had not loved?
Lover loved   What dyd my love tyll your lye was moved?   1365
No lover nor loved   By these two questions it semeth we may make
                       Your love and my lye to parte evenly the stake.
                       Lovyng and lyeng have we brought nowe hyther
                       Lovers and lyers to ley both to gyther.
                       But put case my lye of her deth were true   1370
                       What excuse for your love coulde then ensue?
Lover loved   If fortune – God save her – dyd bryng her to it
                       The faute were in fortune and in love no whyt.
No lover nor loved   The hole faute in fortune? by my sheth, well [hyt];
                       God sende your fortune better then your wyt.   1375
Lover loved   Well, syr, at extremyte I can prove
                       The faute in fortune as much as in love.
No lover nor loved   Then fortune in lyke case with love nowe joyne yow
                       As I with lovyng joyned lyeng even now.

                                  176

And well they may joyne all by ought that I se   1380
For eche of all thre I take lyke vanyte.
But syns ye confesse that your part of such payne
Cometh halfe by love, and that it is certayne
That certayne paynes to loved lovers do move,
In whiche the faute in nothyng save onely love –   1385
As dred and jelousy eche of which with mo
To your estate of love is a dayly fo –
And I clere out of love declaryng such show
As in my case no payne to me can grow,
I say this consydred hath pyth suffycyent   1390
In profe of my parte to dryve you to judgement.

<table>
<tr><td>Lover loved</td><td>Nay [f]yrst a fewe wordes, syr, though I confes</td><td>E2</td></tr>
</table>

That love bryngeth some payne, and your case paynles
By meane of your contented quyetnes,
Yet thactuall pleasures that I posses   1395
Are as farre above the case that ye profes
As is my payne in your ymagynacyon
Under the pleasures of contentacyon.
Thus wade how ye wyll one way or other,
If ye wynne one way ye shall lese another.   1400
But if ye intende for ende to be brefe
Joine wyth me herein for indifferent prefe:
A tree ye knowe wel is a thinge that hath life
And such a thinge as never feleth payne or strife
But ever quiet and alway contented.   1405
And as there can no way be invented
To bringe a tree dyspleasure by felinge paine
So no felinge pleasure in it can remayne.
A hors is a thinge that hath life also,
And he by felinge felith both welth and wo.   1410
By dryvinge or drawinge al day in the mier
Many paynefull jorneys hath he in hier.
But after al those he hath alway at night
These pleasures folowing to his great delyght:
Fyrst, fayre washt at a river or a weyre   1415
And straight brought to a stabel warme and fayre,
Dry rubbyd and chafed from hed to hele,
And coryd tyll he be slyke as an ele.
Then he is littrid in maner nose hie,
And hey as much as will in his belie,   1420
Then provender hath he otes, pese, benes, or brede,
Which feding in felinge as pleasaunt to his hede
As to a covetous man to beholde

177

	Of his owne Westminster Hall full of golde.	
	After which feding he slepeth in quiet rest	1425
	Dewring such time as his meat may degest:	
	Al this considred, a hors or a tree	
	If ye must chose the tone, which woulde ye be?	
No lover nor loved	When the hors must to labour, by our Lady,	
	I had lever be a tree then a hors I.	1430
Lover loved	But howe when he resteth and fylleth his gorge?	
No lover nor loved	Then wolde I be a hors and no tree, by saint George.	
Lover loved	But what if [ye] must nedes sticke to the tone?	
[No lover nor loved]	Which were then best? By the masse, I can name none.	
Lover loved	The first case is yours and the next is for me.	1435
	In case lyke a tree I may liken ye,	
	For as a tree hath lyfe [without] feling	
	Wherby it felith pleasing no[r] displeasing	E2v
	And can not be but contented quietly,	
	Even the like case is yours now presently.	1440
	And as the hors feleth paine and not the tree,	
	Lykewyse I have paine and no paine have ye;	
	And as a hors above a tree felyth pleasure	
	So fele I pleasure above you in rate sure;	
	And as the tre felith nother and the hors both	1445
	Even so pleasure and paine betwene us twaine goeth.	
	Sins these two cases so indifferently fall	
	That your selfe can judge nother for perciall,	
	For indifferent ende I thinke this way best:	
	Of all our reasoning to debarre the rest,	1450
	And in these two cases this one question	
	To be the issue that we shal joyne on.	
No lover nor loved	Be it so.	
Lover loved	Nowe are these issues cowched so nie	
	That both sides I trust shall take ende shortly?	
Lover not loved	I hope and desire the same, and syns we	1455
	Were fyrst harde, we both humbly beseche ye	
	That we in like wise maye have judgement furst.	
Lover loved	I graunt.	
No lover nor loved	By the masse, and I, come best or wurst.	
Lover loved	Though nature force man styfly to encline	
	To his owne parte in ech particuler thing,	1460
	Yet reason wolde man, whan man shal determine	
	Other mens partes by indifferent awarding,	
	Indifferent to be in al his reasoning;	
	Wherfore in this parte cut [we] of affeccion	
	So that indifferency be [our] direccion.	1465

178

No lover nor loved	Contented with that and by ought I espy
	We may in this mater take ende quickly.
	Scan we theyr cases as she did apply them
	That we may perceive what is ment by them.
	He loveth unloved a goodly one, 1470
	She is loved not lovinge of an ugly one,
	Or in his eye his lover semeth goodly
	And in her eye her lober semeth as ugly;
	Her most desyred angels face he can not see,
	His most lothely hell houndes face she can not flee. 1475
	He loveth, she abhorreth, wherby presens is
	His life, her deth, wherby I say even this:
	Be his feling paines in every degre
	As great and as many as he sayth they be,
	Yet in my judgement by these cases hath she 1480
	As great and as many feling paines as he.
Lover loved	When mater at full is indifferently leyd E3
	As ye in this jugement have leyd this nowe,
	What reason the tyme by me shulde be deleyd?
	Ye have spoken my thought wherfore to you 1485
	In peysing your paines my consciens doth alowe
	A just counterpaise, and thus your paynes be
	Ajudged by us twaine one paine in degre.
Lover not loved	Well, sins your conscyens driveth you thus to judge,
	I receive this judgement without grefe or grudge. 1490
Loved not lovyng	And I in like rate, yelding unto you twaine
	Harty thankes for this your undeservid paine.
Lover not loved	Nowe [maistres], may it please you to declare
	As touching their partes of what minde ye are.
Loved not lovyng	With right good will sir, and sure I suppose 1495
	Their partes in fewe wordes maie come to pointe well.
	The two examples which he did disclose
	All errours or doubtes do clerly expell:
	The estate of a tre his estate doth tell,
	And of the hors his tale wel understande 1500
	Declareth as well his case nowe in hande.
	For as nothing can please or displease a tre
	By ani pleasure or displeasure feling,
	Nor never bring a tre discontent to be
	So like case to him not loved nor loving 1505
	Love can no way bring pleasing or displeasing;
	Live women, die women, sinke women, or swim,
	In all he content, for al is one to him.

And as a horse hath mani painefull jorneis,
A lover best loved hath paines in like wise   1510
As here hath apered by sondry weys,
Which sheweth his case in wurst part to rise:
But then as the horse feleth pleasure in sise
At night in the stable above the tre,
So feleth he some pleasure as farre above ye.   1515

In some case he feleth much more pleasure then he
And in some case he feleth even as muche lesse.
Betwene the more and the lesse it semeth to me
That betwene their pleasures no choise is to gesse,
Wherfore I give judgement in short processe: 1520
Set the tone pleasure evin to the tother.

No lover nor loved Womanly spoken maistres, by the roodes mother.

Lover not loved Who heareth this tale wyth indifferent minde,
And seeth of these twaine eche one so full bent   E3v
To his owne parte that nother in harte can finde   1525
To chaunge pleasures with other, must nedes assent
That she in these wordes hath gyven ryght judgement:
In affirmance wherof I judge and awarde
Both these pleasures of yours as one in regarde.

Lover loved Wel syns I thinke ye both without corrupcion, 1530
I shall move no mater of interrupcion.

No lover nor loved Nor I, but [maystres], though I say nought in this
May I not thinke my pleasure more than his?

Loved not lovyng Affeccion unbridled may make us al thynke
That eche of us hath done other wronge,   1535
But where reason taketh place it can not sinke
Syns cause to be percial here is none us amonge;
That one hed that wolde thinke his owne wit so strong
That on his judges he myght judgement devise,
What judge in so judging coulde judge hym wyse?   1540

Lover loved Well myne estate ryght wel contenteth me.
No lover nor loved And I with myne as well content as ye.

Lover not loved So shulde ye both likewise be contented
Eche other to see content in such degree,
As on your partes our jugement hath awarded   1545
Your neyghbour in pleasure lyke your selfe to be.
Gladly to wishe Christes precept doth bynde ye:
Thus contentacion shulde alway prefer
One man to joy the pleasure of an other.

Lover loved	True, and contencion may be in like case	1550
	All though no helth, yet helpe and greate relefe	
	In both your paynes, for ye havyng such grace	
	To be contented in sufferaunce of grefe	
	Shall by contentacion avoide much myschiefe,	
	Such as the contrary shall suerly bring you:	1555
	Payne to paine as painefull as your paine is nowe.	

Thus not we foure but al the worlde beside
Knowledge them selfe or other in joy or payne,
Hath nede of contentacion for a gyde;
Havinge joy or payne, content let us remayne.   1560
In joy or payne of other fee we disdaine;
Be we content welth or woo, and eche for other
Rejoyse in the tone and pyte the tother.

Lover not loved Syns such contencion may hardly acorde
In such kynde of love as here hath ben ment,   E4
Let us seke the love of that lovyng Lorde   1566
Who to suffer passion for love was content,
Wherby his lovers that love for love assent
Shall have in fyne above contentacyon
The felyng pleasure of eternall salvacyon.   1570

Which Lorde of lordes, whose joyfull and blessed byrth
Is now remembred by tyme presentyng
This accustomyd tyme of honest myrth,
That Lorde we beseche in most humble meanyng
That it may please hym by mercyfull hearyng   1575
Thestate of this audyens longe to endure
In myrth, helth, and welth, to graunt his pleasure.

AMEN

PRYNTED BY W. RASTELL
1534
CUM PRIVILEGIO REGALI.

*A new and a very mery enterlude of all maner wethers
made by Johan Heywood.*

The players names

Jupiter, a god
Mery Reporte, the vyce
The Gentylman
The Marchaunt
The Ranger
The Water Myller
The Wynde Myller
The Gentylwoman
The Launder
A Boy, the lest that can play.

Jupiter   Ryght farre to longe as now were to recyte   A2
The auncyent estate wherin our selfe hath reyned,
What honour, what laude gyven us of very ryght,
What glory we have had dewly unfayned
Of eche creature whych dewty hath constrayned,   5
For above all goddes syns our fathers fale
We Jupiter were ever pryncypale.

If we so have ben as treuth yt is in dede
Beyond the compas of all comparyson,
Who coulde presume to shew for any mede   10
So that yt myght appere to humayne reason
The hye renowme we stande in at this season?
For syns that heven and erth were fyrste create
Stode we never in suche tryumphaunt estate

As we now do, wherof we woll reporte   15
Suche parte as we se mete for tyme present,
Chyefely concernynge your perpetuall conforte
As the thynge selfe shall prove in experyment,
Whyche hyely shall bynde you on knees lowly bent
Soolly to honour oure hyenes day by day.   20
And now to the mater gyve eare and we shall say.

Before our presens in our hye parlyament
Both goddes and goddeses of all degrees
Hath late assembled by comen assent
For the redres of certayne enormytees   25
Bred amonge them thorow extremytees
Abusyd in eche to other of them all,
Namely to purpose in these moste specyall:

Our foresayd father Saturne, and Phebus,
Eolus and Phebe, these four by name,   30
Whose natures not onely so farre contraryous
But also of malyce eche other to defame,
Have longe tyme abused ryght farre out of frame
The dew course of all theyr constellacyons
To the great damage of all yerthly nacyons,   35

Whyche was debated in place sayde before.   A2v
And fyrste as became our father moste auncyent
Wyth berde whyte as snow, his lockes both cold and hore,
Hath entred such mater as served his entent,
Laudynge his frosty mansyon in the fyrmament   40

184

To ayre and yerth as thynge moste precyous,
Pourgynge all humours that are contagyous.

How be yt he alledgeth that of longe tyme past
Lyttell hath prevayled his great dylygens,
Full oft uppon yerth his fayre frost he hath cast   45
All thynges hurtfull to banysh out of presens,
But Phebus entendynge to kepe hym in sylens
When he hath labored all nyght in his powres
His glarynge beamys maryth all in two howres.

Phebus to this made no maner answerynge   50
Wheruppon they both then Phebe defyed,
Eche for his parte leyd in her reprouvynge
That by her showres superfluous, they have tryed
In all that she may, theyr powres be denyed.
Wherunto Phebe made answere no more   55
Then Phebus to Saturne hadde made before.

Anone uppon Eolus all these dyd fle
Complaynynge theyr causes eche one arow
And sayd to compare none was so evyll as he,
For when he is dysposed his blastes to blow   60
He suffereth neyther sone shyne, rayne nor snow.
They eche agaynste other, and he agaynste all thre,
Thus can these foure in no maner agre.

Whyche sene in them selfe, and further consyderynge
The same to redres was cause of theyr assemble.   65
And also that we, evermore beynge,
Besyde our puysaunt power of deite,
Of wysedome and nature so noble and so fre –
From all extremytees the meane devydynge,
To pease and plente eche thynge attemperynge –   70

They have in conclusyon holly surrendryd   A3
Into our handes (as mych as concernynge
All maner wethers by them engendryd)
The full of theyr powrs for terme everlastynge,
To set suche order as standyth wyth our pleasynge,   75
Whyche thynge, as of our parte, no parte requyred
But of all theyr partys ryght humbly desyred.

To take uppon us wherto we dyd assente.
And so in all thynges wyth one voyce agreable
We have clerely fynyshed our foresayd parleament   80

To your great welth whyche shall be fyrme and stable,
And to our honour farre inestymable.
For syns theyr powers as ours addyd to our owne
Who can we say know us as we shulde be knowne?

But now, for fyne, the reste of our entent   85
Wherfore as now we hyther are dyscendyd,
Is onely to satysfye and content
All maner people whyche have ben offendyd
By any wether mete to be amendyd.
Uppon whose complayntes declarynge theyr grefe   90
We shall shape remedy for theyr relefe.

And to gyve knowledge for theyr hyther resorte
We wolde thys afore proclaymed to be
To all our people by some one of thys sorte
Whom we lyste to choyse here amongest all ye   95
Wherfore eche man avaunce and we shall se
Whyche of you is moste mete to be our cryer.

Here entreth Mery Reporte.

Mery Report	Brother holde up your torche a lytell hyer!
	Now I beseche you my lorde, loke on me furste.
	I truste your lordshyp shall not fynde me the wurste. 100
Jupiter	Why, what arte thou that approchyst so ny?
Mery Report	Forsothe, and please your lordshyppe it is I.
Jupiter	All that we knowe very well, but what I?
Mery Report	What I? Some saye I am I perse I.
	But what maner I, so ever be I, 105
	I assure your good lordshyp I am I.
Jupiter	What maner man arte thou, shewe quyckely. A3v
Mery Report	By god, a poore gentylman dwellyth here by.
Jupiter	A gentylman? Thy selfe bryngeth wytnes naye,
	Bothe in thy lyght behavour and araye! 110
	But what arte thou called where thou dost resorte?
Mery Report	Forsoth my lorde, mayster Mery Reporte.
Jupiter	Thou arte no mete man in our bysynes
	For thyne apparence ys of to mych lyghtnes.
Mery Report	Why can not your lordshyp lyke my maner, 115
	Myne apparell nor my name nother?
Jupiter	To nother of all we have devocyon.
Mery Report	A proper lycklyhod of promocyon!
	Well than, as wyse as ye seme to be,
	Yet can ye se no wysdome in me. 120
	But syns ye dysprayse me for so lyghte an elfe

I praye you gyve me leve to prayse my selfe.
And for the fyrste parte I wyll begyn
In my behavour at my commynge in,
Wherin I thynke I have lytell offendyd   125
For sewer my curtesy coulde not be amendyd.
And as for my sewt your servaunt to be
Myghte yll have bene myst for your honeste;
For as I be saved, yf I shall not lye,
I saw no man sew for the offyce but I.   130
Wherfore yf ye take me not or I go
Ye must anone whether ye wyll or no
And syns your entent is but for the wethers
What skyls our apparell to be fryse or fethers?
I thynke it wysdome syns no man forbad it   135
Wyth thys to spare a better – yf I had it.
And for my name, reportyng alwaye trewly
What hurte to reporte a sad mater merely?
As by occasyon for the same entent
To a serteyne wedow thys daye was I sent   140
Whose husbande departyd wythout her wyttynge –
A specyall good lover and she hys owne swettynge –
To whome at my commyng I caste such a fygure,
Mynglynge the mater accordynge to my nature
That when we departyd above all other thynges   145
She thanked me hartely for my mery tydynges.
And yf I had not handled yt meryly   A4
Perchaunce she myght have take yt hevely,
But in suche facyon I conjured and bounde her
That I left her meryer then I founde her.   150
What man may compare to shew the lyke comforte
That dayly is shewed by me, Mery Reporte?
And for your purpose at this tyme ment
For all wethers I am so indyfferent,
Wythout affeccyon standynge so up ryght –   155
Son lyght, mone lyght, ster lyght, twy lyght, torch light,
Cold, hete, moyst, drye, hayle, rayne, frost, snow, lightnyng,
                                                        thunder,
Cloudy, mysty, wyndy, fayre, fowle, above hed or under,
Temperate or dystemperate – what ever yt be,
I promyse your lordshyp all is one to me.   160

Jupiter   Well sonne, consydrynge thyne indyfferency,
           And partely the rest of thy declaracyon,
           We make the our servaunte, and immedyately
           We woll thou departe and cause proclamacyon

187

Publyshynge our pleasure to every nacyon   165
Whyche thynge ons done, wyth all dylygens
Make thy returne agayne to this presens.

Here to receyve all sewters of eche degre
And suche as to the may seme moste metely
We wyll thow brynge them before our majeste.   170
And for the reste that be not so worthy
Make thou reporte to us effectually
So that we may heare eche maner sewte at large.
Thus se thow departe and loke uppon thy charge.

Mery Report   Now good my lorde god, Our Lady be wyth ye!   175
Frendes, a fellyshyppe let me go by ye!
Thynke ye I may stand thrustyng amonge you there?
Nay by God, I muste thrust about other gere.
                    Mery Report goth out. At thende of this
                    staf the god hath a song played in his
                    trone or Mery Report come in.

Jupiter   Now syns we have thus farre set forth our purpose
A whyle we woll wythdraw our godly presens   180
To enbold all such more playnely to dysclose
As here wyll attende in our foresayde pretens.
And now accordynge to your obedyens   A4v
Rejoyce ye in us wyth joy most joyfully,
And we our selfe shall joy in our owne glory.   185
                    [Jupiter withdraws.]
                    Mery Report cometh in.

Mery Report   Now syrs, take hede for here cometh goddes servaunt.
Avaunte, carterly keytyfs, avaunt!
Why, ye dronken horesons, wyll yt not be?
By your fayth, have ye nother cap nor kne?
Not one of you that wyll make curtsy   190
To me that am squyre for goddes precyous body,
Regarde ye nothynge myne authoryte?
No 'welcome home' nor 'where have ye be?'
How be yt yf ye axyd I coulde not well tell,
But suer I thynke a thousande myle from hell.   195
And on my fayth I thynke in my conscyens
I have ben from hevyn as farre as heven is hens,
At Louyn, at London and in Lombardy,
At Baldock, at Barfolde and in Barbary,
At Canturbery, at Coventre, at Colchester   200
At Wansworth and Welbeck, at Westchester,
At Fullam, at Faleborne and at Fenlow,

	At Wallyngford, at Wakefeld and at Waltamstow,	
	At Tawnton, at Typtre and at Totnam,	
	At Glouceter, at Gylford and at Gotham,	205
	At Hartforde, at Harwyche, at Harrow on the hyll,	
	At Sudbery, Suthampton, at Shoters hyll,	
	At Walsyngham, at Wyttam and at Werwycke,	
	At Boston, at Brystow and at Berwycke,	
	At Gravelyn, at Gravesend and at Glastynbery,	210
	Ynge Gyngiang Jayberd, the paryshe of Butsbery.	
	The devyll hym selfe wythout more leasure	
	Coulde not have gone halfe thus myche I am sure.	
	But now I have warned them, let them even chose,	
	For in fayth I care not who wynne or lose.	215

Here the Gentylman before he
cometh in bloweth his horne.

Mery Report	Now by my trouth, this was a goodly hearyng.	
	I went yt had ben the gentylwomens blowynge,	
	But yt is not so as I now suppose,	
	For womens hornes sounde more in a mannys nose.	

[Enter Gentylman.]

Gentylman	Stande ye mery, my frendes everychone!	B1
Mery Report	Say that to me and let the reste alone.	221
	Syr, ye be welcome and all your meyny.	
Gentylman	Now in good sooth my frende, God a mercy!	
	And syns that I mete the here thus by chaunce,	
	I shall requyre the of further acqueyntaunce.	225
	And brevely to shew the this is the mater:	
	I come to sew to the great god Jupyter	
	For helpe of thynges concernynge my recreacyon	
	Accordynge to his late proclamacyon.	
Mery Report	Mary, and I am he that this must spede.	230
	But fyrste tell me what be ye in dede.	
Gentylman	Forsoth, good frende, I am a gentylman.	
Mery Report	A goodly occupacyon, by Seynt Anne!	
	On my fayth your mashyp hath a mery lyfe.	
	But who maketh al these hornes, your self or your wife?	235
	Nay, even in ernest I aske you this questyon.	
Gentylman	Now by my trouth, thou art a mery one.	
Mery Report	In fayth, of us both I thynke never one sad,	
	For I am not so mery but ye seme as mad.	
	But stande ye styll and take a lyttell payne	240
	I wyll come to you by and by agayne.	
	Now gracyous god, yf your wyll so be.	
	I pray ye let me speke a worde wyth ye.	

Jupiter	My sonne say on, let us here thy mynde.	
Mery Report	My lord, there standeth a sewter even here behynde,	245
	A Gentylman in yonder corner,	
	And as I thynke his name is mayster Horner.	
	A hunter he is and comyth to make you sporte,	
	He wolde hunte a sow or twayne out of this sorte.	

Here he poynteth to the women.

Jupiter	What so ever his mynde be, let hym appere.	250
Mery Report	Now good mayster Horner, I pray you come nere.	
Gentylman	I am no horner, knave, I wyll thou know yt.	
Mery Report	I thought ye had, for when ye dyd blow yt	
	Harde I never horeson make horne so goo.	
	As lefe ye kyste myne ars as blow my hole soo.	255
	Come on your way before the god Jupyter	
	And there for your selfe ye shall be sewter.	

[*The Gentylman approaches
Jupiter's throne.*]

Gentylman	Moste myghty prynce and god of every nacyon,	
	Pleasyth your hyghnes to vouchsave the herynge	
	Of me, whyche accordynge to your proclamacyon	B1v
	Doth make apparaunce in way of besechynge	261

Not sole for my selfe, but generally
For all come of noble and auncyent stock ,
Whych sorte above all doth most thankfully
Dayly take payne for welth of the comen flocke, 265

Wyth dylygent study alway devysynge
To kepe them in order and unyte,
In peace to labour the encrees of theyr lyvynge
Wherby eche man may prosper in plente.

Wherfore good god, this is our hole desyrynge: 270
That for ease of our paynes at tymes vacaunt
In our recreacyon – whyche chyefely is huntynge –
It may please you to sende us wether pleasaunt:

Drye and not mysty, the wynde calme and styll,
That after our houndes yournynge so meryly 275
Chasynge the dere over dale and hyll
In herynge we may folow and to-comfort the cry.

| Jupiter | Ryght well we do perceyve your hole request, |

	Whyche shall not fayle to reste in memory.	
	Wherfore we wyll ye set your selfe at rest	280
	Tyll we have herde eche man indyfferently,	
	And we shall take suche order unyversally	
	As best may stande to our honour infynyte	
	For welth in commune and ech mannys synguler profyte.	

[Jupiter withdraws in his
throne.

Gentylman	In heveri and yerth honoured be the name	285
	Of Jupyter, whome of his godly goodnes	
	Hath set this mater in so goodly frame	
	That every wyght shall have his desyre doutles.	

	And fyrst for us nobles and gentylmen,	
	I doute not in his wysedome to provyde	290
	Suche wether as in our huntynge now and then	
	We may both teyse and receyve on every syde.	

	Whyche thynge ones had for our seyd recreacyon	
	Shall greatly prevayle you in preferrynge our helth,	
	For what thynge more nedefull then our preservacyon	295
	Beynge the weale and heddes of all comen welth.	

Mery Report	Now I beseche your mashyp, whose hed be you?	
Gentylman	Whose hed am I? Thy hed. What seyst thou now?	
Mery Report	Nay, I thynke yt very trew so god me helpe	
	For I have ever ben of a lyttell whelpe	B2
	So full of fansyes and in so many fyttes,	301
	So many smale reasons and in so many wyttes	
	That, even as I stande, I pray god I be dede	
	If ever I thought them all mete for one hede.	
	But syns I have one hed more then I knew,	305
	Blame not my rejoycynge – I love all thynges new.	
	And suer yt is a treasour of heddes to have store.	
	One feate can I now that I never coude before.	
Gentylman	What is that?	
Mery Report	By god syns ye came hyther	
	I can set my hedde and my tayle to gyther.	310
	This hed shall save mony, by saynt Mary,	
	From hens forth I wyll no potycary,	
	For at all tymys when suche thynges shall myster,	
	My new hed shall geve myne olde tayle a glyster.	
	And after all this then shall my hedde wayte	315
	Uppon my tayle and there stande at receyte.	
	Syr, for the reste I wyll not now move you,	

	But yf we lyve ye shall smell how I love yow.	
	And syr, touchyng your sewt here depart when it please you,	
	For be ye suer as I can I wyll ease you.	320

Gentylman	Then gyve me thy hande that promyse I take	
	And yf for my sake any sewt thou do make	
	I promyse thy payne to be requyted	
	More largely then now shall be recyted.	

[Exit]

Mery Report	Alas, my necke, goddes pyty, where is my hed?	325
	By Saynt Yve, I feare me I shall be ded!	
	And yf I were, me thynke yt were no wonder	
	Syns my hed and my body is so farre asonder.	

Entreth the Marchaunt

| | Mayster Person, now welcome by my lyfe! | |
| | I pray you, how doth my mastres your wyfe? | 330 |

Marchaunt	Syr, for the presthod and wyfe that ye alledge,	
	I se ye speke more of dotage then knowledge.	
	But let pas syr, I wolde to you be sewter	
	To brynge me yf ye can before Jupiter.	

| Mery Report | Yes, mary can I, and wyll do yt in dede. | 335 |
| | Tary and I shall make wey for your spede. | |

[He goes to Jupiter's throne.]

	In fayth good lord, yf it please your gracyous godshyp	
	I muste have a worde or twayne wyth your lordshyp.	B2v
	Syr, yonder is a nother man in place	
	Who maketh great sewt to speke wyth your grace.	340
	Your pleasure ones knowen, he commeth by and by.	
Jupiter	Bryng hym before our presens sone, hardely.	

[Mery Report returns.]

| Mery Report | Why, where be you? Shall I not fynde ye – | |
| | Come a way, I pray god the devyll blynde ye! | |

[He ushers the Marchaunt
to Jupiter's throne.]

Marchaunt	Most myghty prynce and lorde of lordes all	345
	Ryght humbly besecheth your majeste	
	Your marchaunt men thorow the worlde all	
	That yt may please you of your benygnyte,	
	In the dayly daunger of our goodes and lyfe,	
	Fyrste to consyder the desert of our request –	350
	What welth we bryng the rest to our great care and stryfe –	
	And then to rewarde us as ye shall thynke best.	

What were the surplysage of eche commodyte
Whyche groweth and encreaseth in every lande,
Excepte exchaunge by suche men as we be   355
By wey of entercours that lyeth on our hande?

We fraught from home thynges wherof there is plente
And home we brynge such thynges as there be scant.
Who sholde afore us marchauntes accompted be?
For were not we, the worlde shuld wyshe and want   360

In many thynges, whych now shall lack rehersall.
And brevely to conclude, we beseche your hyghnes
That of the benefyte proclaymed in generall
We may be parte takers for comen encres,

Stablyshynge wether thus, pleasynge your grace: 365
Stormy nor mysty, the wynde mesurable,
That savely we may passe from place to place
Berynge our seylys for spede moste vayleable;

And also the wynde to chaunge and to turne
Eest, west, north and south, as beste may be set,   370
In any one place not to longe to sojourne,
For the length of our vyage may lese our market.

Jupiter   Ryght well have ye sayde and we accept yt so,
               And so shall we rewarde you ere we go hens;
               But ye muste take pacyens tyll we have harde mo   375
               That we may indyfferently gyve sentens.
               There may passe by us no spot of neglygence.
               But justely to judge eche thynge so upryghte   B3
               That ech mans parte maye shyne in the selfe ryghte.
                              [Jupiter withdraws in his throne.]

Mery Report   Now syr, by your fayth, yf ye shulde be sworne   380
               Harde ye ever god speke so syns ye were borne?
               So wysely, so gentylly hys wordes be showd.
Merchaunt   I thanke hys grace my sewte is well bestowd.
Mery Report   Syr, what vyage entende ye nexte to go?
Merchaunt   I truste or myd lente to be to Syo.   385
Mery Report   Ha ha, is it your mynde to sayle at Syo?
               Nay then, when ye wyll, byr lady ye maye go
               And let me alone wyth thys. Be of good chere –
               Ye maye truste me at Syo as well as here;
               For, though ye were fro me a thousande myle space, 390

193

I wolde do as myche as ye were here in place.
For syns that from hens it is so farre thyther
I care not though ye never come agayne hyther.

Merchaunt Syr, yf ye remember me when tyme shall come
Though I requyte not all, I shall deserve some. 395

           Exeat Marchaunt.

Mery Report Now farre ye well, and god thanke you by saynt Anne!
I pray you marke the fasshyon of thys honeste manne:
He putteth me in more truste at thys metynge here
Then he shall fynde cause why thys twenty yere.

          Here entreth the Ranger.

Ranger God be here! Now Cryst kepe thys company! 400
Mery Report In fayth ye be welcome evyn very skantely.
Syr, for your comynge, what is the mater?
Ranger I wolde fayne speke wyth the god Jupyter.
Mery Report That wyll not be but ye may do thys:
Tell me your mynde, I am an offycer of hys. 405

Ranger Be ye so? Mary, I cry you marcy!
Your maystershyp may say I am homely,
But syns your mynde is to have reportyd
The cause wherfore I am now resortyd,
Pleasyth it your maystershyp it is so: 410
I come for my selfe and suche other mo
Rangers and kepers of certayne places
As forestes, parkes, purlews and chasys,
Where we be chargyd wyth all maner game.
Smale is our profyte and great is our blame. 415
Alas for our wages, what be we the nere?
What is forty shyllynges or fyve marke a yere? B3v
Many tymes and oft where we be flyttynge
We spende forty pens a pece at a syttynge.
Now for our vauntage whyche chefely is wyndefale, 420
That is ryght nought there blowyth no wynde at all,
Whyche is the thynge wherin we fynde most grefe
And cause of my commynge to sew for relefe,
That the god, of pyty, all thys thynge knowynge,
Maye sende us good rage of blustryng and blowynge. 425
And yf I can not get god to do some good
I wolde hyer the devyll to runne thorow the wood
The rootes to turne up, the toppys to brynge under.
A myschyefe upon them and a wylde thunder!

Mery Report Very well sayd. I set by your charyte 430
As mych in a maner as by your honeste.

194

	I shall set you somwhat in ease anone –	
	Ye shall putte on your cappe when I am gone,	
	For I se ye care not who wyn or lese	
	So ye maye fynde meanys to wyn your fees.	435
Ranger	Syr, as in that ye speke as it please ye,	
	But let me speke wyth the god yf it maye be –	
	I pray you lette me passe ye.	

[He tries to approach the throne.]

Mery Report	Why, nay syr, by the masse, ye!	
Ranger	Then wyll I leve you evyn as I founde ye.	440
Mery Report	Go when ye wyll, no man here hath bounde ye.	

Here entreth the Water Myller
and the Ranger goth out.

Water Myller	What the devyll shold skyl though all the world were dum,	
	Syns in all our spekynge we never be harde.	
	We crye out for rayne, the devyll sped drop wyll cum.	
	We water myllers be nothynge in regarde.	445

No water have we to grynde at any stynt.
The wynde is so stronge the rayne can not fall,
Whyche kepeth our myldams as drye as a flynt.
We are undone, we grynde nothynge at all.

The greter is the pyte as thynketh me	450
For what avayleth to eche man hys corne	
Tyll it be grounde by such men as we be.	
There is the losse yf we be forborne.	

For touchynge our selfes, we are but drudgys	454
And very beggers, save onely our tole,	B4
Whyche is ryght smale and yet many grudges	
For gryste of a busshell to gyve a quarte bole.	

Yet, were not reparacyons, we myght do wele:
Our mylstons, our whele with her kogges and our trindill,
Our floodgate, our mylpooll, our water whele,   460
Our hopper, our extre, our yren spyndyll.

In thys and mych more so great is our charge	
That we wolde not recke though no water ware,	
Save onely it toucheth eche man so large,	
And ech for our neyghbour Cryste byddeth us care.	465

Wherfore my conscyence hath prycked me hyther
In thys to sewe accordynge to the cry

195

	For plente of rayne to the god Jupiter,	
	To whose presence I wyll go evyn boldely.	
	[*Mery Report prevents him.*]	
Mery Report	Syr, I dowt nothynge your audacyte	470
	But I feare me ye lacke capacyte,	
	For yf ye were wyse ye myghte well espye	
	How rudely ye erre from rewls of curtesye.	
	What, ye come in revelynge and reheytynge	
	Evyn as a knave myght go to a beare beytynge!	475
Water Myller	All you bere recorde what favour I have.	
	Herke how famylyerly he calleth me knave.	
	Dowtles the gentylman is universall,	
	But marke thys lesson, syr, you shulde never call	
	Your felow knave nor your brother horeson,	480
	For nought can ye get by it when ye have done.	
Mery Report	Thou arte nother brother nor felowe to me,	
	For I am goddes servaunt – mayst thou not se?	
	Wolde ye presume to speke wyth the great god?	
	Nay, dyscrecyon and you be to farre od.	485
	Byr lady, these knavys muste be tyed shorter.	
	Syr, who let you in, spake ye wyth the porter?	
Water Myller	Nay, by my trouth, nor wyth no nother man,	
	Yet I saw you well when I fyrst began.	
	How be it, so helpe me god and holydam,	490
	I toke you but for a knave as I am.	
	But mary, now, syns I knowe what ye be,	
	I muste and wyll obey your authoryte,	
	And yf I maye not speke wyth Jupiter	494
	I beseche you be my solycyter.	B4v
Mery Report	As in that I wylbe your well wyller.	
	I perceyve you be a water myller	
	And your hole desyre, as I take the mater,	
	Is plente of rayne for encres of water,	
	The let wherof, ye affyrme determynately	500
	Is onely the wynde, your mortall enemy.	
Water Myller	Trouth it is, for it blowyth so alofte	
	We never have rayne, or at the most not ofte.	
	Wherfore I praye you, put the god in mynde	
	Clerely for ever to banysh the wynde.	505
	Entreth the Wynd Myller	
Wynd Myller	How? Is all the wether gone or I come?	
	For the passyon of God, helpe me to some!	
	I am a wynd myller as many mo be –	
	No wretch in wretchydnes so wrechyd as we!	
	The hole sorte of my crafte be all mard at onys,	510

196

The wynde is so weyke it sturryth not our stonys,
Nor skantely can shatter the shyttyn sayle
That hangeth shatterynge at a womans tayle.
The rayne never resteth, so longe be the showres
From tyme of begynnyng tyll foure and twenty howres,   515
And ende whan it shall, at nyght or at none,
An other begynneth as soone as that is done.
Such revell of rayne ye knowe well inough
Destroyeth the wynde, be it never so rough;
Wherby, syns our myllys be come to styll standynge,   520
Now maye we wynd myllers go evyn to hangynge.
A myller? Wyth a moryn and a myschyefe!
Who wolde be a myller? As good be a thefe.
Yet in tyme past when gryndynge was plente
Who were so lyke goddys felows as we?   525
As faste as god made corne we myllers made meale.
Whyche myght be best forborne for comyn weale?
But let that gere passe! For I feare our pryde
Is cause of the care whyche god doth us provyde,
Wherfore I submyt me, entendynge to se   530
What comforte maye come by humylyte.
And now at thys tyme they sayd in the crye
The god is come downe to shape remedye.

Mery Report   No doute he is here even in yonder trone.   C1
But in your mater he trusteth me alone,   535
Wherin I do perceyve by your complaynte
Oppressyon of rayne doth make the wynde so faynte
That ye wynde myllers be clene caste away.

Wynd Myller   If Jupyter helpe not, yt is as ye say.
But in few wordes to tell you my mynde rounde,   540
Uppon this condycyon I wolde be bounde
Day by day to say Our Ladyes sauter:
That in this world were no drope of water
Nor never rayne, but wynde contynuall,
Then shold we wyndemyllers be lordes over all.   545

Mery Report   Come on and assay how you twayne can agre –
A brother of yours, a myller as ye be.

Water Myller   By meane of our craft we may be brothers,
But whyles we lyve shall we never be lovers.
We be of one crafte but not of one kynde   550
I lyve by water and he by the wynde.

                 Here Mery Reporte goth out.

And syr, as ye desyre wynde contynuall,
So wolde I have rayne ever more to fall,

Whyche two in experyence ryght well ye se
Ryght selde or never to gether can be.   555
For as longe as the wynde rewleth, yt is playne
Twenty to one ye get no drop of rayne;
And when the element is to farre opprest,
Downe commeth the rayne and setteth the wynde at rest.
By this ye se we can not both obtayne,   560
For ye must lacke wynde or I must lacke rayne.
Wherfore I thynke good before this audyens
Eche for our selfe to say or we go hens.
And whom is thought weykest when we have fynysht,
Leve of his sewt and content to be banysht.   565

Wynd Myller   In fayth, agreed. But then by your lycens
Our mylles for a tyme shall hange in suspens.
Syns water and wynde is chyefely our sewt
Whyche best may be spared we woll fyrst dyspute.
Wherfore to the see my reason shall resorte   570
Where shyppes by meane of wynd try from port to port,
From lande to lande in dystaunce many a myle –
Great is the passage and smale is the whyle.
So great is the profyte as to me doth seme   Clv
That no mans wysdome the welth can exteme.   575
And syns the wynde is conveyer of all,
Who but the wynde shulde have thanke above all?

Water Myller   Amytte in thys place a tree here to growe
And therat the wynde in great rage to blowe;
When it hath all blowen – thys is a clere case –   580
The tre removyth no here bred from hys place.
No more wolde the shyppys – blow the best it cowde –
All though it wolde blow downe both mast and shrowde,
Except the shyppe flete uppon the water
The wynde can ryght nought do – a playne mater.   585
Yet maye ye on water, wythout any wynde
Row forth your vessell where men wyll have her synde.
Nothynge more rejoyceth the maryner
Then meane coolys of wynde and plente of water,
For commenly the cause of every wracke   590
Is excesse of wynde where water doth lacke.
In rage of these stormys the perell is suche
That better were no wynde then so farre to muche.

Wynd Myller   Well, yf my reason in thys may not stande,
I wyll forsake the see and lepe to lande.   595

198

In every chyrche where goddys servyce is
The organs beare brunt of halfe the quere iwys.
Whyche causyth the sounde – [or] water or wynde?
More over, for wynde thys thynge I fynde:
For the most parte, all maner mynstrelsy   600
By wynde they delyver theyr sound chefly.
Fyll me a bagpype of your water full.
As swetly shall it sounde as it were stuffyd with wull.

Water Myller   On my fayth, I thynke the moone be at the full,
For frantyke fansyes be then most plentefull,   605
Whych are at the pryde of theyr sprynge in your hed,
So farre from our mater he is now fled.
As for the wynde in any instrument,
It is no percell of our argument.
We spake of wynde that comyth naturally   610
And that is wynde forcyd artyfycyally,
Whyche is not to purpose. But yf it were,
And water in dede ryght nought coulde do there,
Yet I thynke organs no suche commodyte   C2
Wherby the water shulde banyshed be.   615
And for your bagpypes, I take them as nyfuls –
Your mater is all in fansyes and tryfuls.

Wynd Myller   By God, but ye shall not tryfull me of so!
Yf these thynges serve not, I wyll reherse mo.
And now to mynde there is one olde proverbe come: 620
'One bushell of March dust is worth a kynges raunsome.'
What is a hundreth thousande bushels worth than?
Water Myller   Not one myte, for the thynge selfe, to no man.

Wynd Myller   Why, shall wynde every where thus be objecte?
Nay, in the hye wayes he shall take effecte   625
Where as the rayne doth never good but hurt,
For wynde maketh but dust, and water maketh durt.
Powder or syrop, syrs, whyche lycke ye beste?
Who lycketh not the tone maye lycke up the reste.
But sure who so ever hath assayed such syppes   630
Had lever have dusty eyes then durty lyppes.
And it is sayd syns afore we were borne
That drought doth never make derth of corne.
And well it is knowen to the most foole here
How rayne hath pryced corne within this seven yere.   635

Water Myller   Syr, I pray the, spare me a lytyll season
And I shall brevely conclude the wyth reason.

Put case on somers daye wythout wynde to be,
And ragyous wynde in wynter dayes two or thre:
Mych more shall dry that one calme daye in somer   640
Then shall those thre wyndy dayes in wynter.
Whom shall we thanke for thys when all is done?
The thanke to wynde? Nay, thanke chyefely the sone.
And so for drought, yf corne therby encres,
The sone doth comforte and rype all dowtles.   645
And oft the wynde so leyth the corne, God wot,
That never after can it rype, but rot.
Yf drought toke place as ye say, yet maye ye se
Lytell helpeth the wynde in thys commodyte.
But now, syr, I deny your pryncypyll: 650
Yf drought ever were, it were impossybyll
To have ony grayne, for or it can grow
Ye must plow your lande, harrow and sow.
Whyche wyll not be, except ye maye have rayne   C2v
To temper the grounde, and after agayne   655
For spryngynge and plumpyng all maner corne
Yet muste ye have water or all is forlorne.
Yf ye take water for no commodyte,
Yet must ye take it for thynge of necessyte
For washynge, for skowrynge, all fylth clensynge.   660
Where water lacketh, what bestely beynge!
In brewyng, in bakynge, in dressynge of meate,
Yf ye lacke water what coulde ye drynke or eate?
Wythout water coulde lyve neyther man nor best,
For water preservyth both moste and lest.   665
For water coulde I say a thousande thynges mo,
Savynge as now the tyme wyll not serve so.
And as for that wynde that you do sew fore,
Is good for your wyndemyll and for no more.
Syr, syth all thys in experyence is tryde,   670
I say thys mater standeth clere on my syde.

Wynd Myller   Well, syns thys wyll not serve, I wyll alledge the reste.
Syr, for our myllys, I saye myne is the beste.
My wyndmyll shall grynd more corne in one our
Then thy water myll shall in thre or foure –   675
Ye, more then thyne shulde in a hole yere,
Yf thou myghtest have as thou hast wyshyd here.
For thou desyrest to have excesse of rayne,
Whych thyng to the were the worst thou coudyst obtayne,
For, yf thou dydyst, it were a playne induccyon   680
To make thyne owne desyer thyne owne destruccyon.

200

For in excesse of rayne at any flood
Your myllys must stande styll – they can do no good.
And whan the wynde doth blow the uttermost,
Our wyndmylles walke a-mayne in every cost.   685
For as we se the wynde in hys estate
We moder our saylys after the same rate.
Syns our myllys grynde so farre faster then yours,
And also they may grynde all tymes and howrs,
I say we nede no water mylles at all,   690
For wyndmylles be suffycyent to serve all.

Water Myller   Thou spekest of all and consyderest not halfe.
In boste of thy gryste thou arte wyse as a calfe!
For though above us your mylles grynde farre faster,   C3
What helpe to those from whome ye be myche farther?   695
And of two sortes, yf the tone shold be conserved,
I thynke yt mete the moste nomber be served.
In vales and weldes where moste commodyte is,
There is most people – ye must graunte me this.
On hylles and downes, whyche partes are moste barayne   700
There muste be few – yt can no mo sustayne.
I darre well say, yf yt were tryed even now
That there is ten of us to one of you.
And where shuld chyefely all necessaryes be
But there as people are moste in plente?   705
More reason that you come seven myle to myll
Then all we of the vale sholde clyme the hyll.
Yf rayne came reasonable as I requyre yt,
We sholde of your wyndemylles have nede no whyt.

                                        Entreth Mery Reporte.
Mery Report   Stop, folysh knaves, for your reasonynge is suche   710
That ye have reasoned even ynough and to much.
I hard all the wordes that ye both have hadde –
So helpe me God, the knaves be more then madde!
Nother of them both that hath wyt nor grace
To perceyve that both myllys may serve in place.   715
Betwene water and wynde there is no suche let,
But eche myll may have tyme to use his fet.
Whyche thynge I can tell by experyens,
For I have of myne owne, not farre from hens
In a corner to gether, a couple of myllys   720
Standynge in a marres betwene two hyllys –
Not of inherytaunce but by my wyfe.
She is feofed in the tayle for terme of her lyfe,

201

The one for wynde, the other for water,
And of them both I thanke god there standeth nother,   725
For in a good hour be yt spoken
The water gate is no soner open
But 'Clap!' sayth the wyndmyll, even strayght behynde.
There is good spedde, the devyll and all they grynde.
But whether that the hopper be dusty,   730
Or that the mylstonys be sum what rusty,
By the mas, the meale is myschevous musty.
And yf ye thynke my tale be not trusty   C3v
I make ye trew promyse – come when ye lyst,
We shall fynde meane ye shall taste of the gryst.   735

Water Myller   The corne at receyt happely is not good.

Mery Report   There can be no sweeter, by the sweet rood.
Another thynge yet whyche shall not be cloked,
My water myll many tymes is choked.

Water Myller   So wyll she be though ye shuld burste your bones,   740
Except ye be perfyt in settynge your stones.
Fere not the lydger, be ware your ronner.
Yet this for the lydger or ye have wonne her –
Perchaunce your lydger doth lacke good peckyng.

Mery Report   So sayth my wyfe and that maketh all our checkyng.   745
She wolde have the myll peckt, peckt, peckt every day,
But by god, myllers muste pecke when they may.
So oft have we peckt that our stones wax ryght thyn
And all our other gere not worth a pyn.
For wyth peckynge and peckyng I have so wrought   750
That I have peckt a good peckynge yron to nought.
How be yt yf I stycke no better tyll her
My wyfe sayth she wyll have a new myller.
But let yt passe – and now to our mater.
I say my myllys lack nother wynde nor water –   755
No more do yours as farre as nede doth requyre.
But syns ye can not agree, I wyll desyre
Jupyter to set you both in suche rest
As to your welth and his honour may stande best.

Water Myller   I pray you hertely remember me.   760

Wynd Myller   Let not me be forgoten, I beseche ye.

                                  Both myllers goth forth.

Mery Report   If I remember you not both a lyke
I wolde ye were over the eares in the dyke!

	Now be we ryd of two knaves at once chaunce –	
	By saynt Thomas, yt is a knavyshe ryddaunce.	765
	The Gentylwoman entreth.	
Gentylwoman	Now good god, what a foly is this!	
	What sholde I do where so mych people is?	
	I know not how to passe in to the god now.	
Mery Report	No, but ye know how he may passe into you.	
Gentylwoman	I pray you, let me in at the backe syde.	770
Mery Report	Ye, shall I so, and your foresyde so wyde?	C4
	Nay, not yet! But syns ye love to be alone,	
	We twayne wyll into a corner anone.	
	But fyrste I pray you come your way hyther	
	And let us twayne chat a whyle to-gyther.	775
Gentylwoman	Syr, as to you, I have lyttell mater –	
	My commynge is to speke wyth Jupiter.	
Mery Report	Stande ye styll a whyle and I wyll go prove	
	Whether that the god wyll be brought in love.	
	[He approaches Jupiter's throne.]	
	My lorde, how now, loke uppe lustely,	780
	Here is a derlynge come, by saynt Antony!	
	And yf yt be your pleasure to mary	
	Speke quyckly, for she may not tary.	
	In fayth I thynke ye may wynne her anone,	
	For she wolde speke wyth your lordshyp alone.	785
Jupiter	Sonne, that is not the thynge at this tyme ment.	
	If her sewt concerne no cause of our hyther resorte,	
	Sende her out of place; but yf she be bent	
	To that purpose, heare her and make us reporte.	
Mery Report	I count women lost yf we love them not well,	790
	For ye se god loveth them never a dele.	
	Maystres, ye can not speke wyth the god.	
Gentylwoman	No, why?	
Mery Report	By my fayth, for his lordshyp is ryght besy	
	Wyth a pece of worke that nedes must be doone.	
	Even now is he makynge of a new moone:	795
	He sayth your old moones be so farre tasted	
	That all the goodnes of them is wasted –	
	Whyche of the great wete hath ben moste mater,	
	For olde moones be leake, they can holde no water.	
	But for this new mone, I durst lay my gowne,	800
	Except a few droppes at her goyng downe,	

Ye get no rayne tyll her arysynge
Wythout yt nede and then no mans devysynge
Coulde wyshe the fashyon of rayne to be so good,
Not gushynge out lyke gutters of Noyes flood,   805
But smale droppes sprynklyng softly on the grounde
Though they fell on a sponge they wold gyve no sounde.
This new moone shal make a thing spryng more in this while
Then a old moone shal while a man may go a mile.
By that tyme the god hath all made an ende   C4v
Ye shall se how the wether wyll amende.   811
By saynt Anne, he goth to worke even boldely!
I thynke hym wyse ynough, for he loketh oldely.
Wherfore maystres, be ye now of good chere,
For though in his presens ye can not appere,   815
Tell me your mater and let me alone:
May happe I wyll thynke on you when you be gone.

Gentylwoman   Forsoth the cause of my commynge is this:
I am a woman ryght fayre, as ye se,
In no creature more beauty then in me is,   820
And syns I am fayre, fayre wolde I kepe me.

But the sonne in somer so sore doth burne me,
In wynter the wynde on every syde me,
No parte of the yere wote I where to turne me,
But even in my house am I fayne to hyde me.   825

And so do all other that beuty have,
In whose name at this tyme this sewt I make,
Besechynge Jupyter to graunt that I crave
Whyche is this: that yt may please hym for our sake

To sende us wether close and temperate,   830
No sonne shyne, no frost, nor no wynde to blow.
Then wolde we get the stretes trym as a parate –
Ye shold se how we wolde set our selfe to show.

Mery Report   Jet where ye wyll, I swere by saynte Quintyne,
Ye passe them all both in your owne conceyt and myne.   835
Gentylwoman   If we had wether to walke at our pleasure,
Our lyves wolde be mery out of measure.
One parte of the day for our apparellynge,
Another parte for eatynge and drynkynge,
And all the reste in stretes to be walkynge,   840
Or in the house to passe tyme wyth talkynge.
Mery Report   When serve ye God?

204

Gentylwoman	Who bosteth in vertue are but daws.	
Mery Report	Ye do the better, namely syns there is no cause.	
	How spende ye the nyght?	
Gentylwoman	In daunsynge and syngynge	
	Tyll mydnyght and then fall to slepynge.	845
Mery Report	Why, swete herte, by your false fayth, can ye syng?	
Gentylwoman	Nay nay but I love yt above all thynge.	

Mery Report	Now by my trouth, for the love that I owe you,	D1
	You shall here what pleasure I can shew you.	
	One songe have I for you, suche as yt is,	850
	And yf yt were better ye shold have yt, by gys!	

Gentylwoman	Mary syr, I thanke you even hartely.	
Mery Report	Come on, syrs, but now let us synge lustly.	

Here they synge.

Gentylwoman	Syr, this is well done, I hertely thanke you.	
	Ye have done me pleasure, I make god a vowe.	855
	Ones in a nyght I longe for suche a fyt,	
	For longe tyme have I ben brought up in yt.	
Mery Report	Oft tyme yt is sene both in court and towne,	
	Longe be women a bryngyng up and sone brought down.	
	So fete yt is, so nete yt is, so nyse yt is,	860
	So trycke yt is, so quycke yt is, so wyse yt is!	
	I fere my selfe, excepte I may entreat her,	
	I am so farre in love I shall forget her.	
	Now good maystres, I pray you let me kys ye.	
Gentylwoman	Kys me, quoth a! Why nay, syr, I wys ye!	865
Mery Report	What, yes, hardely, kys me ons and no more.	
	I never desyred to kys you before.	

Here the Launder cometh in.

Launder	Why, have ye alway kyst her behynde?	
	In fayth good inough yf yt be your mynde.	
	And yf your appetyte serve you so to do,	870
	Byr lady, I wolde ye had kyst myne ars to.	
Mery Report	To whom dost thou speke, foule hore, canst thou tell?	
Launder	Nay, by my trouth – I syr? Not very well.	
	But by conjecture this ges I have,	
	That I do speke to an olde baudy knave.	875
	I saw you dally wyth your symper de cokket –	
	I rede you beware she pyck not your pokket.	
	Such ydyll huswyfes do now and than	
	Thynke all well wonne that they pyck from a man.	
	Yet such of some men shall have more favour	880
	Then we that for them dayly toyle and labour.	

205

But I trust the god wyll be so indyfferent
That she shall fayle some parte of her entent.

Mery Report   No dout he wyll deale so gracyously
That all folke shall be served indyfferently.   885
How be yt – I tell the trewth – my offyce is suche   D1v
That I muste reporte eche sewt lyttell or muche.
Wherfore wyth the god syns thou canst not speke,
Trust me wyth thy sewt – I wyll not fayle yt to breke.

Launder   Then leane not to myche to yonder gyglet,   890
For her desyre contrary to myne is set.
I herde by her tale she wolde banyshe the sonne
And then were we pore launders all undonne.
Excepte the sonne shyne that our clothes may dry
We can do ryght nought in our laundry –   895
Another maner losse yf we sholde mys
Then of such nycebyceters as she is.

Gentylwoman   I thynke yt better that thou envy me
Then I sholde stande at rewarde of thy pytte.
It is the guyse of such grose queynes as thou art   900
Wyth such as I am evermore to thwart,
Bycause that no beauty ye can obtayne,
Therfore ye have us that be fayre in dysdayne.

Launder   When I was as yonge as thou art now
I was wythin lyttel as fayre as thou   905
And so myght have kept me yf I hadde wolde
And as derely my youth I myght have solde
As the tryckest and fayrest of you all.
But I feared parels that after myght fall,
Wherfore some besynes I dyd me provyde   910
Lest vyce myght entre on every syde,
Whyche hath fre entre where ydylnesse doth reyne.
It is not thy beauty that I dysdeyne
But thyne ydyll lyfe that thou hast rehersed,
Whych any good womans hert wolde have perced.   915
For I perceyve in daunsynge and syngynge,
In eatyng and drynkynge and thyne apparellynge
Is all the joye wherin thy herte is set.
But nought of all this doth thyne owne labour get.
For haddest thou nothyng but of thyne owne travayle,   920
Thou myghtest go as naked as my nayle.
Me thynke thou shuldest abhorre suche ydylnes
And passe thy tyme in some honest besynes.

206

	Better to lese some parte of thy beaute	
	Then so oft to jeoberd all thyne honeste.	925
	But I thynke rather then thou woldest so do,	D2
	Thou haddest lever have us lyve ydylly to.	
	And so no doute we shulde, yf thou myghtest have	
	The clere sone banysht as thou dost crave;	
	Then were we launders marde, and unto the	930
	Thyne owne request were smale commodyte.	
	For of these twayne I thynke yt farre better	
	Thy face were sone-burned and thy clothis the swetter,	
	Then that the sonne from shynynge sholde be smytten	
	To kepe thy face fayre and thy smocke beshytten.	935
	Syr, how lycke ye my reason in her case?	

Mery Report   Such a raylynge hore, by the holy mas,
              I never herde in all my lyfe tyll now!
              In dede I love ryght well the ton of you,
              But or I wolde kepe you both, by Goddes mother,   940
              The devyll shall have the tone to fet the tother!
Launder   Promise me to speke that the sone may shyne bryght
              And I wyll be gone quyckly for all nyght.

Mery Report   Get you both hens, I pray you hartely.
              Your sewtes I perceyve and wyll reporte them trewly   945
              Unto Jupyter at the next leysure
              And, in the same, desyre to know his pleasure;
              Whyche knowledge hadde, even as he doth show yt,
              Feare ye not, tyme inough ye shall know yt.

Gentylwoman   Syr, yf ye medyll, remember me fyrste.   950
Launder   Then in this medlynge my parte shalbe the wurst.
Mery Report   Now I beseche Our Lorde, the devyll the burst!
              Who medlyth wyth many I hold hym accurst.
              Thou hore, can I medyl wyth you both at ones?
                              Here the gentylwoman goth forth
Launder   By the mas, knave, I wold I had both thy stones   955
              In my purs yf thou medyl not indyfferently
              That both our maters in yssew may be lyckly.

Mery Report   Many wordes, lyttell mater and to no purpose,
              Suche is the effect that thou dost dysclose,
              The more ye byb the more ye babyll,   960
              The more ye babyll the more ye fabyll,
              The more ye fabyll the more unstabyll,
              The more unstabyll the more unabyll,

	In any maner thynge to do any good.	
	No hurt though ye were hanged, by the holy rood!	965
Launder	The les your sylence the lesse your credence,	D2v
	The les your credens the les your honeste,	
	The les your honeste the les your assystens,	
	The les your assystens the les abylyte	
	In you to do ought! Wherfore, so god me save,	970
	No hurte in hangynge suche a raylynge knave!	
Mery Report	What monster is this? I never harde none suche,	
	For loke how myche more I have made her to myche	
	And so farre at lest she hath made me to lyttell.	
	Wher be ye launder? I thynke in some spyttell.	975
	Ye shall washe me no gere for feare of fretynge.	
	I love no launders that shrynke my gere in wettynge.	
	I pray the go hens and let me be in rest.	
	I wyll do thyne erand as I thynke best.	
Launder	Now wolde I take my leve yf I wyste how.	980
	The lenger I lyve the more knave you!	

[Exit the Launder.]

Mery Report	The lenger thou lyvest, the pyte the gretter,	
	The soner thou be ryd, the tydynges the better!	
	Is not this a swete offyce that I have,	
	When every drab shall prove me a knave?	985
	Every man knoweth not what goddes servyce is	
	Nor I my selfe knew yt not before this.	
	I thynke goddes servauntes may lyve holyly	
	But the devyls servauntes lyve more meryly.	
	I know not what god geveth in standynge fees	990
	But the devyls servauntes have casweltees	
	A hundred tymes mo then goddes servauntes have.	
	For though ye be never so starke a knave,	
	If ye lacke money the devyll wyll do no wurse	
	But brynge you strayght to a nother mans purse.	995
	Then wyll the devyll promote you here in this world	
	As unto suche ryche yt doth moste accord.	
	Fyrste, '*pater noster qui es in celis*',	
	And then ye shall sens the shryfe wyth your helys.	
	The greatest frende ye have in felde or towne	1000
	Standynge a typ-to shall not reche your crowne.	

The Boy comyth in, the lest
that can play.

| [Boy] | This same is even he by al lycklyhod. |
| | Syr, I pray you, be not you master god? |

Mery Report	No in good fayth sonne, but I may say to the	
	I am suche a man that god may not mysse me.	D3
	Wherfore wyth the god yf thou woldest have ought done,	1006
	Tell me thy mynde and I shall shew yt sone.	

Boy	Forsothe syr, my mynde is thys, at few wordes	
	All my pleasure is in catchynge of byrdes	
	And makynge of snow ballys and throwyng the same.	1010
	For the whyche purpose to have set in frame,	
	Wyth my godfather god I wolde fayne have spoken,	
	Desyrynge hym to have sent me by some token	
	Where I myghte have had great frost for my pytfallys	
	And plente of snow to make my snow ballys.	1015
	This onys had, boyes lyvis be such as no man leddys.	
	O, to se my snow ballys lyght on my felowes heddys	
	And to here the byrdes how they flycker theyr wynges	
	In the pytfale, I say yt passeth all thynges.	
	Syr, yf ye be goddes servaunt or his kynsman,	1020
	I pray you helpe me in this yf ye can.	

Mery Report	Alas, pore boy, who sent the hether?	
Boy	A hundred boys that stode to gether,	
	Where they herde one say in a cry	
	That my godfather, god almyghty,	1025
	Was come from heven by his owne accorde	
	This nyght to suppe here wyth my lorde.	
	And farther he sayde, come whoso wull,	
	They shall sure have theyr bellyes full	
	Of all wethers, who lyste to crave –	1030
	Eche sorte suche wether as they lyste to have.	
	And when my felowes thought this wolde be had,	
	And saw me so prety a pratelynge lad,	
	Uppon agrement, wyth a great noys	
	'Sende lyttell Dycke!' cryed all the boys,	1035
	By whose assent I am purveyd	
	To sew for the wether afore seyd.	
	Wherin I pray you to be good, as thus,	
	To helpe that god may gyve yt us.	

Mery Report	Gyve boys wether, quoth a! Nonny nonny!	1040
Boy	If god of his wether wyll gyve nonny,	
	I pray you, wyll he sell ony	

	Or lend us a bushell of snow or twayne	
	And poynt us a day to pay hym agayne?	
Mery Report	I can not tell, for by thys lyght,	D3v
	I chept nor borowed none of hym this nyght.	1046
	But by suche shyfte as I wyll make	
	Thou shalte se soone what waye he wyll take.	

| *Boy* | Syr, I thanke you. Then I may departe. | |

The Boye goth forth.

| *Mery Report* | Ye, farewell, good sonne, wyth all my harte. | 1050 |

Now such an other sorte as here hath bene
In all the dayes of my lyfe I have not sene.
No sewters now but women, knavys, and boys,
And all theyr sewtys are in fansyes and toys.
Yf that there come no wyser after thys cry   1055
I wyll to the god and make an ende quyckely.

[*He makes proclamation.*]

Oyes, yf that any knave here
Be wyllynge to appere
For wether fowle or clere,
Come in before thys flocke,   1060
And be he hole or syckly,
Come shew hys mynde quyckly,
And yf hys tale be not lyckly
Ye shall lycke my tayle in the nocke.
All thys tyme I perceyve is spent in wast   1065
To wayte for mo sewters, I se none make hast,
Wherfore I wyll shew the god all thys procys
And be delyvered of my symple offys.

[*He goes to Jupiter's throne.*]

Now lorde, accordynge to your commaundement,
Attendynge sewters I have ben dylygent   1070
And, at begynnyng as your wyll was I sholde,
I come now at ende to shewe what eche man wolde.
The fyrst sewter before your selfe dyd appere,
A gentylman desyrynge wether clere,
Clowdy nor mysty nor no wynde to blow,   1075
For hurt in hys huntynge. And then, as ye know,
The marchaunt sewde for all of that kynde
For wether clere and mesurable wynde,
As they maye best bere theyr saylys to make spede.
And streyght after thys there came to me in dede   1080

210

An other man, who namyd hym selfe a ranger,
And sayd all of hys crafte be farre brought in daunger
For lacke of lyvynge, whyche chefely ys wynde fall.
But he playnely sayth there bloweth no wynde at al, D4
Wherfore he desyreth for encrease of theyr fleesys 1085
Extreme rage of wynde, trees to tere in peces.
Then came a water myller, and he cryed out
For water, and sayde the wynde was so stout
The rayne could not fale, wherfore he made request
For plenty of rayne to set the wynde at rest. 1090
And then, syr, there came a wyndemyller in
Who sayde for the rayne he could no wynde wyn.
The water he wysht to be banysht all,
Besechynge your grace of wynde contynuall.
Then came there an other that wolde banysh all this – 1095
A goodly dame, an ydyll thynge iwys;
Wynde, rayne, nor froste, nor sonshyne wold she have,
But fayre close wether, her beautye to save.
Then came there a nother that lyveth by laundry,
Who muste have wether hote and clere, here clothys to dry. 1100
Then came there a boy for froste and snow contynuall,
Snow to make snowballys and frost for his pytfale,
For whyche, God wote, he seweth full gredely!
Your fyrst man wold have wether clere and not wyndy;
The seconde the same, save cooles to blow meanly; 1105
The thyrd desyred stormes and wynde most extermely;
The fourth all in water and wolde have no wynde;
The fyft no water, but all wynde to grynde;
The syxst wold have none of all these, nor no bright son;
The seventh extremely the hote son wold have wonne; 1110
The eyght and the last, for frost and snow he prayd.
Byr lady, we shall take shame, I am a frayd!
Who marketh in what maner this sort is led
May thynke yt impossyble all to be sped.
This nomber is smale – there lacketh twayne of ten – 1115
And yet by the masse, amonge ten thousand men
No one thynge could stand more wyde from the tother.
Not one of theyr sewtes agreeth wyth an other.
I promyse you here is a shrewed pece of warke –
This gere wyll trye wether ye be a clarke. 1120
If ye trust to me, yt is a great foly
For yt passeth my braynes, by Goddes body!

Jupiter   Son, thou haste ben dylygent and done so well,
That thy labour is ryght myche thanke worthy. D4v

	But be thou suer we nede no whyt thy counsell,	1125
	For in our selfe we have foresene remedy,
	Whyche thou shalt se. But fyrste depart hens quyckly
	To the gentylman and all other sewters here,
	And commaunde them all before us to appere.

| Mery Report | That shall be no lenger in doynge | 1130 |
| | Then I am in commynge and goynge. |

Mery Report goth out.

Jupiter	Suche debate as from above ye have harde,
	Suche debate beneth amonge your selfes ye se.
	As longe as heddes from temperaunce be deferd,
	So longe the bodyes in dystemperaunce be.	1135
	This perceyve ye all, but none can helpe save we.
	But as we there have made peace concordantly,
	So woll we here now gyve you remedy.

Mery Reporte and all the
sewters entreth.

Mery Report	If I hadde caught them
	Or ever I raught them,	1140
	I wolde have taught them
	To be nere me.
	Full dere have I bought them,
	Lorde, so I sought them,
	Yet have I brought them	1145
	Suche as they be.

Gentylman	Pleaseth yt your majeste, lorde, so yt is:
	We as your subjectes and humble sewters all,
	Accordynge as we here your pleasure is,
	Are presyd to your presens, beynge pryncypall	1150
	Hed and governour of all in every place.
	Who joyeth not in your syght no joy can have,
	Wherfore we all commyt us to your grace
	As lorde of lordes, us to peryshe or save.

Jupiter	As longe as dyscrecyon so well doth you gyde	1155
	Obedyently to use your dewte,
	Dout ye not we shall your savete provyde.
	Your grevys we have harde, wherfore we sent for ye
	To receyve answere, eche man in his degre.
	And fyrst to content most reason yt is	1160
	The fyrste man that sewde – wherfore marke ye this:

Oft shall ye have the wether clere and styll   E1
To hunt in, for recompens of your payne.
Also you merchauntes shall have myche your wyll:
For oft tymes when no wynde on lande doth remayne,   1165
Yet on the see plesaunt cooles you shall obtayne.
And syns your huntynge maye reste in the nyght,
Oft shall the wynde then ryse, and before day lyght.

It shall ratyll downe the wood in suche case
That all ye rangers the better lyve may.   1170
And ye water myllers shall abteyne this grace:
Many tymes the rayne to fall in the valey,
When at the self tymes on hyllys we shall purvey
Fayre wether for your wyndmilles, with such coolys of wynde
As in one instant both kyndes of mylles may grynde.   1175

And for ye fayre women that close wether wold have,
We shall provyde that ye may suffycyently
Have tyme to walke, in and your beauty save.
And yet shall ye have, that lyveth by laundry,
The hote sonne oft ynough your clothes to dry.   1180
Also ye, praty chylde, shall have both frost and snow.
Now marke this conclusyon, we charge you arow:

Myche better have we now devysed for ye all
Then ye all can perceyve or coude desyre.
Eche of you sewd to have contynuall   1185
Suche wether as his crafte onely doth requyre.
All wethers in all places yf men all tymes myght hyer,
Who could lyve by other? What is this neglygens
Us to atempt in suche inconvenyens?

Now on the tother syde, yf we had graunted   1190
The full of some one sewt and no mo,
And from all the rest the wether had forbyd,
Yet who so hadde obtayned had wonne his owne wo.
There is no one craft can preserve man so,
But by other craftes, of necessyte,   1195
He muste have myche parte of his commodyte.

All to serve at ones, and one destroy a nother,   E1v
Or ellys to serve one and destroy all the rest –
Nother wyll we do the tone nor the tother,
But serve as many or as few as we thynke best.   1200
And where or what tyme to serve moste or lest,

213

The dyreccyon of that doutles shall stande
Perpetually in the power of our hande.

Wherfore we wyll the hole worlde to attende,
Eche sort on suche wether as for them doth fall.　　　　1205
Now one, now other, as lyketh us to sende.
Who that hath yt, ply yt, and suer we shall
So gyde the wether in course to you all
That eche wyth other ye shall hole remayne
In pleasure and plentyfull welth certayne.　　　　1210

Gentylman　　Blessyd was the tyme wherin we were borne,
Fyrst for the blysfull chaunce of your godly presens,
Next for our sewt! Was there never man beforne
That ever harde so excellent a sentens

As your grace hath gevyn to us all arow,　　　　1215
Wherin your hyghnes hath so bountyfully
Dystrybuted my parte, that your grace shall know
Your selfe sooll possessed of hertes of all chyvalry.

Marchaunt　　Lyke wyse we marchauntes shall yeld us holy
Onely to laude the name of Jupyter　　　　1220
As god of all goddes, you to serve soolly,
For of every thynge I se you are norysher.

Ranger　　No dout yt is so, for so we now fynde,
Wherin your grace us rangers so doth bynde
That we shall gyve you our hertes with one accorde,　　　　1225
For knowledge to know you as our onely lorde.

Water Myller　　Well, I can no more but, for our water
We shall geve your lordshyp Our Ladyes sauter.

Wynd Myller　　Myche have ye bounde us, for as I be saved,
We have all obteyned better then we craved.　　　　1230

Gentylwoman　　That is trew, werfore your grace shall trewly
The hertes of such as I am have surely.

Launder　　And such as I am – who be as good as you –
His hyghnes shall be suer on, I make a vow.

Boy　　Godfather god, I wyll do somwhat for you agayne.　　　　E2
By Cryste, ye may happe to have a byrd or twayne!　　　　1236

214

And I promyse you yf any snow come,
When I make my snow ballys ye shall have some.

Mery Report   God thanke your lordship. Lo, how this is brought to pas!
Syrs, now shall ye have the wether even as yt was.   1240

Jupiter   We nede no whyte our selfe any farther to bost,
For our dedes declare us apparauntly.
Not onely here on yerth in every cost,
But also above in the hevynly company
Our prudens hath made peace unyversally.   1245
Whyche thynge, we sey, recordeth us as pryncypall
God and governour of heven, yerth, and all.

Now unto that heven we woll make retourne,
Where we be gloryfyed most tryumphantly.
Also we woll all ye that on yerth sojourne –   1250
Syns cause gyveth cause – to know us your lord onely,
And now here to synge moste joyfully,
Rejoycynge in us; and in meane tyme we shall
Ascende into our trone celestyall.   1254

[Song as Jupiter ascends and withdraws.]

FINIS

PRYNTED BY W.RASTELL
1533
CUM PRIVILEGIO

EDITORIAL NOTES TO *WITTY AND WITLESS*

The Text

Manuscript   British Library MS Harley 367, fols. 110ʳ–119ʳ.

No title in MS. Humphrey Wanley, who catalogued the manuscript for Harley between 1708 and 1726, named it *Witty and Witless*. Colophon: 'amen qd John Heywod.'

The copy, including the colophon, is in a mid-Tudor secretary hand which is not Heywood's autograph (Reed, p. 123, and plate opposite p. 124). The manuscript, once separate, was collected by John Stowe (1515–1605), and incorporated before Robert Harley acquired the collection in 1705 from the library of Sir Simonds D'Ewes.

A 'pleye of wytles' was entered in the Stationers' Register in 1560–1 (Arber, I, 154).

Facsimiles   J.S. Farmer, *Tudor Facsimile Texts*, 1909; reprinted New York, 1970.

Peter Happé, *Two Moral Interludes*, Malone Society Reprints, Oxford, 1991.

Editions   F.W. Fairholt, *A Dialogue on Wit and Folly by John Heywood*, Percy Society vol. 20, London, 1846.

J.S. Farmer, *The Dramatic Writings of John Heywood*, London, 1905; (modernized); reprinted 1966.

Rupert de la Bère, *John Heywood, Entertainer*, London, 1937, pp. 117–43.

Editorial treatment of the manuscript

The ten leaves of the manuscript (approximately 318mm x 210mm) are numbered in pencil on each recto. Fol. 110ᵛ is soiled and darkened. The leaves have been folded vertically so that the blank fol. 119ᵛ has at some time been an outside cover. The watermark, found most clearly in fol. 119, and also in fols. 111, 114, 116, and 117, consists of a hand with fingers together and thumb outstretched, and a five-petalled flower or star at the extension of the longest finger. In the palm and wrist of the hand are the number '3', and the initials 'HA'. This corresponds with Briquet nos. 11377–82. E. Heawood identifies this watermark in manuscripts from 1531 to 1574, and suggests an origin in north-west France. ('Sources of English Paper Supply,' *The Library*, Fourth Series, X (1930), pp. 427–54).

The handwriting is typical Tudor secretary in such letters as tailed *h*, the long *s*, and the *c* in two strokes. The letter *y* is almost always dotted following medieval scribal practice. Two other characteristics affect the reading: the reversed *e*, which is often flattened to a mere dash, particularly after *h*; and the manuscript letter which represents *re*, as in *repyng* (Wy94), and which should be distinguished from representing *r*, as in *rynge* (Wy53) – *ressurrectyon* (Wy572) exemplifies both. The consideration of these features makes the present edition different from its predecessors, and implies a revision of many words in the *Concordance*, the *OED*, and critical work in general. Nevertheless the scribe is consistent in the pursuit of these conventions. His deletions and occasional smudgings out bear witness to attentive workmanship, as does his practice of separating with an oblique stroke, often minute, words inadvertently joined. There are cases of 'eye skip' where words or phrases are caught up from the following line, as in Wy288–9. The correction of these and many other literals usually follows immediately indicating that his dissatisfaction or error was acted upon at once. Many of these are ignored here, though a note is made of some outstanding cases. His concern with spelling and changes to it is discussed separately below.

There are virtually no full stops, but the scribe uses a slash or virgule (/) for some breaks within the line: these are syntactical rather than metrical. There is one semicolon, and many 'pen rests' which seem to have no value. Numbers and some isolated capitals are separated by stops before and after. In this edition the punctuation has been modernized and made as light as possible. In places the virgules have served as guides. The whole play is in couplets, except the last 35 lines which are separated into rhyme royal stanzas. This layout has been followed, but the first letter of each line has been capitalized, the copy being inconsistent. Speech heads have been moved from the right margin to the left, and the freehand lines across the page at the end of each speech omitted. Except for the instruction about three staves at Wy675, there are no stage directions: two have been supplied in square brackets.

The scribe's letter thorn þ (th) and the abbreviation for (-es) have been replaced. Conventional manuscript contractions have been expanded as follows: þe the, þ^t that, w^t wythe, w^che, whyche, yor yowr, ⱹ pro, p^a pra, g^ece grace. In common with many Tudor manuscripts this text contains bars over words like *hym*, and *concludyd*, many of them decorative (see A.G. Petti, *English Literary Hands from Chaucer to Dryden*, 1977, nos. 19 [Wyatt], and 20 [Surrey]). These have been ignored unless there is no doubt about a missing letter, as in *nobyr* Wy79, in which case the letter is supplied and the manuscript form noted. In the case of words which appear in modern English as *comm-* the scribe is inconsistent. In some he writes *com-* (with bar), but the procedure here has been to print *com-*, and to give the form with bar in the notes.

Since the date of the play is assumed to be before 1530, individual words in notes and glossary for which the first *OED* citations are 1530 or later are marked with a dagger †. *OED* gives 1546 for citations of this play.

A Note on Spelling

Even though the scribe was not Heywood himself, the spelling in the text may be considered under two general aspects: the difference between the conventions in the manuscript and those of the printed plays, and the visible changes made by the scribe by way of correction.

For the former, the *Concordance* is invaluable. It reveals that the commonest difference is in the 25 words containing *w* or *ew* in Wy which become *u* in the printed texts, e.g. argewment, cawse, conclewd, nowght, plesewrre. This may be accounted for by a shortage of *w* in Tudor type cases. More significant perhaps are the scribe's choice of medial *v* instead of *u* as in evyn, gyve, have, hevyn, love, prove, his use of *c* in words like schall and schow, and of *oo* in woordes, woorse, toonge, and u in wurke and cum.

The treatment of majuscule *I/J*, which is not apparent from the *Concordance*, manifests an interest in orthography and suggests that the scribe was moving towards the modern convention. He has two distinct forms: one with a rounded back which he may have thought of as J, and one with a broken back which may have corresponded with modern I. However his practice is inconsistent, and if this is a transition, it is incomplete. For details see MSR *Two Moral Interludes*.

Many deletions in the manuscript can be deciphered. Together with interlineations and omitted letters above carets, they indicate that the scribe changed his mind over a considerable number of spellings.

     5 changes: way to wey; w- to wh-
     4 changes: o to oo
     3 changes: mayny to many; reson to reason; best to beast
     2 changes: wh- to w-; layte to late; and u to ew
     doubled letters: tt (3); rr (2); ll (once): wytt becomes wyt twice.

There are of course instances where the original form is left unaltered, with resultant inconsistency, but these examples indicate his intention to alter systematically.

The scribe is undecided over think/thing: he has thyngke Wy80, 463; he correctly changes thyngke to thynke Wy336, and thyngks to things Wy464; but erroneously he leaves thyng for thynk Wy147. There is also inconsistency over words which in modern English end -ble: honorabull Wy105, unmesewrabull Wy222, tabyll Wy 106, sensybyll Wy465, resonabyll Wy499, resonable Wy450.

Explanatory Notes

Wy1 Apparently the conversation has already begun, cf. began Wy4 and see textual note to Wy1.

Wy3 Erasmus asked 'If you had to die tomorrow, would you rather die more foolish or more wise?' 'The Abbot and the Learned Lady' (1524) in *Colloquies*.

Wy4 *seay*: say. Also at Wy206; this sp. not in OED.

Wy10 *vuewer*: inspector; OED viewer 1 cites this as vewer, 1540 (from Fairholt). See textual note.

Wy12–16 '. . . that [even] the wittiest, to whom nothing has been left by friends now dead, and for whom no living friends have made provision, must find their own means of support by much physical and more mental payne unless they are to die.'

Wy17 *as who saythe the sott*: which is to say the sot.

Wy17–21 'And as for the witless, which is to say the sot, called the natural fool or idiot, the sot remains in a secure state of life [free] from all kinds of labour which involve pain, as far as the necessities of life are concerned.'

Wy24–26 *yet . . . sustayne*: . . . yet where is there any [fool] who does not endure more pain for that one pleasure [security of living] than the witty feels who has to work hard [for his living]?

Wy28 *yf ye marke hyt*: if you remark it [the matter] properly.

Wy29 'Whoever walks past the sot, or whoever he walks past . . .'

Wy31 *bob*: buffet, OED v².1, associated with the beating and mocking of Christ-as-fool.

Wy38 *crampe*: squeeze, compress; †OED v³ (1555).

Wy40 *lowte*: mock, OED v.3 (c.1530, Redford, *Wit and Science*, 799).

Wy41 *whysk*: beat with a rod of twigs; 'Yf any childe be . . . stubburne . . . let it . . . be whysked with a good rodde.' OED v.4 (1530).

Wy43 *Somer*: Will Somer, an artificial fool rather than a natural idiot, is said to have come to Court in about 1525 (*DNB* s.v. Sommers), and to have continued in favour until his death, 15 June 1560. Reputedly he outwitted Wolsey, consoled Henry VIII, and was popular with Queen Mary. Records survive for the provision of a purse and clothing (*L&P*, 1539, ii 77, 333), and of a chain and clothes (1551–2: Feuillerat, pp. 55, 67, 73, 77). Robert Armin said 'Few men were more belov'd than was this foole', *A Nest of Ninnies* (1608) in H.F. Lippincott, *A Shakespeare Jest Book* (Salzburg, 1973) pp. 119–20. See also Welsford, pp. 166–71, and Sandra Billington, *A Social History of the Fool* (Brighton, 1984), pp. 33–5. Heywood's apparently harsh attitude to Somer (Wy523, 533) has not been explained. The relationship may not have been acrimonious however, and, as they were at Court together for a very long period, it may have been an amusing public pose. The references to Somer suggest c.1525 as the earliest date for *Witty and Witless*.

Wy44 *new schoole*: new [harsh] discipline.

Wy46–7 'The witty often contrive another kind of all-consuming affliction for the witless.'

Wy48 *yerfull*: angry, possibly causing anger; OED obs. for ireful. See also yere Wy67.

Wy48–9 'In addition to the torments [above] invented out of angry intention, the fool is also made to suffer by flattery.'

Wy50 *his brayne . . . wrowght*: his brain exercised erroneously.

wyde: missing the point, going astray †OED adv.5b (1534, More): also adj. Wy62.
wrowght: †OED p.pl.a. 5 (1585).

Wy51 *myght*: mite, smallest coin worth ⅛ old penny.

Wy53 *Walsyngam rynge*: The shrine of Our Lady at Walsingham Abbey, Norfolk, second in popularity only to Becket's tomb in Canterbury, was notorious for its spurious relics. Erasmus visited Walsingham in 1514, and mentions its trade in tin and lead keepsakes, 'Pilgrimage for Religion's Sake', *Colloquies*, p. 208.

Wy54 *dystemperans*: disturbance of mind, OED distemperance 4, More 1529.

Wy57–60 'The sot's joy [in, say, the ring] is such that if a man contrived to take it from him – as any child could – then man or child might see that the sot's true condition allows him to experience nothing but painful sorrow.'

Wy61–2 'By this little argument someone of small wit may understand that witty men would be wide of the mark [of happiness] if they wished themselves to be witless.'

Wy62 *wyde*: (adj) missing the point, going astray †OED adj 10.b. (1561); for adv see Wy50; cf. wydely Wy436.

Wy70 *dystempryd wythe dystemperat joy*: confused and disordered with excessive joy; †OED distemperate 2 (1548) applied to the humours.

Wy71–2 'That his intense feeling of pleasure brings as much pain as the most painful irritation.'

Wy76–8 'Yes, but if witty and witless are both worked upon by some appropriate discomfort to feel pain, witty [because of his nature] will feel the pain most: nevertheless each will individually boast [of his pain].'

Wy79–82 'Consider the whole quality and number of witty [people] – and I don't think there are many of them who do not of necessity suffer in body and mind . . .'

Wy83 *to all . . . favor*: in comparison with all those that fortune favours [with being free from labour].

Wy85–6 The argument based upon the presumed pain of mind suffered by witty (below Wy258, 302) may be scriptural: 'For in Wisdom is much vexation, and the more a man knows the more he has to suffer,' *Ecclesiastes* 1:18.

Wy86 *harde gest*: heard guessed.

Wy87–90 'And in case both pains, of mind and body, are too tough for you to argue about at the same time, and presuming that the lesser pain is adequate grounds for dispute, let us put together both forms of bodily pain – the fool's greater and the witty's lesser pain.'

Wy89 *nody*: fool. First citation in †OED Heywood, *Love*, L800.

Wy96 *stareyng*: glaring in madness, astonishment, or perhaps here exhaustion OED v.3

Wy98 *swete*: sweat. They are so hot with labour that they would sweat even in the shadow of a cold cave.

Wy101 *warme*: become warm.

Wy105 *wurshypfull*: one holding important office, OED 3.c (1450).

Wy106 *temprately*: not experiencing the extremes of Wy103.

Wy107 *reckyn the hole rabyll*: considering the whole lot of them (the labours). *rabyll*: string or series, usually contemptuous, OED.

Wy108 *babyll*: fool's bauble, a stick with carved head and asses' ears. Somer was provided with one at the Court revels, Dec–Jan 1551/2, Feuillerat, p. 73.

Wy116–7 *Ye schall . . . wyttles*: You will have to search as far to find ease in [the life of] the witty man as of the witless . . .

Wy119 'Sots are beaten by others, the witty man beats himself.' *coylde*: beaten, OED coil v² 1530, possibly figurative here.

Wy120 *elfe*: suggests mischief and small stature of James.

Wy123–4 'The witty who punish themselves by overwork may often advantage themselves in violent exertions.'

Wy131–2 'Witty can, by his wit, arrange what he must do to suit himself, but the fool must accept whatever those cleverer than him impose upon him by way of beating.'

Wy142–4 'For though the things witty had or hoped for are by some considerations greater than what the sot enjoys, they are not better, and the feelings inspired are equally strong – unless of course witty has the greater suffering.' James twists his argument in the last clause.

Wy152 'As the sot enjoys the receipt of his Walsingham ring . . .'

Wy154 *to seeke*: to be sought for and not found. (Gerundial infinitive): elusive.

Wy155 *gyfte*: the thousand pounds, Wy148.

Wy163–4 'To the same extent, as far as their discomfort arises from instability, as you previously showed the witless to be disturbed.' See Wy68–74.

Wy168 'To cause difference of temperament to have little importance.'

Wy181–3 i.e. A positive demonstration that one thing is *better* than another does not mean that it is the *best*.

Wy184 'In making that accusation you overstep your right.'

Wy185–8 'But the wit who boasts the extent of his triumph as though he could predict the outcome at the beginning – that wit will reveal precisely, by this lack of wit, why he cannot keep company with true wits.'

Wy189 *for the myds*: James, using 'mids' to indicate the midpoint in the debate, establishes that so far ('not for thende') he has proved his case. He goes on to the next stage at Wy199.

Wy194 'To make your downfall more acceptable by careful treatment.'
stayer after stayer: step by step, by degrees.

Wy196 *parte*: party (legal sense).
softe and fayer: quietly and securely, †OED soft adv.8.b (1576).

Wy197 *for owght . . . make*: to interpret your words in the most precise way.

Wy199 *thys myds*: see Wy189 note.

Wy207–10 Play on 'sey' – nine instances.

Wy217 'It was clever of you to make that exception to the proposition [and so to delay having to grant the main point].'

Wy221–4 'In order to get to that point, as a moderate course may bring what is unmeasurable into compass, as some say, one may bring together things in similar proportion, as may be intended, by comparing the average labourer to the average student.' Play on *mean*: (1) average (2) ungenerous (3) intention.

Wy229–30 'The labourer's toil instantly matches that in the enjoyment he has of the fruits of his labours.'

Wy229 *at a whyppe*: instantly. †OED whip sb.10 a (1553). 'The hare at pinch turnth from him at a whip', Heywood *100 Epigrams* 15:16.

Wy233 *dreue*: drive. OED does not give this spelling, but it appears in More, *Confutation*, in *Works* VIII i 424.

Wy238 *hansome*: appropriate. First citation in †OED adj.1 Tyndale 1530.

Wy244 James argues that the harm of study goes direct to the heart and brain, whereas the labourer suffers ill effects only in his outward parts.

Wy249 'as regards the average examples now put forward on both sides.'

Wy251–8 '[Even if] you can set about making clear connections in certain respects between labour of body and mind, they are not connected in such intimate ways that one may not be separated from the other; and you claim that both kinds of labour are as similar as wit can devise, [but] once they are both searched it will be found evident that the worst pain arises in labour of the mind.'

Wy255 *arecte*: allege, OED aret v.3.

Wy263 *insydently*: as a side issue; OED incidently adv. (More, 1527).

Wy270 *put . . . purs*: keep silent. Proverbial, earliest citation by †Tilley, T399.

Wy275–6 '. . . relates only to the witty, because the witless cannot possibly experience that pain of mind.'

Wy281/2 *devyce/devyse*: conceive OED.v.10. Two spellings of the same word.

Wy283 In relating the lack of mental power of the fool to the animals James anticipates his later argument, Wy456, 505–6, 517.

Wy284 *Cocke my hors or Gyll my mare*: ? Proverbial, hence cock horse in children's game, OED 1540–1.

Wy285 This reason disposes of the pain of mind [supposedly suffered] by witless.'

Wy289 *plummets*: weights of a clock, †OED 5.b.(1594). They moved round like a watchman (Wy290) going round a tower.

Wy290–2 'Imagination behaves like a watchman, and goes around in such a manner [as the weights of a clock]; consideration [?anxiety] is so sensitive to the sound that there is never any peace in the mind of the witty.' Cf. L283–4.

Wy293 'A person of little wit may [by chance] guess, but no single wit can [rationally] judge . . .'

Wy297 This summary by James suggests that John has lost the argument.

Wy298 *have reles*: are not liable to.

Wy299–300 The second is that witty has direct experience of all mental pain, and that witty brings it about himself.

Wy301 *alewdyng*: alluding to, †OED 4 (More, 1553).

Wy302 *as . . . conclewdyng*: as a conclusion.

Wy307 *envey*: make conclusion, perhaps from OED envoy v. obsolete.

Wy308 *wagge*: move, go, OED v.1.i.

Wy317 'Let us consider pleasures only on both sides.'

Wy319–20 Possibly double meaning, implying a long debate and a sexual encounter.

Wy323–4 'Just now you quite rightly [as in *wytyly* Wy76] claimed that the reasoning must depend on short argument.'

Wy326 *that . . . ley*: that brings support to my point of view.

Wy337–8 Heywood is echoing the traditional Catholic view of baptism re-iterated by More in which the child receives grace at baptism and is changed by it. 'For though they come to the baptysme and be receyved to the font in the fayth of theyr fathers and of the hole chyrch that offreth them: yet with the baptysme is there by God infounded into them his grace.' More, *Confutation* in *Works* VIII ii 822. More also indicated that original sin is removed by baptism, pp. 754–5, and note VIII iii 1655.

Wy341 'Whereby, until wit can grow from the root of true moral discrimination . . .'

Wy343 'Wherever the innocent are involved in debate over innocent matters.'

Wy353–4 *That . . . wyttles*: That 'if' alters a great deal the outcome of my argument in favour of witless [because witless has no moral judgement].

Wy365 *goose . . . hys*: This goose does not appear to be proverbial. A comic tone is implied, perhaps similar to Ignorance saying 'hiss' in *Wit and Science*, 485–8. James is talking to the audience, formally summarizing the argument under three heads. He addresses John only very briefly at Wy385.

Wy368–9 'In which he admits that his point of view is not partly wrong but entirely incorrect.'

Wy386 *holde me wagge*: keep me at bay, †OED wag sb[1] 2.

Wy388 *stamynge*: stemming, keeping vessel on course, OED stem v³ 1.e.

Wy392–3 'Those in the estate of sots have no requirement to account for their worldly actions, so that God imputes no evil to them.'

Wy394–6 'And the witty's account gets worse every day; the Auditor's wit who sees all in making up the account – he [God] does not forget one word in a thousand years.'

Wy397 *the least wytt here*: the meanest intelligence in the audience.

Wy404–8 John concedes that it is better to be witless than witty, thus bringing about a turning point. However, by suggesting at Wy406 that John is a fool, Heywood opens up the second part of the play.

Wy409 Jerome's intervention depends upon his knowing the previous argument, as he says at Wy433. Though such unrealistic awareness is common in interludes, he may have been waiting seated in the audience, or visible to the audience, as are the characters in Sir David Lindsay's *Ane Satire of the Thrie Estaitis* (see s.d.'s at 1086, 1935–6, 1951, 2399). *Jerome*: Whilst the names James and John are apostolic, Jerome suggests rather the learning of St Jerome, who established the Vulgate.

Wy414 *wysdom and folly*: Jerome's case turns upon this substitution of wisdom for wit. Joel B.Altman points out that Jerome thus provides a counter-thesis to the defence by James of the proposition 'Better ys for man that man be wyttles/ Then wytty.' (Wy5–6), p. 112.

Wy416 *wysdom nowhyt*: no scrap of wisdom. See *Book of Wisdom* 1:4, and Wy613 and note.

Wy417 'Wit [or commonsense] is the agent of all cognition.'

Wy419–22 'There may be as much wit involved in the most wicked things as in the best things wit can aspire to – I mean vice or virtue – and wit receives no harm where it is the servant of wisdom.'

Wy429–30 'Yet by as much as wisdom towers above wit you conceded too quickly more than you needed.'

Wy431 *freshe comonar*: newly arrived student, not clever enough to be a scholar. †OED cites this line for commoner 6, but attributes to Thomas Heywood, 1613.

Wy432 *the pryncypyll that plantyd thys jar*: the main dispute which originated this dissension. †OED jar sb¹ 6; *Dial. Provs.* II v 1487–9.

WY436 *wydely*: wrongly, misguidedly †OED 4 (1688); first citation for all senses 1663. *wayd*: weighed.

Wy440 K.W. Cameron suggests that the superiority of the Fool over Solomon was developed in OE and ME dialogues of Solomon and Marcolf, printed versions of which he cites as appearing in Antwerp in 1492, and Paris in 1515, *Witty* p. 10; see also Welsford, pp. 36–40, and J.M. Kemble, *The Dialogue of Salomon and Saturnus*, 1848. More mentions writing additions to a play about Solomon, E.F. Rogers (ed.), *St Thomas More: Selected Letters* (1961), 1–2; for conjecture on this see Lancashire, nos. 262 and 1259. This is the last word from James; possibly he remains to hear the conclusion of the debate.

Wy441–2 'Do you give judgement before you hear my case? Lo how he is carried away by what he desires to believe!'

Wy447 *For entre wherto*: As a start to this.

Wy449–51 Man is separated from animals by reason in *Psalm* 31:9 (Vulg.). Thomas Whythorne who worked for Heywood 1545–8, reports that in his lost play Heywood 'mad Reazon to chalenʒ vnto him self þe siuperiorite and government of all þe parts of Man.' Whythorne, p. 74. See *Four Elements* 211–3; *Gentleness and Nobility* 379–80.

Wy451 *By and sell*: suggests an awareness of betrayal. OED buy (v.) 11b.

Wy454 *sped*: brought to an end, OED speed 9.b.

Wy463 *whyse and wherforrse*: †OED why I.6 sb. (1590). See Tilley W331, W332.
thyngke: think. This sp. not in OED. See note on spelling.

Wy469 *or*: before.

Wy470 *twygde*: beaten with twigs, †OED v^1 (1550).

Wy474 *racke*: to go at a rack, 'a shambling half trot, half canter.' †OED rack sb^6 (1580); racking vbl.sb^4 (1530), v^4 (1589).

Wy480 *owt of thacownt of mans estate*: not to be considered as human beings (e.g. slaves, perhaps).

Wy487-8 Cameron, *Witty* (pp. 28-9), cites Pico della Mirandola, *On the Imagination*, trans. H. Caplan (New Haven, 1930), 43, which describes the power of imagination for good or evil, and stresses that it must be controlled. Heywood may well have encountered this work through More.

Wy489-90 '[Imagination] brings to man much pleasure in considering the pleasing content of every pleasurable thing man has at command for his own benefit.'

Wy492 'Beasts have things because they are necessary, but there is no pleasure beyond that.' ·

Wy504 'And let us consider the whole condition of both.'

Wy505 *varyete*: difference †OED 3 (1548).

Wy514-5 *That . . . reason*: that to all intents the senses are not at the disposal of reason. *to all yntents*: practically, †OED intent 6.c (1546).

Wy517 The link between fools and brute reason is made by Erasmus: 'if they be veraie brute Naturalles, now they sinne not, as doctours doe affirme.' *Folie* p. 48 [G2].

Wy521 *the nomber*: the majority.

Wy525 *do yn drugery*: work in drudgery.

Wy529 *have other conseyts*: are thought of differently.

Wy530 *foole . . . flocke*: Proverbial?

Wy534 *for rest*: as far as anything else in concerned. Somer doesn't even work like the mill horse or other men's fools (Wy522), but he is still to be considered among the beasts.

Wy537 *to gether conferd*: taken together.

Wy548 *dyssolvyd*: resolved †OED dissolve v.12 (1549).

Wy551 *mere*: pure, unmixed †OED (1535).

Wy551-4 'Although the pure merit of our redemption rests upon Christ's passion, yet by the justice of God we shall miss redemption unless we use our time and our intelligence to keep his commandments.'

Wy555 *in whyche*: in the commandments.

Wy556 *ymps*: shoot or slip used in grafting, OED imp 2.

Heywood here adopts the orthodox Catholic position regarding good works as a means by which salvation is earned, together with the notion of degrees of beatitude. The implied perfectibility of man is given by Erasmus, who placed more emphasis upon moral choice, and by More, 'good wurkes . . . be very profytable towarde obtaynynge of forgyvenesse and getynge reward in hevyn,' (*Confutation*, in *Works* VIII i 402).

Wy559 *Cryst in the gospell*: John 14:2.

Wy562 *Saynt Awstyne*: 'nullus eorum alienabitur ab illa domo ubi mansionem pro suo quisque accepturus est merito . . . Sed multae mansiones diversas meritorum in una vita aeterna significant dignitates.' *In Joannis Evangelium Sancti Augustini* in *PL* XXXV col. 1812.2. Cameron offers further minor similarities, *Witty*, pp. 15-17. The reference to a patristic exegesis accords with Jerome's learned stance.

Wy568 *faythe*: *PL* XXXV cols. 1813.3

Wy570 *Seynt Powle*: 1 *Corinthians* 15:41-2. Paul also discusses the difference between animal body and spiritual body (*1 Corinthians* 15:44–9), which might well have contributed to Heywood's separation of bodily and spiritual functions.

Wy574 *That . . . ure*: 'That "what" comes into practical consideration immediately.'

Wy583 *Yff . . . yt*: If it were only a matter of wishing for it.

Wy588 *in lott*: as his portion or fate.

Wy592 'I wish I had the sot's certainty of the lowest joy in heaven,' as in Wy351–2, 362–4.

Wy593 *makythe wythe thys*: tells in favour of this, †OED make with 82a (1559).

Wy594 Proverbial, Heywood, *Dial. Prows.* I xi 925; Tilley B363.

Wy605–8 'Because of this fear you desire rather the certainty of even the smallest joys there [in heaven] than take a chance on winning all, and, I think, you chose this so readily [because] the least joy there is more than man can apprehend.'

Wy611–4 'God permits – but does not will – any man to sin, and God wishes no death for a sinner unless he is in such a final state as to be rejected by God because his endless malice precludes penitence.' This follows the Catholic doctrine of free will: 'Nolo mortem impii, sed ut convertatur impius a vita sua et vivat,' *Ezekiel* 33:11.

Wy613 *males*: malice. Whythorne offers a link between the obdurate sinner and Solomon, 'And Solomon in þe first chapter of hiz book of wizdom saith that wyzdom shalnot enter into a malisiows mynd . . . A witty man may be wicked assoon az good, and þat a wys man iz a perfekt good man,' *Autobiography*, p. 72.

Wy614 *reprobate*: rejected by God. †OED sb and adj (1545, Bale). OED cites reprobation (More, 1532), but most other theological citations are Protestant texts.

Wy619 *hopes chayer*: the chair of hope. See 4P351 and note.

Wy620 *brede presumpsyon*: To presume salvation was held to be the sin against the Holy Ghost. '. . . the over great regarde of his mercy turneth truste into presumpcyon and maketh men the more bolde in synne,' More, *Confutation*, in *Works* VIII i 513.

Wy624 *yll wyllynge wyll*: malice against God as in Wy613.

Wy626 *scrypture saythe* as in Wy559–61.

Wy631–2 Cameron *Witty* (p. 25) draws a parallel with the Collect for the Eleventh Sunday after Pentecost: 'Almighty and everlasting God who from the abundance of your mercy exceeds both the merits and prayers of those who beg.'

Wy635 *schow of that feare*: manifestation of the fear of losing heaven (Wy591).

Wy638 *hasthe as in post*: hastens like a express messenger.

Wy639–40 The argument depends on God's willingness to offer mercy (Wy626, 637–8), and on the effect of contrition producing instant forgiveness (Wy629, 639–40).

Wy643–4 'As a result of this my [proper] fear of God is in accordance with love and hope; no desperate fear now grasps my heart.'

Wy647 *the byrder*: i.e. God.

Wy657 *my mate . . . sayde*: James at Wy440.

my lords: Presumably the noble audience, of which Henry VIII may have been one, see Wy675 s.d.

Wy666–7 'In the managing of God's gifts in accordance with the limits under the normal guidance of wisdom, whereby the following shall occur . . .'

Wy669–70 'The words of advice which I was just discussing I apply solely to him to whom they were directed [and not to the present company].'

Wy672–5 'This distinguished company being assembled, need no exhortation, at least not from me. They possess God's wit by nature and a like measure of wisdom joined to it by grace.'

Wy676–82 'And as by God's grace gifts may shine most in them, so their affairs shall be evidence of God's influence. If God's glory [or gloss] does not shine brightly in every respect in those who, having a realm to govern, exercise their rule to the glory of God, charitably helping their subjects of every rank, where else shall we find the shining of God's gifts?' The transition from ordinary men to kings is abrupt, but it could be gracefully bridged by a simple gesture if the King were present.

Wy678 *glos*: lustre, †OED sb[2] (1538).

Wy685–6 R.C. Johnson (p. 74) suggests that this compliment refers to the Pope's bestowal of the title Fidei Defensor upon Henry in recognition of his *Assertio septem Sacramentorum* (1520) against Luther.

Wy687 'Since wit is lacking here to encompass a full account.'

Wy689 *passyng the same*: in passing over the King's fame somewhat superficially.

Wy690 *pryns . . . owr pryns*: Christ . . . Henry.

Wy692–4 Henry is to achieve the full heavenly reward for faithful service (*use*) as mentioned for John Wy637.

Wy697 *Contynewans wherof*. If the three stanzas were omitted in the King's absence, the sense would be that grace (Wy675) would continue. With the insertion, it is the King who would benefit from a higher degree of 'joyes' (Wy695). The final stanza seems more appropriate to ordinary mortals than to the King.

Wy701 *thydyll sot*: if there is a rivalry with Somer (as above Wy523, 533), Heywood might here single him out from the King's entourage for a final fling.

Textual variants and doubtful readings

These notes record changes made from the manuscript together with some doubtful readings. There is also selective information about scribal changes in spelling, corrections of errors, brevigraphs, and changes to speech heads. Significant variants in Farmer are noted.

Wy1 The conversation appears to be already in progress (Wy4), but not much can be lost since the argument appears complete and balanced. The speech head *John* is centred, and this accords with other pages where a speech is begun at the top (fol. 116, 117[v], 118[v]): in such cases the normal speech head also appears in the right margin at the foot of the previous page.

Wy6 *Ye . . . wyttines*] added in r. margin, with speech head. The next two speech heads (Wy7,22) were originally reversed, and had to be corrected.

Wy8/10 *vuewe . . . vuewer*] wewe . . . wewer. Initial w is here used according to the medieval scribal convention, for the voiced sound vu.

Wy24 *leve wythe owt*] levew[r]owt

Wy26 *wyty*] altered from wytt, as in wytyly Wy76. The change relates to the scribe's concern for spelling.

Wy27 *havyng*] havȳn

Wy39 *cuff*] ? read cuff hym

Wy42 *Wythe*] The scribe first wrote Whythe, and crossed out [1]h; he then began a new line with Wythe, leaving the abandoned word uncancelled.

Wy43 *gracys*] g[a]cys

Wy48 *yerfull*] yerefull

Wy76 *wytyly*] altered from wytt or wyttly

Wy79 *nombyr*] altered from nomber

Wy80 *thyngke*] think, see note on spelling.
the nombyr] the nōbyr

Wy85   *bothe*] body
Wy96   *thy eyse*] thyese
stareyng] e interlined
Wy100   *plesaunttly*] [1]t interlined
Wy113   *Feor*] e interlined above caret, its intended position not clear.
Wy125   After this line the scribe copied and cancelled Wy128.
Wy129   *alwey*] altered from alway; see note on spelling.
Wy135   *may*] interlined
Wy141   *wyttl[e]s*] wyttls, probably altered from wytty or wyttyles.
Wy147   *Thyn[k]*] Thyng
Wy169   *dyfferens*] dyfferēs
Wy174   *conclewde*] coclude deleted
Wy181   *wytt*] wytty deleted
comparatyve] cōparatyve
Wy183   *clayme*] y interlined above caret
Wy190   *reason*] a interlined; see note on spelling.
Wy193   *feare*] fierce Farmer
Wy199   *prove*] ? prowe; w/v blotted
Wy206   *seay*] ? say, a perhaps intended to substitute for e
Wy207   *I*] 'J' form deleted; see note on spelling.
Wy220   The scribe began Wy221 and cancelled it.
Wy227   *plesauntly*] plesāutly
Wy230   *hys*] ? read of hys
Wy232   *neate*] a interlined above caret; see note on spelling.
Wy237   *common*] cōmon
Wy247   *whyche*] [1]h inserted
Wy249   *John*] Jh cancelled
Wy259   *John*] Jo altered from Ja
Wy260   *dylate*] altered from dylayte
Wy261   *therin*] r interlined above caret
Wy271   *woorde*] [1]o interlined
Wy276   *wyttles*] [2]t interlined
Wy277   *Why*] on left of text in
Wy281   *devyce*] perhaps devyne
Wy287   *an*] and
Wy288–9   *never*] The scribe skipped to *never* in Wy289 and continued with *to ground*, which he subsequently deleted, interlining *standythe styll* in different ink.
Wy294   *many*] altered from mayny; *theyre*] y interlined
Wy301   *at*] ar
Wy308   *to*] interlined; *wey*] e substituted for a
Wy309   *of*] altered from to
twayne most payne] interlined above *have most plesewre*, eyeskip from Wy310.
Wy313   *promyse*] ℘myse; beginning of m not a second o.
payment] paymēt
Wy315   *prove*] ℘ve
Wy332   *partts*] [1]t interlined
Wy335   *James*] a altered from o
Wy336   *thynke*] thyngke with g deleted; see note on spelling.

Wy344 *woorddes*] [1]o interlined
Wy345 *dyscernyng*] dysnernyng
Wy347 *dysernythe*] dyservythe deleted
Wy348 *thynosent*] thȳnosent
Wy358 *conclewde*] w interlined
Wy361 *have*] lacke deleted
Wy368 *partt*] [2]t added
Wy374 *bothe*] ?bothye
Wy392 *carnall*] [1]r interlined
Wy418 *indyferent*] indyferēt
Wy420 *thyngys*] [2]y obscured by s and possibly deleted
Wy423 *alwey*] e interlined above deleted a, see note on spelling.
Wy433 *dothe*] altered from nothe
Wy434 *ye*] altered from he
Wy436 *saying*] i interlined above caret
Wy446 *when*] altered from ween
Wy455 *woolde*] [2]o possibly added
Wy456 *John*] speech head centred as well as in right margin
Wy458 *beast*] a interlined; see note on spelling.
Wy459 *Were*] altered from Where, also Wy477
Wy460 *Jerome*] [1]e altered, possibly from o.
Wy462 *Why*] at beginning of following line, as in Wy277
Wy463 *wherforrse*] [3]r added
Wy464 *things*] thyngks deleted
Wy469 *beasts*] altered from bes
Wy472 *Drawyng*] Drowȳng
Wy477 *Were*] altered from Where
Wy483 *twayne*] y interlined
Wy484 *compare*] cōpare; compayrre cancelled
Wy490 *plesaunt*] plesaūt
Wy491 *commandynge*] cōmandynge
Wy494 *commodyte*] cōmodyte
Wy506 *John*] James deleted
Wy507 *reason*] a interlined; see note on spelling.
Wy519 *grawnt*] grāwt deleted
Wy524 *many*] altered from mayny
Wy528 *whyppyd*] altered from w(?y)ppyd
Wy535 *Therefor*] The for
Wy539 *r[e]sonabyll*] rosonabyll
Wy541 *answere*] [1]e interlined
Wy554 *commandments*] cōmandements
Wy555 *who*] altered from ho
Wy561 *many*] altered from mayny
Wy569 *commandment*] cōmandment
Wy574 *and*] interlined
Jerome] in centre as well as in right margin at foot of fol. 117.
Wy579 *compare*] cōpare
Wy581 *desyrusly*] discernfully Farmer

Wy587 *commandyd*] cōmandyd

Wy589 *folks*] ?folkes

Wy600 *thencres*] the chance Farmer

Wy611 *sofereth*] sofether; willeth he, Farmer

Wy616 *Owrr*] The scribe first wrote the beginning of Wy617, and wrote this over the cancelled words.

Wy621 *of*] altered from or; *alwey*] altered from alway

Wy623 *commandments*] cōmandments

Wy629 *instant*] altered from instanc

Wy635 *feare*] frare

Wy639 *wrowght*] wrowght/. See Explanatory Note.

Wy646 *John*] s.h. in centre as well as right margin

Wy659 *woolde*] wolde corr. woolde

Wy666 *governans*] governās; *gyfts*] t indistinct, but by analogy with Wy575, 668 it is intended.

Wy667 *alwey*] altered from alway

Wy676 *gyfts*] see note to Wy666. *may*] man, Farmer

Wy682 *wheer*] ? whear

Wy683 *of*] ? ofe

Wy689 Farmer moves this line to the next stanza.

Wy690 *Prayng*] praynge deleted above, presumably to allow larger space between stanzas.

Wy698 *of*] ? ofe

Wy699 *late*] altered from layte

EDITORIAL NOTES TO JOHAN JOHAN

The Text

Original   *A mery play betwene Johan Johan the husbande, Tyb his wyfe, and syr Johan the preest.* [Colophon] Impryntyd by Wyllyam Rastell the xii day of February the yere of our lord Mccccc and xxxiii. Cum Privilegio.
2° A–B⁴ [No separate title page].
Two copies : Bodleian Library (A), Pepys Library (P).
Black letter.
(STC 13298). Greg 13.

Facsimiles   J.S. Farmer, *Tudor Facsimile Texts*, 1909; reprinted New York, 1970.
G.R. Proudfoot, Malone Society Reprints, Oxford, 1971.

Editions   Alois Brandl, *Quellen des weltlichen Dramas in England vor Shakespeare*, Strassburg, 1898.
A.W. Pollard, in C.M. Gayley, *Representative English Comedies*, 2 vols., London, 1903; vol. I.
J.S. Farmer, *Dramatic Writings of John Heywood*, London, 1905; (modernized); reprinted 1966.
J.Q. Adams, *Chief Pre-Shakespearean Dramas*, Boston, 1924.
Rupert de la Bère, *John Heywood, Entertainer*, London, 1937.
Edmund Creeth, *Tudor Plays: An Anthology of Early English Drama*, New York, 1966.
David Bevington, *Medieval Drama*, Boston, 1975.

The present text follows, with permission, the Pepys copy (P) which contains ten press corrections to the Bodleian copy (Ashmole 1766 – A). The Ashmole variants are noted. The copies have the same misassigned speech heads, recorded in the Notes; these have been corrected. There are no commas in the original. The virgule (/), used sometimes in its stead, has been replaced by a comma. Full stops are very rare, even at the end of speeches, as are question marks: both have been supplied, though sparingly. Contractions are expanded.

    Mid-line speech heads reduced to initial letters have been expanded to the most frequent form. Greg notes the typographical similarity with PF. The pilcrow to mark the beginning of speeches has been omitted, but where it is used to indicate paragraphs an indentation is substituted.

Explanatory Notes

Heading *Syr Johan*: 'A familiar or contemptuous appellation for a priest.' OED John 3 (Chaucer *NPProl*, 44). Around 1500 he has a reputation as a seducer: 'O Lord, so swett Ser John dothe kys.' Greene, *Early English Carols*, 456.1. The name Johan Johan is probably modelled on the diminutive in French farce (*La farce de messire Jehan Jenin*, see Maxwell, *French Farce and John Heywood*, Melbourne, 1946, pp. 68–9). One of Heywood's fellow servants of the King had a strikingly similar name. The Treasurer of the Chamber's Accounts from 1 October 1529 record payments of 50 shillings to Heywood and also to 'John de John, priest, organ maker' (*L&P* V 306).

J5 *go a gaddynge*: rove idly. gad OED vbl.sb² 1545. Robinson (1589) speaks of 'No wandring unto waks, those dayes did women use, / Nor gadding into greens, their life for to abuse.' Bale rails against 'gadders, pylgrymes and ydoll sekers.'

J6 *Lyke an Anthony pyg*: close at heel. Cf. *Pasté* 10–1. In England 'The Officers . . . of the Markets did take from the Market Pigs starved, or otherwise unwholesome for Man's sustenance. One of the Proctors of St Anthonies tyed a Bell about the neck, and let it feed on the Dunghills; no man would hurt or take it up; but if anyone gave to them bread, or other feeding, such would they know, watch for and daily folloe . . . Whereupon was raised a Proverbe, Such an one will *follow* such an one and whine as *it were an Antonie* pig.' J. Stow, *The Survey of London*, 1595, 190 (quoted by J.S. Farmer, *The Dramatic Writings of John Heywood*, p. 221). Tilley S35. St Anthony's Hospital in the parish of St Benet Frink had an establishment of King's Minstrels in the 15th cent. and was treated as a Royal Free chapel. In the 1530s it was raising money by selling hallowed bells for cattle. The pigs were a constant cause of complaint (VCH *London* I 583n).

On St Anthony see We78. St Anthony of Egypt (3–4 cent.) patron of swineherds and of the Order of Hospitallers, founded c.1100, dedicated to pilgrims suffering ergotism (St Anthony's fire). He is shown with T-staff, bell, book and pig by his side, walking on fire. J is much earlier than OED reference (1662). *Pasté* refers to him at 109, 209, 226.

J9 *gogges blod*: God's blood. gogges †OED 1553 (Udall), probably used on stage to avoid blasphemy.

J10 *our lady of Crome*: ? shrine at Crome, Kent (Farmer).

J14 *trayne*: (v.) drag. OED v¹ c.1450.

J24 *the devyll spede whyt*: even the devil himself would not achieve that! OED whit 1.b for negative sense; also Skelton *Magnyfycence*, 1006.

J26 *No, shall*: Yes I shall. An affirmation, contradicting a previous negative, as in the elliptical form no had J624.

J30 *cokkes blood*: common oath, euphemistic for God's blood.

J40 *Walke her cote*: beat her hide. See OED walk v.², to beat or press woollen cloth in the felting process. Also at J667, GN719.

J45 *this . . . wyst*: the following should be considered.

J58–9 *And if . . me*: And if I were to put up with her ways, nothing would be of any use to me, I assure you.

J59 *waster*: club. †OED sb².2; in the 15 cent. a wooden sword for practice.

J64 *top . . . fote*: Proverbial, Dent C864.

J73 *stynke lyke a pole kat*: Proverbial, †Tilley P461. Shakespeare uses polecat for contemptible person, prostitute (MWW IV.2.195).

J76 *every nyght ones*: at least once a night.

J80 *toppe and tayle*: a cliché, but perhaps here literally 'from head to buttocks'.

J84 *blacke and blewe*: discoloured by beating; common in ME. Proverbial, Dent B160.

J86 *holde a noble*: bet a noble (gold coin worth £1/3 at this time).

J89 *enrage*: grow angry, (J'enrage, *Pasté* 91).

J90 *our gentylwoman*: familiar domestic usage, sometimes ironic.

J95 *weare a fether*: wear badge of a fool. †OED 8b feather 1588. Proverbial, Dent B717.

J96 'But yet I have no need to fear at all.'

J97–100 *gossyp*: godfather, godmother, or baptismal sponsor; one having spiritual affinity of kinship. The play is between OED sense 1 (a) and 1(c). 'How can Sir Johan be a gossip of hers since she hasn't any children for him to have sponsored?'. *Commere* and *comperage* used similarly in *Pasté* 99, 101.

J104 *case*: poosibly an indecent pun, codpiece.

J108 *She shall have her payment styk by her syde*: I shall beat her on the flank with this stick. There may be a further play on 'payment styk' as tally and penis, cf. Chaucer, *ShT* 416: 'I am youre wyf, score it upon my taille' and *WBPr* 132–3:

> 'Now wherwith sholde he make his paiment,
> If he ne used his sely instrument?'

J110 *to go a catter wawlyng*: to seek sexual adventures like a cat. More writes: 'prestes, freres, monkes & nonnes be taught that euangelycall lyberty, that they may runne out a caterwawynge' (*Confutation*, in *Works* VIII i 8/16). He plays on the same idea in condemning Luther: 'for a shewe of holy matrymony, frere Luther and Cate calate hys nonne lye luskynge togyther in lechery' (*ibid.* 181/2–4). The expression is Proverbial, Dent C192. Chaucer (*WBPr* 348–54) seems to have suggested to Heywood the identification of the lustful wife with cat-on-heat:

> Thou seydest this, that I was lyk a cat;
> For whoso wolde singe a cattes skyn,
> Thanne wolde the cat wel dwellen in his in;
> And if the cattest skyn be slyk and gay,
> She wol nat dwelle in house half a day,
> But forth she wole, er any day be dawed,
> To shewe hir skyn and goon a-caterwawed.

This is developed later, in J129, J588–9.

J111   *Tyb* becomes typical name for a woman of lower class and a strumpet.

J114   *stokfysshe*: fish, usually cod, preserved by drying and salting, beaten preparatory to use in the lean season in Lent. A bawdy sense is probable. Proverbial, Dent S867.
Temmes Strete: parallel to the River Thames on the north bank through the City of London. Stowe (p. 74) notes that stockfishmongers traded there.

J120   *this worke*: his carrying on (J118–9). But, Johan Johan's prompt and conciliatory explanation that he has lit the fire, suggests that Tyb expects him to work in the house; her later commands to prepare the table support this.

J127   *lay a swan*: wager a swan (a valuable, royal bird).

J129   *fatched of hym a lyk*: 'Wele wotith the cat whos berde she likkith,' Skelton *Garland of Laurel*, 1438. Tyb has come in from caterwauling to warm herself by the fire, having had a good 'lick' of Syr Johan.

J138   '. . . he won't find anything to please him.'

J146–9   *saynt Dyryk*: Possibly St Theodoric (d.533 A.D.) Abbot of Mont d'Or, or Tewdric, S. Welsh saint. More interesting in the context is the noted hangman c.1600 (OED), hence *derrick*: hanging, the gallows, a machine for hoisting heavy weights. Dyryk may be one of Heywood's burlesque saints.

J153   *Poules*: St Paul's cathedral.

J163   *lylly*: pure, fair. *lily wounds* †OED *Roister Doister* IV vii 72.

J164   'The biggest bawd from here to Coventry.' Proverbial, though the place varies, see J466. Tilley H429 (common in interludes).

J168   'I have something about which I would like to appeal to you.' OED move 12.

J175–8   Perhaps not an aside, but not meant to be heard clearly by Tyb, hence the double-take at J179–81.

J183   *too too*; excessively. This line spoken by Wife in *Pasté*.

J188   *What . . . I?* What the devil do I care?

J189/90   *and*: if.

J201   This line lacks a rhyming pair.

J202   'I assure you that would be right.'

J204   *go to hym ryght*: go directly to him.

J211   Proverbial, Tilley D298; also We941.

J212   *he . . . curate*: he has spiritual care of my soul.

J222   *make some chere*: give you a good time.

J240   *I . . . whether*: I don't mind which of the two.

J250, 252, 254   *you . . . he . . . ye*: he selects different spectators.

J264   *out of the way*: unprepared, in the wrong place.

J274–5   *lyttell . . . thus*: Proverbial, Dent T141.11.

J280 *with . . . face*: and may mischief descend upon you. OED light v¹ 10c. Proverbial, Dent M1003.

J293 'It is a hard thing to please a cantankerous fool.'

J304 *gyve a strawe*: care. Proverbial, Tilley S917, and PF357.

J307 *in the space*: in the intervening time.

J308 *and . . . ryght*: if I were to do what you deserve.

J313 Proverbial, Tilley D278, also Heywood, *Dial. Provs.* II vii 2065.

J313 s.d. Though there is little information in the text about staging, the change of location indicates two centres of action, as in *Pasté*.

J327 'I will not accept because it may lead to strife.'

J341–4 Quatrain, abab.

J343 *Now . . . yow*: God reward you for it.

J344 'and send you good health in return for your good deeds.'

J345 'I am much beholden to you, whatever it pleases you to do.'

J350 *lye uppon*: importune, press: with sexual innuendo, continued in J352.

J353 *lest . . . nyne*: Proverbial, see J.M. Lothian and T.W. Craik (eds.) *Twelfth Night* III ii 64 note. Dent C87.11.

J361 *intyce*: stir up, but perhaps with suggestion of allure or seduce.

J366 *savyng your reverens*: Proverbial, Dent R93.

J372–4 'And now he shows himself to be innocent, and I here see he tries as if he would give his life to bring the quarrel between me and my wife to an end.' Johan is apparently taken in by the Priest.

J384 *agaynst this nyght*: in anticipation of this night.

J391–4 Quatrain, abab.

J398 *bespake*: ordered, arranged for. †OED v.5 (1583).

J401 *masshyp*: mastership, not this spelling in OED; mashyp 4P641.

J408 'She thinks the time I take to return too long.'

J410 *take in*: intransitive here.

J413 *as . . . heve*: as big as I can lift.

J417 *whyt*: no OED citation refers to liquids.

J419 *fast as a snayle*: Proverbial, Tilley S579, and S583; haste like a snail Heywood *Dial. Provs.* I ix 504.

J421–2 Spoken sarcastically.

J425 'Go away, curse you, and consider yourself politely requested to do it.'

J426 The 11-line delay in Tyb's welcome of Syr Johan, like the broken-off confidence of J438, is an excellent example of Heywood's stagecraft.

J427 *Welcome myn owne*: the conventional endearment may allude to a contemporary song. See Redford, *Wyt and Science* 989–1020.

J430 *abateth my chere*: makes me downhearted.

J439 *what . . . here*: Proverbial, Dent W280.2.

J442 *have done*: stop talking.

J447 *clyfte*: split or slit with sexual reference. 'In the sexual double entendre, the bucket and its slit are Tib and her sexual appetites, which Johan is unable to keep filled or satiated. The wax represents his phallus which his wife suggests he rub or chafe as a sexual substitute' (Bevington). Cf. the extended double entendre in We719–54.

J454 'It would be a shame to help him,' (because she enjoys his predicament.)

J455 *canst . . . shyfte*: can you not think of a solution?

J457–8 'to pull one's wire': masturbate, 19th-cent. slang (see E.H. Partridge, *The Routledge Dictionary of Historical Slang*, 1973).

J465 *by my holydome*: by what I hold sacred. †OED.

J466 *erranst*: most notorious (from arrant).

betwene this and Rome: for parallel structure see J164 and note.

J478 *whyle thou art well*: while you are still in one piece (a threat).

J480 *Benedicite*: beginning of grace, interrupted by Johan's *Dominus*, apparently his blessing, see J482–3.

J484 *Mych good do it you*: the good wishes are ironical; Syr Johan returns the compliment a J497.

J487–91 Quatrain, abab.

J488 *wodcok*: Proverbial for fool, see L323.

J490 *gyveth . . . mok*: plays a scornful trick on me.

J492 'And I think to myself – in order to increase your pleasure . . .' (sarcastic).

J514 *make . . . ape*: make her husband a fool. Proverbial, †Tilley A273.

J522 *patter*: mutter rapidly, as in saying prayers, especially Pater Noster, OED v¹.

J523 *and . . . shyft*: and struggle against difficulties.

J526 *wedlok . . . yoke*: 16th-century emblem books show Matrimonio as a youthful figure bearing a yoke. Cf. J675.

J531 'To entertain us by conversation.'

J536 'You must indeed do some things that your wife requires.'

J544 *comen . . . was*: returned home.

J556 *thou lettest the worde of God*: you are impeding the speaking of God's word. Cf. PF262, 419.

J561 *to Saynt Modwin*: Irish virgin saint, probably of 7 cent., patron of a Benedictine Abbey church at Burton-on-Trent from which Henry VIII's commissioners sent to London 'the image of seint Modwyn with her red kowe and hir staff, which wymen labouryng of child in those parts were very desirous to have with them to lean upon', (Farmer). The woman's pilgrimage must have been to Burton-on-Trent. The offering of a 'lyve pyg' by the barren but promiscuous woman links with Tyb (J6, 588–9, 675).

J566 *as moche as I*: just like me. This points more directly to misbehaviour by the Priest than does *Pasté*.

J572 *knave*: male, with play on knavish/knave's.

J581–2 'As though she had gone a further five months to full term. See, here are five months saved!' The assumption is that a pregnancy lasts ten (lunar) months. Syr Johan 'saved' the five months by intervening five months before marriage.

J588–9 Heywood's alterations to *Pasté*, where the Wife exclaims 'I have seen our cat produce a litter of kittens in seven weeks', are striking. *pus* is the earliest use of the conventional call-name for a cat. But why 'my cat' where one might expect 'our'? Tyb is throughout JJ associated with a cat on heat (J73, 110, 118, 129, 588): she goes 'catter wawlyng', comes in by the fire having 'licked' Syr Johan. The suggestion of a double-entendre in J588–9 is strengthened by a possible secondary meaning to *kytlyns*. Kittling, glossed *titillacio* in 1483, occurs frequently in the phrase 'kitlynge of þaire flesch' to denote sexual arousal. Though the slang term 'pussy' (*pudendum*) is not attested until the 19th cent., there may be a suggestion of 'heat periods'. Tyb (another cat name from the 18th cent.) has no children, and marvels at 'kytlyns eyghtene' in a year which might work out at one 'kytlyn' every three weeks. It was a common view in the middle ages that a lustful woman will not be able to bear children (Vera L. Bullough, 'Medieval Medical and Scientific Views of Women,' *Viator* IV (1973) 493).

J588–9 Tyb means that there are disadvantages in over-productivity. *kytlyns* †OED kitlings, first citation for domestic kittens.

J592 'Damn it, I have not had one mouthful of it.'

J595 Proverbial, Tilley P56.

J596 *doth . . . you*: doesn't it come to your memory?

J597 *clerke*: one who assisted in church offices.

J607 *to mych*: too much.

J608 'And kiss me instead of saying grace for the meal.' They are standing having risen from the table.

J613 'This is not the kind of food I usually have.'

J614 *served*: given food, treated. The play on the word also implies Johan's sexual humiliation.

J624 *no had*: didn't you really?

J630 *so mote I the*: as I hope to thrive.

J642 *for my suffysaunce*: sufficient for my needs.

J644–5 *with . . . me*: with a vengeance as for as I am concerned.

J649 *dystaf*: staff used to hold fibre for spinning, often a yard in length.
clyppyng sherys: shears for cutting wool or cloth: †OED clipping shears (1874), though *clipping* and *shears* appear separately in ME.

J657 By calling Johan a cuckold, Sir Johan concedes his own adultery.

J662 *it . . . bought*: you'll pay for it dearly.

J664 *Saynt . . . borow*: may St George be my helper!. An appropriate battle-cry.

J664 s.d. *fyght by the erys*: fight vigorously, at close quarters. †OED ears sb¹.1.d.(1539); proverbial Heywood, *Dial. Provs.* II i 1413; Tilley E23. Cf. PF515.

J667 *walkyd*: beaten, see J40 note.

J672 *Spyte of my hart*: in order to hurt my feelings the more.

J675 *then had I a pyg in the wors panyer*: i.e. I would have made the wrong choice and lost my pig (wife). Proverbial, Tilley P301. 'Who that hath either of these pygs in ure, / He hath a pyg of the woorse panier sure.' Heywood, *Dial. Provs.* II ix 2737–8. The paniers of the proverb need to be equally strong and balanced, or else the load cannot be carried. Johan Johan may also allude to the iconographic tradition of marriage as a yoke.

Colophon 12 February 1534. On the printing of the play, see Introduction p. 3.

Doubtful readings and variants

J22 *an hundred*] a .C. P, A. Cf. J303.

J111–4 *Tyb . . . Johan*] These four speech heads one line earlier in P; corrected by a ? 16th-cent. hand in A. Errors in speech heads occur on A2, A3, and A4.

J152 *Mary percase*] My pcase P, A. My as an elliptical exclamation is not attested until 1707 (OED).

J153 *churche*] churthe P, A.

J166 No speech head for Tyb in P, A.

J182 No speech head for Johan in P, A.

J191 *the*] P, A; thy Farmer.

J195 No speech head in P, A. Jhan added in manuscript in P.

J202–3 Speech heads reversed in P, A.

J241 *to*] No punctuation in P, A. ? Read go to!

J252 Speech head *Johan* repeated before this line in P, A. *Pasté* 265–6, corresponding to J252–3, are attributed to Wife. J241–65 follow the distribution proposed by R.C. Johnson, 'A Textual Problem in *Johan Johan*,' *N&Q*, 215 (1970), 210–1.

J258–9 These lines attributed to Tyb, P, A.

J260 This speech attributed to Johan, P, A.

J340 *her now*] her/now P, A.

J343 *good*] god P, A.

J365 *my*] me P, A, cf. J376.

J374 *styn[t]*] stynk P, A.

J375 *though[t]*] though P, A.

J376 *my*] me P, A.

J410 *in*] P, A; it in Farmer.

J453 *Tusshe*] P; Tusshr A.

J468 *chafe*] P; chase, A.

J470 *ywys*] P; yvys A.

J471 *Ye . . . chafe*] P; Je . . . chefe A.

J511 *And*] Áud P, A.

nat] P; uat A.

J513 *Tyb*] P; at J512 A.

J521 *. clatter*] clatier.

J523 *chafe*] thafe P, A.

J524 *ryft*] P; ryftt A.

J536–7 Both these lines begin with a pilcrow, indicating either a change of speaker, or marking the beginning of Syr Johan's recital.

J540 *beyond se*] beyondse P, beandse A.

J544 *But*] P; Bnt A.

J552 *Beyond*] P; Beyand A.

J567 *wonderous*] monderous P, A.

J600 *withstandyng*] withstankyng P, A.

J610 *it waxte* P, A. MSR suggests is waxte, or it waxeth.

J656 *the*] thy P, A.

J661 *nought*] nonght P, A.

J664 *you*] your P, A.

J675 *wors*] woyrs P, A.

EDITORIAL NOTES TO
THE PARDONER AND THE FRERE

The Text

Original   *A mery play betwene the pardoner and the frere, the curate and neybour Pratte.* [Colophon] Imprynted by Wyllyam Rastell the .v. day of Apryll the yere of our lorde 1533, Cum privilegio.

2°, A–B4. Black letter. Two copies: Pepys (P), Huntington (HN). (STC 13299) Greg 14.

Facsimiles   J.S. Farmer, *Tudor Facsimile Texts*, London, 1909; reprinted New York 1970.

A mery playe . . . etc., printed by George Smeeton, St Martin's Church Yard, London [c.1820] (line 39 and some virgules omitted).

G.R. Proudfoot and J. Pitcher, Malone Society Reprints, Oxford, 1984.

Editions   F.J. Child, *Four Old Plays*, Cambridge, 1848.

J.S. Farmer, *Dramatic Writings of John Heywood*, London, 1905 (modernized); reprinted 1966.

Rupert de la Bère, *John Heywood, Entertainer*, London, 1937.

The present text is transcribed, with permission, from the copy in the Pepys Library, and checked against Huntington and MSR. The two copies contain no press variants and a similar degree of show-through. One fount of black letter (bâtard) is used throughout, except for the head-title and the speakers' names when they are centred. Speakers' names, sometimes abbreviated, are usually in the left margin, while the beginning of a speech is sometimes marked with a paragraph or indented, occasionally neither. The pilcrow sometimes marks divisions within a speech. Staging directions are centred. Some lines run over and the printer had recourse to contracted word forms. The speech heads at 321–25 are misassigned. At PF265 the omitted speech head 'Pardo.' has been added in both copies, though the hands and inks are different. Line 518 lacks a couplet, apparently omitted by Rastell's printer.

The most striking feature of Rastell's punctuation is the abundant use of the mid-line slash or virgule (/). This is remarkably consistent throughout three-quarters of the text and seems to have been suggested by the way in which Heywood's source in Chaucer's *Canterbury Tales* was printed in 1526 (STC 5086) and 1532 *Workes* (STC 5068). The slashes may derive from Heywood himself rather than from Rastell's printer. In the manuscript copy of Bale's *King Johan* the scribe (corrected by Bale himself) used a non-syntactical mark to indicate a metrical break at the mid-line. These mid-line slashes appear to distribute stress in the line (and may incidentally reveal something about the way in which Heywood read Chaucer). We have adopted the convention used in *The Complete Plays of John Bale* (Tudor Interludes) to represent the line-break with an additonal space.

Explanatory Notes

PF1 *Deus hic*: God be here! Formulaic blessing by which 'houseless' friars sanctified the places where they preached or begged. Cf. Chaucer, *SumT* 1770. After the Reformation, it is used with patent irony in the interlude of Robin Hood and the Friar (pr. 1553–69):

Deus hic! Deus hic! God be here!

Is not this a holy worde for a frere?

and by the Ranger in We400.

PF6 *rent*: reward, perhaps in kind (e.g. grain) as opposed to money.

PF9 *to poll nor to shave*: to clip hair nor to shave heads, i.e. to tonsure new friars. But the phrase seems also to have the figurative sense 'to fleece'('Their tenauntes . . . whom they poll and shave to the quycke by reysing theyr rentes,' *Utopia* 1551 trans. Robinson).

PF14 *edyfye*: instruct †OED 3.b. cites PF. Cf.PF561.

PF15 *we freres*: the Frere is probably conceived as a Dominican (Black Friar) or preaching friar. The other mendicant orders of men were Franciscans or Friars Minor (Grey Friars), Augustiniáns, and Carmelites (White Friars).

PF21 *serche mennes conscyens*: elicit confession by systematic questioning. This function was particularly associated with the footloose Dominicans and Franciscans.

PF22 *We may not care for grotes / nor for pens*: we are not allowed to be concerned with worldly wealth, however small. An ironic sense is also found in the collection taken by the vices in *Mankind* 457: 'He lovyth no grotis, nor pens of to pens'. A grote was worth 4 pence.

PF26 *the gospell vary*: deviate from the gospel (Matt.10:9–14:
> Provide neither gold, nor silver, nor brass in your purses . . . .
> And when ye come into an house, salute it. And if the house be worthy, let your peace come upon it: but if it be not worthy, let your peace return to you.
> And whosoever shall not receive you, nor hear your words, when ye depart out of that house or city, shake off the dust of your feet.)

This is paraphrased in PF37–53. Cf. Mark 6,8–11, Luke 9,3–5.)

PF43 *electe*: chosen by God. Possibly the preaching Friar associates himself with Protestant heresies. Note, however, that it is the house, not the people who are 'electe'.

PF54 *Wherfore*: Printer's paragraph sign indicates a new section in the speech.

PF57 *harty chere*: the Friar is looking for a good meal.

PF61 *were*: a normal Rastell spelling – where.

PF68 *almyght*: almighty. Archaic form, long (for metrical reasons) the common form in poetry.

PF70 *A symple colacyon*: an informal discourse or homily (OED 5b) with, perhaps, the lurking primary sense of gathering money. The word is rare in English and occurs also in *La farce du Pardonneur* (Maxwell pp. 79–80).

PF78 s.d. *pardoner*: person licensed to sell papal pardons or indulgences.

to declare what eche of them ben: each section of the Pardoner's exposition refers to a different relic and is marked with a paragraph sign: 105 *sheep bone*, 128 *mytten*, 140 *great too of the Holy Trynyte*, 145 *Our Lady bongrace*, 154 *All Helowes . . . jaw bone*. There is no paragraph sign for PF134 *the blessed arme of swete saynt Sondaye* or 162 *the brayn pan of saynt Myghell*.

PF79 *Saynt Leonarde*. It is not clear why the Pardoner invokes this saint, who is not mentioned by Chaucer or the *Farce du pardonneur*. St Leonard, feast day 6 Nov., was first saint of the crown of France, a Limousin noble of the 11th cent., widely venerated in Europe. His miracles include deliverance of captives, pregnant women in confinement, and those possessed of evil spirits. St Leonard was special patron of prisoners in medieval England (E.J. Dobson, *The Origins of Ancrene Wisse*, Oxford, 1976, pp. 243–50). By Heywood's time he may well have become disreputable. Bale's Idolatry attributes to him the well-being of ducks (*Three Laws* 512). He is generally depicted as holding chains. A story current in 1535 associates St Leonard with prayers for deliverance from the gallows (Robert Whiting, *The Blind Devotion of the People*, Cambridge, 1989, p. 62). On his chapel see PF207.

PF82–83 The Pardoner's prayer that his audience resemble 'the ymage' of their creator states the idée fixe of his professional calling. The hostility of Pardoner and Friar embodies (but does not necessarily represent) the opposition of image and word which had already been taken as a key-note in Lutheran polemic and which excercised More in his controversy with Tyndale (Margaret Aston, *England's Iconoclasts* I, Oxford, 1988, ch. 5). Cf. PF243.

PF84 'And that you save that within you which Christ bought (your souls)'.

PF91 *his bulles under lede*: Papal edicts sealed with leaden seals (*bulla*). While the medieval church regularly cursed 'þo þat falsen þe popis bulle or bischopis letteris', Wyclif denounced bulls themselves and the paraphernalia of pardoners as unchristian: 'Also þe proude prest of Rome settiþ ymagis of Petre and Poul in his leed, and makiþ Cristene men to bileve þat alle þat his billes speken of is don bi her auctorite and Cristis.' (*De Pontificum Romanorum Schismate*, cap. xvi, *Select English Works*, ed. T. Arnold, 3 vols. Oxford, 1869–71, III 308.)

PF93 *grotes or els pens.* Cf. 22, 132, and PP B Prol.68ff.

PF97–138 and 173–82 closely follow Chaucer's Pardoner (*PardPr* 335–88).

PF98 *all and some*: the whole sum. The phrase (OED all *adj* 12b) confuses some and sum.

PF99 *lyege lorde seale*: the seal of our liege Lord (and King).

PF100 *my body to warant*: to give authority to my personal presence here.

PF105 *a holy Jewes shepe*: possibly Jacob (Gen. 30:31). Cf. Chaucer, *PardPr* 351. The use of a 'shulderboon of a sheep' for conjurations by enchantours or nigromanciens in bacyns ful of water' is condemned in the *ParsT* X 603. Heywood may have been sent to Chaucer by a passage in More: 'For what reuerent hounore is there dayly done . . . to some old rotten bone yt was happely some tyme as Chaucer sayth a bone of some holy Iewes shepe' (*Heresies* I 17, *Works* VI i 98).

PF111 *And yf any worme have your beestes stonge*: Chaucer's 'That any worm hath ete, or worm ystonge' (355) suggests that *worm* has the generalised ME sense of creeping things, including insects.

PF121–22 *His beestes and his store shall multeply*
    And, maysters all, it helpeth well
These lines do not rhyme. Chaucer (*PardPr* 366) has:
    'And, sires, also it heeleth jalousie'.
Heywood's effect may be deliberate, to conclude a paragraph, beginning the new one with an internal half-rhyme (all/well), but this seems unlikely. More likely is that after the printing of 122 a line was omitted. The paragraph may have ended with a coda:
    And maysters all
     It helpeth well
    [jalousie]

PF123 *be foule in jelous rage*: be wickedly in a jealous rage. MSR suggests foule = fallen.

PF126 *Thoughe he in sothe the faut by her wyst*: though he should know the truth about her failing. Chaucer *PardPr* 370 has 'Though he the soothe of hir defaute wiste'.

PF127 *Or had she been take with freres two or thre*: If she had been taken in adultery with two or three friars. The alteration of Chaucer ('Al had she take prestes two or thre') points the insult at the Friar on stage, suggesting flagrantly public misconduct.

PF128–9 *mytten . . . myttayn*: change of spelling to rhyme with grayn.

PF131–2 *otys/grotes*: Cf. Chaucer, *SumT* 1963–5.

PF134 *The blessed arme of swete saynt Sondaye*: apparently a rendering of Sanctus Dominicus (St Dominic), due to confusion with *dies dominica*. The intention may be to associate the Pardoner with the Dominican friars. The first of the absurd and bizarre relics marks Heywood's departure from his Chaucerian source, prompted perhaps by knowledge of the French tradition of *Le Pardonneur, le Triacleur et la Tavernière* (*Ancien Théâtre françois* ed. M. Viollet-Leduc, 10 vols. Paris, 1854–57. II 50–63). There the first of the Pardonneur's relics are 'des ouyes / De sainct Couillebault confesseur / Et de sainte Velue, sa soeur' and others are in a similar vein of burlesque 'phallic' saints. However, none of the specific details corresponds to Heywood's.

PF140 *The great too of the Holy Trynyte.* The same relic is introduced with more elaborate and graphic stage business in 4P508–17.

PF146 *Her bongrace which she ware with her french hode.* The bonegrace (Fr. moufflet: Palsgrave 1530) was a shade or curtain at the front of women's bonnets, caps, or the fashionable French hood, to protect the complexion from the sun. Among the relics of Chaucer's Pardoner is a 'pilwe-beer [pillow case] Which that he seyde was our Lady veyl' (*GenPr* 694–95).

PF148 *Women with chylde, whiche be in mournynge*: possibly in the sense 'have painful longings' (OED 3). That this is one group of women, not two, seems evident from the promise that they shall be 'sone easyd' and 'of theyr travayll full sone also releasyd' by kissing the bongrace. Cf. St Leonard's powers, PF79.

PF154 *Of All Helowes the blessyd jaw bone.* The same relic is introduced in an identical line by the Pardoner in 4P497, where protracted scurrility suggests topical reference to the notorious stronghold of heresy in Honey Lane (see note to 4P503). In summer 1532 blood was shed there when two priest fought, and no service could be performed until they did penance before a general procession (Brigden, *London* p. 213).

PF170 *crouche and crepe*: as in 'creeping to the cross'. The old sense to cross oneself (as in Crouchmas) seems unlikely.

PF173–82 follows Chaucer, *PardPr* 377–86.

PF181 *out of suche blame*: free from such reproach.

PF182 *Com hyther to me*: possibly an echo of Chaucer's Pardoner: 'Ful loude he soong "Com hider, love, to me!" ' (*GenPr* I 672).

PF188 s.d. *evyn at the same tyme* In Rastell's folio the speech heads alternate, line by line; the Friar leads and each of the Pardoner's lines is marked by a paragraph sign. The stage direction, together with the layout of subsequent speeches, make clear that *simultaneous* delivery is intended. In performance there are various possibilities (see The Plays 4).

PF189 *Date et dabitur vobis*: give and it shall be given unto you (Luke 6:38), glossed tendentiously at PF196–98.

PF190 *place of scrypture*: text, extract (OED 7b 1526).

PF193 *Pope Leo the tenth*: Leo X (Pope 1513–1521) licensed the sale of indulgences to raise money for his building program in the Vatican, a practice attacked by Luther publicly in 1517. When Henry VIII wrote his *Assertio septem sacramentorum adversus M.Lutherum* in 1520 (pr. Pynson, London, 1521), it was Leo X who granted him the title 'Fidei Defensor '. Leo's death in 1521 has sometimes been taken as a terminal date for composition of *Pardoner and Frere*, taking PF193 to refer to a living pope. This is by no means certain, since Heywood plays games with names of popes (see below PF217, 223). More quotes the King's view of Leo X as a good man several times in *Responsio ad Lutherum* (1523) (*Works* V i 327–33).

PF195 *under lede*: bearing lead seals cf. PF91.

PF197 *bothe quycke and dede*: The Pardoner's papal edict addressed to both living and dead seems to send up his authority.

PF199 *Ten thousande yeres and as many lentes of pardon.* Those who give a penny or a charitable offering (*almes dede*) are promised as reward (*guardon*) ten thousand years of pardon and as many periods of forty days (*lentes*).

PF205 *Put to theyr handes to the good spede*: give a hand in furthering the success ...

PF207 *the holy chapell of swete saynt Leonarde*: the Chapel of St Leonard, destroyed by fire 'late', cannot be identifed with certainty. Of medieval London parish churches of St Leonard the likeliest was at Foster Lane, on the corner of Cheapside and Aldersgate, just across the road from St Paul's Cross (VCH *London* I 179, 245). During 1529–32 its rector was demanding tithes in absentia and parishioners petitioned Cromwell (Brigden, *London and the Reformation* pp. 53, 201). After the Reformation Stow (*Survey of London*,

1603) refers to this as 'a smal parrish church by Pope lane end'. Possibly the London citizen who gave his name to the lane had been forgotten in the 16th cent. in favour of the Pope. But Heywood's Pardoner derives his authority from Rome and may refer to a real or imagined building burned by the 'heretics' in the sack of Rome in May 1527.

PF210 The syntactical break signals a shift in acting mode and is the first textual indication the Friar gives that he is aware of the Pardoner's presence. See note to PF188.

PF217 *Pope July*: There has been no Julius VI. Julius II was Pope 1503–13 and laid the cornerstone of St Peter's. Bale is scathing about him (see note to *Three Laws* 647). Perhaps the point is merely the Pardoner's comic ignorance.

PF223 *Pope Bonyface the ninth also*: Boniface IX, Pope 1389–1404, was notorious among the schismatic Avignon popes for his attempts to replenish the papal treasury.

PF225 *Pope July, Pope Innocent*: the vagueness seems deliberate. The eighth Pope Innocent died in 1492.

PF228 *How Dives Epulus reygnynge in welfare*: enjoying everlastingly an abundance of food and drink (welfare OED 2b). The story of the rich man (*dives*) and Lazarus is in Luke 16:19–31. The Vulgate says merely *epulabatur*: 'he feasted'; hence the epithet Epulus.

PF235, 237 *Any monye into the pardoners cofer . . . Or any money up unto it offer* Apparent tautology, but the distinction is between a private act and a public demonstration of piety.

PF243 *ymage or letter*: sacred object (badge, effigy, relic) or letter (of indulgence).

PF249 *quyte you well your mede*: requite you with your reward.

PF262 *lettyth the worde of God of audyence*: obstructs the hearing of God's word. Cf. PF419.

PF263 *Standeth accurst in the greate sentence*: stands anathematised by excommunication (the 'great curse', pronounced by the Pope, 'with bell, book, and candle': Foxe AM V 20–1).

PF271–74 The Pardoner claims royal authority, witnessing the king's 'brode seale', i.e. the Great Seal of Westminster, used for sealing letters patent of open authority. Henry VIII's view on pardons is not specified in his *Defence*, but might be inferred to be orthodox (cf. PF99).

PF276 *set fast by the fete*: in the stocks.

PF277 *more mete*: better fitted. Cf. *meter* PF283. The boast contains the seed of the contest in *Foure PP* to establish who teaches the best way to salvation.

PF292 *clene purgacyon*: perfect purification.

PF298 *after another rate*: in another manner.

PF311 *clene rejecte*: completely expelled.

PF313 *It forseth not for the wordes of a knave*: a knave's words are of no importance.

PF316 *I shewed you ere whyle of almes dede*: some time ago I told you about gifts of charity.

PF325 *And forgyven*: omission of the grammatically necessary 'be' is hardly noticeable in performance.

synnes seven: pride, wrath, envy, avarice, gluttony, lechery, sloth.

PF331 *mysse*: go without (OED 6) Cf. *Pricke of Conscience* 5266–67:
> And for þe godhede es ful of blisse
> þar for þe sight of it þai sal misse.

PF335 *rydder*: deliverer. †OED ridder 2.1. The older word ridder means a sieve and Heywood's usage here may be metaphorical.

PF340 *lymytacyon*: licensed circuit of an itinerant preaching friar.

PF347–49 These lines confirm that the Pardoner's interruptions are simultaneous and suggest too that he keeps up a continuous noise.

PF353 *Maledictus qui audit verbum dei negligenter.* Translated in PF355. Possibly a Protestant riposte to *Jer.* 48.10: 'Maledictus qui facit opus Domini fraudulenter'.

PF354 The Friar picks up his earlier request (PF315) before the interruption.

PF356 *syr daw.* The jackdaw with its noisy and limited vocabulary is a by-word for folly in literature of the period. Cf. *100 Epigrams* 94.

PF357 *I care nat for the an olde straw.* Proverbial *Gentleness* 415, Tilley S917.

PF360 *thou standest and prate.* Rhythm in an already overlong line requires ellipsis of 'thou standest and dost prate'.

PF358–61 'I would rather you were hanged by a rope than have to stand knocking outside the gate while you stand prating.'

PF367 *That pardoners from you may not be spared:* that you can't afford to do without pardoners.

PF376 *For of our own propre we have no propre thynge:* to call our very own we have no real property.

PF380 *fryers thre score and three.* The significance of this number is revealed in John Lydgate's satirical *Order of Fools*, line 6: 'Noumbre in this frary told iij skore and thre' (*Minor Poems* p. 449). There may also be an allusion to the Fraternity of the Holy Trinity and of the Sixty Priests in Leadenhall Chapel (VCH *London* I 578).

PF384 *wylfull charyte professe:* profess to live willingly on charity.

PF385 *though ye had slayne bothe father and mother:* cf. More's 'ensample of Iak slouche . . . ye defoylyng of hys mother And also the poysenynge of hys father' (*Confutacyon, Works* V 495/4).

PF417 'It does not befit you one bit, you knave.'

PF419 *And let the worde of God of audience:* and hinder the hearing of God's word. Cf. PF262.

PF420–1 'Hinder God's word', says he! No, let the idiotic kitchen-knave spout here all day – a rotten plague on him!' Cf. J655.

PF422–3 *thy sermon goth on covetyce:* Chaucer's Pardoner preaches 'no thynge but for coveitise' on the text 'Radix malorum est cupiditas' (*PardPr* 334).

PF442 'The gifts of good men do them [beggars] much harm.'

PF443 *fables dere inoughe a flye:* Proverbial, 'not worth a fly' Tilley F396. Cf. L985.

PF447 *in the twenty devyll waye:* in the name of the devil twenty times over. An intensification of the normal oath, 'in the devil way', by an indefinite number. But cf. *Chester Plays* III 219: 'in twentye devylles waye'.

PF448 *hardely:* assuredly. Possibly still trisyllabic.

PF449 *hardely do your cost:* confidently put your trust and money.

PF458 *prebends:* pittance; portion of the revenues of a cathedral or collegiate church granted to a canon or member of the chapter as his stipend.

PF460 'We are forbidden to undertake any worldly service' [such as teaching, looking after the sick].

PF461 *the fyve solempne festes:* Farmer names Christmas, Circumcision, Epiphany, Purification, Annunciation – all immovable feasts.

PF463 *A masse and dirige:* A masse and dirge (Farmer). The English 'dirge' comes from the first word of the Latin antiphon, 'Dirige, Domine, Deus meus, in conspectu tuo viam meam,' (Direct my path, O Lord, in thy sight) at Matins in the Office of the Dead.

PF468–70 Cf. Chaucer's comment on his Friar (*GenPr* 229–30):

> For many a man so hard is of his herte,
> He may nat wepe, althogh hym soore smerte.'

PF469 *herse:* hearse (OED 2), an elaborate frame originally intended to carry lighted tapers and other decorations over the coffin when placed in church.

PF479 *Twelve pore people*: in remembrance of the twelve apostles, as in the Maundy Thursday service. Charitable orders and hospitals, such as St Anthony's, typically provided for 'twelve poor men'.

PF484 *For the more of religion, the more herde of our Lorde*: the more members in a religious order, the better are they heard by God. The maxim may play against the medieval proverb, 'The nere to the churche, the ferther from God' (Heywood, *Dial.Provs*. I ix 483).

PF486 'And that it should be so accords well to reason.'

PF489 *in decay*: on hard times.

PF490 *parte with your charitie*: give your alms.

PF505 *sticke nat for a peny*: 'Don't be unwilling to give a mere penny'. †OED stick 15b: to be grudging or stingy.

PF508 *stynt thy clappe*: cease your chatter. Cf. Chaucer *MilPr* I 3144.

PF509 *Pull me down the pardoner with an evyll happe!* Pull down the Pardoner for me – and ill luck to him! The Pardoner has been standing on a stool (512) to gain an advantage in preaching. The a stool may be a sign of his attempt to give himself spurious spiritual authority. Cf. Bale, *Three Laws* 675–77, where a stool is used for a stage confession:

> Here is a stoole for the
> A ghostlye father to be
> To heare *Benedicite*.

Cf. More, *Confutacyon*: 'wolde [a man] not wene that yt were a sorte of freres folowynge an abbote of mysrule in a Christemas game that were prykked in blankettes, and then sholde stande vp and preche vppon a stole and make a mowynge sermon' (*Works* VIII i 42/2).

PF511 *while ye be in rest*: i.e. 'while I am not attacking you'. *rest* (OED 4e) freedom from molestation.

PF515 *Or by Jys Ish'lug the by the swete eares*: 'By Jesus I shall pull you by your precious ears'. *Ish'lug*: phonetic reduction of 'I shall lug' (usually used of animals). A play (lug sb²: ear) may be intended.
swete: dear to the person himself †OED 8d (1621).

PF518 *And I shrew thy herte and thou spare*: I curse your heart if you hang back. The missing partner (518a) of this unrhymed line may have ended with *hair*.

PF519 *thou slouche*: 'a term of disparagement without precise significance' (OED 1511). But in the *Confutacyon* More's repeated use of the word 'slouche' forges a strong association with heresy. He imagines a grown-up heretic of Tyndale's faith, 'a great slouen slouche, that of hys boyes age is twenty wynter stepte into hys knavys age' (*Works* VIII ii 492/30) and 'a nother slouche of hys acuayntaunce hys owne mayster Master Luther' (494/5).

PF520 *And yf thou playe me suche another touche*. The phrasing suggests stylisation of the bout in the idiom of fencing.

PF521 *costarde*: literally a kind of large apple, applied humorously or derisively to the head (OED 2 cites Palsgrave 1530 as first ex.).

PF522 '*Mary, that wolde I se!' quod blynde Hew*: Whiting H629 gives this as first use of the proverb or Wellerism.

PF532 *some good body*: This cry to the audience takes the same form in *Calisto* 791.
hengar: dagger, short sword, originally hung from the belt. Perhaps a Chaucerian echo.

PF542 *lye the*: lay thee. Lie (OED III:15) used causatively or in error for lay.

PF549–50 'Before you leave you shall both repent with every drop of your blood as bitterly as you ever regretted anything.'

PF553 *To publysh his ragman rolles with lyes*: to proclaim publicly the lies in his rigmarole. Farmer notes: 'Ragman-roll or rageman-roll was the name given (OED) to a statute of 4Ed.I, appointing justices to hear and determine complaints of injuries done within 25 years previously. Concurrent and derived meanings are numerous – a roll, list, contract, official document, discourse, rhapsody, &c – many of which have apparently been influenced by *rageman*= the Devil.' The main sense here seems to be the physical object, roll with pendant seals, such as Langland gives his pardoner (*PP* C I 73). More refers several times to 'a Ragman roll of a rable of heretykes' (*Works* VIII i 181/29) and 'all the heresyes that they haue in all theyr whole Ragmans roll' (VIII ii 657/13).

PF556 *But he wolde here no more than the man in the mone*. In the well-known ME poem (Harley MS 2253, f.114v) the Man in the Moon is said to be deaf.

PF557 'Why should I allow you to preach any more than you do me?'

PF565 *thy lyvynge is nought*: your way of life is vicious.

PF566 *Thou art an apostata, yf it were well sought*: 'If the matter were properly inquired into, you would be found to be an apostate (i.e. a member of a religious order who has deserted without legal dispensation). Cf. More *Confutacyon*: 'monkys & freres, and now apostatas & lyuynge wyth harlotes' (*Works* VIII i 42/2).

PF567–8 Note rhyme inoughe/sloughe.

PF569 *in a couche*: in bed. An oddly sinister detail recalling Chaucer:
    'Al were it good no womman for to touche
    He mente as in his bed or in his couche . . .' (*WBPr* 87–8)

PF570 *thou no man shall touch*: The Pardoner points out that the Frere preached only against homicide and so thought nothing of stabbing a woman. The Frere's sermon has not mentioned the commandments against murder and adultery. Ironically, it is the Pardoner who offered deliverance from 'every cryme', 'Ye, though ye had slayne bothe father and mother' (PF385) and 'Though that he had all his kyndred slayn' (PF393).

PF572 *lurche*: swindle. †OED lurch 4 cites this as earliest ex.

PF575 *egetoles*: edge-tools, sharp instruments.
than had it ben wronge: then an injury or crime would have been committed.

PF578 *nyse fraye*: foolish conflict.

PF585 *that laye knave*: The Pardoner is a lay officer, not an ordained priest nor a tonsured cleric. Langland's satire points to the frequent usurpation: 'þer prechede a pardoner/ as he a prest were' (*PP* C Prol.65)

PF586 *this gentylman*: the Frere. The ironic use is as old as the rhyme. For the pairing of knave/gentleman see 4P1049.

PF587 *I shall borowe upon prestholde somwhat*: I shall presume on my priest's authority a little.

PF589–91 Either, 'It is a good deed to punish such men as an example to others, if they should mix it in combat (OED mell 6) in a similar fashion to these wretches' Or, 'It is a good deed to punish such men as an example to others, showing them that they shall fare in similar fashion to these wretches'.

PF601 *Nay, I am ones charged with the*: No, I have been definitely given the charge of arresting you.
ones: in any circumstances (OED 2)

PF603 *scouryd a pare of stokys* Cf. *Mankind* 634: 'Me semyth 3e have scoryde a peyr of fetters'. OED scour v^2.1.f. rub against.

PF604 'He believes all this is just a joke.'

PF607 *this seven yere*: sg. for pl. is common in the colloquial attributive phrase. †OED cites Shakespeare, 2H6 II i 2 as earliest ex. Cf. We635.

PF611 *it wyll not be for your honesty*: the result will not be good for your reputation.

PF617 *churle preeste*: ignorant peasant priest. The 'gentylman' Frere asserts his social superiority. Cf. 4P1049.

PF621 *wylt thou be there?* suggests that the Frere has already struck his opponent.

PF623 *And thou, Syr Frere, yf thou wylt algatys rave.* Either the Parson is interrupted by the Frere, 'And you, Sir Frere, if you are determined at all events to rave' Or this is a challenge: 'If you want to, by all means, rave on!' taking *rave* as imperative and *algatys* in the sense 'altogether' (OED 4).

PF626 *by and by*: at once. Cf. 4P779–80.

PF630 *elfe*: tricksy, malicious person. †OED cites *Roister Doister* (c.1553) as earliest use. Cf. Wy120, We121.

PF636 *I have more tow on my dystaffe than I can well spyn.* Proverbial for 'trouble in store'. Cf. Chaucer, *Mil.T.* 588; Heywood, *Dial. Provs.* II v 1929–30):
'If they fyre me, some of them shall wyn / More towe on their distaves, than they can well spyn.'

PF640 *Than adew, to the devyll, tyll we come agayn.* The former combatants speak for the first time in unison. There is appropriate irony in that the farewell curse, addressed to the Curate, Pratt, and the audience, suggests that, until they 'return to the place,' the Pardoner and Friar will be found in hell. *tyll we come agayn*: the actors' conventional promise to return to 'the place'.

Doubtful readings and variants

PF s.h. *The frere.* centred. In right margin of Huntington a 16th-cent. hand has written 'Hum.Dyson'.

PF1 *Deus*] D is ornamented, 25mm sq.

PF33 *suche*] luche F

PF61 *were*] F

PF70 *colacyon*] colacyou F.

PF71 *presence*] prese F

PF78 s.d. printed the whole width of the page in same type as the dialogue.

PF82 *I pray God*] I pray good/ F

PF142 *He*] Ge F

PF143 *brede*] birde F

PF154 *Of*] Hf F

PF163 *for the*] forthe F

PF193 *the tenth*] the .x. F

PF208 *dampnable*] damynable F, y possibly broken p

PF217 *the sixth*] ye .vi. F

PF221 *lende*] l broken or poorly inked at top F

PF223 *the ninth*] the .ix. F

PF224 *these*] In both copies of F the first e apparently broken type and bears a tail.

PF225 *Pope July*] The line, unusually, has two virgules, after July and after Innocent F.

PF236 *ryche man*] rycheman F

PF242 *angels*] F (both copies); a is broken, hooked as if overprinted on r.

PF265 *acurst, knave*] a curst / knave / F; a cursed knave (Farmer) s.h. lacking. Pardo. added in HN and Pepys in dissimilar 16th-cent hands.

PF285 *carest*] earest F

PF300 *gydes*] MSR suggests guide, ? guider

PF303 *Thou*] thon F

PF304 Thou pratest in fayth / even lyke a pardoner F The first r is lettre bâtard, the second the more normal Gothic textura.

PF316 *shewed*] swewed F; *almes dede*] ? almesdede F

PF320 *thynge*] tkynge F

PF321–5 In F the speech heads for these lines, which begin a new recto page (B1), are mis-assigned as follows: 321 frere. 322 pardo. 323 frere. 324 pardo. 325 frere.

PF344 In F a long line: *sone* runs over on to 345.

PF378 *peoples gettynge*] people's giving (Farmer)

PF388 *wordly*] F. A Rastell spelling, cf. *Gentleness* 720.

PF405 In Huntington this line, the first of B2, is cropped very close.

PF416 For my pleasure ? nay F. The same printer's mark serves for questions and exclamations, see PF420.

PF417 It becometh the knave / never a dell F. It becometh the knave never a deal (Farmer).

PF420 Let the word of god qda? nay let a horsō drevyll F

PF436 *pratyng*] parting (Farmer)

PF440 *lyvynge*] lyuyuge F

PF486 And that is / so shulde / good reason doeth accorde F

PF489 The top of this line, the first on B3, is cropped in Huntington.

PF495 *monethes*] first e faint in Pepys

PF498 *and*] aud F

PF512 *knave*] kuaue F

PF518 The missing partner of this unrhymed line may have ended *hair*.

PF528 s.h. poorly inked in Pepys.

PF538 s.d. Than the fyght. F

PF566 *art*] are F

PF570 *thou*] y° F; yᵗ MSR

PF575 *egetoles*] egoteles F

PF576 *synge*] syuge F

PF602 *Johan*] Iohn F

PF604 *weneth*] wenoth F

PF641 *a myschefe*] s broken F

PF Colophon *Cum privilegio*] Cum priuilegis (Farmer)

EDITORIAL NOTES TO *THE FOURE PP*

The Text

Originals

The playe called the foure PP. A newe and a very mery enterlude of a palmer, a pardoner, a potycary, a pedler. Made by John Heewood. [Colophon] Imprynted at London in Fletestrete at the sygne of the George by Wyllyam Myddylton [1544?]
4°, A–E⁴. Black letter. One copy. British Library.
(STC 13300) Greg 21a (Q1)

The playe called the foure P. A new and very mery enterlude of A Palmer, A pardoner, A Potycary, A Pedler. Made by John Heewode. [Colophon] Imprinted at London by Wyllyam Copland [1560?]
4°, A⁴ B–E⁴. Black letter. Two copies: Bodleian; Yale.
(STC 13301) Greg 21b (Q2)

The Playe called the foure P. A very mery Enterlude of A Palmer, A Pardoner, A Potycary, A Pedler. Imprinted at London at the long Shop adioyning vnto S. Mildreds Church in the Pultrie, by John Allde. Anno Domini 1569 Septembris 14. FINIS q. Jhon Heywood.
4°, A–E⁴. Black letter. 3 copies: British Library; Pepys; John Rylands University Library, Manchester.
(STC 13302) Greg 21c (Q3)

Facsimiles

J.S. Farmer, *Tudor Facsimile Texts*, London 1909; reprinted New York 1970.
L.M. Clopper and G.R. Proudfoot, Malone Society Reprints, Oxford, 1984

Editions

R. Dodsley, ed. *Old English Plays* I, London, 1744.
J.S. Farmer, *Dramatic Writings of John Heywood*, London, 1905 (modernized); reprinted 1966.
J.Q. Adams, *Chief Pre-Shakespearean Dramas*, Boston, 1924.
Rupert de la Bère, *John Heywood, Entertainer*, London, 1937.
M.F. Ashe-Jones, An Edition of Two Plays by John Heywood. Unpublished B.Litt. thesis, Oxford University 1975.

The present edition is based on that of Middleton's quarto (Q1). This is printed, apart from the title, in one fount of black letter. Directions and speakers' names are centred with an ornament, and the beginning of each speech is marked with a paragraph or ornament. The type and ornaments of Q1 are identical with Middleton's quarto of *Wether* suggesting that the two were companion pieces (Greg I 90, 95).

It is likely that Rastell printed a folio *Foure PP* and some typical Rastell spellings (not, woll) appear in defiance of Middleton's practice (nat, wyll). Middleton's alterations to characteristic Rastell house spellings have been helpful in establishing dubious readings. Q2 makes some obvious corrections and introduces a good deal of error. Q3 corrects many readings, but modernizes idiom and spelling, smoothes rhythm, and introduces a great deal more error. In view of a number of unique readings the editor's problem is what authority, if any, to give to Q3.

At the time of Q3 (Allde) 1569 Heywood was in exile and well over seventy. It is unlikely that he had anything to do with the reissue. However, Ashe Jones discusses the textual relations of the quartos and explains its superior readings in a number of places by arguing that its compositor had direct access to the lost folio. But he does not distinguish the kinds of error and change introduced by Q3. His argument rests heavily on Q3's inclusion of 1072a, a rhyme line missing from Q1, 2.

Thre of the wysest and thre of the shrewdest
[Thre of the cheefest and thre of the lewdest]

Q3 clearly recognised that Heywood's 8-line leash of balanced opposites was unbalanced and supplied a line which cannot be proved unworthy or inauthentic. But this single fortunate restoration is insufficient to warrant importation of all Q3's modernisations. In the case of line 999, all quartos lack a first line to the couplet (4P998a).

>   And oft with them longe tyme maryed

Q3's emendation required no great privileged knowledge. Q1's 'long time married' makes sense, though it may not be what Heywood wrote (see Textual Note on 4P999). If, *pace* Ashe-Jones, Q3's printer was correcting his quarto copy with reference to an 'original' Rastell folio, it is hard to explain why he did not restore the couplet entirely.

Even if, as is remotely possible, Heywood were responsible for some of the corrections in Q3 (and it is scarcely credible that he would have countenanced the Protestant reformulation in 4P1163):

>   To synge and praye for soule departed   Q1
>   To synge and say the sarvyes apoynted   Q3

Allde's edition also introduces a vast amount of error. It also alters the spelling and idiom so drastically that the text appears almost two generations younger than its language and dramatic idiom. Substantive variants in Q2, 3 are noted, together with spelling variants which might affect syllable count or rhyme.

Explanatory Notes

Title 4PP was pronounced 'four Pees'. A copy of the play belonging to John Dudley, lord Lisle, is marked 'a play called ye 4 pees' (Lancashire 102). For possible origin of the idea of the Ps in Dante's *Purgatorio*, see above p. 42.
The title may allude to an enigmatic phrase in Stephen Hawes' *Conforte of Lovers*:

>   Yet the trouthe knowynge / the good gretest P
>   May me releace / of all my /p/p/p/ thre.   (139–40)

(*The Minor Poems* ed. Florence W. Gluck & Alice B. Morgan, EETS Oxford, 1974; notes to lines 140 and 559–60). Hawes' three ps may stand for sins (*peccata*) of thought, word, and deed; the Lover anticipates release through God (Pater) or the Lady (Pusell). A penitential interpretation is supported by an apocalyptic passage in the same poem:

>   Many one wryteth trouthe / yet conforte hath he none
>   Wherfore I fere me / lyke a swarme of bees
>   Wylde fyre wyll lyght amonge a thousande pees.   (558–60)

4P1 *Nowe God be here!* Cf. PF1, We400.
4P4 'My rudeness shows me to be unrefined now' (the actor's 'now' picking up the 'now' of lines 1–2). Cf. The sentiment is paralleled in *Calisto and Melebea* 313.
4P9 The actor refers to his dress, traditionally a palmer's cloak and staff. Pilgrims returning from the Holy Land carried palm branches in token.
4P13 The Palmer's catalogue begins very properly with holy places associated with Christ; proceeds to Rome and then to a mixture of English and continental places, often associated by alliteration.
4P17 *To Josophat and Olyvete*: the vale of Josophat, Mount of Olives. Palms which strewed Jesus's way into Jerusalem were said to have been taken from a tree in the valley of Josophat, 17 km from Jerusalem.
4P22 *the stacions*: the seven stations of Rome, i.e. the basilicas of St Peter, St John Lateran, Jerusalem Holy Cross, St Mary the Great, and, without the walls, St Paul, St Lawrence, St Sebastian. The ME *Stacions of Rome* (ed. F.J. Furnivall, EETS o.s. 25, 1867) describes in detail the relics preserved at each station and the years of pardon granted to pilgrims seeking them.

4P23 *Saynt Peters shryne*: in the crypt at St Peter's in Rome.

4P29 *the Rodes*. The fortress city on Rhodes fell to the Turks on 21 Dec 1522 and an account was published by R. Copeland in 1524 (STC² 15050). island was repossessed by the Turks in 1524. According to More, the church of St John Baptist possessed the Holy Thorn ('Yf ye wolde haue gone to the Rodes . . .' *Heresies* I 13, in *Works* VI i 84). There were Knights Hospitallers of the Order of St John of Jerusalem at Henry VIII's court. There may be a pun on roads/roods.

4P30 *Amyas*: Amiens cathedral in northern France was a favourite of English pilgrims. Ashe-Jones notes that there was a chapel of 'Notre Dame Englesque' there. 'For at Amyas is saynt Iohans hed the baptyste as men call it in talkynge . . . But . . . the nether iowe [jaw] lacketh.' (More, *Heresies* II 9, *Works* VI i 221).

4P31 *At Saynt Toncomber and Saynt Tronion*: St Uncumber, better known as Wilgefortis, had a shrine as St Paul's in London, where suppliants offered her oats. More writes of her names: 'Whereof I can not perceyue the reason / but yf it be bycause she shold prouyde an horse for an euyll housbonde to ryde to the deuyll vpon. For that is the thynge that she is so sought for as they say. In so moch that women hath therfore chaunged her name / and in stede of saynt wylgeforte call her saynt Vncumber / bycasuse they reken that for a pecke of otys she wyll not fayle to vncumber theym of theyr housbondys' (*Heresies* II 10, *Works* VI i 227–35). Cf. Bale, *Three Laws* 532.

Saynt Tronion: Chaucer's Pardoner swears by 'Seint Ronyan' (*PardPr* 310). According to Malcom Jones (in a forthcoming paper on 'Burlesque Saints' communicated to the editors), St Ronion 'certainly has no connexion with the (historical) Scottish 7th-cent. saint . . . but is one of a class of burlesque phallic saints popular in the late Middle Ages'. He suggests an etymology from rognon=kidney, pointing to the thematic context in Chaucer. Ashe-Jones draws attention to Geffraie Fenton's *Certain Tragical Discourses* (1567), ed. R.L. Douglas (1898), I 232: 'Papistes in Fraunce performe their ydolatrous pilgrimage to theyr ydoll Sainct Tronyon upon the mont Avyon besides Roan.' 'Saincte Tronnion' is also mentioned in *Respublica* V ix 32.

4P32 *Saynt Bothulph*: sixty-four ancient churches were dedicated to this 7th cent. saint who was a favourite in Lincolnshire. Saynt Anne of Buckston: famous shrine of Virgin's mother, widely revered in England, at Buxton in Derbyshire, where the hot springs were dedicated to her.

4P33 *see*] sawe Q2, 3. ME see for pa. t. is by this time old-fashioned. Armony: Armenia. The hills of Armenia with Mount Ararat were the biblical grounding place of Noah's ark.

4P34 *with*: in the company of. Job's tomb was variously identified by medieval writers (*Egeria's Travels*, trans. by John Wilkinson, London, 1971, pp. 108, 281–3; *Mandeville's Travels*, ed. M. Letts (1953), pp. 73, 285. (Ashe-Jones)
Saynt George in Suthwarke: the church of St George, Martyr, rebuilt in 14th cent.

4P35 *Waltam*: Waltham Cross, Essex. There was an ancient cross there in the time of K. Canute. Edward I erected one of his twelve 'Eleanor Crosses' there; it survives. Waltham Holy Cross had a priory, later an abbey.
Walsyngham: the shrine of Our Lady of Walsingham in Norfolk, second only to Canterbury in popularity at this time, object of Erasmus's irony in his dialogue 'Pylgremage' (1526, English trans. 1536), based on visits made 1512–14. More refers to it several times ('they wyll make comparysons betwene our lady of Ipswyche and our lady of Walsyngam' *Heresies* I 17, *Works* VI i 99) The road leading to the church and chapel was called Palmer's Way. Henry VIII's anxiety to produce a male heir prompted him to make the pilgrimage there barefoot (Aston p. 138). Cf. We208, Wy53.

4P36 *rood of Dagnam*: in the parish church of Dagenham in Essex. Ashe-Jones notes reference to the 'holy rood' in a will of 1531.

4P37 *Saynt Cornelys*: Pope Cornelius, d.253. The tomb of 'Cornelius Martyr' is still visible in the crypt of Lucina in Rome. A screen painting of him with triple cross and horn is in Portleham church in Devon.

Saynt James in Gales: St James of Galicia (at Santiago de Compostella), as popular as Jerusalem and Rome. Chaucer's Wyf of Bath had been there (CT I 466).

4P38 *Saynt Wynefrydes well in Walles*: Welsh virgin saint, whose shrine is at Holywell, venerated also at Shrewsbury and at Canterbury.

4P39 *Our Lady of Boston*: Lincolnshire. Cf. Bale, *Three Laws* 1667 and note.

Saynt Edmundes Byry: Bury St Edmunds's, Suffolk; the great Benedictine abbey named for Edmund, Saxon King of East Anglia killed by Danes in 869. His shrine was established in 925 by King Athelstan. Over sixty English churches are dedicated to him.

4P40 *Saynt Patrykes purgatory*: the church said to have been built by St Patrick in 5th cent. at Station Island, Lough Derg, Donegal, at the place where Jesus had shown him a pit and taken him on a tour of purgatory. It was closed on St Patrick's Day 1497 as a result of a complaint to the Pope about deceptions (D.D.R. Owen, *The Vision of Hell*, Edinburgh, 1970, p. 46; Owen discusses the medieval narratives on the subject). Erasmus in his *Adagia* compares Trophonius' cave to saint Patrick's purgatory (Erasmus, *Praise of Folie*, trans. Sir Thomas Chaloner, ed. C. Miller, EETS Oxford, 1965, p. 7/15–16 and note).

4P41 *Rydybone*: the priory of Redbourn near St Albans, Hertfordshire with a cult of St Amphibal since the 12th cent.

the blood of Hayles: Hailes, Gloucestershire, the Cistercian abbey to which Joseph of Arimathia is said to have brought the blood of Christ in a phial. The blood could not be seen by those in mortal sin, to whom the confessing priest would turn the opaque side of the phial. Hence, 'pylgrymes paynes' were rewarded by being shown the clear side. The relic was publicly destroyed in 1539. Cf. Chaucer, *PardT*: 'By the blood of Crist that is in Hayles' (CT VI 652); Bale, *Three Laws* 833.

4P43 *Saynt Davys*: shrine of the patron saint of Wales at St David's, Pembrokeshire, dating from 13th cent.

Saynt Denis: shrine of St Denis, first bishop of Paris, beheaded on the hill of Montmartre c.280, where the great abbey was named after him.

4P44 *Saynt Mathew*: cathedral of San Matteo in Palermo, built 1084, with his relics in the crypt.

Saynt Marke in Venis: church of San Marco in Venice, with his shrine. A pilgrim lodging was next to it.

4P45 *At mayster Johan Shorne, at Canterbury*: Possibly there was a shrine or image of 'Saint John Shorne' in Canterbury (Q3), but there seem to be two separate places named in the line. John Shorne, rector of N. Marston, Buckinghamshire, c.1290–1314, was renowned for his miracles (striking the ground with his staff to produce Shorne Spring) and for conjuring the devil into a boot. A shrine was erected over his tomb and his body was moved to St George's Chapel, Windsor, in 1478. (VCH *Buckinghamshire* IV (1927) 176. Cf. Bale, *King Johan* 1225, Foxe AM V 197, 464.

Canterbury: England's prime pilgrimage place, with the tomb of Thomas à Becket.

4P46 *great God*: Ashe-Jones emends to Rood. The 'great rood' usually consisted of the carved wooden figures of Christ crucified, flanked by the Blessed Virgin St John, and positioned above the screen separating the nave and chancel (Brigden, *London* pp. 11–12). But god=image (OED 2) seems to have been current in the period (Chester's Midsummer Show had a 'god in strings' (L. Clopper ed., *Chester* REED, Toronto & Manchester, 1979, p. lx).

Katewade: Catway, Catterwade, or Cattywade bridge, linking Manningtree (Essex) and Brantham (Suffolk) over the River Stour. At the time of Edward I the Crown still claimed forest in this region. (VCH *Essex* II 617).

Kynge Henry: the saintly Henry VI, d.1471, buried in the Benedictine monastery at Chertsey, Surrey. His body was removed by Richard III to St George's Chapel, Windsor, but remained a pilgrimage haunt.

4P47 *Saynt Savyours*: St Saviour in Bermondsey (founded as a Cluniac priory, made an abbey in 1399, and possessing a miracle-working rood) was another popular shrine that was controversial at Heywood's time. Elizabeth Sampson, cited for heresy in 1509 by Bishop FitzJames, is said to have refered mockingly to 'Sim Saviour with kit lips' (Aston, *England's Iconoclasts* p. 136, and below 4P48).

Our lady of Southwell: the collegiate church of the Blessed Virgin of Southwell, on the site of a holy well (VCH *Nottinghamshire* II 152, cited by Ashe-Jones).

4P48 *Crome*: Crome Hill, near the Royal Palace at Greenwich. Cf. J10 'our lady of Crome'.

Wylsdome: shrine of Our Lady of Willesden, Middlesex, the object of 'Lollard' scepticism in 1509 on account of its partial burning. Elizabeth Sampson refered to it as 'a burnt arse elf' (Aston p.136). 'Ye men of London gange on your selfe with your wyues to wyllesdon in the deuyls name' (More, *Heresies* I 17, *Works* VI i 100).

Muswell: Muswell Hill in N. London, site of a healing spring. A.W. Reed notes: 'Muswell, Willesden and our Lady of the Oak (Highgate Woods) were shrines in the Middlesex forest whose booths and stalls were famous to all Londoners' (*Canon* p. 21n).

4P49 *Saynt Rycharde*: Richard de Wych, Bishop of Chichester from 1244, was canonised in 1262; his body was translated to behind the high altar, where it was much visited until 1538, when the shrine was despoiled and the body secretly reburied.

Saynt Roke: Rocco, b. Montpellier c.1350, was famous as a hermit and as a pilgrim once fed by a dog. Patron of plague victims, his relics were claimed by Arles and Venice. The Bishop of Ely had a park at Rokney (VCH *Essex* II 617). St Rokeshill, Sussex is named for him and there are screen paintings in Devon and Norfolk which show him with a sore on his left leg, accompanied by a dog with a loaf in its mouth. More associates him with popular cures for syphilis: 'Saynt Roke we set to see the great sykenes / bycause he had a sore' (*Heresies* II 10, *Works* VI i 227).

4P50 *Our Lady that standeth in the oke*: the shrine of the Virgin was a notable landmark on Hampstead Heath, mentioned in proclamations of Henry VIII concerning hunting rights (VCH *Middlesex* II (1911) 241).

4P61 *thy*: The Palmer previously addresses the audience as 'ye', putting the case of those 'who seketh'. He seems here to single out an individual member of the audience.

4P65 *gostely entente*: spiritual purpose.

4P66 *as wyse as ye wente*: Proverbial, Whiting W395.

4P79 *rehersed or this*: named over previously.

4P85 *mediacyon*: The intercession by souls of dead saints on behalf of the living was one of Church doctrines to come under scrutiny during the Reformation. Q1's Catholic reading was apparently unacceptable to Q2, 3, which read medytacion. See below 1163.

4P100 *Jericho*: pilgrimage place, site of the sycamore which Zacchaeus climbed, and where Joshua threw down the walls.

4P109–10 Proverbial, Whiting (1938), p. 179.

4P112 '. . . you will never leave off magnifying them . . .'

4P115 *selfe thynge*: the actual place.

4P119–23 'But even if you had all the [power of] pardon you wished, and supposing that I had no scrap of pardon granted me in any of the places I have visited, still I would not regret the pains of my journeys.'

4P120 *kepe of*: 'care for' is normal in the negative sense. Q2, 3 found the usage obsolete, substituting 'speak of'.

4P124–6 The Palmer expounds the orthodox Catholic doctrine of salvation by good works, by which acts of pilgrimage are themselves meritorious.

4P128 *late from the ale*: (recently) straight from the alehouse.

4P130 *reasonyng*] Q3, sonyng Q1, 2. *Sonyng* might conceivably be justified as sounding ('Sownynge in moral vertue was his speche' *GenProl* I 307).

4P134–46 *And all that hath wandred so farr*: seems like a non-sequitur. Possibly lines were omitted in the composition of the new page A3v. However the rambling sentence may be construed: ' [Since no one can gainsay your travels] you can lie with impunity, as can all who have strayed so far that they are under no spiritual authority. But, whereas you consider your travail so highly, I say yet again that my pardons are such that even if there were a thousand souls in a heap, I would bring them to heaven at as good a bargain price as you have paid for the least expensive part of your pilgrimage – which still leaves you far short of heaven. In that particular relation your labours and the efficacy of pardons are not to be matched.'

4P136 *controller*: one who restrains, †OED 3 (1541) or, perhaps, censors, †OED 4 (1566).

4P151 s.h. The Potycary's entrance appears improvised ('by stelth' 4P156) and the Pardoner addresses him first as one of the audience, rather than as a professional rival.

4P157 *Saynt Antony*: Cf. 578 and We781. The choice seems dictated by rhyme, unless the saint's patronage of swineherds is intended to insult the audience through whom he pushes (see J6 and note).

4P162 *countest no lete*: reckon no hindrance.

4P164 *procure*: pejorative sense, OED 5.5.

4P165 *If I toke an accyon then were they blanke*: best understood as an aside to the audience: 'If I took the matter to trial (OED 7,8) then these pardons [compared to my power] would prove to be blank, unwritten on (†OED 2, 1547) and [the pardoners] dumbfounded' (†OED 5, 1542).

4P166–8 'Like thieves these unscrupulous bounders steal my credit. As for all the souls safely in heaven, relieved [of their sufferings], shall they thank your skills? No, they should thank me above all.'

4P173–4 'No, everyone comes into our hands [on their way to death] unless you chance to be hanged.'

4P175–6 'In which case (hanging) there will be no question of failing to get to heaven without a helping suppository [because you will be in hell]' Cf. We313, for myster/glyster rhyme.

4P181–2 'There is no choice, if you don't want to deal with the apothecary, but to meet a dishonest end by hanging.'

4P182 *bande*: hangman's noose, more usually shackle, fetter.

4P188 *from state of grace]* out of state of grace. Q3 modernizes the sense.

4P189 *about your neckes*: their necks would be more idiomatic, but the Potycary addresses and engages the audience in his hypothesis.

4P191–4 The relation posited here between good works and salvation is orthodoxly Catholic.

4P193 *one dewty*: one important duty, the essential one good deed necessary for salvation. Cf. 'one vertue' (4P1174).

4P195–6 'It is better to delay something and then achieve it than to set off too early and vainly have to do without it'. Proverbial, Whiting (1938), p. 179.

4P199 *at the fyrst chop*: tout à coup, at the first stroke †OED 4.b (1528 Tyndale).

4P203–4 '[If you are all worthless] then I have gone astray, and yet I was impatient to get here'. The Potycary reassures him the effort was worth it.

4P206–10 The kinship of the 4Ps is here explicitly indicated by the alliteration, the double couplet, and some formal stage business suggesting setting of a military watch.

4P208 *To plante you*: to station you, †OED plant 2c (1693). The implication 'like a watchman' is borne out in the subsequent clowning.

4P211 *well watched]* MSR suggests error for matched. But this would be to repeat the rhyme. The speakers 'keep watch' by the precision of the arrangement; the Pedler chimes in.

4P218 *tryfull*: lying tale, trinket. *medler*: fraudulent dealer in mixed wares. The bawdy sense of meddle (OED 5) is borne out in 219. Cf. J431.

4P228–9 Q2, 3 *For all your walkyng* interpret this pleasantry as 'in spite of all your holy pilgrimages you must have a wench somewhere.'

4P231 *Who lyveth in love or love wolde wynne*. Possibly a snatch of song.

4P235–42 More may also have provided the rationale for including the Pedler in the seventh 'Properte of a Lover', appended to his *Lyfe of Johan Picus* (printed by J. Rastell c.1510 and by Wynkyn de Worde 1525) he writes:

> There is . . . none so small a tryfle or conceyte,
> Lace, gyrdels, poynt or propre glove strayte,
> But that yf to his love it have ben nere,
> The lover hath it precyous, leyfe & dere.
> So euery relyque, image or pycture,
> That doth pertayne to Goddes magnyfycence,
> The lover of God sholde wyth all besy cure
> Haue it in love, honour and reverence . . .

(*The XII Propertees or Condicyons of a Lover by Johan Picus*, Expressed in Balade by Sir Thomas More, St Dominic's Press, Ditchling Common Sussex, 1933).

4P235 *glasses unspottyd*: looking glasses, flawless [to flatter complexions].

4P236 *pomander*: ball of spices, or hollow ball of silver etc. suspended by a chain from the neck or waist.

4P238 *Lace rounde and flat*: lace made in round shapes to lie flat on women's heads. Q3 mistakes lace for laces.

4P241 *sypers*: Cypress satin kerchiefs or bands for a hat in sign of mourning. OED 1c cites 4P.

swathbondes: swaddling bands or binders.

sleve laces: ornamental laces for tying sleeves, or possibly lace trimming.

4P247 *wyfeys*] wyfe ys Q1, wives Q2, 3. Q1's spelling may indicate disyllabic pronunciation, as in the double-entendre on *pynnes* (though OED attests penis only in 1693).

4P251–2 There is no need to suppose with MSR that these lines are transposed: *complayne* is transitive. The speech ends with a variation of the salesman's pitch.

4P253 *well sene*: evident from experience.

4P257 *lettes*: hindrances.

4P258 *nettes*: veils. Proverbial, see L646 and note.

4P259 *frontlettes*: ornamental forehead bands, supporting a hood.

fyllettes: hairbands or ribbons.

partlettes: neck- or throat-pieces made of linen or muslin.

4P260 *poynettes*: poignet, bracelet.

4P262 *That spede is small whan haste is muche*: ME Proverb, see also Heywood *Dial. Provs.* I ii 106.

4P263–78 A passage of intensive double entendre, playing through 'thynge . . . gere . . . tayle pyn . . . prycke . . . stande . . . joynt . . . fall poynt'.

4P267 *tayle pyn*: pin for the tail of a woman's gown.

4P269 *If it chaunce to double*: if [once it is in] it bends or slips out.

4P277 *holde you a joynt*: bet you a joint; a jointure or dowry (OED 12) or simply an item, article (OED 9). In view of the context possibly a sexual pun. Cf. L787–8.

4P278 *at a fall poynt*: (1) completely satisfied (OED full D.d); (2) falling down as in a wrestling or sexual bout (cf. *stande* 4P271). Q2, 3 read full. Cf. the elaborate jesting about insatiable women and male inadequacy in We719–54.

4P280 *poyntes*: (1) qualities (2) tag-ended laces for a woman's bodice or a man's hose. OED A.31 (thread lace made with a needle, 1662) is unlikely.

4P282 *come of*: hurry up.

4P285 *for your mynde*: as you please.

4P291 *Up shall this packe*: I'll close up my pack of wares.

4P293–4 'He who cannot take one day in the week for play may find that it is hard to thrive'. Proverbial, Whiting D66.

4P297 *unyversall*: learned in many subjects (sarcastic). Cf. We478.

4P304 *whyle the shot is tynkynge*: while clinking coins settle the bill.

4P306 *pynkynge*: †OED cites this as first ex. of pink: blink sleepily.

4P312 *brest*: breath. 'Sweet breath' and 'sweet brest' are equally common idiom for good singing, but technical enough to pass the Pedler by.

4P316–9 The unexpected metrical break (abba) sharpens the Pardoner's cynical interjection. Emendation in Q2, 3 smoothes over a pointed dramatic exchange: the Palmer denies *skyll* (training), the Pardoner says that training without *wyt* (talent) is useless, and the Potycary accuses both of being *frowarde* (reluctant), lacking the *wyll* to sing.

4P321 s.d. *Here they synge.* No words or music are given. The practice of importing up-to-date song in performance of interludes was common.

4P333 A *pylgrymage callynge for grace.* There is no reason to suppose an allusion here to the anti-Reformatory pilgrimage(s) of grace 1536–37. Almost certainly the play was written and printed much earlier than this.

4P351 *kepe even his chayre*: (to keep even in his chair Q3) 'He may even get there [to heaven] seated.' A man may stay at home in his chair rather than go wandering on pilgrimages (cf. 4P357). The confessional was known as the 'pardon chair'. Possible allusion to the Proverb 'Though every man maie not syt in the chayre' (Heywood, *Dial. Provs.* I xii 1205).

4P355 *jet*: strut. OED v¹ has sense of ostentation, fitting the Pardoner's scorn for the Palmer.

4P360 'Revealing to us, in his own self-importance'. The 'daw' (4P359 – the Potycary) claims divine revelation (OED reveal 1). The '*dixit insipiens*' theme occurs in *Witty and Witless*.

4P367 It is not clear whether the Potycary admits that his customers die or that men say they do 'now and then'.

4P378 *take me so*: understand me in that sense.

4P378–79 *he . . . you*: both refer to the Pedler, as the Potycary turns gesturally from addressing the audience to address him.

4P386 *proctours*: the needed rhyme for doctours (of theology) disparages these junior university officers who had administrative and disciplinary duties.

4P394–6 The Pedler's Trinitarian solution to the dispute serves for more logic chopping at 4P410.

4P414–5 *good order . . . wayte on.* Early Tudor obsession with social hierarchy and precedent explains the following exchange, in which the Potycary attempts to assume physical domination of the group.

4P416–7 The Potycary's idiom, in agreeing to his own proposal, is quite idiosyncratic (cf. 4P157).

4P418 s.h. Clearly a new speaker is needed for these lines. In Q3 a 19th cent. hand has written in the left margin 'Pardo.' It is simplest to assign lines 418–9 to the Pardoner, though this entails making the speech an aside.

4P419 *Commaunded two knaves be, besyde hym selfe*: The reading of Q1, 2 looks like a printer's repetition of *be*, but can be justified: 'should have commanded two knaves into existence (as well as himself) to stand beside him'.

4P427 *thynge decayed*: decayed may be understood as *pa. p.* rather than a printing error for decayeth: 'everything is – or will be – de-cayed'. Q3 has 'things decay'. A commonplace of Tudor social theory. Cf. the clowning about heads in We285–8.

4P433 *lyke conrynge*: equally skilful.

4P450–1 'though it might gain me £1000 to go against my conscience (by doing the opposite).'

4P455 *be uncontrolled*] lie uncontrolled Q3 is an attractive emendation (suggesting that Q1's compositor may have misread lie as be) but is not necessary. *uncontrolled*: unrestrained OED 1 (1513), undisputed (OED 3, 1534). Cf More, *Supplication of Souls* (1529): 'Sith he knoweth hys tale false: it is wisdome to leve the time unknowen, that hys lye may bee uncontrolled' (*Works* VII 132/19).

4P467 s.d. *Here the Potycary hoppeth*. Hopping for a ring made of rushes was a traditional game of wooing and mock-marriages, but the association with folly is old:

The lenthe fooll may hoppe upon the ryng,
Foote al afforn, and lede of riht the daunce.

(Lydgate, 'Order of Fools', *Works* ed. McCracken, II 450 and R.L. Greene, *Early English Carols*, 2nd ed., Oxford, 1975, Introduction p. xxvi). Note also *Dial. Provs.* I iii 155–6.

Where wooers hoppe in & out, long tyme may bryng
Hym that hoppeth best, at last to have the ryng.

4P469 'This matter won't be decided by hopping.'

4P472–3 'The outcome of any such hopping, I hope and don't doubt, is that I shall hop so well that you will hop without winning the prize-ring.' The sense requires acceptance of Q2, 3 hop for hope in line 473. since the Potycary clearly cannot 'hope . . . to hope'.

4P486 *rule the roste*: have full authority (like the carver's over the roast). The context of discussion is eating and drinking and shows the origins of the expression misinterpreted by modern 'roost'. See 4P523.

4P497 *All Hallows*: the feast is grotesqely made a saint, as at 4P521 and in PF154 (where this line appears unchanged) as a prophylactic against poisons. At Heywood's time London had eight churches dedicated to All Hallows, the most notorious in Honey Lane off Cheapside (which is suggestive in relation to the introduction of bees at 4P546), see below 4P503.

The mockery of relic-peddling is parallelled in PF153–61 (and in its Chaucerian source), in *Thersites* 709–43 and in Erasmus' *Colloquies*, especially 'A Pilgrimage for Religion's Sake': 'there was shewn to us the middle joint of a man's finger; I kissed it and asked whose relick it was . . . he told me it was St Peter's . . . then I took notice of the bigness of the joint . . . Upon which, said I, Peter must needs have been a very lusty man' (*Colloquies*. I 225–36. Thompson p. 294.) It appears that Heywood invented the blasphemous notions of the jawbone of All Hallows, the toe of the Trinity, and the buttock-bone of Pentecost. But he may have followed hints in the *Farce*.

4P500 *Saynt Savyour*: see 4P47. The pun savour/saviour is traditional.

4P503 *All Halows breth stynketh*: Heywood's drawn-out emphasis in 501–6 on the stink of All Hallows suggests a covert reference to the church of Honey Lane, well known as a stronghold for 'the secret sowing and setting forth of Luther's heresies'. Its rector was condemned by More in *Heresies* (VI ii 714). Its infamy reached a pitch in about 1528 (Brigden, *London* p. 113). The repetition of the allusion in PF154 may carry a similar indictment of the stink of heresy.

4P510–11 The rhyme *voweth/moueth* is altered in Q3's vowth/mouth.

4P523 *beshyten the roste*: the roost suggests the perch or 'nest' in which the relic is kept.

4P524 *whipper*: something surpassing, OED cites 4P.

4P526 *the Seven Slepers*: said to have lived at Ephesus in the time of Emperor Dacian, these Christians took refuge from persecution in a cave in Mt Ceylon and fell asleep, waking between 208 and 372 years later in the region of Theodosia. The story is told in *Legenda Aurea*. Their tomb in Asia Minor was a medieval pilgrimage haunt. Cf. Bale, *Three Laws* 1578 ff.

4P538 *the great Turke*: probably the 15th cent. Tamburlane. The legendary 'great Turk' is pictured in contemporary maps (see Rastell, *Four Elements* 832–3).

4P539–41 'Anyone who looks on this prize specimen may possibly lose part of his eyesight, but not all of it – until he goes completely blind!'

4P542 *seeth*: possibly a pun on sayeth, keeping up the play on sight that begins with eye toth (538).

4P546 *humble bees*: According to the Koran there were there bees in paradise, but this sounds like a popular version of Pandora's box.
More associates bees with heresy: 'whether the bees in theyr hyues vse to say matens a mong them. For euen such a nother buzzynge they make' (*Heresies* III 2, *Works* VI i 259).

4P553–5 The Palmer hands the box to the Potycary, who refuses it.

4P556 *yest*: yeast, froth or sediment (cf. 4P570).

4P562 *ye shall be as mete*: it will be as becoming for you.

4P569 *To kysse the pardon bowle for the drynke sake*. There may be a play here on bowl (the glass of 4P556) and bull, and an allusion to the proverb, 'Many kiss the child for the nurse's sake' (Tilley C312).

4P573 *The oftener I kysse the, more lyke to burste*: the more likely to perish from hunger (OED 1c: the sense of burst as 'rupture by internal force' is 18th cent.) The rhetorical context here requires paradox.

4P575 *Hyre me*: hear me. Q1's spelling is supported by 4P697 hyrynge.

4P576 *What, so muche prayenge and so lytell spede?* Such a long prayer and so little success? The cup remains empty. The line requires a pause and stage business in its delivery. There may be an allusion to the miracle of Caana here.

4P578 *Saynt Antony*: see note to J6. The point here may be that, as patron of men and animals, he takes a kindly view of over-indulgence, as a result of his own privations.

4P581 *the*] thy Q3 is an intelligent emendation, but not necessary.

4P588–9 'There is nothing that lies within my professional capacity that would not directly have been carried out for you.'

4P590 'I surpass you as the value of an ace does the other cards.'

4P592 *rebarb*: preserved rhubarb, as purgative.

4P594 *hollydam*: halidom, anything sacred. Cf. J565 and note.

4P600–1 'It makes your stomach roll about so much that you would die long before you were hanged.' The Potycary sustains his running joke against those who escape his ministrations by hanging (4P173–4).

4P606 *diapompholicus*: type of salve used for wounds, ulcers etc. Possibly consisting of (dia) 'pompholix': 'the sperkles or ashes that commeth of brasse tried in the furneis, and is of Apothecaries called Nyll, much used in medicines of the eyes' (Thomas Cooper, *Thesaurus Linguae Romanae et Britannicae*, 1565, cited by Ashe-Jones).

4P609 *shot anker*: sheet anchor, absolutely effective (ironic).

4P612 *syrapus de Byzansis*: syrup of Byzantine, made from some herb (†OED cites Burton, *Anatomy of Melancholie* II iv I.5).

4P614 *scryppull*: scruple, apothecaries' weight of 20 grains.

4P616 *diosfialios*: medicine, unidentified. Arderne (see 4P619) has diaflosmus, a turpentine-based plaster.

4P617 *Diagalanga*: English galangale, from sedge roots, for stomach ills.
sticados: 'sticados citrine is called barba iovis . . . and hercules grasse' (*Great Herbal*, 1529

cited by OED) is said to be 'profitable and good for the diseases of the breste' (Turner, *Herbal*, 1562).

4P618 *Blanka manna*: white juice of manna-ash used as laxative.

diospoliticon] diospolion Q2, 3. Ashe-Jones cites Thomas Cooper, *Bibliotheca Eliotae* (1552): 'a certayne medicine, made of divers thinges, as cummine, pepper, rue, etc.'

4P619 *Mercury sublyme*: mercuric chloride, white crystalline powder used for piles (John Arderne, *Treatises of Fistula in Ano*, ed. D'Arcy Power, EETS o.s. 139, Oxford, 1910, p. 76).

metridaticon: 'a compound against poison or infectious disease in the form of a conserve or paste' (Ashe-Jones).

4P620 *Pelitory*: 'pellitory of Spain', ME pelleter, whose root has a pungent flavour and was used as a local irritant and salivant against toothache. *arsefetita*: asafoetida, a resinous gum, used as an anti-spasmodic.

4P621 *Cassy*: dried leaflets of cassia tree, a common purgative.

colloquintita: colocynth or bitter apple, a kind of wild gourd, whose inner part 'has the natur to purge . . . made in pilles with honied water' (Turner, *Herbal*, 1551).

4P628 *Alikakabus or Alkakengy*: the scarlet-fruited red winter-cherry, whose resin was used medicinally 'agaynst the strangurie, or stoppyng of uryne' (Thomas Cooper, 1548, cited by OED)

4P641 *I besech your mashyp be good to me*. In offering his service, the Potycary craves favour from a social superior in the standard formulae of Tudor society.

4P642-3 *a box of marmelade / So fyne*. Boxes of marmalade appear to have presents at court and to have been considered medicinal. Ashe-Jones notes a New Year's gift to Q. Mary in 1553 by John de Soto, her apothecary, of 'six boxes of marmalade and cordials' (cited by C.J.S. Thompson, *The Mystery and Art of the Apothecary*, 1928, p. 94).

fyne: choice, excellent, contrasting humorously in scale with 'dyg . . . spade'.

4P656 s.h. *Palmer*: Q2, 3 give this line to Pedler, but it is the Palmer who proposes that the greatest lie should be 'in the fewyst wordes' (654). The Pedler keeps aloof.

4P660-1 i.e. the Pardoner's denunciation, if true, disqualifies him from the competition.

4P660-93 The Potycary proceeds to manipulate the others by rapid switching of pronouns, which would be clear if accompanied in performance by a comic routine of gesture and position.

we both: Potycary and Palmer; *ye*: pardoner.

4P664 *Ye*: Palmer; *he*: Pardoner

4P665 *your mashyp*: the Palmer. The Pardoner called them knaves at 4P419.

4P668-70 The Potycary called the Palmer an honest man at 4P655.

4P675 *ye*: Pardoner.

4P681 *lyed out*: lied outright

4P682 *us twayne*] Potycary and Pardoner. Q3 (you) misses the point here.

4P684-9 'Since both you (Pardoner and Palmer) profess your truth, and we both (Potycary and Pardoner) vouch for my lie, and since two out of three agree, and since the liar must be the winner, who could provide such good proof as I have offered in this submission?'

4P689 *pretens*: The sense 'putting forward of a claim' may have been obsolete by mid 16th cent. Q2, 3 replace with the conventional interlude tag 'in this presence'.

4P691 *you*: Pedler.

4P697 *hyrynge*: hearing. Cf. 4P575 'Hyre me'.

4P709 *But Anno domini millesimo*: in the year 1000 A.D. The Potycary claims to be somewhat more than 500 years old. Q3 uses Roman type for the Latin.

4P713 *fallen sykness*: falling sickness, epilepsy, treated at this time with 'gall of a ferret'.

It was thought that in the case of women sexual intercourse was beneficial. Cf. the cure of Tyb's sickness in J130–45.

4P721 *her helys so shorte*: skittish, wanton (†OED short 26, Porter 1599). Cf. 'round hele' L468.

4P731–44 Heywood's expansion here in terms of artillery may possibly have been suggested by *A Mery geste of the frere and the boye*, printed by Wynkyn de Worde [1510–13] (STC 14521). See above, p. 44n.

4P732 *thampyon*: tampon, (1) pessary (2) wood and wadding to fit the bore of a muzzle-loading gun and rammed home between the charge and the missile.

4P741 *bumberd*: bombard, canon shot, with traditional play on bum-beard (Chaucer, MilT. 3742).

4P744 Chaucer has a 'castel of lime and ston' FkT 477.

4P749 *the Regent*: Henry VIII's prize warship, 1000 tons, built 1487–90, served against Brittany, Scotland, and France, carrying 700 soldiers, mariners and gunners. She sank in an engagement with the French on 10 August 1512 in Bertheaume Bay near Brest, fouled with the Cordelière, when her gunpowder took fire, and about 500 English died. The sinking is recalled in *Hick Scorner* 332 (c.1515) and seems to have become legendary. (Ian Lancashire, *Two Tudor Interludes*, Manchester, 1980, pp. 245–6). The Regent is mentioned as evidence of the river's draught, but it may be pertinent to note the context of parodic Rabelaisian explosion and destruction in 4P.

ryden: ridden at anchor, or make passage.

4P751 *castels*: perhaps in the sense 'castellations', since they are plural. Ashe-Jones emends to bastels (OED bastille: small bastion of a castle, a wooden tower on wheels, used during siege operations). The Potycary's treatment suggests also the destruction of the castle of maidenhood by Rabelaisian analogy.

4P754 *But rolled downe so faste the hyll*: unusual word order.

4P762 *in a good houre maye these wordes be spoken*. This formulaic narratorial interjection, appropriate to heralding delivery of an infant, changes the tempo, promising a hasty and happy conclusion.

4P763–4 'After the charge had wreaked havoc on the walls, which piece by piece fragmented . . .'

4P776 *within thys seven yere*: as an indication of recent time, an 'age' of man's life, duration of an apprenticeship etc. Cf. We635.

4P783 *I was thens*: The Pardoner offers an alternative to the last rites, hence the circumstantial excuse for losing one of his flock.

4P789 *so daungerously*: in such peril †OED cites.

4P793 *out of hande*: at once

4P799 *thys gere*: his pardons.

4P802–4 The Pardoner, snobbish as ever, describes his own behaviour as a model of courtesy and authority. In response to the souls' low curtseying, he nods a 'beck' to engage them in his service (retayne OED 2b) – a distinct contrast to his own deferential behaviour in hell (4P821–2). Chaucer's Pardoner describes how, 'est and west upon the peple I bekke' (CT VI 396).

4P812 'I was sure she had not been made a saint in heaven!'

4P813–5 Cf. *Spider and Flie* ch. 9 st.1:

'And here with all (by chaunse) the spider sneezes
Now (quoth the flie) chaunce I win or leese
Christ help, and long helth wel mote ye sneeze.'

4P814 *ley for his fees*: presumably the soul of a lawyer who 'lay there [suffering] as reward [for his dishonesty.' Possibly lay is archaic pa.t. of lie (ME la3e): hence a lawyer 'who had lied for his fees' [and was therefore in hell]. The jibe about lawyers, close to a reference to Coventry (4P832), may point to Heywood's legally trained Rastell in-laws, John and his son William, printer of the plays. A farce in French showing Wolsey in hell was played in January 1531, shortly after his death, at the house of Thomas Boleyn in London (see above p. 44 n15). Wolsey's practices in Chancery are satirized in *Love* (see L801–12).

4P821–2 The Pardoner admits that he has no authority to deliver souls, only power to intercede.

4P823 *And fyrst the devyll*: the idiom is acceptable to all Qq, though Q3 has 'to' inserted by hand in right margin.

4P826 *thys smillyngly*: this said smilingly. Q2, 3 thus is more obviously gestural; the Pardoner imitates the Devil's welcoming grin.

4P830–2 Two Coventry plays from Corpus Christi survive, neither with a devil's part. The Demon of N-Town CC play is presented as a dandy, full of pride in his fine clothes, yet also unkempt. Coventry was native city of John Rastell, Heywood's father-in-law, so that there may be some humorous banter here, involving Rastell's profession as barrister (see 4P814).

4P836 *mayster porter*: On the dramatic tradition of the comic porter of hell see Glynne Wickham, 'Hell-Castle and its Door-Keeper', *Shakespeare Survey* XIX (1966), 68–74.

4P841 *thys daye Lucyfer fell*: In the first 'N-Town' Passion play one of the Demon's functions in the prologue is to relate his fall from heaven (text in Bevington, pp. 479–81). For the possibility that the 'festyvall' was celebration of a royal birthday, see Sources 5.

4P850–1 'Under seal and written in the Devil's hand in generous terms.'

4P852–67 The form of address here – a spoof of the King's letters patent cannot but suggest a mischievous equation of Lucyfer and King Henry VIII.

4P861 *extyncte*: vanished (OED 3, citing 4P).

4P864 *warde*: custody; or perhaps prison, guarded entrance to a fortress (OED 14b).

4P868 *God save the devyll*: parodic of 'God save the King', pointed by the tactless and implausible 'God save thee, devil.'

4P870 'Then act on your trust, prove it.'

in eure: in use

4P879 *Sothery butter*: possibly a form of Surrey (OED); capitalization favours this. Farmer suggests sweet (from sote). Ashe-Jones suggests a compositorial error for mothery: mouldy or feculent (18th cent.). But the context is blandly approving. Perhaps the word should be *sethery*, from seethe; seether: one who boils. Melted butter would be appropriate in hell's kitchen.

4P881 *jacket*: this evidently identifies the 'mayster devyll', renowned for his sartorial elegance, and implies that the tennis-playing devils were in their shirts – a spectacle no doubt modelled on Henry VIII's real tennis court. In summer of 1528 Henry played tennis at Greenwich and was reported as wearing a fine embroidered shirt and afterwards a special tennis coat of blue or black velvet (Ernest Law, *History of Hampton Court Palace*, 1885–91, I 139).

4P882 *racket*: OED sb² cites Lindsay 1529 and 4P; played by hitting a ball against walls with rackettes (4P883) akin to those used in real tennis.

4P886 *Lucyfer laughed*: Heywood's delightful picture of hell seems to recall the mockery of John Frith at the expense of Thomas More: 'Now, as touching the manner how this devil came into purgatory, laughing, grinning, and gnashing his teeth, in sooth it maketh me to see the merry antics of Master More' (Cited by Foxe, AM IV 665).

merely: merrily. MSR suggested emendation to metely is unnecessary, since Heywood often rhymes only the final feminine syllable.

4P894–5 *knelyd . . . beckte*: see 4P802.

4P898 *burres*: burs (OED bur 1, rough or prickly seed-vessel, cites 4P, but notes that derivation from Fr. *bourre*, 'rough hair, flock of wool' is problematic.

4P899 *bushels*: bushel measures, wooden and cylindrical, about 50 cm across.

4P900 *Flastynge*: Q1's spelling may possibly be an unrecorded variant form of flashing (Q3). *nose thryls*: literally 'nose holes'; usually as one word (Q2, 3) in 16th cent.

4P901 *Gnashynge hys teeth*: see note on 4P886.

4P905 *Feutred in fashyon abominable*: sheathed in inhuman appearance (or in detestable style of garment – OED fashion 3b 1529). *Feutred*: from fewter, to put a spear in its (originally felted) sheath. The devil's trendy clothes are skin-tight. The Pardoner's Frenchified address, similar to that of the N-Town Demon, sails close to the wind here.

4P915–6 'And in this bargain, though we cannot be quits, nevertheless I can [offer] something to deserve my part.'

4P918 *controller*: continues the motif of 4P802–4.

4P920 *on my hande*: in my hands.

4P924 *I shall requyte*: We follow MSR in seeing a compositorial misreading of the copytext's t for r, perpetuated by Q2, 3. 'I shall pay back any part of this purchase [or exchange of souls]'. Edwin S. Miller maintains that the audience would know that the Pardoner is exceeding his powers, having control over purgatory and not over damnation ('Guilt and Penalty in Heywood's Pardoner's Lie' *MLQ* X (1949) 58–60).

4P932 *Margery Coorson*: for the rhyme, but Margery is traditional in ME for a common wench. Heywood seems to have picked up a motif from Skelton's *Colin Clout* 876–8:

> [Friars] say propreli they are sacerdotes
> To shryve, assoyle and reles
> Dame Margeries soule out of hell.

(J.W. McCain Jr, 'Heywood's *The Foure PP*: a Debt to Skelton' *N&Q* (1938) CLXXIV 205.)

4P938 *Have more to do with two women*: Traditional antifeminism may cloak a jibe here about the great trouble in the realm caused by Anne Boleyn and Katherine of Aragon.

4P940 'If you would prove yourself to be our friend.'

4P944 *as the fayth goth*: as religious matters are at present.

4P945 *thys dayes*: singular for plural is common in 16th cent. texts.

4P949 *I was hadde into the kechyn*: for this sense 'fetched away', see *Calisto* 636.

4P954–60 Margery turns a spit but is not herself spitted, though she is glad to be relieved. A playful double entendre links her punishment in hell with her sexual life on earth ('here' 955) and the burning diseases associated with it. In addition to the phallic meanings of *spit* implied here, there is also the possible literal sense from ME: fin-spine a fish (OED spit sb1 2.a), since fish course would precede meat course.

4P961–70 An admirable *abbrevatio* of the story.

4P974 *on New Market heth*: The Devil's Dyke near Newmarket, Suffolk, was known as gathering place for witches and an entry to hell (*Thersites* 794).

4P979 'Listening to the adventures you came upon in hell . . .'

4P986 *Frowardly fashonde*: naturally contrary

4P992 *And here so gentyll as farre as I se*: here [in the playing place] they are so gentle as far as I can see.

4P996 *through*: Q3's thorough rhymes more completely with borough.

4P998a–9 See Textual Note and discussion of the implications of a missing line in Editorial Procedure. The rhyme tarried/married occurs in Heywood's *Dial. Provs.* I vii 359–60:

> Those two men, each other so hasted or tarried
> That those two women on one day they married.

4P1006 Feeling the fish bite, the Pedler strikes.

4P1010 *Procede:* legal sense OED v 2c.

4P1013 *In Poules Churche yarde were set on sale.* The centre of London's bookselling trade was renowned particularly for the popular printing – plays, tales, pamphlets – sold from shops beside St Paul's yard.

4P1018 *ye:* Potycary.

4P1028 *ye:* Pardoner.

4P1031 *by these ten bonnes:* i.e. fingers. Cf. *Spider* 44.28; *Thersites* 831; *Jacke Jugeler* 418.

4P1033 *he:* Palmer.

4P1034–37 This mathematical riposte to the Pedler, requires stage antics as the Potycary completes his earlier attempt (414–7) to arrange the others in an order of subservience. The Potycary stands at the centre of an imaginary square and numbers the 'knaves' present and imagined at the corners.

4P1037 *Thou knave:* apparently a game-song or 'catch' (*Twelfth Night* II iii 67ff.).

4P1040 *pryvy tythe:* the Potycary implies that the Pedler would have received a secret tenth as bribe from the Palmer, since the other two are disqualified. Tithing was cause of much anticlerical feeling in London at this time.

4P1043 '. . . that your wife's ten fingers (nails) may gouge your head'.

4P1049 *I wyll thou knowe yf I am a gentylman, knave:* I would have you acknowledge whether or not I am a gentleman.

4P1050–55 In his superior anger, the Potycary expects to be supported by the snobbish Pardoner. He however refuses, politely conceding defeat by means of a curtsy formula offering his service.

4P1061 *his:* the Palmer's lie (1003).

4P1064 *your tale:* the Potycary's.

4P1068 *take thys order:* make a systematic selection.

4P1069 *Amonge the women in thys border:* Separation of the sexes seems to have been common in public seating (Cf. We249 and s.d.).
border: edge of the seating bloc in the hall.

4P1072a *Three of the cheefest and three of the lewdest:* 'three from the highest rank and from the lowest orders'. This line supplied from Q3, though its authority is dubious. Given the paucity of rhymes for shrewdest, it would not have been difficult for Allde to come up with a line of this structure. MSR suggestion of *chastest* for *cheefest* seems inspired by the modern sense of lewd.

4P1075 *fayrest . . . maddest:* gentlest (OED 15) . . . wildest.

4P1076 *fowlest . . . saddest:* most disgusting . . . most dignified.

4P1081 *Hym selfe:* the Palmer.

4P1082 *And oft hath tryed some of thys rowe.* Clearly the player indicates particular women in the audience, originally perhaps his relatives.

4P1095 *of equyte:* in fairness.

4P1105 *horson nody:* a favourite Tudor disparagement for a blockhead.

4P1106–10 In his clowning routine of low bowing (*curtesy:* making reverence by bowing and bending the knee, OED 8) the Potycary apparently makes a circle about the Palmer, as if conjuring. Hence the pertinence of his imprecation, 'And then on eche syde the devyll blynde hym'. Cf. Wakefield *Second Shepherds Play* lines 278–83.

4P1114 *call my mayster 'knave':* The Potycary rejects the recently imposed herarchy with the Palmer as his master.

4P1115–18 Note the 'leash' of four double rhymes.

4P1117–18 'If I were your master I would rather be rid of you than suffer such carrying on'.

4P1121–2 'It would be in no way good for your reputation to have us two knaves strutting about after you.'

4P1126 *thyrde*: pronounced 'turd'.

4P1141 *pylgrymage*: Heywood's orthodox view here runs close to that of Thomas More in *Heresies* I iv (*Works* VI i 60).

4P1142 *ye*: Palmer.

4P1147 *ye*: Pardoner.

4P1155 *That bothe your walkes come to one ende*: There may be a Proverbial sub-text here ('Right as diverse pathes leden diverse folk the righte way to Rome' Chaucer, *Astrolabe* Prol. 40).

4P1156–70 The optimistic Catholic viewpoint of social harmony arising from diversity of individual contributions is consistent with We1194–1200.

4P1160 *wyllfull povertie*: willing (and therefore meritorious) poverty.

4P1163 *To synge and praye for soule departed*. Q2,3 read 'To synge and say the sarvyes apoynted' – a Protestant revision, later than 1547 (cf. 4P85). The second Prayer Book of 1552 forbade prayers for the dead. In 1534 John Rastell affirmed that such prayer 'can in no wise be profitable to them that be dead', while his son William remained Catholic (specifically requesting prayers for the dead on his return to England from Newfoundland in 1554, see Reed, p. 25, 88). Supposing there to have been a folio of 4P printed around 1533–34, it would have been published by William.

4P1165–7 'Though these virtues are distinct and various, they are not all operative in the diversity of human minds, but only in so far as God animates each.'

4P1175–79 '[Let] that man, by the power of that grace [of the holy ghost] apply his particular virtue and so serve God very fully. Yet he should not so distort his effort, out of partiality, that he comes to despise the other virtues. For anyone who forces himself into an alien course will work in vain.'

4P1183–4 'Whoever pursues this path looking to find God, will find that the further they seek the further away from him they are.' Q2, 3 (this way and for God) attempt to clarify the sense of Q1.

4P1185–6 Proverbial, Whiting (1938) p. 179.

4P1188 *I thanke God I use no vertue at all*. Cf. the comic servant 'A' in *Fulgens* 843: 'Vertue? What the devyll is that?'

4P1190–2 Proverbial, Whiting (1938) p. 179

4P1194–6 The serious sub-text here is the Mass: 'If we say we have no sin, we deceive ourselves and the truth is not in us.'

4P1198 *all thys sorte*: the audience.

4P1203–16 The position on credence to be given to relics and suchlike accords with a central Catholic-humanist teaching. It is no accident that the last words of the play are 'churche universall'.

4P1206–10 Cf. *Dial. Provs.* II v 1904,' deme the best, til tyme hath tried the trouth out.'

4P1212 *make no judgement upon ye*: Q2, 3 read take, making the Pedler's lines a warning against exercise of individual judgment. Heywood's normal usage is to 'give' judgment. Since the Pedler is as good as his word, the dramatic issue is left open as in *Wether*.

Textual variants and doubtful readings

Title page   *Johan*] Johñ Q1
4P1 s.h.   *Palmer*] Palmer speaketh Q3
4P4   *now*] MSR; no Q1, not Q2, 3 (cancelled by hand).
4P6   *you*] now Q2,3
4P8   *mynde*] myndy Q1
4P9   *ye*] you Q2, 3
4P10   *hath*] have Q3
4P11   *fayre and farre*] farre and fayre Q2,3
4P13   *Hierusalem*] Jerusalem Q2,3
4P15   *have I*] I have Q3
4P20   *coulde*] would Q2,3
4P29   *Rodes*] Roodes Q2, Rhodes Q3
4P33   *see*] sawe Q2, 3
4P45   *at*] in Q2,3
4P46   *great*] graet Q1; *Katewade*] Kateward Q2, 3; *Henry*] Herry Q2, 3
4P51   *these*] those Q3
4P55   *prayers*] prayets Q1
4P56   *obtayne*] obtaye Q1
4P58   *surely*] assuredly Q3
4P61   *thy*] their Q3
4P64   *ye can*] you canQ3
4P66   *Yet welcome*] Ye will come Farmer
4P71   *payne*] paines Q3
4P73   *or*] ere Q3
4P75   *pray*] yray Q1
4P81   *be recorde*] be ar record Q3, bere recorde Ashe-Jones. Cf. We476
4P85   *mediacyon*] medytacion Q2, 3
4P86   *myne*] my Q3
4P89 s.h.   *Pardoner*] Pardonar Q1. Also at 106, 127.
4P90   *your selfe*] you Q3
4P92   *No nother*] No other Q3
4P102   *at*] to Q2,3
4P103   *ye*] you Q3
4P109   *never*] never. Q1
4P111   *your*] yours Q3
4P119   *scoffe*] Q3, scofte Q1, scofe Q2
4P120   *kepe*] Q1, speke Q2,3
4P127   *the*] this Q2, 3
4P128   *you come*] ye come to Q2, ye came of Q3
4P130   *reasonyng*] Q3, sonyng Q1, 2.
4P131   *ye*] you Q3
4P132   *ye be*] be you Q3
4P137   *ye*] you Q3
4P138   *be*] are Q3
4P143   *is*] as Q2, 3
4P145   *any payne*] pain Q3

4P146 *bryngeth*] bring Q3
4P149 *an*] a Q2, 3; *moste*] the moste/ Q3
4P152 *dyd*] do Q2, 3
4P155 *soules*] soule Q2,3
4P156 *in by*] by Q2, 3
4P157 *I*] we Q2, 3
4P159 *or*] ere Q3
4P164 *lyste*] loste Q2
4P166 *the knaves*] they Q3
4P168 *Nay thanke myn*] nay mine Q3
4P171 *honestlye*] Q2, 3, hostlye Q1
4P177 *ye*] you Q3
4P178 *If*] That Q3; *chaunce*] chaunge Q1
4P181 *fle*] flie Q2, 3
4P184 *is vewed*] vewd Q3
4P188 *from state of*] out of Q3
4P193 *one dewty*] Q1, 2, 3. MSR suggests our duty
4P196 *to*] so Q2, 3
4P198 *The*] Thy Q2
4P199 *even at*] at Q2,3
4P204 *longe*] it long Q3
4P209 *Thou palmer*] Thou a Palmer Q3
4P212 *Were*] Where Q2, 3
4P214 *catchyd*] had catched Q3
4P217 *pedler*] pedled Q1
4P218 *every tryfull*] all kinde of trifles Q3
4P220 *chefe*] chieflye Q2,3
4P224 *thynketh*] thinks Q3
4P225 *were*] where Q2, 3; *be*] buy Q3
4P226 *looser*] a loser Q3
4P227 *Is here*] Is there Q2, 3; *my*] me Q2
4P229 *your*] all your Q2, 3
4P231 *or*] and Q2
4P233 *Where*] Wherin Q3
4P236 *knotted*] unknotted Q3
4P237 *maner*] maner of Q3
4P238 *Lace*] Laces Q3
4P239 *all suche*] suche selye Q3 (Pepys) such other (BL)
4P241 *sypers*] sipets Q3
4P242 s.h.   Q3 prints the next three speech headings one line too soon, though in the right order.
4P243 *theyr*] these Q3 (Pepys), their (BL)
4P247 *wyfeys*] wyfe ys Q1, wives Q2, 3.
4P249 *Great pynnes*] Jette pines Q2, Yet pinnes Q3; *must she*] she must Q3
4P252 *and*] but to Q3
4P255 *arysynge*] uprising Q3
4P259 *partlettes*] Q3, parlettes Q1, 2; *barcelettes*] Q1, bracelettes Q2, 3
4P265 *yet*] it Q3

4P266 *theyr*] of their Q3

4P268 *prycke*] prickt Q2, 3

4P270 *be they*] they be Q3; *swereth*] swere Q3

4P272 *wolde*] wil Q3

4P274 *For when*] When Q3; *they marre*] Q3 marre Q1

4P275 *myche*] nyche Q1, nigh Q2, nie Q3. A printer's error m>n, rather than an idiosyncratic spelling of nigh. In Rastell's printing of *Johan Johan* myche:muche occurs in ratio 5:3, in *Wether* 16:3.

4P277 *you*] with you Q3

4P278 *fall*] full Q2,3

4P283 *my*] me Q2

4P287 *journey*] your ney Q1, iourney Q2, 3

4P294 *is farre*] farre Q2,3

4P297 *ye*] you Q3

4P298 *you*] ye Q2; *ye*] you Q3

4P299 *ye*] you Q3; *to*] for to Q3

4P300 *ye*] you Q3

4P301 *be ye*] are you Q3

4P305 *swymmyng*] swinking Q3

4P308 *ye*] you Q3

4P309 *ye*] you Q3

4P310 *can you*] can ye Q2

4P317 *wyt*] wyl Q2,3

4P319 *wyll*] wyt Q2,3

4P321 *synge*] e broken Q1

4P331 *and nat*] Q2,3; nat and Q1

4P332 *On fot*] One fot Q2

4P337 *our*] your Q2,3

4P344 *that this*] that his Q2,3

4P348 *aske*] s poorly inked Q1

4P354 *can*] may Q2,3

4P356 *then hys*] than is his Q2

4P357 *To walke*] To wake Q1; *syns*] sith Q3

4P360 *Revelynge*] Revilyng Q2,3.

4P368 *ye*] you Q3

4P369 *men*] them Q3

4P370 *nay*] nay as Q2,3

4P372 *Ye, but yet it is necessary*] Ye a but . . . Q2, . . . very necessary Q3

4P374 *ye*] you Q3

4P375 *quyckly*] very quickly Q2,3

4P378 *he*] ye Q3

4P394 *on*] one Q2,3

4P397 *goo*] go on Q3

4P398 *ye*] you Q3; *debite*] deputie Q3. In left margin Q3 has handwritten 'to þe Palmer'.

4P399 *dyscharge*] dyscharde Q1; a case of eye-skip (parde).

4P400 **s.h.** In left margin Q3 has handwritten 'to þe Pardoner'.

4P401 *pardons*] pardon Q2, 3

4P402 *ye*] you Q3; handwritten in the margin 'to þe Pothecary'
4P404 *taste*] taste of Q2, 3
4P409 *Who*] Q2, 3, How Q1
4P411 *be we*] were we as Q3
4P419 *Commaunded*] Commaundes Q3
4P423 *on you*] of you Q2, 3
4P424 *ye*] you Q3
4P427 *thynge decayed*] things decay Q3.
4P432 *But to*] But Q2, 3
4P438 *have I*] I have Q2, 3
4P439 *indyfferently*] in dyfferently Q1
4P440 *nor*] or Q3
4P448 *ye*] you Q3
4P454 *nat cause to feare to be bolde*] no cause to feare, beholde Q2, 3
4P455 *be*] lie Q3
4P468 *hop*] hope Q3
4P469 *syr*] syrs Q2, 3
4P471 *as well as*] aswell as Q1, better then Q3
4P472 *hope*] hop Q2, Q3
4P473 *To hop*] To hope Q1; *hope*] hop Q2, 3; *without it*] without Q1
4P474 *ne*] nor Q2, 3
4P478 *sure*] sute Q1
4P479 *rychesse*] riches Q3
4P480 *maner*] manner of Q3
4P481 *or*] or to Q2,3
4P486 *myght*] Q2, 3, myghe Q1 seems more like error than an unrecognised form of 3 subj. may (ME muȝhe).
4P488 *be*] are Q3
4P492 *be*] are Q3
4P493 *can*] may Q3
4P495 *my*] me Q2
4P496 *ye*] you Q3
4P501 *good*] good to Q2, 3
4P502 *me*] yet me Q3
4P503 *stynketh*] stynktth Q1
4P504 *Ye*] You Q3
4P513 *be ryd of*] never be vext with Q3
4P517 *muche*] as muche Q3
4P518 s.h. *Pardoner*] Potycary Q1; *upon*] on Q3
4P524 *well thys*] wel this, this Q3
4P525 *frendes*] frinde Q2, 3
4P526 *Slepers*] sse pers Q1
4P530 *thys*] these Q2, 3
4P542 *any other*] any Q3
4P543 *devocion*] devacion Q1; *to*] unto Q3
4P556 *yest*] yet Q1
4P564 *Ye*] you Q2, 3
4P569 *drynke*] drincks' Q3

4P570　*loketh*] lookst Q3
4P572　*beholde*] be holde Q1, see Q3
4P573　*kysse the, more lyke*] kysse, þe more I lyke Q2, kisse thee, the more like Q3
4P574　*syns*] sith Q3; *the so*] thee Q2
4P577　*whan*] when that Q3
4P578　*folkes*] folke Q3
4P581　*the*] thy Q3
4P584　*this*] Q2, 3, his Q1
4P589　*in*] on Q2, one Q3
4P591　*Here*] So heer Q3; *in*] in a Q2, 3
4P595　*dram*] deam Q1
4P597　*twenty*] .xx. Q1
4P598　*do*] doth Q2
4P599　*pourgeth*] pourget Q1; purgeth Q2, 3; *clene*] cleue Q1
4P604　*ye . . . ye*] you . . . you Q3
4P605　*If ever*] If Q2, 3
4P608　*or*] be for Q3
4P610　*medecyn*] oyntment Q3
4P611　*bryngeth*] brings Q3
4P612　*is*] is a Q2, 3
4P613　*inough*] I nough Q1
4P615　*Shall*] wil Q3
4P622　*be*] are Q3; *stryfe*] st ryfe Q1
4P627　*is called*] called Q2
4P629　*be*] are Q3
4P630　*these*] thefe Q1
4P636　*syns*] sith Q3
4P637　*in*] in one Q2, 3
4P641　*to*] unto Q3
4P642　*ye*] you Q3
4P651　*and*] now Q3
4P655　*ye be*] you are Q3
4P656 s.h.　*Palmer*] Pedler Q2, 3. *ye*] he Q2, 3
4P664　*Ye*] You Q3; *gave*] gane Q1
4P666　*true*] truthe Q3
4P667　*or*] ere Q3
4P670　*When ye*] Then you Q3; *for no*] for to Q2, to be a Q3
4P671　*our*] your Q2, 3
4P672　*ye*] you Q2, 3; *affyrmacion*] affyrmaciou Q1
4P673　*ye*] you Q3
4P681　*none hath lyed out but*] one hath lyed but Q2, 3
4P682　*us*] you Q3; *hath*] have Q3
4P684　*syns*] sith Q3; *your trouth*] ye the truthe Q3
4P685　*And that we both my lye so witnes*] How that I lyed doo bear witnes Q3
4P686　*thre in one*] three may one Q2, may soon Q3
4P689　*pretens*] presence Q2, 3
4P690　*thynketh*] thynke Q2, 3
4P693　*ye*] you Q3

4P696 *yet*] as yet Q3
4P697 *answered you and geven hyrynge*] answered and given you hearing Q3.
4P699 *your*] our Q3
4P702 *unlyke*] unlikest Q3
4P704 *set in*] set on Q3
4P708 *ago*] a go Q1
4P712 *from*] of Q2, 3
4P713 *fallen*] falling Q3
4P722 *twynglynge*] twynklinge Q2, 3
4P724 *or*] ere Q3
4P725 *practyse, muche*] cunning, but Q3
4P727 *Shulde . . . sowne*] Could . . . swoun Q3
4P729 *payne*] paines Q3
4P732 *thampyon* inconsistent sp. (737 *tampyon* 745 *tampion*)
4P734 *it so*] it was to Q3
4P737 *wyll*] there wil Q3
4P743 *tampion*] champien Q2, thampion Q3; *ten*] .x. Q1
4P750 *tampyon on thys castell*] this thampion at this castle did Q3
4P751 *castels so*] Q1, castele so Q2, 3
4P762 *these wordes*] this Q3
4P770 *ye*] you Q3
4P771 *then marke*] mark Q2,3
4P773 *greater*] great Q2, more Q3
4P779 *so sycke*] sycke Q2, 3
4P782 *of thys*] of his Q2, of Q3
4P786 *I have to heven*] to heaven I have Q3
4P790 *especyally*] specyally Q2, 3
4P802 *how lowe*] how Q3
4P813 *chaunced*] channced Q1
4P821 *outhorite*] Q1, authoritie Q2, 3
4P826 *thys*] thus Q2, 3
4P828 *syns*] sith Q3
4P835 *my returne*] me retourne Q2
4P839 *quoth*] quod Q3
4P841 *For thys daye Lucyfer fell*] For as on this day Lucifer fell Q3
4P843 *Nothynge*] Nothyngc Q1
4P852 *began Lucyfere*] began; I Lucifer Q3
4P855 *every*] to every Q3
4P856 *streyght*] streygyt Q1, strenght Q2, straight Q3
4P858 *named*] maned Q1
4P860 *hys*] any Q3
4P864 *they lye*] the lye Q2
4P865 *fornes*] fiery fornace Q3
4P868 *for playne*] for playue Q1, amain Q3
4P870 *eure*] euer Q1, cure Q3
4P871 *Syns*] sith Q3
4P875 *aray*] Q3, a ray Q1

4P877 *homes*] home Q2
4P883 *they hadde*] had they Q3
4P887 *feendes*] Q2, 3, frendes Q1
4P888 *laugh*] laugh therat Q3; *well togytther*] wel lyke Q2, 3
4P892 *And I*] And Q2, 3; *in*] to Q3
4P893 *Then to Lucyfer low as*] Of Lucifer, then lowe as wel Q3
4P897 *as barne durres*] as a barn doores Q3
4P900 *Flastynge*] Flashing Q3; *nose thryls*] nosethryls Q2, 3
4P901 *vaynglorousely*] vayngloronsely Q1
4P906 *that is*] that it is Q3
4P908 *unworthy*] as unworthy Q2, 3
4P913 *hyther is*] hithers Q2, hither Q3
4P914 *Delivered*] Delyver Q2, 3
4P916 *Yet*] Yet in Q3; *shall*] wil Q3
4P918 *as a*] as Q2, 3
4P924 *I shall requyte*] I shall requyre Q1; ye shall requyre Q2, 3
4P927 *Nowe quoth*] Ho, ho quod Q2,3
4P936 *Were*] wert Q3
4P937 *we devyls*] the devyls Q2,3
4P940 *wyll*] wilt Q3
4P945 *thys dayes to heven I do procure*] thys day to heven I procure Q3
4P946 *be*] ye may be Q3
4P957 *hote*] Q2, 3; hoth Q1
4P960 *for spede*] with speed Q3
4P970 *twentieth*] .xx. Q1,2, twentie Q3
4P975 *yf that*] yf Q2,3
4P978 *ye . . . ye*] you . . . you Q3
4P979 *founde*] had Q3
4P980 *ye*] you Q3
4P985 *By*] Be Q3
4P989 *This*] Thus Q3; *for*] of Q3; *trueth*] ttueth Q1
4P990 *murvell*] murnell Q1
4P996 *through*] thorough Q3
4P999 *maryed*] Q1, 2, taried Q3. Possibly a case of eye-slip, since all editions lack a couplet line (998a). Q3 emends to a more commonplace expression, but surely would have restored the couplet had it been in the copy text.
4P1002 *to*] in Q2,3
4P1004 *great lye*] greatlye Q1
4P1005 *a greater*] greater Q3
4P1010 *ye*] you Q3
4P1012 *tale*] tales Q2
4P1015 *shulde sure*] sure should Q3
4P1018 *ye*] you Q3
4P1023 *ye . . . ye*] you . . . you Q3; *sayd*] said, that Q3
4P1025 *jayles*] ?tayles Q1
4P1026 *fyll*] fild Q3
4P1028 *ye*] you Q3
4P1033 *hath meved*] meeved Q3

4P1034 *lacketh*] lacks Q3

4P1035 *one . . . one*] . i . . . . i. Q1

4P1036 *two . . . two*] . ii . . . . ii. Q1

4P1039 *accomber*] encumber Q3

4P1041 *me thynketh*] my thinke Q2, me thinks Q3

4P1043 *ten*] .x. Q1; *fyve*] .v. Q1

4P1045 *of*] on Q3

4P1046 *ten*] Q1, 3, then Q2

4P1049 *knowe yf*] Q1, knowe Q2, 3; ?yt MSR; *gentylman*] gentyll Q2, 3

4P1051 *beshrew*] be shrew Q1

4P1052 *take*] toke Q2

4P1053 *Our*] one Q1

4P1055 *ye can*] you may Q3; *to*] unto me Q3

4P1059 *consciens*] couscieus Q1

4P1060 *impossyble*] unpossible Q3

4P1061 *farther*] father Q1

4P1072a *Three of the cheefest and three of the lewdest*] Q3. The line is lacking in Q1, 2; Allde's provision of it is the principal evidence for thinking that he had access to an earlier edition than Q1, perhaps to a folio by Rastell (above pp. 247–8).

4P1081 *knowe*] kuowe Q1

4P1084 *paciens*] her patience Q3

4P1103 *never*] nevet Q1

4P1108 *then on*] thenon Q1

4P1109 *I*] ye Q2, 3

4P1111 *brother*] gentle brother Q3

4P1116 *ye . . . ye*] you . . . you Q3

4P1117 *lever*] rather Q3; *ye*] you Q3

4P1118 *Then*] Then to Q3; *ye*] you Q3

4P1119 s.h. *Pardoner*] Poticary Q3

4P1123 s.h. *Potycary*] Pardo. Q3; *ye*] you Q3

4P1128 *Syns*] sith Q3

4P1130 *ye*] you Q3; *beste*] the better Q3

4P1133 *syns*] lyns Q1, sith Q3

4P1134 *dyscharge*] doo discharge Q3

4P1136 *And I lyke wyse I make God avowe*] And likewise I, to God I vow Q3

4P1139 *debate*] Q2, 3, debace Q1

4P1142 *chyefe the*] cheefest Q3

4P1143 *love*] the love Q2, 3

4P1148 *thus*] this Q2, 3

4P1152 *shewe*] shewell Q1

4P1153 *ye*] you Q3

4P1155 *one*] on Q2, an Q3

4P1160 *povertie*] Q2, 3; povetie Q1

4P1161 *other*] like Q3

4P1163 *To synge and praye for soule departed*] depatted Q1, To synge and say the sarvyes apoynted Q2, 3.

4P1175 *one*] one must Q3

4P1176 *plentyfully*] plenteously Q3

4P1177 *Yet nat that*] Yet that Q2, 3
4P1179 *is in*] in Q3
4P1182 *you*] ye Q3
4P1183 *for God wolde fynde hym*] for god & wold fynd hym Q2, 3.
4P1186 *hange*] hang up Q3
4P1192 *mended*] amended Q2
4P1193 *ye be nat*] ye are not Q3
4P1196 *ye . . . ye*] you . . . you Q3
4P1198 *Ye*] you Q3; *beloved*] be loved Q1
4P1200 *and*] ond Q1
4P1202 *knowe*] knowe is Q3
4P1204 *nother*] not Q3
4P1205 *in any suche case*] to any suche thynge Q2, in any case Q3
4P1206 *in any suche*] in suche Q3
4P1210 *In judgynge*] Judginge Q2,3
4P1212 *make*] Q1, take Q2,3
4P1215 *be sure*] be you sure Q3
4P1217 *ye*] you Q3; true a true Q2
4P1218 *faste*] fastt Q1
4P1228 *scape*] escaped Q2,3
4P1232 *you*] you to Q2, 3
Colophon *FINIS*] FINIS q Ihon Heywood Q3
Imprinted at London by Wyllyam /Copland Q2
Imprinted at Lon=/don at the long Shop adioyning vnto S./Mildreds Churche in the Pul/trie, by Iohn Allde Q3

The Text

Originals   *A play of love, A newe and a mery enterlude concernyng pleasure and payne in love*, made by Jhon Heywood. 'Printed by w.Rastell, 1534, Cum privilegio Regali.'
2° A–E4. One copy: Pepys Library. (F)
(STC 13303) Greg, 16a.
Fragment (E1–4) owned by Prof. Ray Nash, Hanover, N.H.

—— Another edition: [Title page lost] 'Printed at London in Farster Laen by John Waley. Cum privilegio ad imprimendum solum.' [1546–1582].
4° A–G4. One copy (STC 13304) Bodleian Library, 4 p. 33(1)Jur. (Q)
One imperfect copy wanting A1: Bodleian Library.
Greg, 16b.

Facsimiles   J.S. Farmer, *Tudor Facsimile Texts*, 1909; reprinted New York, 1970.
J.A.B. Somerset, Malone Society Reprint, Oxford, 1977.

Editions   Alois Brandl, *Quellen des weltlichen Dramas in England vor Shakespeare*, Strassburg, 1898.
J.S. Farmer, *Dramatic Writings of John Heywood*, 1905 (modernized); reprinted 1966.
Rupert de la Bère, *John Heywood, Entertainer*, 1937.
Kenneth Walter Cameron, *The Play of Love*, Raleigh, N.C., 1944.
J.A.B. Somerset, *Four Tudor Interludes*, London, 1974 (modern spelling).
F.E. La Rosa, *A Critical Edition of John Heywood's 'A Play of Love'*, New York and London, 1979.

The present text is transcribed, by permission, from the only surviving complete copy, printed by William Rastell, in the Pepys Library (F). The text is printed in one fount of black letter. Directions and speakers' names are centred, the former with an index, the latter with a leaf ornament; the beginning of each speech is marked with a pilcrow. Greg's suggestion (I 92) that Rastell's printing of *Wether* is closely related typographically is confirmed by Robinson (p. 3).

The second edition of *Love* (Q), probably printed by William Copland for John Waley after 1546 and before 1582, has been collated from the only extant complete copy. It corrects a few errors, especially after L1392 (sig. E2), where the work of a second compositor in F is less accurate, and it adds some new ones. Many of the changes in Q are to modernize spelling, and are here ignored. A few other alterations of significance are mentioned in the Notes. There is no evidence that the revisions are Heywood's.

Alterations to F are placed in square brackets. Punctuation here is editorial, but it is kept as close to F as possible. The virgule (/) is used rarely in F, mostly where the modern convention requires a comma, and it has been changed accordingly. The comma in F is used syntactically, but it occurs more frequently at a mid-line break in the rhythm. Full stops have been supplied, being scarcer in F than in Q. Most of the speech heads are slightly out of line in F, perhaps because they were added. From E2 to E3v they were printed in smaller but similar case. Inconsistencies in their spelling have been normalized to Rastell's most frequent usage.

Explanatory notes

Title page The Greek quotation 'Nothing is sweeter than knowing all things' was inscribed by Thomas Skeffington on at least five of the books which he offered in his will to the library of Trinity College, Cambridge, where he was a Fellow 1571–8. As a lawyer he may have been interested by the legal aspects of *Love*. The play is not mentioned in the full list of his books given by P. Gaskell, *Trinity College Library: The First 150 Years*, Cambridge, 1980, pp. 194–212. [Note by Marie Axton.]

L1 *curtesy*: Perhaps the actor's traditional bow at the beginning of performance. The actor's speech is an intrusion 'unthought uppon' (L3) into a socially superior audience, cf. L711, 1076–7. Also in 4P6. It appears from L2 that no curtsy is forthcoming.

L2 *pretendyng*: offering.

L16 'All these things and their causes are unknown to me.'

L17 *fale*: fall, rimes with shall L15. 15th-cent. spelling.

L20–1 'As one person is all people to me, so every place to me is but one.'

L24 *in the contrary*: on the other hand.

L33–4 *can . . . dyscryve*: can actually realise a true description.

in ure into practice, or performance. †OED sb.I.1b first use followed by infinitive.

L35 *full*: sum total, OED B.3.

L39 *as . . . ryghtly*: if one were to speak truly.

L40 *soole*: undivided. OED 1a celibate.

L43–4 *Wherin . . . all*: Because of this I assume that you all take the following for granted.

L46 'In accordance with what is properly due in return.'

L48–9 Proverbial, Dent L515.

L50–1 *But . . . case*: But my situation is so bad as to be completely the opposite.

L52–6 'No occasion can allow me to present my suit and ease my pain – it's too early before noon and too late at any other time. Thus time forces my worth to be presented at the wrong time [and out of my true rhythm.] For though time may give hope of any grace [or release] it never provides the opportunity in time or place.'

L58 'That death may end my life, which is made like death in this way.' *dedly*: death-like, OED 7a,b.

L63 s.d. In spite of the marked entry here, Loved not lovyng by convention has knowledge of what is said before she appears.

L68–70 'I don't doubt that by this process you, yourself will see, by the following words, the exact oposite of your words proved true.'

L71 *pleasyth it you*: if it pleases you.

L74 'On grounds of reason (or *by* reason) I must and will be corrected.'

L75 *confyrmable*: compliant to (with). See OED conformable 3 (1525).

L76 *in avoydyng circumstaunce*: in avoiding what is inessential.

L79 *of . . . nothyng*: by someone whom I do not love at all.

L80 *standyth our question*: the point of the dispute between us is . . .

L87–8 *more . . . true*: Proverbial, Dent S914.

L109 *harpe*: dwell upon tediously; gnaw (fig.). Proverbial, 'Harp no more on that string,' Tilley S934 (1543, More); Heywood *Dial. Provs.* II iv 1653, ix 2581.

L112 'From the lack of pleasure (dyspleasaunt L111) I would urge that the meaning is actually painful.'

L116 'By admitting that I might experience displeasure you admit that I am in pain.'

L126 'My heart's blood would have disappeared before now.'

L132–3 The executioner traditionally begged pardon of the condemned.

L141 *for shorter end*: to come to a conclusion more quickly.

put case: consider.

L146–7 'If your partiality in the matter I shall discuss will allow your reason to understand fairly.'

L155 'Since neither his absence nor his presence removes my pain.'

L162-6 'Mistress, if your long suffered pain is no stronger than this long argument [which you adduce] against my short [but intense] pain, you are sure to live much longer than the executioner [you just mentioned] who is eager to strike off your head. Yet in order to prevent your thinking I hold your words in contempt . . .'

L179 *Came . . . contynue*: subjunctive, 'If . . .'

L180 *to . . . skyll*: to anyone who can reason it out.

L186-7 'One pang from a single word from her mouth spoken as it were in anger or in witholding of her love which I seek . . .'

L189 *quayle*: (v.trans) destroy put an end to, †OED More 1532 (first citation).

L192-3 'Yet, no matter how short the pain, the sharpness is such that my heart could not withstand being pierced by the slightest of these [pains].'

L199-201 '. . . wish for something which is of such a nature that no scrap of what he wants can be achieved unless you agree.'

L203 'You need not fear death till your pain is stronger.'

L205 'In spite of my agreement to what you have claimed.' Refers to L167-8 above.

L214 *Bred*: is bred.

L215 *malydy*: Not this sp. in OED.

L224 *droppes*: ? tear drops (which make the fire smoulder).

L240-2 *yet . . . compare*: yet it will reveal great cause for you to be ashamed to complain, comparing your counterfeit pains with my true ones.

L243 *mete*: suitable. Perhaps a joke against the audience.

L245 s.d. The song is presumably omitted as the following lines do not seem suitable for singing.

L249-50 *wherby . . . knowe*: by means of which external perception can appreciate within . . .

L253-5 'If these things are properly considered in many cases they indicate that we must reveal ourselves in outward communication so that words and signs procede from us following our thoughts closely.'

L258-9 'To deceive man's inward mind by outward signs may shortly become more common than is commendable.' A serious note of social warning.
fable: no similar transitive use in OED.

L262 'But love always offered signs in accordance with the feelings of the heart.'

L264-6 'As with those who show mirth when in despair of advancement in love or those who receiving grace show sadness – such are not lovers but scorners of love.'

L270-3 'That one suffering from a burning fever may sooner hide its ferocity than he [a true lover] can possibly hide, by any human power, the least of his thousand pains, I dare say.'

L276-80 '[The lover] will be able to pluck the moon down to earth by manipulating a puppet with his finger [an impossible task] as easily as he can hide the radiance of his joy, since the reflection [of that love] shines from his heart to all who look upon him.' Proverbial, Dent M1124.
momet: a doll (OED maumet 2), perhaps having magic qualities. Otherwise an error for moment ('pluck down . . . in an instant').

L283-5 'Yet his external appearance will reveal his inner feelings as a dial reveals the movements of a clock, which might well be considered as an index, giving an abstract of the full circumstances.' Cf. Wy289-92.

L290 *of my such spede*: of my enjoying such success.

L294 'With cleverness I could not invent love as good as I find it.'

L302 *God you good evyn*: good evening. Lit: 'God give you good even' 'Variously mutilated' good even OED; see godigod, *Respublica* lines 59, 60, 61, 63.

woodcock: No lover nor loved develops this title for one proverbially foolish at L323 and L1323–6. The change in to a bawdy tone on the entry of the Vice is marked by a shift into couplets.

L306   *by lyke*: probably, OED belike 1533.

L309   *Or . . . woodcock*: or else [I am] like a woodcock [and] . . .

L312–3   These lines form a monometer couplet and accordingly are here numbered separately. The Vice, following convention, knows what has been said on stage without being present.

L323   *wyse as a woodcock*: Ironic and proverbial, Tilley W746.

L324   *tomd on thy syde*: favourable to your party.

L325   *to use*: to act.

L337–8   'That part you just reiterated is the sole cause of our dispute.'

L339/340   *affirmed/beloved*. Apparently not a true rhyme, but Heywood quite often rhymes final -ed, e.g. *rehearsed/beloved* L369–70.

L350   *at one poynt*: at the same state [of rejecting all women]. See L364. Possibly a pun on one point meaning half unbuttoned.

L351   *smyrkest*: neatest, most agreeable, †OED smirk (adj.).

L351–62   Each line has three virgules (/), here marked by commas, perhaps to aid delivery.

L354   *manerlyest*: most seemly. Skelton uses *mannerly* for polite, OED 1529.

L389   'And if you can bring one who is at all likely.'

L390   *for my parte*: as far as I am concerned.

L392   *scometh me*: impersonal use, not in OED.

L397   *nobs*: beloved, Skelton *Elinor Rummyng* 225.

malous: ? maleys (sickness); MSR suggests malees (malease); ? malice.

L398   *a felyshyp, spede ye*: in our common purpose, hurry up!

L399–406   'I shan't be surprised at whatever sort of rascal that this fool shall bring [to be a judge], and I don't care, provided he is not biased. And yet even if he were a false and foolish knave, I don't care a mite what man should come, provided that it wasn't too much effort to make a jackdaw [or fool] hear and speak correctly. And since I don't doubt my success, why should I spend unnecessary time preparing my case?' The Vice is so certain of victory that he proposes to divert himself and the audience ('for your confort', L415) by the following monologue (L407–690) instead of rehearsing his argument.

L404   *worth . . . myte*: Proverbial, Tilley M1026.

L408   *mummyng*: acting silently. If the actor made a long pause it would give point to his resuming speech by offering 'mere pastyme'.

L412   *all such standyng by*: i.e. the audience.

L422   *Nor never have ben*. In what follows No lover nor loved asserts that he was not in love, but only mocking the beloved, but he protests so much, especially at L612, the crisis of his tale, that it is hard to believe him.

L425   *Sent Savour*: Now cathedral church of Southwark, chosen here for the rhyme and for the 'sweetness' of his punning name.

L427–66   The topos of *descriptio* taught in the *artes poeticae* provides the template from top to toe, cf. *Calisto* 226ff. The dimeter couplets and doublets may be an imitation of Skelton's *Elinor Rummyng*.

L433   He appears to become incoherent with delight here.

L435   'When she was all dressed up.' Possibly 'weryng gere' is head gear.

L444   *clyps*: clasps, OED v^1 3, or trims v^2 [her nails].

L446   *gossyps*: close companions. Her cheeks and lips were red.

275

L449 *hole*: probably an indecent pun, 'it' L450ff.

L452–4 'The mere shadow of her 'whole' beauty in the darkest place could strike men's hearts.'

L464 Is he doing a display or perhaps moving among the audience lifting hems?

L467 *sent Katheryns whele*: St Catherine of Alexandria was tortured on a wheel.

L468 *round . . . hele*: quick to turn round (?dancing), or perhaps over. Cf. 4P721.

L473 *pas . . . sholde*: wherever she might go.

L474 *dyfference . . . golde*: Proverbial, Dent L135.11.

L479 *mete to ges*: prepared to judge.

L481–2 See L422 and note.

L484 'Who was herself perfect and apt in deceiving.'

L485 *to gyve a mock*: play a trick.

L486 *beyonde the nock*: beyond measure, OED nock 1d. Proverbial Tilley N197; but probably indecent (anus), see We1064, L1325.

L487/489 *trysed/tryse*: snatch(ed), pulled away, OED trice. ? defeat at a stroke.

L507–8 *coulde/alowde*; rhymed.

L511 He does not allow lovers to follow the convention of being sleepless (L508) and slovenly.

L514 *were*: where, common spelling in Heywood. Proverbial, Tilley T517.

L523 *in rate*: by their condition, OED rate sb.9.

L527 *fet*: fetched †OED fet 5 (Heywood,1556).

L547 *Hope and Drede*: 'Twene hope and drede / My lyfe I lede.' Skelton, *Garden of Laurel* 1594–5. Shakespeare, Sonnet 144, contrasts 'two loves' as good and bad angels, comfort and depair.

L552 *bloud and bones*: a proverbial asseveration, presumably referring to Christ's body, see OED bone 3.

L561 *in rate*: with the same force.

L566 *in ure*: into the discussion (lit. 'in use').

L568 *wurth an old sho*: of negligible value. Proverbial: nearest citation 'Not worth shoe buckles,' (1670) Tilley S382.

L570 *mockum moccabitur*: the mocker shall be mocked, Job 13:9. Proverbial, Tilley M1031.

L581 'Soon one of us said "I love you" and the other replied the same.'

L583 ' "I love you" and "I love you in return because you love me".'

L585 He conjugates the verb to love in the present tense, mockingly.

L587 *over the eares*: deeply, †OED 1553. He means he was (almost) out of his depth – 'and felt no ground'.

L593 *suche awayt she toke*: she took such careful heed. Possibly with hostile intent, OED await sb.1.

L596 *set the fynger in the eye*: pretended to weep. Proverbial, †Tilley F229. †OED 1590.

L597 *aptnes*: inclination †OED 1548.

L600 'Pretended a similar mood, appearing just like her in every respect.'

L603–4 *lyke a bur*: closely. †Proverbial, Tilley B724, first citation Heywood *Dial. Prous.* II v 1893. Pun on tale/tail.

L606 *dysgysyng*: 'play acting.'

L632 *Mother B*: Apparently refers to 'the auncyent woman' L617. Mother Bee, a farcical old woman, appears in W.S.'s *Gammer Gurton's Nedle* (c.1550) and F. Merbury's *Marriage between Wit and Wisdom* (1579).

L633–4 *bethought . . . betokenyng*: recalled that everything betokened true love in this woman.

L637–8 'Thinking to myself that I should have been treated in just such a cunning way if I had been a genuine lover.'

L643–8 'But you undertook too much in thinking you would make a project of mocking me, especially as I have seen you showing off from the beginning like a fool in a net thinking that he was the only one who could see himself.'

L646 *jettyd in a net*: Proverbial, marking the folly of thinking a net makes one invisible, Whiting N92. Cf. *Mankind* 529–31.

L664 'For trying to teach mockery or tricks to a woman.'

L668 *well sene*: thoroughly experienced.

L672 *the substaunce beyng no greater*: 'There being no evidence that the essential nature of a true lover's experience is of greater import than mine.' This disparaging remark reflects the Vice's contention that he knows all about love even though he has not experienced it fully: the weakness of his case is thus exposed.

L677–8 *wherby . . . swete*: so love is a suitable worm medicine to give infants as it tastes sweet first and afterwards bitter.

L678 *bytter swete*: Proverbial, Dent L505a.

L680 *frantyk worme*: Cf. 'The wylde worm ys com into hys hed,' Medwall, *Nature* 2, 306. Proverbial, Dent W907.

L684 *not worth an onyon*: worthless. Proverbial, Tilley O66.

L686 'I have the means to overcome every one of his arguments.'

L687–8 'Since my part of the business has been accomplished with such success, all you in the audience who take my part should be cheerful.'

L688 *ye*: the audience.

L691 *he that seketh shall fynde*: Matthew 7:8. Proverbial, Tilley S213. First citation Heywood *Dial. Provs.* I ix 609.

L693–5 'But in coming back with such as I have found I would rather try to lose twenty pounds than to commit myself to such a search as I have just undertaken.' A comic view of the difficulty in making up the match of characters demanded by Heywood's scheme.

L699 *great myst*: ? obscurity of mental vision. Possibly Lover loved accuses the Vice of making a smokescreen with his long tale.

L700 *By jys*: mild oath, for 'by Jesu'.
blynde balde cote: The coot (*fulica atra*) was proverbially bald and foolish, but not blind, Tilley C645, and Heywood *Dial. Provs.* 1 v 287.

L701–2 *ryde . . . fyst*: Presumably Lover not loved (male) leads Loved not loving (female) by the hand, hence nag as derogatory term for horse and woman, with sexual innuendo on *ride*.

L711 *curtsy*: The formulaic playing on place and time in the preceding lines (L705–10) is lightened by stage business, with the Vice jumping in front, behind, and at the side, ending with a bow here. The Potycary has similar business 4P1034–7.

L713 *set a broche*: open up; from broche, a bore used for tapping a barrel.

L715–6 *ye both wyll be/Good unto me, and especyally ye*: The formal language of Tudor servility requesting social patronage turns cleverly to insult.

L716 *especyally ye*: i.e. the woman.

L717 *face*: Proverbial, the face is the index of the heart, †Tilley F1 (1586).

L718 *a pore mans case*: this allusion to the Court of Request or 'Court of poor men's causes' anticipates a full-blown satire of Wolsey's style of dealing justice at L801–12 (R.J. Schoeck, 'Satire of Wolsey in Heywood's *Play of Love*', *N&Q* 196 (1951), 112–14).

L726 The Vice sees another opportunity for bawdy suggestion based upon Lover not loving's 'helpe' L724–5.

L734 *gredyly grated*: hotly argued. grate †OED 9 (1542).

L734–5 'Each of us has harped on his own case with such passionate prejudice.'

L741 *that medyll wyll or can*: who is willing or able to be concerned with it.

L752 Proverbial, Dent D395.

L753 *boke*: The nature of the book is not clear, but the Vice uses its supposed loss at L1263. Foly carries a fool's bible in *Magnyfycence* 1220.

L754 *cometh a croke*: is crooked, goes awry.

L756 Proverbial, Whiting D274; *Matt* 7:12, *Luke* 6:31

L762 'Is not a cause for my grief, but may well kill me.' For a similar paradox see Loved not loving, L768.

L770 *on me as wood*: as mad [with love] about me. Cf. 'be these men as mad/On women as they sey?' *Calisto* 637–8.

L775–82 These eight lines, setting out the differing stances of the participants, are paired by assonance, 'loved' being disyllabic.

L779–84 He shows that the pairs are diametrically opposed.

L787–8 'If only he had a carpenter (joiner) to help him they could join the others together very neatly' – with sexual innuendo.

L789–92 'For first I would divide these elements into separate lots (*fleses*), and once they were separated I would fit the units together in similar wholes, so that each part should go away in peace.' By separating out the discordant elements he would be able to reassemble them as uniform wholes.
fleses: shares OED fleece 2 (1602), cf. We1085.

L793 At the end of his dizzying punning the Vice is reminded that, perhaps because he is a child, he is not capable of such a lecherous performance.

L794 *Let passe*: let it go.

L800 *Why where the devyll is this horeson nody?* This concealed stage direction may indicate that the Vice has climbed up above the suitors into a 'seat of judgment'.
†*nody*: fool †OED first citation, but see Wy89; noddy polles, Skelton, *Colin Clout* 1243.

L801–12 *I never syt in iustyce* . . . The Vice's sanctimonious preparation to giving judgment, for which he admits he has no qualifications but his conscience, is satirical of Wolsey's manner in the Court of Requests. Heywood here aligns himself with the common lawyers' hatred of Wolsey, who had no training in either civil or canon law. On the basis of this passage Schoeck suggests as possible auspice for *Love* the Christmas Revels at Lincoln's Inn 1528 or 1529 (Schoeck, pp. 112–14).

L803 *confessyon*: Apart from its satirical point in relation to Wolsey the stage business of the confession relates back to the mocking re-arrangement of roles, L775–92.

L809 'But who can boast his advancement as I can.'

L810 *serjaunt*: senior barrister from whose ranks judges were chosen.

L814 *loke here how they ly*: From his great height the Vice indicates the women in the audience, with obvious sexual innuendo on *ly*.

L815 *beck*: a gesture or nod indicating condescension. Cf. 4P802–4. Cf. Skelton's allusion to Wolsey in *Why Come Ye Nat to Court?* 717: 'In the Ster Chambre he noddis and beks.'

L818–9 'Though one can hear two different tales at once, it is not possible to answer both at the same time.' In the first half of this thought is contained the premise of *Pardoner and Frere*. Cf. L826.

L821 *in havyng ferdest home*: in living furthest away.

L825 'As the other pair agree that we two shall start . . .'

L829–30 'Which [tale] I fervently hope will not advance my case except what is of essential value excluding unimportant details.'

L840 *had lever*: had rather. The Vice cynically insinuates that to say 'no' would pain some women, thus rejecting Lover not loved's point at L838.

L841 *ryde . . . myle*: Proverbial, Dent M927.

L842 *one . . . whyle*: for the brief time it takes to say a *Pater noster*. Proverbial, Tilley P99.

L845 *she say nay and take it*: Proverbial, †Tilley M34; also Heywood 300 *Epigrams* 223.

L858 *dyssymylyng*: pretending. The Vice had pretended not to know the real reason, preferring his own bawdy suggestions at L840, L846.

L864 *in maner*: to some extent.

L867–70 'His dreadful look is so pale that, to relieve my ears from his suit, I hardly dare cast my eye towards him because my eye carries [his] thought straight to my heart and so increases my pain.'

L874–6 'And for that pain [of receiving his thought] if it were a question of my immediate death I could still not agree to him, even if agreeing would save me.'

L889–90 *for . . . were*: for I am the victim and you may be said to signify the hangman.

L894 *of delyghtfull wyll*: in an act of will which must bring you pleasure.

L903–4 'And not only do you love without her attraction compelling you, but you persist in your suit completely against her will.'

L905–14 'Now since your will brought you to love, and by will-power you persist in love, and since by understanding even will sees such pain in love that will's perception would command him to refrain from loving, and [since] you are able to be your own physician and extinguish every symptom of love – unless you are a fool or are trying to make me one – what can you say to give reasonable grounds to make a man think your pain as strong [as you claim, in as much as] you turn your potential remedy into your affliction?'

L922 *my wyll . . . it*: my will cannot command [itself].

L924 *saforne flowre*: saffron, autumn crocus. The contrasts are of weight with frailty, and of dulness with brilliant colour.

L931 *demurrer in lawe*: a deadlock requiring judgement by another court. †OED (1533 More). The first citation in a legal sense is 1547.

L932 'You have progressed from the folly of woodcock to that of a jackdaw.' Proverbial, Whiting W565, Tilley W746.

L938 'the essence of which [tale] claims on your behalf . . .' *your* refers to Loved not lovyng.

L943 *bey*: extremity – the position of a hunted animal OED sb⁴, 3.

L949 'This account exemplifies my case, perceived in every detail.'

L950 *for entre*: for a start.

L955 *Yes* is apparently hypermetrical, and is here numbered separately.

L960/1 *save/have*: an acceptable rhyme: also at L980–1.

L962–3 *wyll . . . love*: Proverbial, Dent L499.

L965–7 'Why isn't it equally difficult for me to will the end of love where will has planted love as for you to plant love where [your] will forbids it?'

L966–7 *let*: 1. ending; 2. hindrance.

L970 *meane*: means. Absence (L974) is the means by which Lover not loved can cool his passion.

L975 'which you have permission to take whenever you will.'

L980–1 'because her presence, although I seldom have it, is the only medicine which saves my life.'

L982–3 'I can wish for her absence as unwillingly as I can wish to stop loving her permanently.'

L985 *worth . . . fly*: Proverbial, Tilley F396.

L987 *layd . . . water*: made worthless, dissipated. Proverbial, Tilley W108. Heywood, *Dial. Provs.* I iii 186–7; *300 Epigrams* 127.

L1004–5 'And then love has put his servants and himself into one bed – all crammed inside my head.' The servants are listed L1006–10.

L1014–7 His distemperature is characterized by excess of all four humours.

L1017 *parched perchment drye*: scorched dry as parchment.

L1022 *your . . . wars*: things are not going to get worse for you.

L1023 *Fo*: 'Phew . . .' foh OED 1542.
Saynt Savour: the word play is traditional, cf. L425.

L1026 *by attorney*: with the help of someone else. The hand of the Vice brings the heat and the cold together.

L1035–7 'In such a way that if your reply gives ground to conclude that the question is fully answered we shall not need arbitration, for I will concede.'

L1046 *Gybbes fest*: ? cat's dinner (Somerset).

L1051 *spytfull*: vexing †OED 3 (1548).

L1054 *ye study*: you are perplexed.

L1055 *women . . . redy*: Proverbial, Dent W696.11.

L1060 *proced*: make the basis for further conclusions.

L1065 'You cannot judge for yourself which [case] is most painful.'

L1075 *wyll . . . harte*: Proverbial, Dent H338.1.

L1078–9 *upper ende . . . neyther ende*: the upper and lower ends of the hall where the performance is envisaged.

L1092 *the ende . . . shall try*: who will finally win can only be decided when both our arguments have ended. (Order will favour no one.) Proverbial, Dent E116.1.

L1103 *secondly*: feebly, in a second-rate way. Pleasure and contentment are of a different order.

L1106 *this in hande*: this we speak of.

L1107 *contentacyon*: contentment with one's lot. Chaucer's Boethian 'suffisaunce'. La Rosa notes Heywood's song 'Be merrye, frendes':

Let contentashyn be decree, / Make vertue of nessessytee.

Works, ed. Milligan, 260.

L1123 *no dell*: in no part.

L1130–1 'My contentment concerns something that as a prior condition I would want for its own sake, if it could be a matter of wishing.'

L1144–6 'I have so many active [or sensory] pleasures beyond contentment that no living person can give an account of them by any cleverness or eloquence.'

L1153 *thorowoutly*: in every respect. OED thoroughoutly.

L1157 'Her love created in return for mine and in circulation.'
coin: †OED, earliest figurative use 1569.

L1162–4 *And this hed . . . harte*: this head is scornful of any eyes which close for longer than it takes my thoughts to think on love and dream of my beloved (i.e. the true lover scorns sleep, except for those brief moments which give instant access to the beloved in dreams).

L1167 'Love is the cross which *must* save me.'

L1174–5 'What could all the devils in hell devise for his pain greater than he has just spoken of?'

L1176–7 'What [additional] pain can those devils bring to that body where the head is controlled by love?' or, taking devyls in apposition to mynysters: 'What pain is brought to that body by devils in the head, because such [diabolic] ministers are always prompted by love?'

L1182 *Without stynt of rage*: with no remission from his mad passion.

L1186-7 *hym . . . you*: Lover not loved . . . Lover loved.

L1193-4 *by loves . . . dystruccyon*: by love's leading you, either by pain or by joy, to the same point of destruction.

L1196 'To have a trick in torture better than the devils.'
cast: skill, trick, OED sb.24.

L1197-8 'For I believe you won't discover that the devil is able to torment man in hell with pleasing thoughts.'

L1201-6 'I assure you that, in the beginning, if God had foreseen as much as I can now tell you, Love would have been the wicked angel cast out; don't doubt it at all that experience since then has given God such perception that if anything untoward should happen to Lucifer, Love will be appointed as the young devil to whip souls on the breeches.'

L1206 *blood*: rake, young devil. †OED 15 (1562). But sense 16: a disease (of sheep) may lurk in L1208-9.

L1207 *he*: Lucifer.

L1210 *blak jawndes*: black jaundice, associated with jealousy which, it is implied, is a manifest condition of lovers.

L1215-8 *for where . . . much*: for whereas you alleged that your pleasures are greater than mine, your displeasures are so great that they affect eating, drinking and sleeping, none of which you do very much . . . .

L1226 *none to me moved*: 'are' elliptical.

L1228 *I quyetly content*: 'am' elliptical.

L1233 'Never mind about my diet, judge me objectively by how I look.' Proverbial, †Tilley M838, cf. Heywood, *Dial. Provs*. II v 1607.

L1240-1 *more . . . wyse*: Proverbial, Dent B506.11.

L1247-52 'You know quite well that a post cannot possibly feel pleasures or displeasures. In respect of the effect of the pleasure we are discussing, I liken you to a post in this instance, in that the pleasure which you experience can be no more than the displeasure you say you feel.'

L1253-6 'Sir, though you suggest that the present pleasure you enjoy is more pleasing than the absence of displeasure for me, how do you account for the present displeasures you suffer in relation to the fact that I never feel pain?' The Vice is setting a trap, see L1260 n.

L1259 *No*: hypermetric, and here numbered separately.

L1260 *in this purs*: A purse could be a bag of any size, here large enough to contain the allegedly missing book. The Vice craftily creates an excuse for leaving in order to concoct a displeasure for Lover loved.

L1264-5 'I pray God I may never go from this spot if it is untrue that I would not rather have paid 40 pence [than forget the book – and have to go hence]'. A specious piece of logic chopping which alerts the audience to his deception.

L1267 *the devyll stretch it*: the devil hang it. Perhaps proverbial. This may be a gesture of the neck-rope sort found for vigorous exits in *Mankind*. Together with the promise that he will 'come agayne anone' (L1269) it suggests the antics of the Vice's performance. Cf. We352-6, 998-9.

L1274 *this fole*: the departed No lover nor loved.

L1278-9 'Though by winning I gain nothing which can increase my pleasure in loving by any amount.'

L1281 *pas with me*: come out in my favour.

L1283 *over trodyn*: trodden down †OED overtrodden (1586).

L1285 'By claiming to show that I experience any pain in my state.'

L1286–7 'Then I knew certainly that the fool must do as he did [and run off] or stay here and be silent.'

L1287 *stande . . . mum*: Proverbial, Dent M1311.

L1290–1 'Any reason based upon his proof for doubting the pain I feel has now been rendered void by his running away.'

L1297 s.d. *copyn tank*: a high crowned hat in the form of a sugar loaf, OED copintank. Origin obscure, early 16th cent. Alexander Barclay, *The Ship of Fools*, 1509, reveals it as a recent women's fashion, perhaps conspicuous for its size:

> Of newe fassions and disgised garments
> And ye Jentyl wymen . . .
> Come to my shyp . . .
> I mean your Copyntanke: And if it wyl do no goode
> To kepe you from the rayne, ye shall have a foles hode. (ed. 1874, I 38)

A Trinity College Inventory 1550–1 lists 'ij copyntankes of clothe/ vj copyntankes of dyverse colors' (A.H. Nelson, *Cambridge*, REED, 1988, I 171).

squybs: firecracker †OED. The stage diagram in *Castle of Perseverance* (c.1425) requires the Devil to have gunpowder in various parts of his costume. See also Nelson, *Cambridge* II 720.

L1303 *To fyre*: by fire.

L1310 *at a flush*: in a sudden burst, OED flush 1529 (of water); possibly confused with *flash* of light or fire (1566).

L1311 *toke my bush*: set alight my head of hair.

L1313 *broker*: dealer. But go-between, procurer, may be insinuated here.

L1317 *gone clere*: has fainted (or died) right away.

L1321 *dubbe*: poke, use for stabbing with a dagger, OED v². The comic rub-a-dub revival of the lover occurs in the folk-play tradition and provides here an opportunity for stage antics, clearly indecent (L1325, nock).

L1323 *wood wood woodcock*: plays on wode (mad), would, wooden.

L1326 *speke parot*: Proverbial, †Tilley P60. Perhaps a reference to John Skelton's *Speke Parott* (1522), where the parrot, in some ways an incoherent babbler, is beloved by the ladies.

L1328 *one undertakes*: one understands.

L1336 *burne*: 1. physically; 2. in hell; 3. in lust.

L1338 *bast*: baste with fat; pun on baste OED v³ thrash.

L1340 *fatte*: perhaps a pun on succulent/dull witted.

L1343 *By mater of recorde*: since it is hereby recorded (legal term for the written evidence of a court's proceedings).

L1346 *convynce*: convict †OED II 4, (1535).

L1350 *defaced*: discredited, OED 4, pun on face L1351.

L1354–7 'That wretch now proves before this audience what I said at my first entry: I alleged that to hide one's thoughts by external appearance [or signs] is improper,' He refers to L1246–59.

L1359 *facyng*: asserting, OED face 2a, 4P1066.

L1360 *eyleth nothyng*: it is not all harmed.

L1361–3 A triplet, but with imperfect rhyme.

L1367 *the stake*: what is at risk, normally a wager. †OED sb² (1540).

L1369 *ley*: punning on lie/lay.

L1370 *put case*: suppose.

L1372 *God save her*: an asseveration to counter the diabolical thought that Fortune might have caused her death.

L1374 *by my sheth*: mild oath, which proves the bawdy sense of *hole*. The Vice apparently has a dagger (L1321) and indulges here in some obscene mime with dagger and sheath. For the tradition of the Vice's dagger cf.

> . . . that's fifty years agone and six,
> When every great man had his Vice stand by him,
> In his long coat, shaking his wooden dagger.
>
> Ben Jonson, *The Devil is an Ass*, I i 83–5 (first acted 1616).

L1381 'For I consider all three to be equally worthless.'

L1386–7 '. . . as in the case of dread and jealousy each of which with other [pains] is the deadly enemy to your estate of love.'

L1388–91 'And I [being] completely free from love and saying so, make evident that since in my case no pain can touch me, I contend that this [carefully] considered is weighty enough proof on my side to force you to judgment.'

L1394–6 Triplet with weak rhyme.

L1399 *wade*: discuss. OED v 2d, see Wy669.

L1402 *indifferent prefe*: impartial proof.

L1409 *hors*: the mill horse is used in a similar argument, Wy456–78.

L1418 *slyke as an ele*: Proverbial, †Tilley E60. Heywood 300 *Epigrams* 285.

L1420 *as will*: as he will.

L1423–4 'As a covetous man would have in beholding Westminster Hall full of gold, all his.' Westminster Hall was the site of the King's Bench, Common Pleas, and Chancery (Nelson, *Medwall* p. 15). This strongly suggests that the 'covetous man' is Wolsey as corruptible judge.

L1447–8 'Since these two cases fall so evenly that you yourself can judge neither has advantage . . .'

L1453 *cowched so nie*: placed so close, drawn together.

L1461–5 'Yet in that man decides cases for others by impartial judgement, reason wishes him to be impartial in all his reasoning: wherefore in this case let us cut off all prejudice so that we may be guided by impartiality.'

L1476–7 'He loves whilst she hates and, because of this, promximity of the lover is life to him and death to her: on this basis my opinion is . . .'

L1493 *maystres*: Lover not loved now consults with the lady, Loved not lovyng.

L1496 *come to pointe*: be summarized.

L1507 *sinke . . . or swim*: Proverbial, Tilley S485; Heywood *Dial. Provs.* II ix 2449.

L1513–4 *in sise . . . above the tre*: of a magnitude superior to the tree. †OED size sb[1] 12.

L1522 *by the roodes mother*: by our Lady of the Cross. Perhaps a traditional rather than an ironic oath.

L1528 *affirmance*: ratification, OED 2 (legal term).

L1534–5 'Personal emotion, unguided [by reason] may incline any one of us to think that the other has done him wrong [by prejudicial judgement].'

L1538–40 'What judge could consider any one wise who has decided that his own wit was so strong that he might judge his judges [infallible]?'

L1547 *Christes precept*: Luke 6:31. Cf. L756.

L1556 'To your [existing] pain pain [will be added] quite as painful as your pain is already.'

L1560–1 *Havinge . . . disdaine*: Whether we are in a state of joy or pain, let us remain content. We will avoid being scornful of the joy or pain of others. However, F's reading *other ffee we disdaine* could be construed: 'We will not accept any other [lawyer's] Fee than [sympathy with] the joy and pain of others.'

L1568 *that love . . . assent*: who give love in return for love.

L1569 *in fyne*: finally after death.

L1571-3 'The Lord of lords whose joyful and blessed birth is now remembered by the time [of Christmas] which brings this customary occasion for honest mirth . . .' *present* pun on bringing forth/current. These lines evidence the play's performance at Christmas.

Textual variants and doubtful readings

L24 *and*] aud F.

L36 *thyng*] F; a thinge Q.

L59 *Alas*] No punctuation F; the sentence runs on, perhaps intentionally, suggesting a self-indulgent afterthought.

L64 s.h. *Loued*] Belovyd F.

L92 s.h. *Loued*] Belovyd F.

L111 s.h. *Lover*] Lovyng F.

L113 *anext*] ? t.

L144 *lenght*] F, Q: common 16 cent. sp., OED.

L159 *me thynke*] F; me thynketh Q

L246 s.h. *loued*] belovyd F.

L266 *skomers*] F; shorners Q.

L274 *lot*] F; loth Q.

L275 *That*] F; And Q.

L277 *momet*] F, Q; ? momēt.

L293 *my*] F; in Q.

L349 *touchyng*] Q; touchyug F.

L351 *smothest*] F; smotest Q.

L397 *malous*] F, Q. Meaning not clear; maleys (sickness). malees (disquiet) MSR.

L470 *no*] F; do Q.

L489 *tryp*] Q; ttyp F.

L514 *were*] F, Q; frequent sp. for where.

L517 *semed*] F; semeth Q.

L527 *fet*] F, set Q.

L550 *Drawe*] ? Drewe.

L578 *in*] i F; in Q.

L590 *loue*] F; lone Q.

L621 *mo*] F; no Q.

L632 *Mother B rendryd*] F; mother brendryd Q.

L645 *jet*] iet F; yet Q.

L649 *at*] F; and Q.

L678 *drynkth*] F; drynketh Q.

L695 *pounde*] Q; punde F (Q restores the rhyme).

L702 *his*] Q; his his F.

L722 *swarve*] F; swarme Q.

L737 *indyfferent*] Q; indyffereut F.

L770 *on*] one F.

L781 *loved nor lover*] F; perhaps read nor loved nor lover.
L791 *partlyke*] F; parte lyke Q.
L793 om. Q.
L801 *syt*] F; om. Q.
L805 *God*] gods Q.
L830 *pyth*] F; pyt Q.
L841 *an hundreth*] on hundreth F, Q.
L850 *Were*] suggested MSR; where F, Q.
L869 *his*] suggested MSR; my F, Q.
L883 *payne*] Q; payue F.
L897 *hangmen*] F; hangman Q.
L899 s.h. *loved*] Q; lovcd F.
L899 *never*] Q; ueuer F.
L906 *love*] F; wyll Q.
L920 *my*] F; me Q.
L925 *weyth*] F; welth Q.
L930 s.h. *loved*] Q; loucd F.
L938 *pyth*] F; pyt Q.
L942 *contynue*] Q; contyuue F.
L965 *dyffycult*] Q; dyflycult F.
L981 *soole*] F; foole Somerset; but soole is adverbial here.
L1018 *moyste*] suggested MSR; moste F, Q.
L1048 *as swete*] F; a swete Q.
L1155 *of*] F, Q, but 'or' would make better sense.
L1160 *receyveth*] F; receyved Q.
L1167 *Christs*] F; Christ Q.
L1169 *goodly*] F, Q, but perhaps godly.
L1209 *phisicyon*] phisicyou F.
L1277 *hym*] F; om. Q.
L1292 *Werfore*] F; Wherfore Q.
L1328 *undertakes*] untertakes F, Q.
L1332 *last*] F; om. Q.
L1374 *hyt*] suggested MSR; yt F; ye Q.
L1389 *As in*] Asin F.
L1392 *fyrst*] Q; syrst F.
L1404 *or strife*] F; nor strefe Q.
L1419 *he is*] F, is he Q.
L1421 *otes*] F; othes Q.
L1422 *in felinge*] Q; infelinge F.
L1431 s.h. *Lover*] Q; Loner F.
L1433 *ye*] Q; he F.
L1437 *without*] Q; within F.
L1438 *nor*] Q; not F.
L1459 *styfly*] Q; styffy F.
L1464 *we*] Q; out F.
L1465 *our*] Q: om. F.
L1475 *flee*] Q; ffee F.
L1488 *Ajudged*] A judged F, Q.

L1493 *maistres*] Q (supported by L1527); maisters F.

L1495 s.h. *Loved . . . lovyng*] Q; Loned . . . louing F.

L1503 *displeasure*] Q; displeasue F.

L1508 *he*] F; the Q.

L1512 *rise*] F; aryse Q.

L1517 *muche lesse*] Q; muchelesse F.

L1532 *maystres*] Q; maysters F.

L1537 *perciall*] F; parcyall Q.

L1538 *one*] F; own Q.

L1550 *contencion*] F; contentacion Q. Though F is obsolete, the reading should stand: OED has contention 6 = contentacion (1519), a state of being contented.

L1556 *paineful*] paiueful F; payneful Q.

L1558 *Knowledge*] F; Knowyng Q. OED knowledge (v) acknowledge.

L1561 *fee*] Q; ffee F, possibly for Fee deriving from MS letter ff.

L1564 *contencion*] F; contentacyon Q. See L1550 and textual note.

EDITORIAL NOTES TO *THE PLAY OF THE WETHER*

The Text

Originals   *The play of the wether. A new and a very mery enterlude of all maner wethers* made by Johñ Heywood. [Colophon] Prynted by w.Rastell. 1533. Cum priuilegio.
2°, A–C⁴ D⁶. Black letter. Two copies: Pepys, St John's College, Oxford (cropped, wants D6)
(STC 13305) Greg 15a (F)

The play of the wether. A newe and very mery enterlude of all maner wethers made by John Heywood. [W. Middleton, 1544?]
4°, A–F⁴. Black letter. One copy: Cambridge University Library (lacks F4).
(STC 13305.5) Greg 15b (Q1)

The Play of the Wether. A New and a very mery enterlude of al maner wethers made by John Heywood. [Colophon] Imprinted at London in Paules Churche yearde, at the Sygne of the Sunne, by [J.Tisdale for] Anthonie Kytson.[c.1560]
4°, A–F⁴. Black letter. One copy: Oxford, Bodleian Library.
(STC 13306) Greg 15c (Q2)

The playe of the weather. A newe and a very merye enterlude of all maner wethers made by John Heywoode. [Colophon] Imprinted at London by Jhon Awdeley dwelling in litle Britayne streete, beyonde Aldersgate. [c.1573] [Assigned from Awdeley to J. Charlewood 15 Jan. 1582]
4°, A–F⁴. Black letter. One copy: British Library.
(STC 13307) Greg 15d (Q3)

Facsimiles   J.S. Farmer, *Tudor Facsimile Texts*, London, 1909; reprinted New York, 1970.
T.N.S. Lennam and G.R. Proudfoot, Malone Society Reprints, Oxford 1977.

Editions   A.W. Pollard in C.M. Gayley, *Representative English Comedies* I, New York, 1903.
F.J. Child, *Four Old Plays*, Cambridge, 1848.
Alois Brandl, *Quellen des weltlichen Dramas in England vor Shakespeare*, Strassburg, 1898.
J.S. Farmer, *Dramatic Writings of John Heywood*, London, 1905 (modernized); reprinted 1966.
J.Q. Adams, *Chief Pre-Shakespearean Dramas*, Boston, 1924.
Rupert de la Bère, *John Heywood, Entertainer*, London, 1937.
Peter Happé, *Tudor Interludes*, Harmondsworth, 1972
M.F. Ashe-Jones, An Edition of Two Plays by John Heywood. Unpublished B.Litt. thesis, Oxford University, 1975.
David Bevington, *Medieval Drama*, Boston, 1975.
Vicki Knudsen Robinson, A Critical Edition of the Play of the Wether, The Renaissance Imagination 27, New York & London 1987.

The present text is transcribed, with permission, from the perfect copy of Rastell's small folio in the Pepys Library, and has been checked against St John's Oxford and MSR. St John's is missing the last leaf (D6), with the final twenty lines and the colophon, and is closely cropped on the outer edge. There is a single press variant: line 187, Pepys' 'cartely' is followed by Q1; St John's 'carterly' is followed by Q2, 3. The loosening of some lines in St John's shows correction in the printing house. So do identical pen-and-ink corrections in the two copies.

The type and ornaments of Q1 are identical with Middleton's quarto of 4P suggesting that the two were companion pieces (Greg I 90). Middleton's alterations to characteristic Rastell house spellings have been helpful in establishing dubious readings in *Foure PP*, in the absence of a folio for that play.

The quartos all descend from Rastell's folio. The probability of lost intermediary editions is discussed by Ashe-Jones (p. 102), by David G.Canzler ('Quarto Editions of *Play of the Wether*' PBSA LXII, 313–19), and by Robinson (pp. 9–15), who also discusses the later editorial tradition.

Although all the quartos correct some of F's errors, they all introduce a great deal more corruption. A number of Q3 readings are independent of F, and of Q1, Q2. These can be explained as intelligent reconstruction (e.g. We326) errors, or metrical 'modernisations'. The omission of We447 and the lame readings Q3 at We211, 314, 410, 673, 981, 999 may be indications that Heywood himself did not oversee Q3. All substantive variants are included in the Textual Notes, together with unusual spellings which might affect pronunciation, metre or rhyme. The alteration of Rastell's characteristic not>nat and woll>wyll are not usually noted.

Rastell's folio is well printed in one fount of black letter (large black letter for the title) except for six stage directions in the left margin and the date in the colophon printed in italic. Robinson (p. 3) follows Greg in noting the absence of capital 'w' and 'y' in both *Wether* and *Love*; whereas these capitals are used in *Johan Johan* and *Pardoner and Frere*. (This would seem to support a printing order JJ, PF, We, L.) Speech prefixes are aligned in the left margin or occasionally centered within the text. Spaces in the text are dictated by verse form, not by change of speaker. This principle has been extended in the layout of the present edition in accordance with practice in the Tudor Interludes series.

Explanatory Notes

We1 s.h. *Jupiter*: Identification of Jupiter with Henry VIII comes and goes throughout the play. Jupiter in Skelton's *Speke Parott* (399, 405–10) 'rules the English realm'.

We4 *dewly unfayned*: as our due and sincerely offered.

We6 *our fathers fale*: the fall of Saturn, deposed by Jupiter, possibly referring to Cardinal Wolsey's fall in October 1529.

We10–12 'Who would dare, no matter how great his reward, describe my present glory in terms comprehensible to human reason?'

We13–15 Jupiter's assertion suggests a recent apotheosis of God-like power, alluding almost certainly to Henry's claim to be supreme head of the Church in England'. See We296 and *Introduction* p. 51.

We15–8 'We will relate only evidence of our power which concerns provision for your comfort and this very matter will become self-evident in the course of the play and in your lives.'

We19 *Whyche hyely shall bynde you on knees lowly bent*. The antithesis and witty play on sound and sense barely conceal a vaunt of absolute power that links Jupiter with the boasting tyrants of the miracle play stage.

We22 *our hye parlyament*. The first Reformation Parliament met in eight sessions between 4 Nov 1529 and 14 Apr 1536 (see Chronology) 'Our foresayd parleament' is said at We80 to be 'clerely fynyshed'. Alistair Fox (*Politics* p. 252) sees allusion to the first session, assembled between 3 Nov and 17 Dec 1529.' For discussion of later possibilities, see *Introduction* pp. 51–2.

We25–8 'These irregularities, which have sprung up in their midst through extremes of behaviour, are the result of abuses in each of the gods to the detriment of all the others.'

We29–30 *Saturne, and Phebus*: gods of cold and heat are paired, Eolus and Phebe, gods of wind and water, likewise. The gods probably have specifically topical reference. In Skelton's *Speke Parott* (283–4, 398–9) Tytan and Eolus probably represent Charles V, Saturne may stand for Francis I (ed. Scattergood, pp. 461, 463). Lucina also appears there. In Heywood's allegory it is possible that 'father Saturne' is Wolsey; Phebe as Anne Boleyn would link with later play upon moons.

We33 *out of frame*: far from their predictable courses. That the departure of the planets from their 'proper' courses caused harmful effects on earth, was a common late medieval view.

We39 *entred such mater*: made such depositions. The language is formal and legal (cf. 'debated in place sayde before' We36).

We40–2 '. . . praising (Saturn's) house in heaven as the repository of coldness, a preciously necessary thing to air and earth, purging them of contagious vapours'. Saturn's mansion is Capricorn, extending from the winter solstice to 21 January. If Father Saturn is to be taken as Wolsey, then his 'frosty mansion' would be appropriate to the palace of Whitehall, which reverted to the King in 1529.

We50 *Phebus*: Apollo, the sun.

We51 *Phebe*: the moon.

We52–4 'Each separately alleged against Phebe, that because of her excessive showers, they had found that their own powers [frost and sun] had been curtailed as a consequence of her greater scope.'

We57 *Eolus*: Aeolus, classical god of winds, dispensing them from a bag.

We58 *eche one arow*: each in turn

We62–3 A specific topical interpretation of the conflict between Jupiter's four planetary counsellors cannot be ruled out. See We29–30.

We66–70 'And also, since we are – besides our almighty power of godhead – everlastingly noble, generous in wisdom and nature, we keep the mean, avoiding extremities and tempering each thing to peace and plenty.'

We71–4 'In conclusion, they delivered into our hands for ever all their powers over the various weathers caused by them.' In terms of temporal and spiritual authority Jupiter's claim to power is absolute.

We76–7 'Which, for our part, we did not seek, but they humbly sought for their own sakes.'

We80 See We22.

We83–4 'Since their powers, now ours, have amplified our own, who [among our subjects] can we say knows us as we should [rightly] be weighed?' Jupiter manages to be pompous, enigmatic, and threatening.

We94 *thys sorte*: the audience. Cf 4P1198. The sequence in which a volunteer is recruited from the audience follows a similar one usually associated with More's youth in the Morton household (*Fulgens and Lucres* 354ff. See Nelson p. 17).

We98 *Brother, holde up your torche a lytell hyer*: spoken to a torch-bearer in – or beside – the acting place, and suggesting evening performance. The address is familiar and commanding; it may be the actor draws attention to his own height, see below We121.

We104 *I am I perse I*: I am unsurpassed, the thing itself (*per se* spoken as one word). There is a play on the letter I standing alone as a word, which sounds like a tag from a schoolboy's ABC. Cf. the grammatical play on pronouns in *Jack Juggler* 497ff.

We110 Mery Report's dress is 'lyght' – frivolous, showy, flimsy, not sober. He may change his costume at We178.

We118 Spoken aside.

We121 *so lyghte an elfe*: so frivolous a little rascal. *Elfe* has the sense 'tricksy or mischievous person' (OED 2b 1553) and also 'dwarf' (OED 3a Palsgrave 1530). Cf.

289

'lyttel whelpe' We300 and the play between Mery Report and the Boy 'the lest that can play' We1002. There would be some comic point here if the part was written for Heywood himself, who was a tall man. Skelton makes comedy out of the small stature of Folly in *Magnyfycence* 1068–70.

We126 'My behaviour could not have been bettered (was incorrigible).'

For sewer: for sure, as a servant.

We128 'It would havé been damaging for you to have overlooked my suit, in the interests of your reputation.'

We129 *For as I be saved*: [I swear] as I hope to be saved.

We134 'In so frivolous a subject, what does it matter whether we wear frise (coarse woollen cloth) or feathers?' Feathers might be appropriate to Jupiter's messenger, 'feathered Mercury'.

We136 *wyth thys*: this apparel.

We143 *caste such a fygure*: created such an impression. The word play swtiches between figures of rhetoric and conjuring as bawdy metaphor (cf.We149: 'I conjured and bounde her;' bound: as with a spell, OED cast 1.2.b).

We169–70 'And such of them as seem to you to be most suitable, we would have you bring into our royal presence.' This is what happens. Only the Gentleman and Merchant are brought into presence; Mery Report solicits Jupiter for the Gentlewoman but he refuses to see her. We487 suggests a laxity in regulations governing access to the King, a subject addressed partly by the Eltham Reforms of 1525. Cf. We587.

We176–8 Spoken to the audience. *thrustyng* and *gere* are gestural 'Vice-words' with sexual connotations.

We178 s.d. in F is placed in the left margin in italic type and must have been added after 'this staf' (Jupiter's stanza, 179–85) had been printed. It gives the musician(s) advance warning of the need to play after 185; placing of the s.d. is followed by all Quartos. Richard Southern *The Staging of Plays Before Shakespeare* (1973) p. 241 suggests there was a raised throne with steps leading up to it, all canopied and curtained, and that a musician might sit on the steps.

We186 Mery Report's reentry suggests a showy display of new livery. As a Mercury figure his dress may include helmet, winged heels, and caduceus. An inventory of 1548 at St John's College, Cambridge, lists a 'starr gilted for Mercury's hedd / A golden face and crowne for Jupiter' (REED *Cambridge* ed. A.H. Nelson, 1989, I 162) and Trinity College in 1550 had 'a caduceus with serpentes' (I 172).

We187 *carterly keytyfs*: ill-mannered wretches. The situation of pushing though a crowd brings to mind the carter's proverbial rudeness.

We189 'By your faith, why don't you take off your caps and bend your knees?'

We191 *squyre for goddes precyous body*: If this is not merely an oath, then Mery Report is claiming an official post in the court as 'squire of the King's person' (a post which may well have been Heywood's – a hint, perhaps, that he played the role). His exit at 178 and the song give him time to change costume.

We195 *a thousande myle from hell*: the boast of Puck-like speed and ubiquitousness is unprompted and seems to recall the Pardoner's journey to hell in *Foure PP*. Possibly the parts were written for the same actor, or for Heywood himself.

We198–211 Heywood's love of lists is also evident in 4P29–50. This geography works by alphabetical association, but a high proportion of Essex names is evident, suggesting places with particular association for Heywood's family. See below, especially We211.

We198 *Lowyn*: Louvain. In 1564 the Heywoods joined the Rastells in exile there.

We199 *Baldock*: Hertfordshire.

Barfolde: uncertain. There are several Barfords in southern England, all small villages, one near St Neot's, Cambridgeshire. Possibly Bardfield, near Braintree in Essex.

Barbary: North Africa.

We200 *Coventre*: for the Heywood and Rastell association with Coventry see Introduction, Life and reference to the play of Corpus Christi in 4P831–2.

We201 *Wansworth*: Wandsworth, Surrey.

Welbeck: Nottinghamshire, celebrated for its abbey.

Westchester: Chester (Ashe-Jones, citing John Speed's *England*)

We202 *Fullam*: Fulham, Middlesex, site of a palace.

Faleborne: possibly Fulbourn, Cambs. or Faulkbourne, Essex.

Fenlow: Ashe-Jones notes that Speed's Northumberland shows a 'Farnlaw'.

We203 *Wallyngford*: Wallingford, Berkshire.

Wakefield: in Yorkshire.

Waltamstow: Walthamstow, Essex.

We204 *Taunton*: Taunton, Somerset.

Typtre: Tiptree, Essex.

Totnam: Tottenham, village 8 km N of London, settled by French artisans, who rioted in 1517. Cf. Heywood's *Dial. Provs.* 394: 'Their faces told toies, þat Totnam was turnd frenche'. In 1542 Heywood purchased a large tract of land in Tottenham (Reed p. 46).

We205 *Glouceter*: Gloucester.

Gylford: Guildford.

Gotham: in Nottinghamshire, celebrated for the foolish 'wise man of Gotham' in popular mythology.

We206 *Hartforde*: Hertford, possibly Hartford End near Braintree, Essex.

Harwyche: Harwich, Essex.

Harrow on the hyll: in Middlesex.

We207 *Sudbery*: Sudbury, Suffolk.

Suthampton: Southampton.

Shoters Hyll: Shooter's hill, near the royal palace at Greenwich, scene of a spectacular encounter on May Day 1515 between Henry VIII's court and 'Robin Hood' (P.R.O., E.36/229, fols.125–37; Anglo, p. 119).

We208 *Walsyngham*: Walsingham, Norfolk, famous for its pilgrimage shrine of Our Lady. See 4P35 and note.

Wyttam: Witham, Essex. Used proverbially for a place where the inhabitants were notably foolish. 'Small wyttam be your spede' (Bale, *Three Laws* 374).

Werwycke: Warwick.

We209 *Boston*: in Lincolnshire.

Brystow: Bristol.

Berwycke: Berwick-upon-Tweed, Northumberland, sometimes thought of as the furthest North in the kingdom (the messenger's speech in *Pride of Life* 285). More tells the story of a blind beggar of Berwyke warned in a dream 'to seke saynte Albon' (*Heresies* I 14, *Works* VI i 86).

We210 *Gravelyn*: Gravelines, just across the Flemish border from the English Pale at Calais.

Glastynbery: Glastonbury, Somerset, known for its abbey.

We211 *Ynge Gyngiang Jayberd, the paryshe of Butsbery*: 'a compound manorial name that was used indiscriminately of the parish and manors which descended to the Blund family, Ginge Johiberd and Ginges Landri now being Great Blunts and Little Blunts respectively' (Ashe-Jones). Heywood's brother William had copyhold lands in this area, and several witnesses to his will are recorded as being of the homage of the manor of 'Inge Gynge Joyberd Laundry, Hertford Stock in the parish of Buttysbury' (Reed, p. 31). The representation of a Laundress in *Wether* may hint at a familiar circle of acquaintance.

We215 s.d. *Here the Gentylman before he cometh in bloweth his horne.* Heywood takes hunting as the mark of a 'gentleman born', but his humour carries no trace of the contempt of a man of letters. Contrast Skelton, *Collyn Clout* 619–21: 'But noble men borne, / To lerne they have scorne, / But hunte and blowe an horne.' Similarly Richard Pace, King's Secretary in *De Fructu* (1517): 'It better becomes the sons of gentlemen to blow the horn properly to hunt with skill, to teach and manage the falcon' (cited by Robert S. Kinsman ed. *John Skelton: Poems*, Oxford, 1969, p. 189).

We219 s.d. *Enter Gentylman*. Bevington adds, 'with a retinue of followers'. From We216–19 it seems several horns are blown. It may be that the Gentylman addresses the audience ('my frendes'), at first conspicuously ignoring Mery Report, who refers at We222 to 'your meyny'. The gentlemen in the audience probably sat together (as did the women We249ff.) and it seems in keeping with the nature of performance, that the actor should mark out a socially distinct group in this way.

We219 *womens homes*: shorter horns with higher pitch. Mery Report's play on horns extends from scatological nuisance (cf. *PP* B V 343) to the plague of cuckoldry (We235, 247, 251).

We232 *I am a gentylman*: The Gentylman's occupation is hunting (cf. *Gentleness and Nobility* 185–6). Mery Report's mocking oath, 'a goodly occupacyon - by Seynt Anne' hints at an envied function of a gentleman of the chamber – to attend the King's favourite.

We234 *your mashyp*: mastership. The abbreviated form, at least when used in writing, apparently implied disrespect. Cf. 4P234.

We235 *al these homes*: the old innuendo about cuckolds requires plural horns; Mery Report may refer to the Gentylman's retinue of huntsmen or may gesture at the audience.

We236 Has the Gentylman laughed or shown anger or indicated that he thinks Merry Report a simpleton?

We238–9 'In faith, it seems to me that neither of us is exactly sober. If I am merry then you seem equally mad.'

We246 *Gentylman*: In F Rastell uses upper case 'G' here, perhaps to underscore the social mockery.

We249 *He wolde hunte a sow or twayne out of this sorte*: This is purely Mery Report's invention to 'make game' with the women's section of the audience.

We253 *I thought ye had*: 'been' understood.

We264–5 '. . . which social group above all others earns thanks by painstaking efforts daily on behalf of the common people.' Heywood catches the note of humbug in the claim to altruism (cf. the Merchant at We351 and Water Miller at We 462–5).

We275–7 '. . . and so that we may follow within hearing of our hounds as they cry joyfully over dale and hill, and may encourage the pack'.

We275 *yourmynge*: baying (verbal sb. or pr. part. of yearn OED 4)

We277 *to-comfort*: encourage. Q3, however, did not recognise the compound form, recasting the line 'and to comfort them cry'.

cry: yelping of hounds in the chase (OED 12, 1535) or a pack (OED 13, 1590)†.

We284 s.d. The Gentylman presumably obeys the god's command to retire (280); his speeches at 285–6 and 289–96 may be addressed to the audience rather than to Mery Report. At 297 Mery Report's 'Now I beseche . . .' seems to interrupt a pompous general utterance.

We286 *whome*] All texts. Grammar requires who, but whome is easier to speak before a vowel (cf. We564).

We290 'I do not doubt that in his wisdom he will provide.'

We293–4 'Granting us these conditions for our recreation will be greatly to your benefit by improving the prosperity of gentlemen.' *prevayle* OED 4.b. *you*: Mery Report, whom the Gentleman treats with civility; or, possibly, the audience, addressed as jury in a pleading.

We296 *weale and heddes*: source of felicity (with a play on well-spring and weal: prosperity) and head (water). The prolonged antic about heads (to 316) may have been occasioned by the currency given to the wording of Henry VIII's Act of Supremacy. After the Southern Convocation on 24 Jan 1531/2 Archbishop Warham inserted the clause (among others) styling the King as 'protector and only supreme head of the English Church'. From then until the passing of the Act in the second session of 1534 the *supremum caput* was a contentious issue. See J. Scarisbrick, *Henry VIII* (1968), pp. 276 ff. On the dating of *Wether* see Introduction, Sources 7.

We298 *What sayest thou now?* Possibly he strikes Mery Report here, or he may interrupt a fit of antic musing, or he may draw himself up to his full height.

We300 *of a lyttel whelpe*: since I was a pup. On Mery Report's stature see We121.

We301-4 'So full of notions and in so many different minds (OED wit 4) that, as I stand here, I pray God I may die if I ever thought they might all fit properly into my one head.'

We306 *all thynges new*: (1) such novelities as this; (2) news (as befits my name).

We310 *I can set my hedde and my tayle to gyther*: Mery Report evidently tries to put his backside as close to the Gentylman's face as possible, so that the actor peers at the audience from between his own legs, as his old head 'disappears'. Cf. the comic routine in *Mankind* 343ff., 434ff.

We314 *glyster*: suppository. The rhyme myster/glyster is found also in 4P175-6.

We316 *stande at receyte*: stand by to receive delivery . . . The scatological play continues through 'move you' (†OED move 5b 1700) to end with 'ease you' (We319-20).

We323-4 'I promise to reward your trouble more generously than I shall speak of here.'

We325 *Alas, my necke*: suggests further acrobatic contortions.

We326 *Saynt Yve*: probably the patron of St Ives, Huntingdonshire, after four bodies were discovered there in 1001, one of them with episcopal insignia. Following a peasant's dream, this was identified as remains of a Persian bishop who supposedly died a hermit in England. The bodies were translated to Ramsey Abbey, where many miracles were attributed to them. St Ivo of Chartres, 1040–1116, was greatly venerated for his learning. But the former seems more likely in context of Mery Report's claim that his head and body as 'farre asonder' (Goscelin *Vita S Yvonis PL* CLV cols. 84–92).

We329 *Mayster Person*: Bevington notes: 'Perhaps the merchant's long cloak and general sobriety give him a clerical mien.' However, in the hierarchy of the estates the audience would expect a figure of Clergy to follow the Gentylman. Mery Report seems deliberately to mistake the merchant's profession, so that Heywood can get in a topical jibe about clerical celibacy and plant the subject of marriage in the audience's minds.

We337 *your gracyous godshyp*: jocular address, modelled on lordship, mocking Jupiter's ecclesiastical pretensions. †OED 1553 Udall.

We353-5 'Just think what [local] excess of every kind of commodity there would be . . . were it not for trade'; (not, *pace* Bevington, 'plentiful supply').

We368 *Berynge our seylys for spede moste vayleable*: Keeping our sails hoisted for the most advantageous speed'. †OED valuable 1589.

We379 *That ech mans parte maye shyne in the selfe ryghte*: in order that each man's share may be clearly evident by the same (OED self B.1.i) equitable treatment (OED right 4). shyne: appear with conspicuous clearness (OED 6).

We385 *I truste or myd lente to be to Syo*. For 'mid Lent' (?1533) see We620-4. Allowing a month for the voyage to Chios in the Aegean, this suggests a performance time between Christmas and Shrovetide (see *Sources* 7). The Merchant's business would be fruit, wine, and mastic, used in making picture varnish and in flavouring liquors. This would be a hazardous journey because of the belligerence of the Turks in the Aegean (see Cameron p. 53). Mery Report's comment merely suggests he is glad not to be going there himself.

We391 *as myche*: i.e. as little. The degree of irony depends on delivery of the lines. We392–3 might be spoken aside.

We395 *Though I requyte not all, I shall deserve some*: though I may not recompense all I owe you I shall pay back some. 4P924, 1098.

deserve: pay back (OED 6).

We396 *Saynt Anne*. Cf. We233, a possible allusion to Anne Boleyn.

We399 *thys twenty yere*: twenty is used as an indefinite number at We557 and in 4P597, 935, 1047.

We399 **s.d.** *Ranger*: forest officer. 'The office of a Raunger doth chiefely consists in raunging and walking the Pourallees [perambulations], and in safe conducting of the wilde beasts, that he shall there find, into the Forest againe, and also in presenting of all offenders and vnlawfull Hunters, and of their trespasses and offences' (John Manwood, *A Treatise and Discourse of the Lawes of the Forrest*, London, 1598, fols. 166r–v. Cameron *Wether* pp. 31–2)

We400 *God be here!* An old-fashioned greeting, associated with friars ('Deus hic!' PF1).

We416 'To say "alas" for our wages doesn't bring us nearer [to being paid]'.

We417 *What is forty shyllynges or fyve marke a yere?* Five marks would be 66s 8d – one third of Heywood's 'pension' in 1528, and would not go far,

We418 *flyttynge*: travelling. The Ranger's nomadic occupations may include re-tethering grazing animals. He may also be a night-owl.

We419 *at a syttynge*: at a stop. With forests to visit all over the country, he incurs expenses for lodgings.

We429 *them*: (?)the trees.

We430–1 'I am impressed by your charity almost as much as by your honesty' i.e. not at all. Cf. We434–5.

We432–3 A hidden s.d. here: the Ranger makes as if to replace his cap and Mery Report keeps him subservient a moment longer.

We442–3 'What the devil good would it do even if all the world were dumb [and we alone could speak in petition], since we are never heard anyway?'

We444 *the devyll sped drop wyll cum*: not a drop, for all the devil's help. Cf. J24, 'Nay, by Our Lady, the devyll spede whyt.'

We446 *at any stynt*: at any restricted rate (OED 5 rather than 7, 'allotted portion of work' citing We).

We453 *There is the losse yf we be forborne*: that is the general loss if we are dispensed with; or 'theirs (each man's) is the loss'. (Theres Q3)

We456–7 'Yet many people grudge to pay us a quart bowl of grain [2 lbs] for grinding a bushel [64 lbs]' i.e. 1/32 or about 3%. Act 12 H7 (1497) laid down 'that the measure of a Bushell containe viii. gallons of wheat'.

We459 *whele with her kogges*: the main driving wheel, geared with wooden teeth, which often broke. The wheel is spoken of as feminine.

trindill: trundle or lantern-wheel, a horizontally mounted cog.

We461 *yren spyndyll*: apparently the vertical spindle keyed into the milling stone; this is the only iron part mentioned.

We462–5 The Water Miller claims that lack of water is the least of his worries in relation to expenditure on repairs, and that it is concern for his fellow Christians that brings him hence. This is patently specious (cf. 268, 351). Millers were universally unpopular, always suspected of cheating.

We467 *accordynge to the cry*: as it was proclaimed.

We474 *reheytynge*: railing, provoking trouble (OED rehayte: behave noisily, or rehete v[2] scold). Ashe-Jones notes 1526 regulations for the Royal Household contained an injunction, 'that no man do rehayte nor use himselfe otherwise in the chamber than to that place doth accord'.

We476 The Water Miller appeals to the audience to witness his poor treatment since entering the place.

We478 *universall*: widely accomplished (OED 9), a know-all.

We483 *For I am goddes servaunt, mayst thou not se?* On Mery Report's dress and appearance see We186.

We485 *to farre od*: too far at variance.

We486 *tyed shorter*: like a dog (or a bear, We475).

We487 The Articles devised by the King's Highness . . . Apud Eltham (1525/26) rule that 'the porters suffer none of their servaunts as nigh as they can to enter into the Kings state' (PRO E36/231 p. 20); they are to exclude 'boyes and vile persons' (p. 25).

We510 *hole sorte of my crafte*: the entire group of my profession.

We512 *shatter*: stir to and fro (OED v[6], cf. clatter v[5]).

shyttyn sayle: (1) the shut sails (canvas-covered slats of the mill sails, closed in very light wind); (2) soiled skirt.

We521 'We might as well go hang ourselves.'

We522 'Miller goes with plague (murain) and trouble (mischief)' – all beginning with M.

We523 Heywood may have helped to form the Proverb, 'Many a miller, many a thief' (Wilson M955).

We527 'Which of the two, growing corn or grinding meal, might more readily be dispensed with in the common good?' The question implies equal importance, since in his view millers are 'goddys felows' (525).

We538 *clene caste away*: right out of luck.

We542 *Day by day to say Our Ladyes sauter*. There may be a reference here to Thomas More's visit to his sister in Coventry in 1520. A Franciscan had established the practice of saying Our Lady's Psalter daily, claiming it as an insurance against damnation. Asked for his opinion, More cast doubt on the practice and was laughed at for a fool (Reed, pp. 2–3). Ashe-Jones notes a possible error on Heywood's part at We1228, when he has the Water Miller not the Wind Miller – mention the psalter to Jupiter.

We566 *by your lycens*: by your leave, with a reminder that mills required licence directly or indirectly from the Crown. Cases of conflicting economic interest and challenges to monopolies are common at this period.

We571 *try*: sail, make trial of wind and sea (OED 17 cites this as first, doubtful usage).

We581 *no here bred*: no hair's breadth

We589 *Then meane coolys of wynde*: than moderate cool breezes.

We597 'The organs surely produce half the sound of the choir.'

We598 *or water or wynde*: is it either water or wind?

We602 Chaucer's Miller plays the bagpipe (*GenPr* 565), but the association may be traditional.

We606 'which flourish at their height', with a possible play on spring, i.e. waxing of the moon (OED spring 5c) and tides.

We607 *he is now fled*: addressed to the audience (a rapid shift from *your* of the previous line).

We614–5 'Still I think that organs are not such a benefit that water should be banished for their sake.'

We618 *tryfull me of*: put me off with trifles.

We620–4 First example of the *olde proverbe*, whose generalised meaning here is: 'Dry [windy] weather in March is worth a king's ransom [because it allows early planting].' The Water Miller replies, 'A hundred thousand bushels of dust remain worthless [unless rain falls on them].' There may be a political allusion here. In March 1533 the Act in Restraint of Appeals 'ransomed' the King by enabling the divorce to be settled by Cranmer in May. On implications for the play's date, see also We385 and Introduction, Sources 7. Shrove-tide 1533 was 25 February. The Merchant's mid-Lent would be about 20 March.

We628 *lycke*: like, with play upon 'lick' (629). Cf. the extended play on hop/hope in 4P470.

We629 'Whoever prefers not to lick [a little of] the one [dust] may lick [much more of] the other [mud].'

We633 *drought doth never make derth of corne*. †Proverbial, Whiting D414, Tilley D22.

We635 *How rayne hath pryced corne within this seven yere*: England had wet summers and poor harvests with high prices of grain in 1523 and 1528. Drought was not known to be a problem. *this seven yere* is used as an index of indefinite time (cf. 4P776), so that *Wether* cannot be precisely dated on this reference. A strict interpretation would put the date of the play 1529–34. See Sources 7.

We637 *conclude the*: confute you

We650 *pryncypyll*: chief claim cf. Wy432.

We656 *plumpyng*: swelling. †OED cites this as first usage.

We674 The claim that (the more modern) windmills are mechanically more efficient than (traditional) watermills is historically true.

We685 *Our wyndmylles walke a-mayne in every cost*: run full speed in every region.

We687 *moder*: moderate, check. OED cites this and More's *Apology*.

We693 *wyse as a calfe*: ? Proverbial.

We696–99 'And if, of the two kinds of mill only one is to be kept, I think it fitting that the greatest population be served. It is in the valleys and rolling hills that there is most prosperity and convenient living, and that there are most people – you must concede this.'

We703 *ten of us to one of you*: As an estimate of the relative numbers of water and wind mills this may be quite accurate.

We706 *seven myle*: see above We635.

We714 *wyt nor grace*: intelligence or (God-given) virtue (OED grace 11e)

We719–54 Technical talk of milling is first made by double entendre to refer to bodily functions and then, through Mery Report's clowning reference to his own matrimonial inadequacy, to have topical reference. The degree of risk would depend on precise timing of allusion to Henry's relations with Anne Boleyn. If the play was performed between Christmas 1532 and Lent 1533 then the question of sexual activity would be extremely topical. They were secretly married on 5 January, as soon as Anne knew she was pregnant. Chapuys' doubts about the King's virility and his ability to father a male child were expressed in April 1533 following a conversation with Henry (Ives p. 238. *CSP Sp* 1531–3, 638, *L&P* VI 351). But Heywood's play would feed such rumours.

We721–4 The scatological double entendre is drawn out: 'The bottom I refer to isn't my own, which I inherited, but is held in the right of my wife. She has life-time possession (an entail) of one 'mill' for wind and another for water – and neither of them stands idle.'

We723 *tayle*: limitation of a freehold to a particular person (OED sb² III.3) and buttocks or pudendum (OED sb¹ 5c; cf. We310 and Skelton, *Magnyfycence* 1346).

Ashe-Jones suggests also 'tail-race, or part of the mill race below the wheel' (OED sb[1] 4f).

We726 *For in a good hour be yt spoken*: at an auspicious time, let it be said. A mild oath or asseveration, used as if to invite credulity and to pace the punchline of the joke. The phrase may have vague associations with childbirth.

We729 'All hell is let loose and there is grinding a-plenty.'

We730 *hopper be dusty*: the receiving vessel may be dirty.

We732 *myschevous musty*: disastrously mouldy (OED musty 1 1530)

We733 *my tale*: play on tail=penis (OED 13c) and backside (OED 5).

We735 *We shall fynde meane ye shall taste of the gryst*: 'You shall try my corn for grinding' or a variation on the familiar *osculare fundamentum* topos (cf. We314). Apparently an invitation directed to the women in the audience. The switch from 'I' to 'We' signals the daring of Heywood's conceit, whereby Mery Report boasts and complains in the regal first person plural. The Water Miller (We736) voices doubts about virility such as were current in Henry VIII's court.

We737 *rood*: Christ's cross, with pun here on rod, lewdly gestural.

We739–45 The extended play on technical jargon of milling invites further specific scatological interpretation. The wife's water channel is choked either by menstruation or is simply unavailable. Both suggest inadequacy in Mery Report and invite the Water Miller's professional counselling. She will continue thus despite Mery Report's sexual efforts, unless he 'sets' his stones (testicles) perfectly. He is told, 'Don't worry about the *lydger* (ledger: passive lower stone) only about your *ronner*' (runner: moving upper stone – the male organ). 'But give a thought to the ledger, before you engage with it, because she may not have been properly tooled with a pecker.' The advice here is more appropriate to an inexperienced partner but Mery Report switches at once to his *own* experience and develops the 'insatiable wife' topos.

We744 *peckyng*: action of making radial grooves in the millstone surface using a *peckynge yron* (We751).

We746 *peckt*: struck with a pointed pick or peck †(OED peck v[1] 5 cites We)

We749 *gere not worth a pyn*: for pyn=penis see 4P267.

We753–4 For the Miller's wife to threaten to 'take a new myller' is the comic inverse of the King threatening to take a new wife. Heywood can pursue this line of banter no further. Mery Report turns to address both of them (*our* 754, *yours* 756).

We758–9 *in suche rest*: 'you will both have peace of mind' and also 'both your mills will be stopped'. Mery Report's promise is thoroughly ambiguous.

We763 *over the eares in the dyke*: Proverbial †OED 1553.

We765 Why Saynt Thomas is invoked is unclear. It may be a contemptuous apellation for Cromwell used among a coterie.

We766 The Gentylwoman's entry, coming immediately after this extended obscenity, is suggestive. She behaves as if she is seeking private audience with the god, and is embarassed by 'so mych people'. Her appearance, played by a boy, provides a fine opportunity by means of dress and manner for taking off a particular lady at court and a further means of compromising Jupiter.

We768 *to passe in to the god now*: spoken on entry to the hall; the audience sits between the Gentylwoman and the dais with its curtained throne.

We769 *ye know how he may passe into you*: Q3's 'he knowes how to' is less intimately knowing. Ashe-Jones notes how the clever verbal alteration of 'in to' in the previous line nudges the phrase to obscenity.

We769–73 For discussion of these lines as evidence for staging the play using a curtained throne, having a front ('foresyde') and a 'back syde', see Introduction p. 27.

We781 *by Saynt Antony*: Cf. 4P157. Heywood seems to invoke this saint in the context of 'wandering women', implying here a sexual motive for the journey. See note on J6. In speaking the line the name Anne is also suggested.

We782–815 *And yf yt be your pleasure to mary* . . . A remarkable sequence of playful allusion to topical circumstance of Henry VIII's behaviour in seeking divorce and remarriage. Interpretation may provide a key to dating the play's composition. The new moon, Jupiter's queen of the night, is clearly Anne Boleyn (hence the oaths by saints Anne and Antony) and the old moon, Queen Katherine, whose 'goodness' is 'wasted' (a sad reference to her age and misfortunes in childbearing). This is the 'moste mater' of the 'grete wete' – the storm over Henry's divorce. On a literal level, this picks up the reference to recent heavy rains which have spoiled the harvests (We635) and which will be reformed. The theme is underscored by proverbial weather lore (Whiting M645):

> 'When the new moon lies on her back
> She sucks the wet into her lap.'

and there is also a possible play on 'making moan' (complaining) in love-songs of the period. The future of the reign is punningly seen to lie in the possible pregnancy of Anne Boleyn ('Ye get no rayne tyll her arysynge') – the 'thing' which will 'spryng' is both a new heir and Henry's waned virility, in which confidence is equivocally expressed ('By Saynt Anne . . . he loketh oldely').

We787 *no cause of our hyther resorte*: no reason for her to have resort to our presence here.

We791 *For ye se god loveth them never a dele*: God does not love women at all (spoken to the audience). An old joke about the cursedness of women (Eve) is turned to ironic reflection: the King is not amorously inclined.

We796 *tasted*: enjoyed sexually †OED 3b 1611.

We798 'This is the major cause (or, consequence) of the heavy rains.'

We803 *wythout yt nede*: beyond strict necessity.

We805 *gutters of Noyes flood*: gutter spouting at the time of Noah's flood.

We808 *in this while*: a knowing hint at imminent fruition for Jupiter and his 'new moon'. See above We782.

We816 *let me alone*: leave me to attend to your suit.

We823 *on every syde me*: 'blows' is understood.

We834 *Saynte Quintyne*: The relics of St Quentin, an early Roman martyr, were translated in 835 A.D. A medieval Life and a shrine survive at St-Quentin, N.France. His feast in England was 31 October. Heywood's choice of saint may be dictated by wordplay (ME queynte: pudendum; quintain: a mark to be tilted at – often used in a bawdy figurative sense). Henry VIII jousted until his accident on 24 January 1536. Cf. Skelton, *Bowge of Court* 511.

We842 *daws*: jackdaws, fools. Proverbial.

We843 'You are better than those fools, in that you do not boast of your non-existent virtue.'

We853 *Come on, syrs, but now let us synge lustly*: probably a call to musicians for instrumental support, rather than to 'join in'. A two-part song would be appropriate. Heywood's musicianship would suit him for the part of Mery Report, the maker of the 'play' and servant of Jupiter, would-be intimate of the Privy Chamber.

We856 *fyt*: section of a song, strain (OED sb¹ 1, 2); 'turn' or bout of (sexual) excitement (OED sb² 2).

We859 Sexual innuendo here suggests orgasm as well as a pointed comment on the fate of young ladies coming to court.

We860–1 *yt*: she. The shift to neuter pronoun suggests that talk of 'bryngyng up' leads Mery Report to treat the Gentylwoman as a child, of whom 'it' would be appropriate. Delivery should be gestural as he fusses about.

We863 *I shall forget her*: apparently anticlimactic, perhaps playing on the expected 'forget myself [and behave improperly towards her]'.

We865 *I wys ye*: I apprehend you (OED wis v²).

We867 s.d. Heywood's choice of Launder as antagonist may have been suggested by the proximity of a laundry to his property in Essex. See note to We211.

We876 *symper de cokket*: flirt; a fanciful formation on simper and coquette. OED cites Skelton *Eleanor Rummyng* 1529 as first usage. Cf. *Dial. Provs.* II i 1344.

We892 *I herde by her tale*: It is not necessary to suppose that the actor entered the hall as long ago as this.

We896–7 'That would be different (and more serious) loss, if we launders were to lose our livelihood, than it would be to such creatures of fashion as she is.'

We899 *stande at rewarde of*: be the object of.

We901 '. . . to be ever at loggerheads with people such as I am.'

We909 *parels*: moral dangers. The Launder's autobiography illustrates early Tudor social commonplace.

We921 *naked as my nayle*: Proverbial, †Tilley N4. In contrast to the Gentylwoman, the Launder wears no gloves.

We933 *sone-burned*: cf. We822. Ladies kept their skins fashionably pale by means of veils and bonegraces (PF146). A clue to the Gentylwoman's costume.

We950 *medyll*: meddle, intercede. The word almost always carries a bawdy connotation ('have sexual intercourse' OED meddle 5).

We954 s.d. follows the placing in Q1, 2, 3. In performance it might be more satisfactory for the Gentylwoman to exit after delivering 950.

We955 *stones*: testicles. But there may be a more literal sense if (as was often the case historically) the suitors were expected to bribe the usher with some non-precious stone.

We956 *purs*: moneybag, vagina. Chaucer's Pardoner is threatened in comparable terms (*PardT* 945–5).

We957 *That both our maters in yssew may be lyckly*: that both our requests may come to a successful conclusion. An absurd hope, since the two are contradictory. The bawdy sense is continued in maters and yssew.

We960 *byb*: word formed by 'imitation of repeated movements of the lips' (OED) suggesting mockery. 'Bybble-babble' occurs in *Spider* 64: 12, 833 and *Gentleness* 175.

We973–4 'Just look how with my "more" I have made too much (of her faults), just as she with her "less" has made too little (of my virtues).' A strictly linguistic interpretation seems adequate, though there may possibly be some horseplay here, linking Mery Report's 'to lytell' with a comic fear of impotence in 'shrynke my gere' (977).

We981 *The lenger I lyve the more knave you*: The lenger thou lyvest the more knave thou (Q3) is a form of the proverb more familiar from Wager's play. Tilley L395. The Launder's parting shot suggests her social discomfort in the hall and also her recovery of sufficient dignity to deliver the proverbial sentence.

We985 *prove me a knave*: a stock turn, cf. the 'knaving' sequences in 4P419, 1034, PF585–6.

We986–9 Heywood keeps up a playful juggling between the sense of god as Jupiter, as Christian God, and as monarch. There may be an autobiographical element in Mery Report's rueful comments on the rewards of royal 'service' here.

We991 *casweltees*: occasional payments (in contrast to 'standynge fees').

We997 'As befits such (newly rich) people who get rich by stealing.'

We998–9 'First you will say your "Our Father which art in heaven", next moment you will be swinging, your heels like an incense boat censing the sheriff.' Images of hanging are frequent in drama of the period. On Heywood's narrow escape in summer 1544 see Introduction p. 7.

We999 *shryfe*: sheriff, King's judicial officer responsible for keeping prisoners and executing death sentences.

We1001 s.d. The Boy is to be 'the smallest that knows how to act'. His entrance is set up by mention of the 'greatest frende ye have' (1000) and the effect of his entrance would be more delightful for the contrast with Mery Report's height (see We98, 101). Cameron (*Wether* p. 33) stresses the originality and freshness of the Boy's speech.

We1003 Speech head is lacking in all Qq. While it is possible, as previous editors have assumed, that Boy speaks 1002 to the audience, assigning the line to Mery Report completes the visual joke about the discrepancy of size between them.

We1005 *mysse*: (1) do without, (2) overlook because of my size.

We1011 *set in frame*: properly arranged

We1012 *godfather god*: possibly an allusion to Henry VIII's role as godfather.

We1013 *to have sent*: to cause to be sent

We1014 In hard frost birds will be lured to baited pitfall traps.

We1023 A *hundred boys*: perhaps the number of boys at St Paul's School at this time.

We1027 *my lorde*: the host of the play and supper. T.W. Craik (*Tudor Interludes*, 1958, p. 22) suggests Henry VIII. More likely, perhaps, the London palace of a bishop or nobleman, with the possibility of the King as guest. Cf. Wy676.

We1030 'If any of them cares to ask.'

We1033 *pratelynge*: innocently loquacious (OED 1530)

We1040 *Nonny, nonny*: Tut, tut, how foolish! 'A meaningless expression, often used as a substitute for an indelicacy' (Bevington). The innocent Boy takes up 'none'.

We1042–4 The Boy's urgency suggests there has been no snow that winter. A date of performance in late winter, would accord with We385 and with two traditional Shrovetide themes in the play: scatology and flouting authority.

We1073 *before your selfe dyd appere*: a reminder that only the Gentleman and the Merchant were admitted to the royal presence – as representatives, perhaps, of the two estates of Parliament.

We1076 *as ye know*: Mery Report's account reminds the audience of those suits presented directly to Jupiter and those made to himself.

We1085 *fleesys*: crops (OED 3b 1513) with a strong suggestion of 'shares of booty' †(OED 2b 1601).

We1105 *cooles to blow meanly*: moderate breezes.

We1113–4 'Anyone noticing how this crowd is directed may be sceptical of everyone succeeding in what they want.'

We1132 *as from above*: 'as you have heard coming from up here in heaven', i.e. the disagreement between the gods, recounted by Jupiter at the beginning of the play. At We1137 Jupiter refers to heaven as 'there'; possibly he descends from his throne to level with the audience 'here' (1138).

We1134–5 'As long as heads shun temperateness, bodies will be distempered too.'

We1139–46 Mery Report may sing here.

We1140 'before I finally reached them'.

We1151 *Hed and governour*: Cf. We296

We1154 *lorde of lordes*: dominus dominantium of scripture: Deut.10:17, I Tim.6:15; dominus dominorum Rev.17:14.

We1187–9 'If men were able to arrange continuation of the weather that they individually want, how could they live together? What sort of selfish thoughtlessness is this, to petition us to such an unsatisfactory outcome?'

We1193–4 'Even so, whoever obtained his suit would have earned his own downfall. No single occupation can sustain mankind.'

We1207 *Who that hath yt, ply yt:* Let each man [in turn] use whatever comes to hand.

We1208–10 Compare Jupiter's claim to act for the common good with the similarly self-interested claims of the others characters (We268).

We1218 'That you alone possess the loyal hearts of all who profess chivalry.' *of hertes of all chyvalry*] omitted by Q1, who apparently found the sentiment old fashioned or unsuitable for a printed text intended for general playing, remote from its original 'gentle' context.

We1228 *Our Ladyes sauter:* in the aftermath of More's visit to Coventry (see note on We542), the Watermiller's promise to say the Virgin's Psalter signals Heywood's affirmation of traditional Catholic piety. The Watermiller means that his 'craft' will recite it for the good of the god-king's soul, rather than that they will present him a copy.

We1233–4 Note that the Launder manages to inject a note of aggressive rivalry even in the harmonious resolution.

We1239–40 It is tempting to see Mery Report's deflating comment as addressed to the audience. The actor's tone would be crucial in suggesting either that there has been a lot of fuss about nothing or, per contra, that politically the change is unwelcome.

Colophon Reed (p. 81) argues for printing at the end of the year 1533. See further our discussion in Introduction p. 6.

Textual variants and doubtful readings

Title page *and a very*] and very Q1
We2 *The*] That Q2, 3
We6 *goddes*] goodes Q1
fale] tale Q1 (t altered by hand to f), fall Q2, 3
We13 *heven*] heueu F
We15 *woll*] wolde Q1
We18 *selfe*] it selfe Q3
We20 *Soolly*] Wholly Q2
We21 *we*] well Q2
We29 *father Saturne*] fathers Saturny Q1
We31 *onely so*] onely are so Q3
We37 *father*] fether Q1
We38 *hore*] hote Q1, 2, 3
We39 *mater as*] matters Q3; *his*] is Q1
We41 *thynge*] thyngs Q3
We43 *yt*] yf Q1
We50 *answerynge*] aunswer Q3
We52 *for*] in
We57 *fle*] flye Q3
We59 *evyll*] euyn Q1
We64 *selfe*] selves Q3
We65 *redres*] the redres Q1
We67 *our*] one Q1; *deite*] diet Q3
We68 *so fre*] fre Q1,2,3
We70 *pease*] peale Q1
We71 *surrendryd*] sundryd Q1, 2, 3
We72 *as concernynge*] concernynge Q1, 2, 3

We73 *maner*] maner of Q1
We74 *for*] from Q3
We76 *thynge as*] thynges of Q1
We82 *honour*] houour F
We92 *And*] As Q3
We95 *choyse*] chose Q1,2, chuse Q3
We104 *perse*] perse F
We107 *shewe*] shewe me Q2
We110 *thy*] the Q2
We114 *to mych*] much Q2,3
We115 *maner*] name Q1, 2 order Q3
We116 *Myne*] My Q3
We117 *nother*] none Q1, 2, 3
We118 *promocyon*] proporcion Q3
We121 *elfe*] elft Q1
We135 *forbad*] for bad F
We139 *by*] be Q1
We141 *husbande*] husbandes Q2; *wythout her*] without Q3
We144 *Mynglynge*] Myngled Q2
We146 *thanked*] thanketh Q2,3
We148 *take*] taken Q3
We155 line missing in Q3
We157 *moyst, drye*] most drye, Q1
We158 *fayre*] fryre Q3
We164 *We*] Q3, Well F, Q1, 2; *woll*] F, wolde Q1, wyll Q2, 3
We169 *to the may seme*] maye seme to thee Q3
We178 s.d. *trone*] torne Q1 (?turn).
We187 *carterly*] F St John's, Q2, 3; cartely F Pepys, Q1.
We191 *precyous body*] body Q1
We196 *in*] on Q1, 2, 3
We198 *in*] at Q2, 3
We199 *Barfolde*] Barforde Q1; *in Barbary*] at Barbary Q3
We201 *and Welbeck*] and at Welbeck Q1; at Welbecke and Q2, 3
We204 *Taunton*] Tawton Q1, 2. Tawcon Q3
We206 *Harrow*] Harcow Q1
We207 *Sudbery*] Sutbere, at Q1, 2, 3; *at Shoters*] and at Shoters Q3
We208 *Walsyngham*] Wallyngham, at Wyttam, Q1
We210 *Gravelyn*] Graveling Q3
We211 *Jayberd*] Jabyerde Q1, 2, 3; *Butsbery*] Butlbery Q1
We213 *thus*] so Q2, 3
We214 *have*] hane Q1
We216 *goodly*] good Q2, 3
We217 *gentylwomens*] gentilwomans Q2
We219 *sounde*] soundes Q1
We223 *sooth*] sythe Q3
We224 *syns*] sythe Q3
We226 *brevely*] prevely Q1 (cf. 362, 637)

We230 *Mary and*] Mary Q1

We231 *be ye*] ye be Q3

We238 *never*] never a Q3

We245 **s.h.** *Mery Report*] Meryreport F

We249 **s.d.** *women*] woman Q2, 3

We252 *thou*] you Q1

We260 *your*] our F, Q2; in both copies of F the *y* has been added, above a caret, by the same hand.

We263 *all*] althat Q3; *come*] came Q1;

We269 *eche man may*] eche may Q3

We276 *dale*] pale Q1

We277 *to-comfort*] comfort Q3; *the cry*] cry Q1, thy cry Q2 (cf. 467)

We285 *the*] thy Q1

We286 *whome*] All texts. Grammar requires who, but whome is easier to speak before a vowel.

We302 *in so*] so Q3

We304 *one hede*] hede Q1, 2, my head Q3

We305 *syns*] sythe Q3

We307 *a treasour*] treasour Q1

We312 *wyll no*] wyll have no Q3

We314 *tayle*] head Q3

We318 *lyve ye*] lyve Q1

We320 *as*] as sone as Q3

We322 *do*] doest Q3

We325 *my . . . my*] me . . . my Q1

We327 *yf I*] yf it Q3

We328 *Syns*] sythe Q3

We328 **s.d.** *Entreth*] Here entreth Q3

We329 *now welcome*] welcome Q3

We331 **s.h.** *Marchaunt*] Marchaunte F

We333 *sewter*] a suter Q3

We335 **s.h.** *Mery Reporte*] Q3, om. F, Q2; Mery re. Q1, printed exceptionally in right margin opposite 334, apparently after the dialogue had been set.

We336 *make*] make a Q2

We345 **s.h.** *Marchaunt*] Marthaunt F

We346 *besecheth*] beseched Q2

We351 *stryfe*] gryfe Q1

We352 *ye*] you Q3

We354 *encreaseth*] Q1, 2, 3; euereaseth F

We355 *we*] ye Q1

We356 *of*] or Q1, 2; *on*] in Q3

We362 *brevely*] preuely Q1

We366 *wynde*] windes Q2, 3

We368 *seylys*] selles Q1

We369 *And*] Aud F

We370 *Eest*] F

We374 *ere*] F, Q2; or Q1, when Q3

We380 *yf ye*] if it Q3

We384 *to go*] go to Q2
We385 *or*] ere Q3
We387 *byr lady*] by lady Q1
We389 *maye*] must Q3
We393 *come*] came Q3
We395 *requyte*] rebuyte Q3
We398 *at thys*] at his Q2, 3
We410 *Pleasyth it your maystershyp it is so*] 1st it om. Q2; Pleaseth your maystershippe so to do Q3
We418 *where*] when Q1
We426 *I*] we Q1, 2, 3
We434 *se*] se well Q1, 2, 3
We440 *founde ye*] found you Q2, 3
We441 *bounde ye* bound you Q3
We442 *dum*] dn Q1
We447 *The wynde is so stronge the rayne can not fall*] line om. Q2, 3
We453 *There is*] Theres Q3
We456 *and yet*] as yer Q2; at it Q3
We457 *gryste*] grynden Q1
We459 *mylstons*] mylstone Q2, 3
We461 *our extre, our*] onr extre onr F (axeltree)
We463 *ware*] were Q2
We466 *prycked*] pycked Q2
We467 *sewe*] shew Q3
We469 *boldely*] bodily Q2, 3
We472 *ye . . . ye*] you . . . you Q1
We473 *rudely ye*] rudly/ye Q3
We479 *lesson, syr*] lesson Q3
We486 *muste be*] shalbe Q2, 3
We487 *ye*] you Q3
We488 *no nother*] none other Q1, 2, 3
We491 *but for*] for Q2,3
We494 In the r.h. margin of Q1 a 16th-cent. hand has written 'lord hares u.curtsy & comand bless'.
We495 *solycyter*] solyter Q2
We505 s.d. *Entreth*] Here entreth Q2, 3
We506 *How*] Ho, Q3
We510 *hole*] holde Q1
We512 *skantely*] skantly Q1
We515 *of*] to Q2,3
We525 *goddys*] good Q3
We527 *myght be*] might not be Q3
We528 *that gere passe for I*] this gere passe I Q2, 3
We538 *ye*] the Q3
We539 *ye*] you Q2,3
We545 *lordes*] lorde
We548 *our*] F, Q3 your Q1, 2
We549 *shall we*] we shall Q3

We551 *he*] yᵉ Q1
We564 *thought weykest*] though weyken Q1
We566 *but*] and Q2, 3
We567 *hange*] stande Q2, 3
We569 *woll*] wyll Q1, 2, 3
We581 *bred*] brede Q2, bredth Q3
We582 *shyppys blow*] shype blowes Q1
We583 *mast and shrowde*] man and shrowde Q2, man and shrow Q3
We587 *synde*] all texts (i.e. assigned)
We595 *lepe*] lepte Q1
We598 *or water*] of water F, Q1, 2, 3
We605 *then*] om.Q3
We610 *spake*] speake Q3; *wynde*] minde Q2, wyne Q3
We617 *all in fansyes*] all fansies Q2
We620 *one*] an Q1
We623 *selfe*] it selfe Q3
We625 *he*] it Q3; *take*] take a Q1
We628 *syrs*] syr Q1
We630 *who so*] who Q1
We632 *sayd*] sayne Q3
We637 *brevely*] prevely Q1
We644 *yf come*] of corne Q1
We651 *it were impossybyll*] it impossible Q2
We652 *or it can*] it cannot Q3
We656 *plumpyng*] plumynge Q1, pluming Q2, plumming Q3; *maner*] maner of Q3
We659 *thynge*] thynges Q1, 2, 3
We660 *skowrynge*] showrynge Q1, 2, scouring, and Q3
We661 *lacketh what bestely*] lacketh, there is beastly Q3
We671 *thys*] the Q3
We672 *the reste*] ye reste F
We673 *our myllys*] wyll Q1, our myll Q2, your myll Q3
We674 *one our*] an houre Q1, 2, 3
We675 *thy*] the Q1
We679 *Whych thyng*] which Q3
We685 *walke*] F,Q2, walde Q1, Q3
We689 *all*] at al Q2, 3
We693 *wyse*] as wise Q3
We695 *those*] chose Q2
We697 *yt*] F, Q3, ye Q1, 2
We704 *all*] and Q1, 2, 3
We709 s.d. *Entreth*] Here entreth Q3
We710 *knaves*] knave Q1
We716 *let*] set Q1
We717 *fet*] fete Q2, feate Q3 (rhyme)
We724 *for wynde . . . for water*] of wind . . . of water Q3
We727 *gate is no*] gates not Q2, gates is not Q3
We730 *whether that*] whether Q3

We741　*settynge your*] settynge of Q1, 2, 3
We742　*ronner*] rynner Q2
We746　*peckt, peckt, peckt*] pect Q3
We752　*no*] not the Q2, 3
We762　*you not*] not you Q3
We767　*where*] were Q1
We769　*ye know how he may*] he knowes how to Q3
We771　*so wyde*] to wyde Q3
We785　*lordshyp*] lordshypen Q1
We795　*of a*] a Q2
We799　*leake*] F, Q3 lyke Q1, 2; *they can*] they Q1
We807　*fell on*] fellon F, fal on Q3
We809　*Then a old*] The a old F. The line was cramped by the turned end of 808 and has two superscript bars for missing n. The printer may simply have neglected one here.
We829　*is this*] is Q2, 3
We831　*nor no*] nor Q1
We832　*get*] let Q2, 3; *the stretes*} streetes Q3
We834　*Jet*] Yet Q1, 2
We835　*passe*] paste Q1
We838　*for our*] of our Q3
We841　*house to passe tyme*] house of passe tyme Q2
We844　*the nyght*] this night Q1
We850　*have I*] I have Q1
We852　*even hartely*] hertely Q3
We853　*but now*] but Q3; *lustly*] lustely Q1
We854　*this*] it Q3
We855　*a vowe*] avowe Q2
We858　*tyme yt is*] tymes is Q1, 2, 3
We860　*so fete yt is, so nete*] so farre it is so nere Q2
We862　*my selfe*] me selfe Q1
We864　*pray you*] pray ye Q1
We871　*Byr lady I wolde ye*] By lady you Q1; *myne*] my Q1
We873　*Nay . . . I syr not*] Now . . . syr I wot not Q3
We876　*dally*] dayly Q3; *symper de cokket*] simper the cocked Q2, 3
We887　*lyttell*] either litle Q3; *or*] of Q2
We897　*nycebyceters*] nyceby ceters Q1
We904　*as yonge*] yonge Q3
We913　*thy*] the Q3
We918　*the*] thy Q3
We923　*thy*] the Q1, 3; *honest*] other Q3
We925　*so oft*] oft Q3; *to*] to be
We926　*so do*] do so Q3
We933　*sone-burned*] sone burned F
We934　*smytten*] smytter Q1
We935　*beshytten*] be shytter Q1
We939　*ton*] one Q3
We940　*I wolde kepe*] I kepe Q1
We944　*pray you*] praye Q3

We948 *show*] knowe Q3

We954 **s.d.** We follow the placing in Q1, 2, 3. In F this direction was placed in the left margin in italic type after the dialogue had been set in black letter, so that it is impossible to locate it precisely.

We959 *thou dost*] thou Q1

We965 *ye*] he Q3

We969 *abylyte*] your hability Q3

We974 *lest*] laste Q1

We979 *thynke best*] thinke it best Q3

We981 *The lenger I lyve the more knave you*] The lenger thou lyvest the more knave thou Q3

We982 **s.h.** *Mery Report*] Meryreport F

We985 *prove me a knave*] call me knave Q1, 2, 3

We989 *devyls*] deuyll Q1

We990 *standynge*] Q1, 2, 3; standynges F is noted by OED as anomalous.

We991 *devyls*] deuyll Q1

We994 *do no wurse*] do worse Q1, 2, 3

We999 *sens the shryfe*] sens the stryfe Q1, sence the strete Q2, 3

We1000 *ye*] you Q2, 3

We1002 *This*] The Q3; *al lycklyhod*] allycklyhod F, Q1, 2

We1002 **s.h.** *Boy*] Mery report F printed at 1002, deleted with a thick inky line in both copies. Q2, 3 omit.

We1012 *godfather god*] god father god Q1

We1018 *flycker*] slyckere Q1, flytter Q2

We1025 *godfather*] god father

We1026 *owne*] one Q3

We1028 *whoso*] whose F

We1029 *bellyes*] bylles Q1

We1043 *lend*] sende Q1, 2, 3

We1049 **s.d.** *goth forth*] goeth out Q1

We1050 **s.h.** *Mery Report*] Meryreport F; *sonne*] soone Q3

We1065 *thys*] F, Q3; his Q1, 2; *is spent*] ye spent Q3

We1066 *mo*] me Q2

We1072 *I come now*] I to me Q2; *at*] to Q3

We1077 *all*] as Q1

We1080 *after thys*] after Q1

We1081 *An other man*] Another Q3

We1082 *all of*] all Q3

We1088 *was so*] was Q2

We1089 *fale*] fall Q1

We1093 *banysht*] banyshe Q1

We1100 *her*] Q2, 3; here F, Q1

We1101 *came*] come Q1

We1102 *pytfale*] pytfall Q1, 2, 3

We1106 *extermely*] F, Q1; extremely Q2, 3

We1107 *in water*] water Q3

We1108 *but all*] but Q3

We1111 *frost*] the frost Q1

We1112 *Byr*] By Q1.

We1115 *lacketh*] lackelh F

We1117 *tother*] F tothet(?), other Q1, 2, 3

We1119 *shrewed*] shrewe Q1

We1123 *ben*] best Q1

We1127 *depart hens*] departe Q3

We1132 *debate as*] debates Q2; *ye*] he Q1

We1133 *debate*] bebate F; *selfes*] selves Q1, 3

We1138 *woll*] wyll Q1

We1139–46 Q1, 2, 3 do not indent these lines.

We1150 *presyd to*] presed as Q2

We1152 *in*] is Q2

We1158 *sent*] sende Q1

We1171 *abteyne*] F

We1176 ·*women*] woman Q2

We1184 *ye all*] ye Q2

We1185 *you sewd*] your sute Q3

We1190 *tother*] other Q1, 2, 3

We1191 *some*] the some Q1, 2, 3

We1194 *no one*] none Q2,

We1199 *tone . . . tother*] one . . . other Q1, 2, 3

We1204 *to attende*] attend Q3

We1207 *and suer*] and serve Q3

We1211 s.h. *Gentylman*] F, Gentylwoman Q1, 2, 3

We1218 *of hertes of all chyvalry*] omitted by Q1

We1219 *we marchauntes*] marchaunts Q1

We1226 *as our onely*] onely as our Q1

We1234 *make*] make god Q3

We1237 *promyse you*] promyse Q2

We1238 *make my*] make Q3; *some*] some[r?] Q1.

Q1 ends, lacking sig. F4. 'What should follow, is wanting' in 19th cent. hand.

We1243,1247,1250 *yerth*] earth Q2, 3

We1248 *make*] most Q2, 3

Colophon Imprinted at Lond/don in Paules Churche yearde, at the / Sygne of the Sunne, by Antho/nie Kytson Q2

Imprinted at Lon/don by Jhon Awdeley dwelling/ in litle Britayne Street, beyonde / Aldersgate. Q3

Verses from a lost Play on the Government of Reason preserved in Thomas Whythorne's *Autobiography* pp. 73–4.

Bekawz I hav heer tofor towched sumwhat of þe government of Reazon & will in mankynd, it seemth vnto me þat I shiuld not pas any furder in þis diskowrs till I hav shewd yow sumwhat mor plainly of þeir properties an[d] governments, wherfor I will heer shew vnto yow þe wurdz of my old master mr Haywood, þe which hee did wryt in A komedy or play þat hee hat mad of þe parts of man, in þe which after þat he hath mad Reazon to chalenʒ vnto him self þe siuperiorite and government of all þe parts of Man, and also to kommaund althings lyving vpon þe earth, hee maketh reazon to say þus (in meeter[)] for him self.

[*as prose*]

And þe diffrens between man þe kommaunder,
and beas[ts] being by man kommaunded,
iz only Reazon in man, þe disserner
of good and ill, þe good in man elekted
by me, and þ'ill in man by mee reʒekted.
man obeing mee shynth in exsellensy,
and disobeing mee, shewth mans insolensy.

Now sin[s I] reazon am þ'[o]nly qu[a]lyte,
þa[t q]ualifiet man [in s]uch A temp[er]ans
az setteth man in plas of prinsipalite
abov all beasts to stand in governans
who but I over man shiuld him self advans,
to govern lykwyz, sins I bring man þerto,
and keep man þerin doing az I bid him do.

The French source of *Johan Johan*

La farce nouvelle du Pasté was probably composed in the second half of the fifteenth century. Its anti-feminist theme and stylistic idiom are those of *Les Quinze Joies de Mariage* from the same period. Our translation is made from the text printed by Gustave Cohen (*Recueil de farces françaises inédites du XV siècle*, 2 vols. Cambridge, Mass. 1949), although occasionally we have preferred the MS readings to Cohen's emendations. The most important instance is in attributing lines 252–71 to the Man, where Cohen gives 261–3 and 265–9 to the Wife.

The *Pasté* is composed mainly in octosyllabic couplets, with some passages of shorter lines and of alternating rhymes. Most interesting are its incorporation of *rondeau* forms. Musically, the rondeau has two figures and these are repeated (with small allowed variations) in an eight-figure pattern:

I II I' I II' II I II

Textually, there are two repeated 'refrain' lines, A and B, and the other lines use the same rhymes:

A B a A a b A B

The farce of the *Pasté* incorporates three complete rondeau passages and one half rondeau.

The play opens (1–8, ABaAabAB) with a rondeau in the form of a *demande d'amour* with the answer given. In the drily pathetic exchange of impotent husband and wife (463–70, ABaAabAB), the 'hole in my bucket' theme is pin-pointed. Finally, (694–701, ABaAabAB) the two chief dramatic actions of the play, chafing the wax and serving the pie, are juxtaposed. The half-rondeau (205–8) uses a traditional refrain, A *vrayment je vous ayme bien*, ironically as part of the Wife's strategy of deception. The pattern ABaA here tails off with re-use of the a,b and B rhymes.

As the pace and violence of action increase, more frequent and apparently random repetition of a 'refrain' (*Je chauffe la cire*) occurs a score of times, at intervals of between three and fifteen lines. This is a feature which Heywood imitates, though he does not adopt the formal structure of repeated lines which make up the rondeau pattern.

The use of rondeaux in the *Pasté* may indicate that song and mime were an integral feature of original performance.

A new, excellent, and very entertaining farce about the pie;
for three persons to play, i.e. Man, Wife, and Priest.

Man begins   *Now guess what it is that I ask*
        And I will tell you what I seek;
        Without anyone ordering you
        Now guess what it is that I ask.
        Since my brain prompts me to it,   5
        To know better what it is I'm asking for,
        Now guess what it is that I ask
        And I will tell you what I seek:
        It is my wife that I am seeking.

        O God, may the devil take her.   10
        She goes about from door to door
        Like a Saint Anthony pig
        With an old woman
        Leading her here and there.
        Heavens, I don't know where she goes;   15
        But, by the holy blood, whoah, no more!
        Just let us come back
        Together in this place!
        By Saint John, I make a vow to God,
        See if I don't set about beating her!   20
        At each blow I want to beat her down,
        And I want to throw her on the ground,
        And drag her about by the hair:
        I'm furious not to be beating her now.
        I shall pay her back properly;   25
        There's not a woman from here to the Loire
        Will ever have been so well thumped.
        Beat her – but what then? If I kill her
        I could well be hanged.
        Heavens, if I beat her body   30
        And receive a hundred blows as punishment
        Do you think that she'll improve?
        Not a bit! I shall not beat her at all.
        But if she does something out of order
        Or neglects her housekeeping,   35
        Shall I not beat her for that?
        By the holy flesh, I'll do it.
        I shall beat her and drag her
        At my pleasure from place to place,
        So much, I swear by God,   40
        That I shall speak with my neighbour thus:
        'Whom are you scolding, Johnny John?'

311

'I am scolding my wicked wife,
The foulest, most notorious –
She only goes gadding about,   45
And I cannot make her keep
To the house, up nor down.'
I reckon he will say, 'Then beat her.'
But if I beat her, when I beat her
I shall make her wickeder   50
And she'll become even worse.
'Then don't beat her at all, John John.'
Not beat her? Why ever not?
Is she not my own to chastise?
If I [do not] beat her soundly   55
And people hear me scolding
They will laugh, that's the point.
'Johnny John, but you don't beat her,
You don't beat her, Johnny John!'
And if I chastise her so   60
That she *does* stay at home,
Wouldn't that be well done – why not?
He is a rotten man
Who spares his wife a beating.
'And so it is by Saint Nicolas,   65
John John, but you do not beat her!'
If I don't beat her, how shall I win?
I'll do it, if I knock her down
Stark dead, because it pleases me.
Beat her – beating is bad;   70
Beat her not, then in that case
She will never do well; so I'll beat her.
If she improves then I'll let her alone.
But if she wants to be the mistress,
Then I'll beat her soundly night and morning.   75
And if she lets John John be
Master of the house?
Then I'll not beat her. Not beat her at all?
Zounds, I shall though.
Come on now, I shall beat her   80
This way and the other way
Right way up and round the back
And all about, my Marion!
Must we all be marrying?
What a blessing marriage is!   85
But where the devil can she be?
I reckon she is at the priest's

And the priest is up on top.
I'm afraid of being deceived –
But still I think that I am not.   90
I get angry because I cannot
See what our little madam is up to,
And yet I know that she goes there.
Many respectable women go there,
But who knows what they do there?   95
And yet it is only amusement.
The wife goes there so often
That I'm worried about this business,
But all the same she is his gossip
And one should not suspect such a thing.   100
But how does this gossiping come about?
My wife has had no children.
So what if I forbid her
To go there any more, she'll still go,
As before, or she'll chose   105
Another place like as not.
Lord, this has gone on and on,
Coming on for a year-and-a-half
By Saint Anthony, I do believe
That he has only to start a meal   110
And already she's dancing attendance.
If he asks for something to be done
I've no doubt it's as good as done.
Just like the third son again!

Now, shortly, by the altar sacrament,   115
She shall have her payment for it,
For I shall rub her in the dirt
So that she will find it hard to move.

Wife, with a pie.   And what are you muttering about?
    Will you never do anything but scold?   120
    What the devil have you to complain of?
    Well, John John, is there something that you need?
Man   I was only saying that
    Your good self would have come
    Before I had kindled the fire.   125
    Now come and get warm, my love!
Wife   Alas! Alas!
Man   Saint Mary!
    Heavens, I shall not complain
    If you've done something untoward –
    I always agree with you completely.   130

Wife	Misfortune on the soul and body	
	Of anyone who stirs things up out of spite.	
Man (aside)	May I be mad and dead	
	If she has not come straight from the priest's.	
Wife	What do you say?	
Man	I just said, to be	135
	An hour or two taking one's pleasure	
	Can only be good.	
Wife	Ha! The master!	
Man	Let's not have any strife.	
Wife (aside)	If he does not scold, strike or thump,	
	If he does not threaten, shout or beat,	140
	There is never anything that can please him.	
Man (aside)	If around you the priest	
	Does not frolic, or lay you	
	Beneath him, you are never at ease.	
Wife	Upon my soul, if you don't mind,	145
	Many times I am upset	
	When you think I'm having a good time.	
Man (aside)	May it please God and Saint Ailment	
	To put you in a fiery furnace	
	And see if I would get you out!	150
Wife	Now guess where I was	
	Before I came in here.	
Man	You were before Saint Maurice	
	On your knees, or at Notre Dame.	
Wife	No I wasn't.	
Man	Well, where then, wife?	155
	I beg you, tell me the truth.	
Wife	Truly, we were making a pie,	
	I and Janet, my gossip,	
	And the priest, our companion,	
	And the daughter of his neighbour	160
	And the nephew of my godmother	
	And the uncle of my two cousins.	
	The priest paid for the chickens	
	And Janet put in the flour.	
Man (aside)	Ha! By the holy womb, she's the finest	165
	Bawd from here to Rome.	
Wife	What?	
Man	But isn't he a fine man –	
	Our priest, Master Guillaume?	
Wife	For goodness sake, husband!	
Man	Say, wife,	
	Without getting angry if you can.	170

Wife	I never go to the priest
	Without his being at his devotions
	Or going in procession
	Or saying some prayer.
Man (aside)	Yes, all around the bed, 175
	Just the two of you, no more,
	And at the end you climb on top
	To bring the procession to its close.
Wife	What did you say?
Man	That he must do so
	For the salvation of souls. 180
Wife	John John.
Man	What is your pleasure, wife?
	By my soul, I love you so much.
Wife	Now I shall tell you straightaway
	What I want you to do.
	This pie, I'll have you know, 185
	We have had made all together,
	As I shall relate to you.
Man	Alright, see here,
	What's it to me if he donates it?
Wife	Put me on all the gibbets
	That anyone could take me from alive 190
	If the priest. . .
Man	Ha! Don't swear.
	What is it? You're getting cross?
Wife	Lord, my dear, you will read in
	To this event something non-existent.
Man	By heaven, I am your little rascal, 195
	Your love, your husband, your everything.
Wife	Heavens, how my blood does boil
	When you get angry hastily.
Man	Upon my faith, this pie is spoiling,
	We must put it on the embers. 200
Wife	If the priest were not so good a man
	Upon my faith, we might eat it
	Without him.
Man	We'll never treat him so.
	Let him eat it, above all!
Wife	*Truly, I love you well* 205
	For the way you love your friend.
Man	What, aren't I his parishioner?
Wife	*Truly I love you well.*
Man	Ha! Thanks to Saint Julien
	For the godfather and his gossip – 210

	I think I can say 'friend'.	
	'Ah, my son, preserve my child!'	
	By heavens, I'm suspicious!	
Wife	Come now,	
	Since you want to invite him in,	
	I beg you to go at once	215
	To look for him so we may eat together.	
Man	See the feast assembling,	
	By Saint Paul and Saint Remy!	
Wife	What did you say?	
Man	That he shall come here,	
	By heavens, as if you had sworn it.	220
(aside)	Let him be plagued with fevers –	
	And anyone who brings him into my house.	
Wife	What's that you say?	
Man	That he is my superior,	
	My confessor and my friend.	
	You go and fetch him, I beg you,	225
	And I will look after the pie.	
Wife	By Saint Anthony, I won't.	
	But you shall go, I beg you,	
	And tell him.	
	Holy Mary!	
	It's not I who should tell him.	230
Wife	But you shall tell him, by Saint Mary.	
Man	You tell him.	
Wife	No, you, by our Lord.	
Man	Ah, truly, you shall have the honour	
	[line missing in the French]	
	And the praise for conveying	235
	This pleasure which we have begun.	
Wife, weeping	I shall be scolded a thousand times	
	For the coming of this worthy man.	
Man	How's that?	
Wife	I understand very well what	
	You fear, but you are mistaken.	240
	Let me die a dreadful death	
	If he is not a true catholic.	
Man (aside)	He is better known by everyone to be	
	A ribald and a rake,	
	A liar and a brothel-monger,	245
	A hypocrite, a bigot, a man of shame,	
	Than you are known to be my wife,	
	By heaven or by the devil!	
Wife	What did you say?	

Man	Let's lay the table	
	And sharpen the knives.	250
Wife	Put up the trestles then.	
Man	Wait, I'll take off my coat;	
	I'm afraid that it will be stolen,	
	I don't know where to put it down.	
[to the audience]	Who says he can look after it?	255
	Ah, it will be safe here.	
	Oh, look, some dog piss there –	
	It would be quite spoiled.	
	I'd put it in the hearth	
	Except that it might get singed.	260
	Sir, put it underneath you	
	Or between you and the wine butt.	
	Well, come out here!	
	Look after it, I'll give it to you.	
	Ha! He is right next to the door,	265
	He could easily bolt from there.	
	I will put it down right here.	
	Don't let a soul walk over it.	
	Remove the torch from up above.	
[to Wife]	Look, now I am ready to leave;	270
	Don't say that I am holding things up.	
Wife	Go at once and tell him to come.	
Man	I'm going.	
Wife	Set the table.	
Man	At once.	
Wife	Go to him.	
Man	Holy Mary, enough!	
	Think about finding some candles.	275
Wife	Come back and set the table.	
	Ah, God! You're a fine one!	
Man	By Saint Peter of Rome. . .	[line missing]
	And the priest and my wife.	
	[part line missing]	
Wife	Go to him!	280
Man	She will not leave off today.	
	The devil fetch him to the house!	
Wife	Come on.	
Man	What do you want?	
Wife	Carry this salt	
	And these candles to the table.	
Man	There you are. And the devil	285
	Take priest and priestess!	

Wife	Go and tell him to get ready	
	And that no excuse will do.	
Man	Upon my faith, the pie is burning.	
Wife	Go and wash these two cups.	290
Man	I'm going. The devil makes you prattle on like this.	
Wife	Go and make him hurry up,	
	And meanwhile I bring everything.	
Man	The pie is burning on this side,	
	Do you see?	
Wife	Go on, go on!	295
Man	I'm going to look for him.	
Wife	Come back!	
	Check that there's some wine.	
Man	The blessing of Saint Martin on	
	Table and priest	
	And wine and bread and pie	300
	And fire and candle	
	And trestles and salt –	
	Here's a curious state of things.	
Wife	Go and tell him to come at once,	
	For upon my faith I'm dying of hunger.	305
Man	I'm going to him.	
Wife	Fetch me that bread	
	Lest it get forgotten.	
Man	It's time to turn over	
	The pie – look to it, my girl!	
Wife	Alas! He has a tongue able	310
	To chatter on about this pie.	
	Go and fetch the priest,	
	I've told you a thousand times.	
Man	If the pie should get cold	
	I swear it's ruined.	315
Wife	He should be back again by now.	
	What are you doing? Be off with you!	
Man	Turn the pie frequently.	
	Shall I put it on the table?	
Wife	Hurry up, for the devil's sake	320
	Haven't you babbled on enough?	
	Upon my faith, this humble pie	
	Is really in a state of bloody grace!	
Man	And just look how the grease	
	Is burning here and all around.	325
	Ha! By our Lady, what a pie!	
	I wish to God I'd tasted it.	
Wife	John!	

Man	I'm turning the pie;	
	I swear that it was spoiling.	
Wife	By God, if you were to get your deserts	330
	You would get it in the teeth.	
Man	Would to God it was already inside	
	And that you had the priest in your belly!	

(Before the Priest's house)

	Hey, *domine!* Shall I come in	335
	To the house? Hallo!	
Priest	Who is there?	
	Ah, John John: *bona vita*	
	Vobis bene veneritis	
	Quomodo.	
Man	*Bene et vobis.*	
Priest	So, what's up?	
Man	Here's the point:	
	My wife and I beg you	340
	Humbly, and entreat you	
	To come this fine night	
	And sup with us.	
Priest	Ah, I cannot,	
	By my faith, forgive me.	
Man	Oh you shall come, if you please,	345
	I implore you, Master Guillaume,	
	At least for the love of my wife,	
	If you're unwilling on my account.	
Priest	Stay here at the presbytery	
	And you shall sup with me	350
	And I shan't go out.	
Man	Alas, why so?	
	For the love of my wife,	
	Is there any trouble	
	Between you two, or some quarrel?	
Priest	To speak just between you and me,	355
	She is a most worthy woman;	
	I have had the charge of her soul	
	For a long time, but I have found her	
	Wise and modest, well-behaved,	
	Without a fault – it is so.	360
	I only know in her one little thing	
	For which I often have reproved her,	
	And she has not taken such a course	
	As to deserve any feeling of anger.	
Man	Ah, priest, may God reward you!	365
	I am much obliged to you.	

Priest	Though she may not appear pure to you
	And a worthy woman as to her body,
	She surely is.
Man	I never doubted it at all,
	Thanks to God and to your teaching. 370
	May I know the root
	Of the quarrel between you and her?
Priest	I will tell you, but keep it
	Safe and secret.
Man	So I will.
Priest	She holds a little grudge against me 375
	But I take no offence.
Man	Why's that?
Priest	Because I often enjoin
	Her to some penance
	In that she scolds you too often.
	She blames me, but it must be done. 380
Man	Upon my faith, saving your presence –
Priest	I am certain that is the matter.
Man	Upon my soul, she does not hate you.
(aside)	But am I not the son of a whore?
	I believed plain and clear 385
	That he loved her to deceive her,
	Yet he proves himself dutiful,
	Like a good and loyal friend.
Priest	If ever she speaks evil to me
	I pardon her, upon my soul 390
	Thank your wife for me
	And say I will not come.
Man	And shall I not know
	Where you have promised to sup?
Priest	Upon my faith, I and my friends 395
	Got together this morning;
	One gave the bread, another the wine,
	Another the meat, another the crust;
	Thus worthily we got together
	For the sake of greater fellowship, 400
	And we had a pie made
	To calm a quarrel I knew about
	Between some women, as I thought,
	And I have promised to sup with them.
Man	Where have you had it taken, 405
	Tell me, Master Guillaume?
Priest	It was given to your wife –
	She had the keeping of the pie.

Man	God's body, has she the keeping of it?
	It is by the fire in my house. 410
Priest	Really! What an excellent thing!
	Who ever could have fetched it there?
	What do you say?
Man	It is a pie
	That Janet, your friend,
	And her father's cousin, 415
	And the priest, Master Guillaume,
	And his two cousins, and my wife
	Have had made – am I not right?
Priest	Ah, it's true! I shall go.
Man	At once
	Let's go; my wife is waiting for us. 420
Priest	If she does not scold me
	I shall be content to be patient.
Man	By God's flesh, if she scolds you,
	If she finds fault or complains,
	I'll put a stick in your hand – 425
	Chastise her as it pleases you.
Wife to Man	The devil took you there, sir –
	Hanging about so long!
	There is no water to wash
	A single hand – what a layabout! 430
	Here, carry this bucket
	And fill it with water, quick!
Man	I hardly ever rest
	For long, God be praised!
Wife	Go for the water.
Man	And the pie – 435
	Is it time to put it on the table?
Wife	Go for the water, for the devil's sake!
Priest	Well, my gossip, is that nicely said?
Man (aside)	May I be cursed by God
	If I would not rather be hanged. 440
Wife, kissing the Priest	You are most welcome.
	Is there someone whom you love?
	Man (aside) How close he is getting!
	I'm not so pleased about that.
Priest (to Wife)	By God, if you had heard 445
	The lies and deceptions,
	The clever words, the mutterings
	That I have made John listen to,
	You would rather have been hanged
	Than kept yourself from laughing, 450

	My dear gossip.	
Wife	At what?	
Priest	I'd have to explain.	
Wife	I know nothing about this gossiping –	
	Leave off this gossip-business	
	Since it's just the two of us.	

Man (to the audience)

What the devil is this, my lords?	455
Zounds! How he holds her	
So close.	

Wife	You're back?	
	There with the water. We'll wash our hands.	
Man	Upon my faith, it was full just now,	
	Only a moment ago, as I thought,	460
	But the reason is it's split,	
	Your bucket – look at the hole.	

Wife	*Then stop it up.*	
Man	*I can't.*	
Priest	*A little wax.*	
Man	*Who's got any?*	
	It all splashed out beside the well.	465
Wife	*Then stop it up.*	

Man	*I can't.*	
	It's split.	
Wife	Where?	
Man	Here.	
Wife	So what?	
Man	Not a drop of water left.	
Wife	*Then stop it up.*	
Man	*I can't.*	
Priest	*A little wax.*	
Man	*Who's got any?*	470

Look at the crack – it is split.	
It has been so often banged,	
Knocked and pushed and pressed,	
That it's shot full of holes.	
Saint Peter bless the bucket	475
And the leak and the split	
And the wax and the canvas	
And the hole and the stuffing	
And the plug and the staff –	
By the holy flesh, I don't know what to say!	480

Priest	Here are two wax candles
	Which Dame Janet, my gossip,
	Gave me yesterday.
Wife	Alas, good sir,
	Isn't it a sin to use them?
Priest	Stop up your vessel:
	No need for fear, I assure you.
Man	How hard this wax is!
Wife	It needs a little rubbing.
[Priest]	The one who gave the candles,
	She's a good little woman.
Wife	Is that my gossip Janet?
Priest	Yes, she's a virtuous body.
Wife	Would to God I were as good
	As I believe her to be.
Man (aside)	She's the biggest bawd,
	By the holy flesh, that I know of.
Wife	What's that you say?
Man	I chafe
	This wax and break my hands on it.
	Take out the pie at least
	So it may be eaten while it's hot.
Wife	But you must warm the wax.
Man	Make him sit down – be seated, sir.
Wife	Go and chafe the wax,
	Meanwhile the priest and I
	Shall sup.
Man	And the pie –
	Shall I eat none, you mean to say?
Wife	Go and chafe the wax
	At once, and say no more.
Priest	*Benedicite!*
Man	*Dominus.*
Wife	Go to the fire, for the devil's sake!
Man	I come to bless this board
	As has always been my way,
	To honour you, Sir Priest.
Priest	John John, you make me laugh.
Man	And good health to the pie.
Wife	Go back to the fire, don't talk so much.
Man	I've turned it over lots of times.
Priest	We must eat, for it is spoiling.
Man	My wife has given you some.
Wife	Go and chafe the wax.
Man	Isn't this a real martyrdom,

	To see others eat and have none yourself?	
	Upon my soul, I've hung about so long,	
	May Saint Peter bless the bowl,	
	The digestion and the eating!	525
	No one could make me laugh at it.	
Wife	What are you doing?	
Man	I chafe the wax	
	And think of how to make you cheer.	
	May Saint Peter bless the bucket,	
	The crack and the hole.	530
	At least if I could eat	
	Just a mouthful, things would be better.	
Wife	I drink to you.	
Man, coming to the table	Anything you need?	
Priest	Nothing at all.	
Man	You've only to ask.	
Wife	Go away and chafe the wax.	535
	We shall hear you well at the table.	
Man	Then do so, by the devil	
	And by his bloody mother!	
Priest, drinking		
	John, my friend,	
	See here my gossip,	540
	Of whom I am so fond.	
Man	Now drink, good sir.	
Priest	What are you doing, my friend?	
Man	I chafe the wax.	
Wife	This is good wine.	545
Priest	This is good chicken –	
	Speak no ill of it.	
Wife	Look at that baboon!	
Priest	What's Johnny John doing?	
Man	I chafe the wax	550
	And fumigate myself alone;	
	I burn myself in clouds of soot	
	And dare not say a word.	
	It is a fine custom –	
	One drinks, the other sups,	555
	I chafe the wax.	
Wife	Upon my word, it's good to laugh	
	At a man whom folly leads.	
	See how John John takes such pains	
	To chafe the wax.	560
Man (aside)	May you be warmed	
	By a feverish plague,	

	And the company assembled here,	
	And you and him, and him and you,	
	And at the first gulp	565
	May the lot of you perish!	
Wife	What are you chattering about,	
	John John?	
Man	I chafe this here wax, do you see,	
	To mend your crack.	570
Priest	John John, that's what one must do	
	If one is stuck in marriage.	
Man (aside)	How he stuffs his belly –	
	I wish he'd choke on the pie.	
Wife	Now tell us the truth:	575
	What are you saying, upon your soul?	
Man	Heavens, woman, I was recalling	
	To myself, as I chafed the wax,	
	A story I heard told	
	By our priest on Sunday night;	580
	But it is not in my power	
	To bring it back to mind.	
Wife	Would it please you to tell us	
	Some honest tale to make us laugh?	
Man	While I chafe the wax	585
	I should take great pleasure in hearing it.	
Priest	I have done eight years of service	
	In the parish, searching for	
	Miracles of the martyr	
	Saint Arnoul which I heard of,	590
	But I never witnessed any myself.	
	But know that three happened to me;	
	I shall tell you about one of them,	
	If you'd care to listen.	
Man	And must I still chafe the wax	595
	Between the braziers?	
Wife	Patience!	
Man	Very willingly.	
Priest	As the scripture informs me,	
	There was a man who took a wife,	
	And the very day that he was married	600
	Saint Arnoul called him	
	To be his helper;	
	And he was put into a brotherhood	
	Apart from his wife the following day.	

	But he had, and this is quite certain,	605
	Fourteen children of this marriage,	
	And never did a stroke to produce them:	
	What a miracle that is!	

Man	Ah, Jesus, mea culpa!	
	Listen to his melodious words!	610
	God and the glorious company of saints	
	Grant you all as much.	
	Ah! What a worthy man!	
Wife	Be quiet.	
	My friend, tell us more.	

Man	As for me, I chafe the wax	615
	Bit by bit, as best I can.	
Priest	Another miracle after that	
	Happened to one of his neighbours,	
	And I have counted more than twenty	
	Who can vouch for its truth.	620
	The first child given	
	To him through the prayers of his wife	
	At the pleasure of God and of our Lady	
	Was when he was fifteen years of age.	
	Of another woman, by whom he had	625
	Another child before that one, I am the son;	
	And that first child, which she	
	Whom he married gave to him	
	Was a beautiful and gracious girl.	
	But, so as not to divide the income,	630
	Good reasons were discovered	
	Why they could not enter into	
	Matrimony and be joined together	
	If they conceived no children of their own.	
	So they came to an agreement,	635
	Because his wife had dedicated her [daughter]	
	To the Most Holy and Glorious.	

Man	Ah! poor wretched sinner,	
	How could anyone be so knowledgeable	
	And possess such profound wisdom	640
	As our illustrious priest!	
Priest	The third miracle was proved	
	By a man who married	
	His wife exactly	
	Three years ago on Thursday last.	645

326

	And the very same night	
	Of the morning on which they were married	
	His wife took an oath	
	To become a member of the sisterhood	
	Of Saint Arnoul: but I can tell you	650
	That in the seventh month from that day,	
	Being in pain then on that day	
	As if her skin, alas, would split,	
	His wife brought forth a child,	
	Fully formed in mouth and nose	655
	And all its proper limbs	
	As perfect in every part	
	As if she had carried it nine months:	
	Look at that – two months gained!	
Man	Marriage is a great thing:	660
	Let no man ever doubt it.	
Wife	Upon my faith, I have seen our cat	
	Produce a litter of kittens	
	In seven weeks.	
Man	Heavens, my dear,	
	God must be praised for all.	665
	But who knows if she had dedicated	
	Her fruit to the Holy Glorious Body?	
Priest	He has performed many a miracle,	
	Of which only a few are talked about.	
Man	Was your pie good,	670
	Sir Priest? Alas!	
	O God, do you not remember	
	That when you used to say the epistle	
	I used to sing with you in the pulpit,	
	And said the *Agnus Dei* alongside you?	675
	You could not have had in the years since then	
	As good a parish clerk as I was to you	
	During the time I sang with you.	
	I have sung there many a time –	
	But all the same, our pie	680
	Is gone and 'nothing to be done'.	
	I am John who chafe the wax –	
	That is my name, so there, by God!	
Priest	To sit for ever in this place	
	Would be too much.	
Wife	Let's leave our seats.	685
Priest	And kiss me instead of grace,	
	And farewell my love, my dear.	
Man	This wax has gone cold again	

	While I have been chattering.	
	You others who have supped,	690
	Why should I have to go to bed	
	And take my leave without eating?	
	Who gets his customary pleasures?	
Wife	*What, haven't you been*	
	Served while you chafed the wax?	695
Man	Whatever have you given me?	
Priest	*What, haven't you been*	
	Served with wine and pie?	
Man	Yes, by God, sure, sure!	
Wife	There's a laugh!	
	What, haven't you been	700
	Served while you chafed the wax?	
Man	Well, the Lord be thanked!	
	Do they think me mad and wicked?	
Wife	Have you not supped?	
Man	Certainly not, wife.	705
Wife	What were you given?	
Man	Nothing;	
	I'm fainting with hunger.	
Priest	Oh, what a shame!	
Man	That's the case, whatever you say.	
Wife	Really?	710
Man	No need to keep repeating it.	
Priest	You were included.	
Man	By our Lady.	
Wife	And had nothing?	
Man	Nothing, grace of Saint James.	715
Priest	Have you drunk nothing?	
Man	Nothing, upon my soul.	
Wife	And where were you?	
Man	Here's my place of suffering.	
Priest	And what are you doing over there?	720
Man	I chafe the wax—	
	That's where I learned	
	The lot of married men.	
	Damn it all!	
	I am fainting with hunger	725
	And I am choking with smoke,	
	And fuming about our bucket,	
	By the smoke-hole where I'm fumed.	

	By the holy flesh, since I'm so angry,	
	Never mind how many buckets with holes	730
	They'll all be bust! Well then, on guard!	
	Damn anyone who doesn't like that	
	And who would make me chafe the wax	
	Until the pie is eaten up!	
Wife	What are you doing?	
Man	I chafe the wax.	735
	I'm breaking it and tearing it.	
	Look at it crumbling into pieces.	
Wife	If I can get hold of a piece,	
	I'll well and truly season you	
	So that your flesh will tear to pieces.	740
Priest	Well, my dear!	
Wife	He's breaking it,	
	But, by God, he'll be ruined for that.	
[Man]	Come on then!	
Wife	Get out of here,	
	Or you will die in pain –	
	You filthy mongrel!	
Man	What about you, woman priest!	745
Priest	You lie, you wretched scoundrel.	
Man	You've been lying, the two of you,	
	Through your teeth.	
Priest and Wife, together	And you through your throat.	
	God save the king!	
Man	God save Saint George!	
	Come on, come on! Ah! Master Priest,	750
	I'll make you clear out of this house.	
	You'll get what's coming, take that, take that!	
	You have eaten up our pie,	
	But you will have to pay for it:	
	I shall see you soundly thrashed.	755
	Up and at him! Come on! Come on!	
Wife	Come on, Father!	
Man	I saw you.	
	Ah! You are too much for me.	
	Ah! By the Holy Body, I'll be off,	
	And let him keep what he wants!	760
Wife	Which way is he going?	
Priest	Over there!	
	I say, let's follow close behind.	

The Man comes back from behind them with a bag full of bread.

[Man]   Go on, priest, follow, follow!
                 Ah, you are spoiling my pie.
                 Go on, priest! Go on, priest!   765
                 At him, at him, at him, at him!
                 Now, my lords, I bid you all farewell.

THE END

GLOSSARY

Line references are normally to the first occurrence, and subsequent references are given only where the meaning is different or in cases of special interest. The part of speech is noted where there might be some doubt. An asterisk * indicates a Note on this line. A dagger † indicates that the OED lists this use as the earliest instance, or that the word is earlier than the first instance listed by OED; details are given in Notes.

a in L398
abashement confusion from shame L241
abredge reduce L1070
abrevyate summarize L1068
accomber overwhelm, embarrass 4P1039
accompted accounted We359
accurst detestable, plagued by trouble We953
accyon action, trial 4P165*
a croke dishonestly, crookedly L754
acte action L1346
affeccion partiality L735
affirmance ratification L1528*
agayne in response L47
agew fever, alternately hot and cold L1019
ale ale house 4P128
†alewdyng alluding to Wy301
alewrthe draws Wy621
algatys nevertheless, altogether PF623*
Alikakabus medicinal resin 4P628*
Alkakengy medicinal resin 4P628*
allonely solely Wy695
almes dede almsgiving PF203
almyght almighty PF68*
almyse alms 4P1159
†amayne violently Wy528
Amyas Amiens 4P30*
amytte admit, grant L169, We578
and if J189/90
apostata apostate PF566*
†appoyntement agreement to meet J383
approve (v.) prove L482
†aptnes inclination L597*
aquyghtall release Wy111
aquyghtyd acquitted, released Wy110
aray rank, order 4P875
arayde dirtied J256
arecte allege Wy255
Armony Armenia 4P33*
arow in turn We58
arsefetita asafoetida 4P620*
assoyled absolved PF310
assyned bound to a master 4P1128
assystens usefulness We968
at to 4P102
attende give heed to We1204
audiens a hearing PF354
avaunt (n.) boast L373
awarded judicially considered L386
awayt (n.) watchfulness L593
ax ask Wy632

bable speak foolishly PF12
bande hangman's noose 4P182
barcelettes bracelets 4P259
bareyng bearing Wy95
barthe bears Wy108
bast baste with gravy L1338*
baulde tonsured J268
bayte (v.) ease up L1115
beck nod of command 4P804*
behofe advantage Wy491
†bespake ordered, arranged for J398*
bey position L943*
blanka manna laxative 4P618*
blanke (adj.)empty, dumbfounded 4P165; worthless 4P565
blood young devil L1206*
bob (v.) buffet Wy31*
bongrace veil, French hood PF146*
borne burn J278
borowe presume authority, pull rank PF587
bote remedy J63
brall scold J48
brawlyng quarrelling J109
breke broach, begin L825; disclose We889
brest breath 4P312
broche opener L713*
broker dealer L1313*
bulle papal edict PF91
bumberd bombard, cannon shot 4P741*
burres burs 4P898*
burste perish from hunger 4P573*
bush (n.) head of hair L1311
by lyke probably L306*
byb talk nonsense We960*
byt (n.) bite J487
Byzansis Byzantine 4P612

canker mouth ulcers PF143
capacyte mental ability We471
carke (v.) labour, take trouble PF446
carkes body 4P20
carnall worldly Wy618
carterly ill-mannered We187
case condition Wy478
cassy cassia, purgative 4P621*
cast skill, trick L1196*
castels ?castellations 4P751*
casweltees occasional payments We991
charyte charitable donation PF366
chasys unenclosed parks We413
checkyng quarrelling, disputing We745

331

chefe chiefly 4P168
chept bargained We1046
chere countenance, expression J542
chere entertainment PF57*
chop blow (fr. coup) 4P199
chose do as (they) please We214
clappe (n.) noisy talk PF508*
clarke learned man, divine We1120
clatter chatter J301; prattle, talk idly PF12;
    clatterrynge PF255
clene (adv.) completely PF311
clere clearly proven, evident We671; clearly
    4P377
clyped called PF35
clyps clasps, trims L444*
cokkes God's J30
colacyon discourse PF70
colloquintita colocynth, purgative 4P621
color choler 4P599
come of hurry up 4P282
comen welth common good, prosperity
    We296*
commodyte provision for needs Wy494;
    utility, convenient living We698; benefit
    We658; profit We931; livelihood We1196
†comonar student Wy431*
compas range We9
comynycashyon ? discussion Wy358
conclude confute We637
condicions characteristics 4P985
condyscende (v.trans.) agree with L244
condyt conduct, passport 4P848
confyrmable compliant to L75*
connyng(e) skill PF39, L933
consequent following logically L159
consyderatyon power of thought Wy278
contentacyon contentment L1107*
    contentatyon satisfaction Wy496
controller censor, spiritual guide 4P136
†convynce convict L1346*
coolys breezes We589
copyn tank tall hat L1297 s.d.*
Cornelys Cornelius 4P37*
coryd curried L1418
cost land We1243
costarde apple PF521
counterpaise balance L1487
cownterwaylth equals Wy112
coylde beaten Wy119*
†crampe squeeze, compress Wy38*
cratche scratch Wy38
crome crumb 4P604
crowne tonsure J628
cry (n.) yelping of hounds We277*
    proclamation We467
curate priest in charge PF544 s.d.
curst cantankerous, shrewish J35
    curstest most shrewish L359
curtsy politeness L325
curyosytie hairsplitting 4P320

daw jackdaw, fool PF356*, L403

dawcock male jackdaw, fool L1268
debarre exclude L1450
debate quarrel J356
declare reveal Wy559
dedly death-like L58
defaced discredited L1350*
defarre defer, put off 4P273
    deferd We1134
dele, dell bit We791, PF417; detail L949;
    part L1123
deme judge Wy293
†demurrer in lawe legal deadlock L931*
departe distribute PF196; separate J428, part
    (trans.) 4P974
deserve pay back We395
desyrusly eagerly Wy581
determinately finally L318; resolutely We500
determyne (v.) end L58
devyce, devyse conceive Wy281, Wy282,
    Wy663
devyse (v.) meditate L10
diagalanga galangale 4P617*
diapompholicus salve 4P606*
diosfialios ?herbal medicine 4P616
diospoliticon medicine 4P618*
dirige dirge PF463*
dotage foolishness We332
doubt fear L203
drab whore J36
dreve drive Wy233*
drevyll, dryvyll knave, imbecile,
    kitchen servant PF420, J655
dubbe poke L1321*
dusty dirty We730
dyght prepared, decked PF469
dyscryve describe, write down L34
dysdayne cause for anger J331
dysease (n., v.trans.) discomfort L194,
    L832
dyspend expend Wy149
dyspensys disposes of Wy285
dyspleasaunt disagreeable L111
†dyssolvyd resolved Wy548*
dyssymylyng pretending L858
dystemperans disturbance of mind Wy54
dystemperat Wy70
dystempereth disturbs L1186

earyng ploughing Wy93
†edyfye benefit, instruct PF14*
egall equal L1134; egally equally Wy201
eke also J320
electe chosen of God PF43*
†elfe tricksy, malicious person PF630*,
    Wy120*
encres increase We364
endure prolong L1576
enormytees hostilities We25
ensewe (v.trans.) follow 4P1157
entendyd intending to, bent on PF68
entre beginning L950
entrete plead J65

332

envey conclude Wy307*
erranst most notorious J466*
estate condition PF452, We686
euer (n.) use 4P870
exhibition maintenance, allowance PF458
exteme estimate We575
extermely extremely We1106
extre axle-tree We461
extynct(e) extinguish L910, extinguished;
  L57; vanished 4P861*
ey always L1327

fable, fabyll (v.) tell tales PF13; deceive
  L258; talk idly Wy540
facte deed L1347
facyng asserting L1359*
fale fall L17*, We6
fallen syknes falling sickness 4P713*
falls lapses into sin Wy590
fancy ? deceiving imagination Wy409
fare behave J137
farforth to such an extent PF216
fashyon behaviour Wy72
fatched fetched J129
favour reception We476
fayn(e) (adj.) content PF361; (v.) feign,
  pretend L256; (adv.) eagerly L165
fayre clean J420; fayrest gentlest 4P1075;
  feare fair Wy193
feately skilfully Wy194
feofed endowed We723
feor for Wy113
ferdest furthest L821
ferythe fears Wy27
fet customary action We717
fet fetch L527*, We941
feutred sheathed 4P905*
fewmyng making angry Wy45
fistela fistula 4P608
fle fly away Wy601
fleesys plunder, shares of booty We1085;
  fleses shares L789*
flete float We584
†flush (n.) sudden burst L1310
flycker flutter We1018
flyttynge moving camp, travelling We418
for in spite of Wy271
forbeare refrain from J435
forborne gone without We527
foresyde front We771
forlorne utterlost We657
fornes furnace 4P865
forseth (v.) matters PF313
foule (adv.) foully, nastily PF123
founde provided for PF497
frame order We287; set in frame properly
  arranged We1011
fray(e) quarrel J209; affray, commotion
  PF578
freatyng discomfort Wy114
frettyng, fretynge vexing Wy45; rubbing to
  shreds We976

fro from J128
frontlettes headbands 4P259
frowardly contrarily 4P986
frustrate (adj.) irrelevant L1069
fryse coarse woollen cloth We134
fryse freeze Wy103; frysyth freezes L1178
full (n.) sum total Wy185, L35; fullest extent
  L853
fygewre example Wy195; fygure impression,
  shape We143
fyll fell L481
fyllettes hairbands 4P259
fyndyng maintenance Wy15
fyne conclusion We85; choice 4P643
  in fyne finally Wy585
fyt turn, bout We856*

gaddynge wandering J5
Gales Galicia 4P37
gastfull dreadful L867
gayre gayer 4P711
geare, gere preparation J394; matter We528;
  genitals We749*
gest guessed, supposed J121
gest (v.) mock, scoff PF312
get jet, strut We832
glasses mirror 4P235*
†glos lustre Wy678*
glose fawn, wheedle PF11
glyster suppository 4P731, We314
godshyp godly lordship We337*
†gogges God's J9*
gossyp godfather, baptismal sponsor J97;
  close companions L446*
governall authority Wy679
grace sense We714*
grated harped on L734*
graunted to agreed to J207
Gravelyn Gravelines We210*
greves griefs L60
grope grasp Wy644
grote fourpenny coin PF22*
guardon (v.) reward PF201
gyglet giglot, wanton woman We890
†gyssypry spiritual relationship J99*

hadde into brought, fetched 4P949
hande, out of – at once 4P793
†hansome appropriate Wy238*
happy fortunate J187
harborow lodging PF481
hard(e)ly firmly, boldly PF362; assuredly
  PF448*; fiercely, vigorously J16
harde heard J180
harpe dwell upon tediously, gnaw (fig.) L109*
hasthe hasteth Wy638
heale (n.) health, salvation PF8
hengar dagger, short sword PF532*
here hair J14; hair's We581
here hear J228
here her We1100
herse hearse PF469*

333

holde wager 4P277*
hol(l)ydam halidom 4P594*; relics We490
honorabull distinguished person Wy105
hove wait, linger L918
hye go J281; hyed hastened PF67
hyerd heard 4P737
hyre wages PF606
hyre hear 4P575*
hyrynge hearing 4P697

incontynently immediately L68
†indyfferency impartiality We161
    indyfferent We154;
    indyfferently L238
inestimable worthless 4P906, We695
insydently by the way L984; as a side
    issue Wy263*
intreate (v.) treat, handle PF610
intyce stir up J361*
invencyon fabrication 4P359; invented
    discovered L1406
Ish I shall PF515*
Iwys, ywys certainly J298/9

jakes privy L1329
jangelynge chattering L121
†jar dissension Wy432*
jet (v.) show off L645; jetthe goes, strolls
    Wy472; jetter swaggerer 4P1120
job (v.) prod, poke Wy32; jobbynge Wy66
joll strike Wy32; jollynge Wy66
joy (v.) rejoice in Wy151
joynt ? jointure 4P277*
Jys Jesus PF515

kepe (v.) guard J215
    kepe of care for 4P120*
keytyfs wretches, peasants We187
knakkes dodges J622
knockylls knuckles Wy247
know acknowledge We1226
knowledge acknowledge L1558

lad led L545
lasses laces 4P236
laude praise We3; laudynge praising We40
lay wager We800
leake leaky We799
lede lead L474
lees lose Wy585; leesyng loss, losing Wy155
leman lover J609*
lentes periods of 40 days PF199*
lese lose, waste L1352
lesse lose L695
lesynges lies L1297
let(e) (n.) ending L967; hindrance,
    obstruction 4P162, We500;
    lettes hindrances 4P257
let (v.) desist J49, 4P112; fail J358; hinder
    PF419; lettyth obstructs PF262
leve (v.) live Wy24
leve (v.) allow, permit Wy481

lever rather PF358
lewdenesse ignorance L303
ley (v.pa.t.) lay, ?lied 4P814*
ley allege, bring in argument L685
    adduce L1111; leyde alleged Wy138
leyth flattens, knocks over We646
litterature acquaintance with books PF192
littrid given straw for bedding L1419
lober(s) lubbers, louts L511, L1473
lode (v.) weigh Wy201*
lodyn loaded L1282
longyng belonging L1121
lore teaching PF49
lose (v.) loosen PF539
losell scoundrel L306
lothely loathesome L1475
Louyn Louvain We198
lowte mock Wy40*
lug pull, haul PF515
†lurche (n.) cheat, swindle PF572
luste happiness 4P767
lybertye domain PF597
lycke like We628
lydger ledger, lower millstone We742*
lye lay PF542
lyege liege, superior PF99
lyght frivolous We110
†lylly pure, fair J163*
lymd illuminated as in manuscript
    Wy232
lymytacyon district PF340*
lyst (v.) wishes Wy628; please J46

maculate (v.) pollute, defile PF454
malediction curse J267
malous ? spite L397*
maltman maker of malt Wy455
malydy illness L215*
manner kind of L1099
manerlyest most seemly L354*
marke 6s 8d or 2/3 of £1 We417
marres marsh We721
martreth (v.) martyrs L995
mashyp mastership We234
maystry contest for supremacy 4P476
meale flour PF7
meane means L970
meanly moderately We1105
meanyng intention L655
mede reward Wy604, 4P365
mediacyon intercession 4P85
medler dealer 4P218*
medyll meddle, intercede, go between
    We950*
mell mingle in combat PF590
ment purposed We153
†mere pure, unmixed Wy551*
mesurable moderate We366
mete well fitted PF277 equal Wy205; suitable
    L243*; mete to ges prepared to judge L479;
    meter better fitted PF283
metridaticon nostrum 4P619*

meve speak to J168*
mo more Wy448
moche (adj.) similar J566
†moder moderate We687 CHECK
mokkes derisory tales J432
moryn plague We522
mournynge sorrowing in confinement PF148
moyster moisture L1031
mummyng acting, doing a turn L408*
mursell mouthful J520
musty fetid We732
myche much J5
myckyll large L457
myght mite Wy51*
mylpooll mill pool We460
mynion darling, favourite L930
myschefe, myschyfe (n.) misfortune, disaster
    PF547, PF641; myschevous disastrously
    We732
mysdemed though erroneously L518
myshap misfortune L1001
mysse (v.) do without PF331, We1005
myster fail 4P175*; be necessary We313

nettes veils 4P258
nobs beloved L397
nock measure L486; notch, arsehole L1325
†nody fool Wy89, 4P466, L800*
nones, for the indeed L1019
nonny, nonny tut, tut We1040
nother neither Wy104, PF32
nought wicked PF565
nycebyceters dainty, fashionable women
    We897
nyest nearest 4P1074
nyfuls fictitious tales J432, We616
nyse foolish PF578

objecte objected to We624
od discrepant 4P144
of off 4P282
offyce duty 4P950
omytte (v.trans.) forbear L9
ones in any circumstances PF601
openly publicly, plainly PF16
oppressyon weight We537
or ere, before J444
other either Wy105
ought owed L611
ought (pron.) anything PF221
our hour We674
out outright 4P681
†over trodyn trodden down L1283*
oweth owns PF117
owre hour Wy149

paine trouble L1492
parate parrot We832
parell peril Wy246; parels moral dangers
    We909
parte party Wy196
partlettes neck-pieces 4P259*

parvert (adj.) wicked PF45
pas with succeed L1281
passhynyd impassioned Wy160
passyonate irascible L524
pastaunce entertainment, social intercourse
    L473
patent open letter of authority PF99
patter mutter rapidly J522*
peckt pecked, grooved We746*
pelitory pellitory (salve) 4P620
percase perhaps PF528
percell parcell We609
perde by God, indeed Wy506
perpetuall continuing We17
pewre pure, unassailable Wy407
peyse (v.) weigh, be worth Wy56
peysing weighing L1486
place religious house PF502
    place of scrypture text, extract PF190
†plumpyng swelling We656
ply (v.) use, exercise We1207
pockes pustules PF114
poll (v.) fleece PF9
pomander ball of spices 4P236
porte social position, bearing L7, L31
in post full speed Wy638
potage thick soup PF124
pourget purgeth 4P599
poynettes bracelets 4P260
poynt appoint We1044
poynt devyce perfect L513
poyntes laces 4P280
prately cleverly L635
pratelynge innocently loquacious We1033
pratyng (adj.) chattering, babbling J479,
    PF436
prebendes pittance PF458
predycacyon preaching PF564
preparatyve first dose L1154
prerogatyve right, limit Wy184
presents presence 4P565
preservatyfe prophylactic medicine PF163
prest ready 4P296; gathered together L25
prestholde priesthood PF587
presyd pressed Wy156; urged We1150
presysely precisely Wy178
pretendyng offering, extending L2; claiming
    L1285
pretence submission 4P1147
pretens intention We182
prevayle benefit We294
preveth proves J312
of preyse worth praising Wy426
procede proceed legally 4P1010
proces argument L314
processe statement L1520
proctour law enforcement officers 4P386*
proporte property Wy490
propre (n., adj.) belongings PF376; (adj.)
    real, regular PF376*
proses argument Wy219
prosses argument or narrative Wy61

335

pryde flowering We606
pryncyple chief argument L208;
pryncypyll chief claim We650
purgacyon purification PF292
purlews edges of forests, used as game
  preserves We413
purporthe brings, sets forth Wy355
purs moneybag, ? vagina We956
purveyd provided We1036
pyck steal We879
pyld(e) bald J289, J527
†pynkynge blink sleepily 4P306*
pytfallys bird traps We1014

quayle (v.trans.) destroy, put an end to L189*
queynes whores We900
quycknes vitality Wy239
quyght quit, free 4P817
quyghthe (v.) balances Wy229
quyte requite PF249
quytyth acquits J372
quyte completely L126

rable collection, confused medley J291
rabyll string or series Wy107
†tracke go at half trot Wy474*
racket tennis racquet 4P882
rage (v.) speak wildly 4P68
ragman rolles lists catalogues PF553*
ranger forest officer We399 s.d.
rate scold J136
rate estimated worth L1135; manner PF298,
  4P824
rather earlier, sooner 4P566
raught reached We1140
rave shout madly PF312
ray (v.) soil, defile J510
realynge railing PF426
rebarb rhubarb 4P592
rebounde (sb.) return L278
receyve bring down game We292
recure recover, cure 4P716
reformacyon correction L73
refrayne (v.trans.) restrain, check Wy527
refuse reject, avoid J235
reheytynge railing, behaving noisily We474*
rejecte expelled PF311
rent reward PF6*
requyre ask J398
reseyte receipt Wy152
resorte companionship L1147
revell riot We518
rise (v.) arise, originate L1512
rode (n.) cross J224
ronner upper mill stone We742*
roste roast 4P486, 4P523
rusty rancid We731
rydder deliverer PF335*
Rydybone Redbourn 4P41
ryfe frequently L548

saddest most dignified 4P1076

sadnes seriousness J530
saforne saffron L924*
sans dowte without doubt Wy357
sauter psalter We1228
save safe 4P848
sayle sail (skirt) We512
Saynt Toncomber St Uncumber 4P31*
scouryd rubbed gainst PF603*
scrat scratch PF543
scryppull scruple, apothecaries' weight 4P614
seay say Wy4*
secondly at second rate, feebly L1103
seelde seldom Wy158
selde infrequent L212
selde whan (adv.) seldom L980
sene evident 4P253
senow sinew L994
sensybly with the senses L1247
sensybyll that can be felt Wy465
sentence meaning, gist PF401
sentens judgement We376
senyght week J539
serves service L892
sethe sees Wy59
sew sue We668
sewer sure Wy357
seyng (n.) saying L330
seyng seeing Wy653
seyth says L5
shatter flap We512
shot anker sheet anchor 4P609
shreude bad tempered J415
shrewe (v.) curse J216
shryfe sheriff We999*
shyfte (n.) device We1047
shyne appear We379
shyt shut L621
skannyng examining L775
skant scarcely, hardly J640
skantely barely We401
skathe harm Wy66
skyl avail We442
skyll (v.) understand L180
slake decrease PF110
slouche lout, villain PF519*
sloughe slew PF568
slydder slippery PF297
smake smack L1029
smatterynge chattering PF254
†smyrkest most agreeable, neatest L351*
snape injure Wy37
sod boiled J555
sojorne dwell, remain L153
sojoner dweller L1306
solycyter intercessor We495
a sonder apart 4P1077
sone at once We342; soon We1007
soole undivided L40; solely L981
sort(e) crowd, gathering 4P1198; company
  Wy672
Sothery ?seething 4P879*
sott fool Wy17

336

sow ingot L924

sowne swoon, faint J627, 4P727

space time, meanwhile J307*

specyall (adj.) specific 4P636

sped brought to an end Wy454; achieved L132; helped to prosper We1114

sped (verbal n.) help We444

spede (n.) prosper PF136

spede (v.) prosperity 4P88

sperys spears L123

sprynge waxing We606*

spryngynge germinating We656

†spytfull vexing L1051*

spyttell hospital, leper house We975

†squybs firecrackers L1297 s.d.*

stacions pilgrimage places 4P22*

stack(e) stuck Wy388, L604

†stake what is at risk, a wager L1367*

stale stole, went L607

†stamynge stemming Wy388*

standynge fees retainers We990

stark(e) rigid Wy102; bold outright We993

stewes brothels J234

sticados stechados (medicine) 4P617*

sticke (v.) begrudge PF505*

stole stool J273

stones testicles We955

stop (n.) impediment 4P200

store (n.) livestock PF121

storve die Wy15

strayth soon, immediately PF240

strene strain Wy242

study are perplexed L1054

stuffe stores, materials PF560

styfly stubbornly L1459

stynt leave off PF508

stynt lessening L1182; rate We446*

suer sure We1234

sufferaunce endurance L1118

suppose allege L232; conclude L295

surplusage excess (legal) L137; We353*

suspect (n.) suspicion J170, J230

suspection suspicion J193

swathbondes swaddling bands, binders 4P241

swete sweat Wy98

swete precious PF515*

syckest most subject to strong feeling L362*

syght insight, skill 4P311

symper de cokket (n.) flirt We876*

synde assigned We587*

Syo Chios We385*

sypers Cypress kerchief 4P241

syrapus syrup of Byzantine 4P612*

syse limit Wy666

syth since PF319, L1272

tacle genitals J554*

tallest most virile 4P726

†tasted enjoyed sexually We796*

tayle tail We723*

terys tears L124

tewell anus 4P732

teyse chase We292

thampyon plug, tampon 4P732*

the thee J117, L643

then than Wy6

thether thither J386

thorowoutly thoroughly L1153*

thryls thirls, holes 4P900*

†thwak thrash J31*

thwart cross, oppose We901

thylke the same PF44

to too L852

to-comfort encourage We277*

tole toll We455

tolle ring out Wy235

ton(e) the one Wy65, J62, We629

too (n.) toe PF140

too too excessively J183*

torne turn J469

tother the other J62

towe too Wy438

toys tricks J432

trase harness Wy474

travayle labour, journey 4P161

trayne (v.) drag J14*

trindill trundle, lantern wheel We459*

trow think, believe, swear Wy445, PF582

try sail We571*

tryacle nostrum, remedy 4P584

trycke pretty We861 tryckest prettiest We908

tryed put to proof We702

tryfull, tryfyls lying tale(s), trinket J431, 4P218

tryfull..of (v.) put off We618

tryme scold 4P1038

tryse(d) snatch(ed), pulled away L487, L489*

turmentry torment L1220

†twygde beaten with twigs Wy470*

twynglynge twinkling 4P722

tyckyll ticklish, delicate L458

tyll to We752

tynkynge clinking 4P304*

undertakes understands L1328

universall widely accomplished 4P297, We478

unneth hardly, with difficulty L867

ure, in ure in practical experience Wy299; into practice L33

usage custom J562

variaunce disagreement 4P328

vary dissent from PF26; differ L900

varyeng quarrelling J415

†varyete difference Wy505*

vauntage perquisite We420

†vayleable valuable We368*

verdyt judgement, conclusion L928

very true PF260, L572, We3

veryfy prove to be true L61

vuewe (v.) view, consider Wy8

vuewer (n.) viewer Wy108

wade discuss L1399*
wagge move, go Wy308
wagge joker Wy386*
walke, walkyd beat J40*, J667
Walles Wales 4P38
walope gallop Wy474
walter roll about 4P600
warant authorize PF100
warde keeping, custody 4P864*
ware (v.) were Wy55
†twaster club J59*
wawlyng wailing like a cat J118
way consider Wy562
wayd weighed Wy436
weldes rolling country We698
welfare abundance PF228*
wene think J623
went wened, thought J307, We217
wete wheat PF131
weyke weak L413
weyre pond L1415
whether which of two J240
†whipper something surpassing 4P524*
whyle (n.) duration J435, We573
whyle eare formerly Wy634
whysk beat Wy41*
whyt drop J417;
    no whyt not at all L78
whyt white L430
with in company of 4P34
without outside PF361, L622
witsafe vouchsafe PF466
wode mad, angry 4P270
wonders wondrous 4P977
wondreth is amazed L1003
wone one Wy293
wordly worldly PF388
worme insect PF111*

worshyp (n.) honour J224
wot knows L13
†wrabbed perverse 4P986
wrawlyng screeching J363
wreste distort 4P1177
wroken discharged 4P763
wronge injury PF575*
wryngth suffers Wy92
wull will Wy544
wurshypfull (n.) one holding important
    office Wy105
†wyde (adv. and adj.) missing the point,
    going astray Wy50*, Wy62*, 4P342;
    wanton We771
wydely wrongly, misguidedly Wy436*
wyght(e) person PF159, L1145
wyle trickery J436
wyllfull willing PF23, 4P1160
wyndefale windfall We420
wynkyng napping 4P303
wys apprehend We865
wyt whit 4P205
wyt(te) understand PF85; find, ascertain
    4P847
wyttyly in the right way, cleverly Wy137

ye yea Wy455, PF543
yere anger Wy67
yerfull angry Wy48*
yerthly earthly We35, L1158
yest yeast 4P556
ymagynacyon opinion 4P198
ynduckshyn induction Wy195
ynsydent inessential Wy215
yournynge baying, yelping of hounds We275
yvyll evil J338
ywys for sure, surely PF554

TUDOR INTERLUDES

ISSN 0261-9199

Lightning Source UK Ltd.
Milton Keynes UK

172419UK00001B/13/A